The Boys
From The Mersey

The Boys From
The Mersey

Nicholas Allt

MILO BOOKS LTD

First published in hardcover in March 2004 by Milo Books

This paperback edition published March 2005

ISBN 1 903854 50 4

Typeset in AGaramond by Avon DataSet Ltd,
Bidford on Avon, Warwickshire, B50 4JH

Printed and bound in Great Britain by
Cox & Wyman Ltd, Reading, Berkshire

MILO BOOKS LTD
info@milobooks.com

Contents

Acknowledgements

A thank you and a half goes out to Gary Allt and Matt for jogging my memory button, plus Mono, Waller, Booey at EDT, Sully and Jockey for photo opportunities and albums shared. A tip of the hat goes directly to the story-makers, as in the lads I've travelled all over Europe with since 1976 and who are still going strong, along with the ten lads I know of who departed this life too early after starting out as young, red rag-arses like myself. The Ninety-Six – well, it goes without saying. I'd also like to give recognition to Sammo for his counsel and Dave Kirby for applying his size nine Samba to my Levi back pockets, giving me the kick up the arse I badly needed, along with the sacked dockers' club, the Casa on Hope Street, Liverpool, for the use of the rooms above – if you need me, you'll get hold of me there. Last, I'd like to thank me ma and da for not chaining me to the floor every time the Reds were bang in Europe, otherwise I wouldn't have any story to tell. If you've got a good ma, da and girl standing alongside, then you're always in with a shout. See yer when I get there.

More than anything: Sue, Nikita, Caitlin-Rose and Joseph Connor (the bin lids) – this is for you.

Glossary

Bag off	To leave with a girl
Beaut	Total idiot
Birmos	Birmingham bags
Bizzies	Police
Blowse	Fake or phoney
Brasses	Prostitutes
Brewstered	Wealthy (from the film *Brewster's Millions*)
Briefs	Tickets
Custy	All's well or looking good
Door-hinge	Mingebag, tight
Flock	Bed
Golf ball	Thick or dim-witted
Goosed	Knackered, clapped out
Grock	Big, tough-looking guy, well set
Head-worker	Anyone who uses his loaf; a schemer
Hoffman	To disappear or 'get off, man' (also known as a 'Dustin')
Igloo	Rhyming slang for not a clue
Inman	A way to get inside a stadium or show without paying
Jarg	Counterfeit

Me	My
Minty	Stinking, filthy
Nosebag	Meal
Oul	Old
Paraffin lamp	Tramp
Pazzy	Passport
Scally	Young tearaway
Sheepsville	Where everyone's the same or where woollybacks live
Skin	Hooligan, someone who likes a fight
Spaceman	Dressed or acting like he's in a world of his own
Ted	Lost the plot clothes wise
Tom	Jewellery ('tomfoolery')
Tonking	A hammering, to get well beaten
Trainees	Training shoes
Wheels	Shoes
Whopper	Big fool by itself, can be good or bad depending on text.
Woollyback	Not from a large city, especially rural Lancashire and Yorkshire (oop North), or anyone with a combine harvester accent (Ipswich)
Yer	You or your
Zapper	Pickpocket

Introduction

WHEN I SPOKE with a few of the boys at the game about whether or not I should write this book, I knew I'd have to take into account the people it might upset, as the truth usually upsets somebody. Then I thought about the people who, like me, were there, you know, really there, but who had never had a voice; thousands of lads who would one day say 'You'd never believe the things we used to get up to' to disbelieving kids or grandkids. That was it; I was doing it, simple as that.

Here was a motley crew of larger-than-life young wise-arses who today are mostly touching forty and whom I got to know from our mutual excursions around the country and abroad with Liverpool Football Club. And let me tell you, from the mid-Seventies onwards, the Anfield Road End terraces produced some of the maddest lads you could ever bump into in any circle of life. I believe that this set of football pioneers, head-workers and lunatics should be down on the Liverpool logbook, because whether the club (known for its conservatism) likes it or not, this bunch of scallywags played their part too in making Liverpool FC the most successful football team in British soccer history.

For me, and thankfully for people like Milo Books, these people had to have a voice. Not a journalistic voice, mind you, but a voice that was truly one of their own. While telling this story I've tried to incorporate the voice I had at the time a certain cup was being lifted or something was going off outside the game. For instance, the voice I had at the early European finals had changed considerably after Heysel and Hillsborough, quite understandable really. After seeing people die at football matches your outlook and mindset were bound to change. So for anyone out there struggling with the Liverpool lingo you'll just have to don a pair of Adidas and bear with me, as it wouldn't sound right in plain, old English, for me and my kind, it never does. My decision to get on with the writing graft was finally brought to a head after reading yet another one of those 'blag accounts' of football days gone by; written by some second-guesser who kept telling me how 'hard' he and his mates were and what a lovely thing violence was, when all the time he'd probably never had a straightener in his life and in his heart of hearts he knew that he'd always been down at the back of the crew pushing all the other terrace-loons up to the front. No, I had no interest in writing another 'tit for tat' hooligan type book, as all they seemed to be saying was 'We legged you – no you never – we legged you' and all that palaver from page 1 to page 250, and I think we've seen enough of those over the last ten years, don't you think boys. I've tried to be a little more innovative than that, well you know what they say about Scousers always trying to be different.

Quite a few of the books written about being part of a football crew tend to make the lads look and sound like a bunch of Benny Hill-type cavemen, running around to that tune he plays at the end of his show, only wearing padded jackets, baseball caps and spaceman trainees; in the judge's words, absolutely off one's trolley. Now, concerning the majority of the Liverpool boys that is one utter load of cack. Most of the lads I knew at the match came from the Phil Silvers/Bilko school of terrace thinking, and some of the wisest, smartest, funniest lads you could ever wish to meet learned a lot of life's early lessons down at the football.

A lot of the 'we legged you' authors also try to put across their own view of Scousers, often negative. This is usually down to narrow-mindedness, as a result of seeing their own beloved team being constantly beaten at Anfield, or themselves having been beaten up after bumping into a crew of urchin rag-arses somewhere down at the game. Other blag accounts have tried to steal the Liverpudlian thunder for being the first real dressers, the first real travellers and the first real set of football fans ever to write the 'big book' on going to the match. I unashamedly say that nobody ever had a crew like our crew. While we were busy working out how to rob sledges and sheepie mitts just before Chrimbo in places like Zurich and Vienna, everybody else was running around playing third-round League Cup ties at the likes of Carlisle and York City. Now whether your Tuesday nights took you to Boothferry or Boundary Park, neither place was bound to broaden your horizons in quite the same way, was it? Well, was it?

Nowadays, almost every Thomas, Richard or Harold can get abroad with ease if they fancy taking in a game, duly returning home to take the poseur's walk through customs with nothing to declare except some tasty clobber folded neatly inside their flashy designer carrier bags. But, and this is a big Mike Tyson of a butt, once everybody can get there willy-nilly, it has just about finished as far as being high on the fun agenda goes. It's like your favourite nightclub getting totally ruined by hordes of visiting out-of-towners and you don't feel like going there again – a bit like Anfield today come to think of it – or your favourite local band becoming massively famous and not belonging to precious little you any more.

Well Europe, for the Annie Road End crew, felt like 'ours' in the Seventies and early Eighties. By the Nineties it was completely goosed. Even though some other teams' supporters did cross the English Channel now and again in those early days, they were never there almost permanently, like it felt for our firm. Their teams were never lifting trophies on a regular basis to help them get over to the snazzier grounds and shops of the Continent, so they ended up spending too long in stack-heels and long leathers. But progress is progress, and once the authorities clamped down on football followers, and Liverpool in particular, after Heysel in 1985, then Dustin Hoffmans abroad were never going to be as sweet or as carefree ever again. The clubbed-up, membered-up and subscriptioned-up replica-top wearers of the country can all hop abroad these days and generally come back telling tales of how fantastic it was, plane-in, plane-out style. Well it's not. I should know, I've tried it enough times lately. It's the same for the 'think they're hard' Burberry contingent who all believe they're so different to the replica-shirt wearers; well you're kidding yourself. The only distinction I can make is maybe slightly in the check.

Travelling abroad to watch your team on the official rip-off trip has never been as good as when you venture out your own way. Take it from an Alan Whicker of an expert. Yet with all this Bin Laden bollocks going on, deciding to skedaddle last minute to travel between countries will never be as simple again. If you get caught bunking to a match nowadays while carrying a small holdall and no passport, chances are the French or German authorities are likely to mistake that Scouse accent for Algerian terrorist back-slang, and surmise that the change of clobber is really an Adidas bag full of guns. With so many foot-brawls kicking-off over the past twenty-years, being a bit of a lad or a travelling fan is never going to be the enjoyable off-the-cuff experience it once was. We're living in a time of instant jail for any would-be hooligans, with category letters ranging from C for top skins down to whatever letter it is for when you fart too loud outside the ground. The politically correct brigade rule the roost and won't rest until we've all knuckled down to play by their rules, or we've all paid in full for the times they were called spotty face, fat twat or fruitcake when they were at school. Due to these liberal lunatics now taking over the asylum and having far too big a say in our Saturday afternoon entertainment, for me and most of my generation, football today feels watered down to fuck: no atmosphere, no tackling, no massive swaying mobs to create that atmosphere and no real down to earth heroes to score then adore.

Maybe it'll sound like some cynical, jaded ex-hoolie when I tell this story. If it sounds like that in your head, then tough shit, go and read Geri Halliwell's autobiography. Funny thing is, contrary to what I'm saying I still go the games – it's in your blood isn't it, even though I'm hanging on by the skin of my teeth. And me, I'm like an open book for new experiences; but I'll tell you this, I'm not getting any good ones at the moment. Win, lose or draw, each game you go to feels like an Armani eleven of whingeing foreign pop stars versus the Prada all-stars team of minted Lexus drivers, all twenty-two players dreaming about their next photo-shoot and next big-earner. 'Kick the ball out for our opponent Sol; I think he scratched his knee when he tripped over his wallet,' while we're thinking, *just play on and let the bastard die.* It's a different mindset mate, about thirty grand a week different. And after the initial buzz of a new signing has worn off, it's as though half of them start thinking, *if it's a bit muddy and nobody passes to me, I might ask for a transfer*. If these are the kids' new mercenary, money-mad heroes, I feel sorry for the kids. Everything seems to be geared towards the individual, the celebrity, not the collective team and its city, and as the gorgeous Paul Daniels once said as he looked in the mirror, 'Now that's sad.' Agents and money, money and agents, I don't think anybody would give a flying fuck if more money meant more loyalty and effort, but more often than not it seems to equate with becoming a bigger ponce or another Merc-driving Jack the lad.

I'm starting to rattle now, so I'll end this introduction by saying this: the real know-the-score lads are wise to the fact that the Annie Road End boys were doing it quite a few moons before all the other werewolves of the terraces, and whether you're an ex-ICF chicken-runner, headhunting ex-Shed-singer, Kippax City Cool Cat, donkey-jacketed wor-lass tatt merchant, Baby-Squaded, Soul-Crewed, Zulu'd-up, Bushwhacked-down Park Ender, feather-cutted Gelderd Ender, Brummie car-fixing Holte Ender, cross-the-picket-line Trent Ender, star-jumper-wearing ex-Scoreboard Ender or some other cranked-up, fucking doolally bell-ender, if you were ever in the know, or once knew the dance and could be a teensy-weensy bit honest for two seconds, then you'd know that those rag-arse Scouse urchins definitely wrote the book an' all that, and only the Liverpool boys truly had the right to say what I'm saying now. Yeah, you know where I'm coming from.

We were the boys.

PART ONE

The Annie Road End

CHAPTER ONE

We Were the Boys

WE WERE THE boys, we were always the boys and anyone worth his salt and honest enough to admit it knew that we were the boys. You see, nobody had ever had the opportunity to continually travel abroad like us, because nobody had ever had the team to follow all over Europe and sometimes the world like us. Along with all these lads I'd gotten to know, we were the true, original football gypsies; this was our team's heyday and we were going to travel. We'd cottoned on that we were the absolute beginners with this new clobber lark, and with this in-and-out-of-Europe lark, and once the Road End boys got to notice the bigger picture, other than the one they were used to on the banks of the Mersey, then no lack of money, no border control and no Thatcher-loving police force was ever gonna stop us from venturing out along the strasses, boulevards and autobahns of Europa to broaden our horizons. Here we were back in the smoke, it was 'Dustin Hoffman' time again – time to get 'off, man' – and, as usual, we were all 'on one'.

The year was 1978, we were about to go 'gathering cups in May', as one banner read, and tonight all roads led to Wembley for our second European Cup Final on the bounce and our fourth final in six years. Only we didn't need the usual passports and boat-bunking to get to this one. Anyway, here's me, busy keeping an eye on a couple of London bizzies, who themselves were busy, bizzie, busy keeping an eye on hordes of boisterous Liverpool supporters singing and dancing under the hot London sun. In these days of no promotion play-offs and no Ronald McDonald cups, when only the best were allowed to perform on the Wembley and European stages, then big-time yearly football parties only happened when you had a truly successful team, and we had the very best, so you had to make the most of it while it lasted. That was the over-used motto that I lived by, but at the time, with me being just seventeen, I mean, how was I to know it was going to last so fucking long?

Seeing as the sweat had started to drip from my brow, I lifted my two-tone mohair jumper over my head to tie it around my waist. I was sorely tempted to drop me kecks and join the hundreds of other boys who'd decided it was undies-only time as they splashed about in the Trafalgar Square fountain to cool off. I thought better of it; I still hadn't made any dough yet, and these FC Bruges coaches were starting to pull-up alongside the Square just so they could witness the scene. 'ALLEZ LES ROUGES, ALLEZ LES ROUGES, ALLEZ.' Nobody else sang those triumphant European ditties like us, and for the past few years foreign chants and songs had become our jubilant sounds of choice. It had been funny listening to some lads having a bash at ordering a cup of tea across the Channel in the earlier rounds. You had to laugh, I mean, French and German for 'milk and three sugars', come on, these were fellas who could just about speak Scouse.

The famous London landmark was playing host to thousands of dancing Scousers, but as I looked across to the ticketed Belgium supporters, all I was thinking was, *hold yer horses, kiddo, there might be something in this*. From the corner of my eye I caught sight of a huge flag draped across one of the lions. It simply read, 'Yer Belgian Lace Won't Stop Jimmy Case.' As Admiral Nelson looked down at the Jimmy flag, I began to think maybe it would be nice if dear old Nelson could order the hot-shot Liverpool number eight to fire one of his legendary, bullet-like free kicks straight at the Belgian coaches, and as the Case-ball crashed through the leading coach window screen it would duly create a diversion for Mr Ticket-less here to jump on board via the emergency back door. Then it would be a simple case of rifling through the travel bags of the mesmerised Belgians until I found my hidden treasure: a ticket for the 1978 European Cup Final. Football, football, eh, the lengths some people will go to, all for the sake of a game of footy.

As I approached the first coach, a fella who looked like a Rottweiler walked past. When I say Rottweiler I really mean his face and walk. He was a fridge-freezer with a Rottweiler's head, about six foot two with muscles as good as Austrian Arnie's without doing the weights. In Scouse terms, he was a fucking 'grock'. He was wearing a red scarf that reached down to his belly button and I'm sure he was Biffa Bacon's da, long before he turned into a Geordie in that comic called *Viz*. I'd seen him before: he was one of the Breck Road Firm, one of Liverpool's main firms of boys.

He clocks me and says, 'That fella standing at the front of the coach is a Belgian tout.'

So I go, 'Oh yeah, how d'you know that mate?'

'Coz he's gorra wad of tickets, an' he's just asked me if I wanted to buy one for a little bit extra.'

'Oh a tout, I see, and yer not arsed coz you've already got one?'

'No I am arsed mate, I'm just going to get me boys so we can do him in an' have his tickets off.'

'I'm with yer there mate.'

From the moment he headed back to his crew, I'm thinking, *better be quick*. Once the Rottweiler came back with his pups, it was bound to be one big scramble. I knew the dance with these ticket scrambles; it was like a Scouse version of the Moonlight Waltz, only it went something like this: firstly, take your partner or the Belgium Tout by the body or arms and give him a good thump; secondly, make things easy on yourself by flattening him into a Belgium waffle; thirdly, lift his deadened arms to commence with the most important part of the dance, the part which led to him having a set of turned-out pockets and an aching head, with both his waffle crumbs and his cup final tickets spread all over the concrete dance-floor.

Jean-Claude Loadsatickets was standing in the coach doorway on the bottom step, and as I came up close, I heard Gerry Rafferty singing 'Baker Street' on the driver's radio. This immediately had me thinking about which direction I needed to head-off to, just in case a serious 'hoffman' was about to take place.

'Alright mate, have yer got any tickets to sell?'

I was speaking to a typical Belgian; when I say typical, I mean he had the usual pallid skin with that chip-pan black hair. In fact his rug was so fucking greasy it looked like he'd washed it in margarine shampoo. It was slapped on top of a gob that had that anorexic Johan Cruyff look about it. He muttered something back in what I presumed to be Belgian. So I asked again, only a little slower this time.

'Er, 'scuse me monsieur, have you got any tickets to sell?'

'Parlez-vous Francaise? Ah, sprechen sie Deutsch?'

Fuck-sake, this is going nowhere and the Rottweiler's bound to be back crewed-up soon. I'll have to try another one.

'Do . . . you . . . speak . . . English?'

'Yes of course I do. Why didn't you say so?'

'But . . . I did.'

And Jean-Claude goes, 'Ah, I'm sorry, I didn't know that, ah, you were speaking English, I thought you were, ah, speaking another language, maybe, ah, German.'

I'm thinking, *cheeky cunt, this Belgian balls, now show us the tickets, lard fringe.* But I decided to say, 'Can . . . I . . . buy . . . a . . . final . . . ticket . . . from you?'

'Why yes, of course. Ah, now, where would you like to sit? And ah, don't speak so slowly.'

So it's a Belgian Bossy boots, is it? And the hard-faced twat thinks he speaks better English than me, does he? Okay, we'll see about that.

'I would like an expensive seat for the football game, yes, is that okay?'

'Yes sure, ah, now, wait here.'

As he walked back into the coach, I went to follow, just to have a bit of a mooch.

And he goes, 'No, ah, you must wait by the door, yes?'

'Oh sorry, I understand, Mister Belgian Bossy Balls, ah yes.'

He gave me a funny look. I did an about turn and began to walk really slowly off the coach, just so my eyes could scan for anything that might be holding a ticket. *Nah, there's nothing much on here except for a few FC Bruges scarves and some smelly Belgian Alsatian sarnies.* On turning my head back towards Jean-Claude, I noticed that he was taking a small black bag down from the overhead shelf above the back seat. I was tempted to return there to try to get a glimpse of the hidden treasure, but realised at the last second that this would be the wrong move, as the driver was still sitting in his seat and staring at the strange passenger walking towards him. I gave him a wink as I left the coach and he made a half-hearted attempt at smiling back. As his thick blubbery lips opened up, I blimped a seriously bad set of Sugar Puff peggies. I'm thinking, *What is it with the Belgians? They're just like those Australian Aborigines. Why're their railings always fucked-up? Too many sweets or not enough dentists? God knows.* The brief movement had slightly dislodged his newspaper, revealing a fifty-inch waistline that told me he'd been absolutely hammering the Belgian chocolates. Judging by the belly and the nashers, when he wasn't lodged in the driver's seat he probably spent most of his spare time lying around all day trying to chew the buttons off his Belgian Chesterfield couch. It got me thinking again, *fat coach drivers and fat taxi drivers, what does that tell you? It must be something to do with sitting on the job. How else do you explain having an arse like a burst beachball?* Then I'm wondering why I'm thinking so much, and why me brain's doing overtime. I double-clocked the tub of lard, confirming there was no way he was going to give Speedy Gonzales any trouble in the hoffman stakes. One down, one to go.

From the moment my feet touched the pavement, I scanned Trafalgar Square for the Breck Road boys. Still no sign of the Rottweiler or any of his crew, and those two London bizzies were well occupied. *Come on Jean-Claude, me oul china, get a move on.* The tasselled loafers at the top of the stairs told me he was back in town and hopefully he'd be carrying the ticket, or tickets, that would soon have my Adidas Samba trainees sprinting through the streets of London in true Ralph McTell style. He sat down on a doorway step, pushed his margarine fringe to one side and produced part of the hidden treasure. It was a seat for the 1978 European Cup final. I looked at it; I was mesmerised. He told me in a far-off voice that he also had standing tickets, which were not so expensive. Thinking intently, I knew that the treasure was in his black bag he had placed on the stair behind him. Biding my time, I asked him whether or not they were forgeries, but he didn't understand the question, so I repeated myself.

'Are . . . you . . . sure . . . they . . . are . . . not . . . for . . . geries?'

'Ah, what is this four jerries?'

I was tempted to state the obvious punch line that it was a German pop group but decided to say, 'Are . . . you . . . sure . . . the . . . tickets . . . are . . . okay?'

'Ah, yes, now I understand. Let me show you. Ah, see, I used to be a footballer in the Belgian professional league . . . yes?'

'Oh yeah.' I'm thinking, *that's funny, I don't remember Johan Cruyff playing any footy in the Waffle League.* He smiled, then I smiled, then he smiled back again; fucksake, it was like European Happy Families. I knew this smiley culture thing was never going to last, as the more predatory, shark-like side of my brain kicked in. *Might be your last smile of the day, Jean-Claude.*

With no more cheery grins on offer, he reached behind to the top of the entrance stairs for the bag. He brought it back down to rest on his legs, which he had swivelled protectively inside the door. As he put his hand inside the bag, I craned my neck to try to have a gander, but he half-turned his back on me so I couldn't see inside. That was it; time's up, Mr Tout.

DOOOF, I dove headlong into the gap where he held the bag and snatched it from his grasp. As I tried to get away I tripped over his legs, or he tripped me, and he started to shout for help. All the time he was grabbing and holding on to my clothing for all he was worth. PING. *You bastard!* The buttons had popped off my Fred Perry, and as we fell from the coach the comprehension hit me that maybe we were having the first

Bruges versus Liverpool inter-continental wrestling Match of the Day. A final glimpse of the lard-arse driver told me the Belgian belly was stuck in his seat, seeing as he wasn't making any attempt to intervene. Maybe he didn't like touts either. Nah, don't think so; he was simply a fat, greasy cunt, sitting there sweating out the Stella, and couldn't be arsed with the graft.

Jean-Claude was hanging onto my tattered Fred Perry t-shirt like Tarzan on a rope, but made a fateful mistake when he swung and landed a punch to the side of my head. Now I definitely didn't want any assault charge but it was red-mist time, and as I felt my arms and then fists pump with blood, I thought about delivering a swift uppercut, cos believe you me, this Jean-Claude was no Van Damme. While seriously contemplating going for the quick knockout, I finally loosened his grip on the last remnants of my rag of a t-shirt, pushed him back with a swift kick to the shins; it was then, and only then, that Speedy Gonzales took over.

Andale! Andale! Arriba! Arriba! It was off. *Come on me oul Adidas Samba, take me to freedom.* The chase was on and Jean-Claude was no slouch, as he proved by keeping up for the first 100 yards or so, and I mean, I'd just turned seventeen and could have given Linford Christie a hard time at that age. But lo and behold, who is this overtaking Jean-Claude and moving up into second place? It's hard to tell, as his purple and white Bruges scarf keeps jumping up from his bare belly over his face. *OH NO! You bastard . . . It's the Rottweiller.* And he's shouting something, but I'm struggling to hear as I'm so intent on getting away. Fucksake, half the Rottweiler's crew are coming up on the rails in their undies; some bad pairs of boxies in that firm.

'WAIT FER ME, WAIT FER ME.'

The hard-faced twat: wait for me he's shouting; as if . . . I'm waiting for no one. The turbo engines kicked in and my Samba went into overdrive. WAAHEY! Soho, land of the baggy fannies, here I come.

I shot past the National Gallery, which borders Trafalgar Square. I was no London cabbie but I knew where Soho was, so that was the immediate direction I took. If I outran Jean-Claude, I could take a rest by stashing myself away in one of those sleazy peep shows somewhere in the heart of Soho. *Big pair of milky tits and a breather, yeah, sounds about right to me.* But this Belgian guy, even though he was lagging behind in third or fourth place, just wouldn't give up. Maybe he really was an ex-footballer. I ran straight through Chinatown and started to get a bigger lead when it dawned on me that I no longer had my mohair jumper, and to this day I don't know where we parted company.

From the moment I caught my second wind, I flew through Soho. Sex shops, peep shows and beckoning brasses all went whizzing past before I finally came to a halt. When I looked around there was no sign of the ticketless tout or the Breck Road boys, so I quickly slipped behind one of those black curtains as some spotty hostess, prozzy, brass, or whatever you want to call her, beckoned me in. She looked like a porno version of one of Ken Dodd's Diddymen, with her little fat tits stuffed into some cheap black dress. The dress looked like it contained 1,000 DNA samples from her past six months' sexual encounters, as well as a few Heinz Beans stains from last night's tea, the fucking minty cow. She could've run her gladrags through the washing machine for European Cup Final day.

I now knew I was safe. The heart of Soho was littered with similar seedy gaffs and finding which black curtain I'd gone behind would have been like trying to find a spare final ticket in Liverpool. It was two o'clock in the afternoon and the match didn't kick-off at Wembley till 7.30. I'd lost me mates but that was a small price to pay if this bag was holding what I thought it held. It was a bit dark inside my wanking cubicle and the fishy smell was making me baulk, but thinking about the contents of the bag had me forgetting the bad smell and I soon got used to it. Finding the desired coin, I dropped it into the slot and spotty Shirley immediately started to wriggle her bare bum in front of my narrow viewing window. I wanted her to move her saggy arse out of the light so I could see more clearly, as there was only one zip I wanted to open and it definitely wasn't the one on my Lois jeans. *Get yer big spotty arse away from the window Shirley, I'm trying to find me treasure.* Looking beyond those white, lumpy cheeks, I could see other letterbox-size viewing holes. Each open slot contained a set of pervy eyes peering out excitedly at the girl's omelette of an arse. Two more opened up, which instantly took Shirley across the large red bed that stood in the middle of the room. She started to dance provocatively in front of her new customers as I got a rear-end view of her hanging bush. I have to admit that that gave me a bit of a tickle, but with the tout's black bag now well out of sight from any prying eyes, I decided it was time to stick my hand inside, hopefully to pull out a decent bit of treasure.

I found my treasure all right, and a lot more beside. Inside were fifteen European Cup Final tickets, £125 sterling, some Belgian francs that I estimated to be worth roughly £55, and two passports. One of the pazzies showed the picture of the greasy-fringed Belgian tout. The other showed the face of some Turkish wrestler I'd never seen before. Then BANG, the oul Catholic guilty conscience popped up, with its little silver toffee hammer jabbing away inside my head. It was the sweet white angel on one shoulder versus the little black devil on the other. My sweet white angel told me that by taking the passports

back, then some of my sins would be washed away, as the rest
of the booty in my angel's eyes was a fair cop, yer know, seeing
as he was only a Belgian spiv an' all that. But the little black
devil was saying, 'Fuck the two greasy Belgians, rip the pazzies
up and throw them in the sponk bin.' After a brief pause, I
realised I had to go back. The little white angel was always the
stronger in the Catholic Conscience Cup.

Fifteen European Cup Final tickets – I was rich.

The fact that a lot of the items from my treasure chest
ended in a five was a good omen, seeing as we'd won football's
biggest club trophy for the first time on the 25th of May last
year. The 25th of the 5th eh, in fact I wanted good luck all
round, so I kidded myself by converting the francs my way so
they ended in a five.

My allotted time had run out and the shutter on my
letterbox came down. I inserted another 50p to see Shirley's
arse and to shed some light onto my new riches. Riches, ha!
The tickets cost £2.50 each, apart from a couple of more
expensive seats, so if I thought I was rich I obviously mustn't
have had a pot to piss in, in 1978.

Once I'd organised myself and made sure that the black bag
was empty, I stashed it in the wanking bin among a stack of
glued-up tissues. *Careful, careful, didn't need to touch any of that
multi-nation papier mache heaped up inside the bin.* It was a 101
wank-yous from twenty different countries. Yeah, five wanks
per country, sounds about right to me. And the odd one over –
probably some hard-up spaceman who'd fell in love with
Shirley's big fat arse, because it deffo wasn't me.

On leaving the peep show I darted into the first restaurant
in Chinatown and washed my hands at least five times before
heading back towards Trafalgar Square. A large grandfather
clock in the restaurant showed that I'd been gone roughly

forty-five minutes; the lads should still be there. The Chinese lady at the door seemed unusually pleasant, at a time when a lot of restaurant people in London would scowl at you for just using the toilet, especially when my body language had blagged her that I was about to eat. I never asked for permission, as most of them would only refuse; that's the warmth of the big city people, eh?

Hopefully, if I stood on the other side of the square and the lads were still knocking about, I could shout one of them over. Whoever approached could then hand the pazzies over to a passing Officer Dibble, who could make sure that they got back into the hands of their rightful owners. If it hadn't been for the oul Catholic Conscience Cup kicking of inside me barnet, I'd have been one ruthless young man. No wonder some people say religion is an invention of the controlling authorities. Yer know, invented to keep the more exuberant of the under-funded down at heel. It deffo kept me in check, otherwise I'd have lashed the pazzies in the bin and gone about me business, but the little white angel just wouldn't leave me alone. She kept nagging at me, 'No need to cause any extra grief for somebody who'd already been through enough upset.' Typical thoughtful woman eh; meanwhile, the little devil fella couldn't give a shit for no one.

Retracing my steps, I kept an eye out for my mohair jumper. I also removed my polishing rag of a t-shirt. I'd have removed it earlier but I had visions of one of Shirley's bouncers entering my cubicle once she'd snitched about my topless state. Therein they would have found a lone, semi-naked young Scouser, with a large bump in his kecks, carrying a small black handbag. If you think it sounds iffy, try imagining how it would have looked as the cubicle door opened.

I luxuriated in the feeling of warm sun on my shoulders as

thousands of Liverpudlians stood out among the passing West London crowds. It was our annual cup-gathering month of May and the Redmen were back in the final. My pockets were feeling fuller than they'd ever felt, and as I walked on I began to wonder why there couldn't be more days like this. Things were looking up. Oooh, oooh, oooh, what a life.

As I neared Trafalgar Square, my walk back became as shifty as a prison escapee. My eyes scoured the street for any sign of the Rottweiler and his crew, or the probably suicidal ticketless tout. He'd no doubt be trying to focus in on one particular Liverpudlian as thousands danced before his eyes, a job that would be all the more difficult with a long greasy fringe.

The corner of the National Gallery presented me with the scene I'd just fled from, and as I looked to where the coaches were parked I could clearly see Jean-Claude speaking to two well-interested Cockney plod with the listening dibbles' car parked in close attendance. I automatically turned on my heels and started to walk back around the massive building, enabling me to enter the square at a different angle. My new approach brought my two mates into view; they were lazily lounging about enjoying the sun but they were too close to the coaches for me to make a comfortable re-entry back into the square. The nearest approachable-looking person was a young, good-looking girl dressed in the bright red of Liverpool from the waist up. She had red ribbons in her hair and a large European Cup rosette pinned to her blouse. She definitely looked the friendly type, so I spoke up.

'Hey girl, here a minute.'

She clocked me warily.

'No, I'm not a weirdo, just come here a minute.'

She looked at her two mates, who giggled, then encouraged her to walk over. Her two friends smiled coyly and were definitely thinking, *this fella's trying for a cup final cop off. Seeing as it was such a fine day in the merry month of May, maybe they were also thinking that there might be a little bit of romance in the air, and hopefully they had me down as Anfield Road's answer to Paul Newman. Ha! Wake up soft lad, she's staring at yer.*

'I'm not being a weirdo or nothing, them dibbles are on my case.'

And she goes, 'And what?'

'Well, see them two lads sitting there?'

As I'm pointing, she's going, 'There's lads everywhere, soft shite, who d'yer mean?'

'There, them two there, the two with the black Adidas Samba.'

'Oh I see. The ones who look like two bottles of milk.'

'Ha ha ha! Yeah, that's them. Anyway, what's yer name?'

'Angela. Why?'

'I'm only asking. Can yer go and get them for us Angela? Cos I don't want them bizzies to see me, yer see. Go on girl, I'll say pretty please if yer want.'

'Go on then.'

'Err, all right. Pretty please.'

'Alright, hang on.'

Watching her walk down the steps, I clocked her bum. She was wearing a pair of tight Lois jeans and I liked her style. My immediate thought was of how her lovely backside made saggy Shirley's look like a five-year-old bag of spuds that'd been left on the larder floor inside a boarded-up fish and chip shop.

She turned on the steps and caught me clocking her bum. She smiled and said, 'What's your mates' names?'

'Ken Dodd and Arthur Askey.'

She half laughed and carried on down the stairs, saying, 'Sounds like you're the real comedian out of the three.'

When she touched me mate Eddie on the shoulder, he gave a jump, as he looked like he'd been in a bit of a trance. Eddie spent half his life in trance. Joey O, meanwhile, was well aware of his white torso. On rising, he immediately put on his Levi clip-button shirt as though he read Angela's mind about the bottle of milk joke. Angela pointed up in my direction and they shaded their eyes from the dazzling sun by raising a hand salute-style, before joint smiles of acknowledgment could be seen.

Walking lazily up the stairs, they tried to act dead cool but kept breaking out into little fits of laughter. Up close, I noticed they were both nudging each other as Angela's bum swayed from side to side. She was walking slightly ahead of them and I'm thinking: *I know boys; it's a whopper isn't it?*

Joey O spoke first. 'Where've you been, soft lad?'

'Angela, this is Liverpool's answer to Starsky and Hutch. Lads, this is Angela.'

Once everybody was introduced, Angela shouted her two mates over. She told us they'd come down by train with their dads as chaperones, and as she pointed them out, I think the three of us recognised that the daddios were already clocking us with that cynical 'keep yer eyes off my daughter's arse' look. Not wanting to linger in Daddy's glare, we said our farewells with a promise to have a bevvy up in Liverpool one day (and believe you me that day did arrive).

All the time we were speaking to the girls I was still keeping a wary eye on the coaches, but I'd lost sight of Jean-Claude and for a moment I got a bit edgy. I think Angela sensed this and gave me a peck on the cheek, saying, 'That's for the Reds, now have a good time.'

I whispered into her ear, 'Have youse all got tickets?'

'No, we're a couple short.'

I reached into me pocket and squeezed two terrace tickets into her hand. She looked at them amazed, legged it down to her da, who quickly produced the required fiver. Bombing back up the stairs, she eagerly stuffed the note into my hand to send us on our way. No freebies in 1978 I'm afraid; except for me and me mates that is.

I'd smelled alcohol on Angela's breath and clicked that she must've been having a sly sip of the hard stuff when her dad's cynical eye wasn't doing the rounds, otherwise she wouldn't have come forward to give me a kiss. Years later we laughed about it, and cynical Daddio, apparently after her divorce several years later from some fella who thought he was Toxteth's answer to Warren Beatty, had said, 'I told you Ange, you should've married that kid with the final tickets, you don't meet many of them in this life.'

But that's a different story. All I was interested in then was getting the news across to Starsky and Hutch, who'd already fathomed that something good had happened. Once we'd all given our farewells, I go:

'Who's hungry?'

And the two of them go, 'Starving, starving, starving,' or words to that effect.

'Come on, I'm taking youse for a Chinese, it's only round the corner and . . .'

'And where'd you get the money to be buying scran?'

'Slow down, Fast Eddie. Come on, let's get over to Chinatown. Haven't you heard that patience is a virtue?' In my best Max Bygraves voice, I added, 'I wanna tell you a little story . . .'

On the walk back to Soho I started to explain to the lads what had happened, and just as I'm getting to the best bit, who appears from nowhere.

'Aaagh, for fucksake.'

Eddie and Joey O looked mystified; they didn't understand that the Breck Road Rottweiler was back in town.

'Alright mate, how many tickets did yer cop for?'

'Five mate, three for us, one for me sister back in Trafalgar Square, and there you go, one for you. How's that for yer?'

'Ah cheers mate, I won't forget it. That's me sorted. I can see why yer didn't wait for us, you've gorra look after yer mates, haven't yer?'

'That's it lad, you know the score.'

His final words before he departed were three loud 'yee-ha's'. He punched the air, then he was gone. I still see him now and again on the doors of a few Liverpool boozers. He must be touching fifty, as he was ten years older than me on that sunny London day back in '78.

We sat down inside the same Chinese scran-house where I'd just washed my hands, right next to the big grandfather clock, with the same smiley, happy lady serving up the banquet. We walloped the food, before meeting the rest of our little firm outside the metal gates of Buckingham Palace. Here, we all made a mental note of how the bona fide big-time robbers really live. We all had a final ticket each for the first time in our lives, sold six others for face value, including my own (I was already a double-click expert: two through the turnstile for the price of one), gave Joey O and Eddie twenty nicker each, Dalglish chipped the Bruges goalie in front of the 80,000 Redmen among a crowd of 92,000 in a glorious 1–0 victory, whilst one pasty-faced Belgian tout probably looked on in dismay, staring miserably at a telly in a London boozer. The BIG cup was back in Liverpool for the second year in a row, and it all suddenly dawned on me the next day in bed. *Fuck the apprenticeship, fuck the nine to five, this footy's the one; this is going to be my ticket out to where the real life is, you know, where something's really happening.*

To make a life, some people choose social climbing, some people choose family connections, and some jammy bastards get to choose Mummy and Daddy's lovely big silver spoon. Well, I never had those choices when it concerned life matters, and although I didn't know it at the time, the day after that European Cup Final, I simply chose football. I suppose it was a bit like that Renton skaghead in *Trainspotting*, where he said he chose heroin, but that always seemed like a cop-out in my 'fight back against Thatcher' book. Footy was my drug of choice, much cleaner and it let you stamp around the Southern part of England shouting 'You dirty stinking Tory cunts' at every match-day opportunity. Politics and sport don't mix? Ha! They do where I come from. Our firm of boys wanted to be seen and heard all around Europe, whereas heroin meanwhile meant you only ended up shouting at your own family or the local shopkeepers who would always be on your case, and that was just wasting precious time.

And anyway, I had no aspirations to become just another 'Saturday's Kid' like The Jam later sang about. You know, nine to five, Monday to Friday, then betting office and clobber-shopping to stare at the passing Sharons and Traceys every Saturday afternoon, followed up by a spot of boozing every weekend night, to try and cop for those same Sharons and Traceys, where you might be lucky to get your 'bare tit' at half three in the morning. Nah, that typical young teeny-bopper lifestyle wears off as a weekend sideshow after one or two-year stint, while the football trips, for me, never did. I still need a good football dosage pumped into me system three or four times a week, otherwise I'm turkeying, and we're talking thirty-odd years on. Now that's a bit of a habit.

I'd travelled down to Wembley in me da's motor with me pockets bare to the bone. I returned home by bunking the train with me pockets full to the brim. I was seventeen and it was time to venture out. I didn't go to the match with me da again.

CHAPTER TWO

Haydock Roundabout

THAT HAYDOCK ROUNDABOUT on the M6 has got a lot to answer for. I mean, once the council planners had moved thousands of families out of the centre of Liverpool to the surrounding suburbs of Kirkby, Croxteth, Huyton, Halewood and Speke, hitchhikers' mayhem would erupt every time Liverpool played away. The battle was on to find your own speck as hundreds of young, penniless Liverpudlians scrambled for a thumbing space at the huge motorway interchange, all hoping for a lift to watch the Redmen play away.

Many a ship or plane-jumping Scouser now based on the distant shores of Australia, New Zealand or America started his first real journey away from home by using his thumb at that vast Haydock roundabout. The first time you ever got a decent lift, mileage-wise, felt like the first time the umbilical cord had completely snapped. This was the big world, rather than the few streets you were used to outside your front door. You were finally out on your own; no more giggling at the back on school day-trips to North Wales. It was a bit spooky at first, but the scary feeling wore off after a season or so and you'd start bunking off school early if it was a long-distance, mid-week night game. For me, footy beat Maths and Biology hands-down. I could hardly shake a leg for school, but I could sprint as fast as anybody when it came to football.

Our school was called Saint Kevin's and was one of the biggest boys-only comprehensives in Europe; in fact, with well over 2,000 boys, it may have been the biggest. It was a breeding ground for talented people, with world champion boxers in John Conteh and Paul Hodkinson – two world champs from one school; well I suppose you had to learn to look after yourself on that playground – famous footballers like Terry McDermott, Mike Marsh (Liverpool & Coventry), Paul Cook (Coventry & Burnley) and the Villa captain Dennis Mortimer – tennis pumps and tennis balls was how they learned to play, no schools of so-called excellence in those days – *Grange Hill* and *Brookside* creator Phil Redmond, the pop group China Crisis, actor Andrew Schofield (Scully) and comedian Sean Styles, along with other lesser known sports stars, actors and musicians. The only lessons I enjoyed turning up for were Games, because we always played football like Macca and Mortimer, and English, because you learned how to spell all the different footballers' names. Besides, you had to practise your autograph for when you became a Liverpool player, didn't you?

I'd see the older Kop skins heading off to the away games in their Crombies, button-downs, half-mast parallels and red-painted Air Wair, and I'd envy the freedom they had and the tasty clobber they wore. At the time I was a little ten-year-old suedehead, seriously monkey-booted, check Ben-Sherman'd and two-toned trousered-up. Junior school ollie (marble) collector or not, I was already chomping at the bit, so as soon as me and me mates felt brave enough, we headed up to Haydock roundabout to find our place among Shankly's, and then Sir Bob Paisley's, Red Army. It was watch-out time for the service stations up and down the M6 as the first LFC Scouse Urchins were on the march, pockets empty and all. For most travelling people the first hitchhiking question would probably be, 'Where's the best place to get a lift?' I think my first thumbing question was, 'Do they sell ollies in the service stations?'

Most of these mainly skint young lads were a different breed of Liverpudlian to the ones who'd travelled away in the early Sixties. They had been mainly city-centre-dwelling townies. Now the townies were being outnumbered by the shoved-to-the-outskirts council estate boys. These were the sons of dockers, seamen and factory workers who, now that they had smelled the freshly cut fields of grass and also the not so fresh horseshit on the farmers' fields, had become less wary of venturing out than many of their forefathers, seamen excluded. Some ex-town dwellers, on getting the odd sniff of horseshit, immediately vacated their new council houses and moved back to the tenements of town, their reasoning being that if it didn't smell like a roast dinner or the chippy, then it had to be 'bad for yer'. Other families enjoyed the luxury of a new house with an upstairs bog and the open fields too much to ever contemplate a return. Though most of the Lancashire farming folk were not too happy to see a load of Scouse rag-arses settling along their perimeter fences, as you could rest assured that for these new council estate settlers there was never going to be any kind of potato famine for them to deal with. Some of the poorer families, who basically lived on chips and pans of Scouse, didn't always have to go to the shops for carrots, cauliflowers and spuds. It was nigh on 100 years since thousands of starving Irish families had sailed away from home to settle on the banks of the Mersey; a large slice of these Kirkby people were the descendants of those families as the migration continued inwards.

One of my earliest memories, which was also one of the funniest sights I've seen, happened around 1969, when I saw a fat, wellied-up farmer with a face like a squashed tomato and a belly like the front of the Royal Iris legging three young kids in scruffy oul Liverpool kits (the one with the pink collar after a wash) as they dropped spuds, lettuces and other bits of veg they'd just dug up from his fields. I'd lay odds that, like a lot of lost Lancashire souls, he was a Man U fan, if not during the building of the council estate then definitely after it was completed. These Lancashire farmers had been growing and picking produce in peace for an absolute eternity, probably since the Vikings fucked off back to Norway; now all of a sudden hundreds of young Scousers were popping their eyes over the fences surrounding their acreage and declaring, 'Fuck me Jimmy, you don't have to go the shops for a lettuce round here.' You've heard of the Jocks and the Geordies battling at the border, well in the Sixties and Seventies it was the Scousers and the Farmers round our way.

From the early Fifties to the start of the Sixties, the population of Kirkby grew from 3,000 to 52,000. The small Lancashire village had been swamped by ex-townies. It was like Little Liverpool in the fields and, with one of the largest concentrations of young people in the whole of Europe, mobs of youths started to trek the surrounding areas to discover their new place of occupation. Gangs formed around the four different districts of Northwood, Westvale, Southdene and Tower Hill. Sociologists became fascinated with the place and documentaries were made for TV by Ray Gosling, the well-known film producer. Huge gangs of bootboys, sometimes numbering 300, would roam across the new battleground to look for fights with the neighbouring districts of Croxteth, Fazakerley and Cantril Farm. If they couldn't find a battle, they'd go back to their own area, regroup and fight with each other. At ten years of age I'd witnessed a few mass battles and thought they were superb viewing, although walking to a distant newsagents for me da's paper when the local shop was sold out could be daunting at times. You'd always have the snivelling little shit at the back of the mob waiting to spit in your face and rob your money. Mounted police were eventually drafted in in 1974 to quell the bootboy wars, and they based the hit TV series *Z Cars* (the Seventies version of *The Bill*) on Kirkby New Town

The real bizzies had already been shipped in in large numbers a few years earlier during the Tower Hill rent strike, which was beamed across the nation via the main news bulletin almost every night of the week. Here was 'Nob Hill', as we used to call it, an area not much bigger than two square miles, that defied a whole Government and its new legislation for a higher rent; some would say that that amounted to rebellion of the highest standard. People who wouldn't budge ended up in jail and some, unbelievably, are still in debt to this day for not giving in. It was obvious to any part-time sociologist that the place was almost totally made up of a unionised, socialist population. Most people were in low-paid employment, with large companies like Birds Eye, AC Delco, English Electric and Kraft housing the majority of the clocking-on cards. Once the Tories came to power in the late Seventies, those jobs and the larger companies started to close for good, or move their operation down south to the less rebellious and more obedient Conservative heartlands.

The vast majority of the people I grew up with were absolute salt of the earth and would go out of their way to help a new family settle, but with me being confrontational and always having one eye out on the street, it's the bootboys, the nutters and the shitbags at the back of the gang I remember. Even the local pubs had mobs sixty strong. Without doubt it could be an intimidating and at times violent playground. Though I say that, I wouldn't have missed it for the world. It was a good place to grow up and toughen up, with fresh air and fields in abundance, where burglars or muggers got battered and old people got looked after. At the end of the day fresh air and fields affect people in different ways. I thrived on it. Kirkby was alive and bouncing with characters and that's the way I liked it.

Most Reds supporters in the past never had the money or the means to get to distant away games every second Saturday. Maybe Bolton, Manchester or Yorkshire were okay to travel to, but places like Aberdeen, Southampton and Norwich could seem like the other side of the world. It would probably have seemed as easy to get to America on a ship leaving Liverpool docks than to travel by car to a place like Norwich during the first sixty football seasons. A train trip to the cup final in London, that says maybe, but the vast majority could not afford to catch the train every second week to watch the boys in Red, and most of the travelling Kop had more chance of seeing Queen Lizzie's bare arse than of ever owning a car.

However, our council estate generation could now see the trees and not just the River Mersey, and whereas Liverpudlians, they said, often tended to look out to sea, travel-wise and inspiration-wise this new generation could also look inland with much greater ease. Motorways, public transport and football specials were making other parts of Britain and Europe more accessible. Financially, though, things hadn't changed much and me and me mates were always looking for spare coppers. Bread rounds, paper rounds, milk rounds, you name it, we tried it.

Me ma and da had decided that they didn't want to beat a

hasty retreat back to Gerard Gardens, an infamous block of tenements at the back of Liverpool Museum in town, because they could see that me and me brothers liked the open fields, and once we could see the motorways beyond, there was no stopping us. By the time I had hairs on me sui mais and was getting too big for me Raleigh Chopper, I was an all-round council estate kid: I had two thumbs, so I was going to use them.

Me oul fella had started taking me and me middle brother to home games when he was ten and I was eleven, around the 1971/72 season. It was our Boys' Pen apprenticeship. Our youngest 'kidda' was still too busy riding his Raleigh Chipper around the bootboy-lined streets of Kirkby. We were Slade and LFC mad: it was a bad case of 'Cum On Feel the Noize' in our house during the week and a more serious case of come in and feel the noise every time we walked into the Boys' Pen corner of the Kop on a Saturday. The Boys' Pen was a breeding ground for Scouse tear-arses, as in the arse ripped out of your jeans variety, and from the moment your da dropped you at the 'turnies' (turnstiles) before he entered the adjacent Kop, it was fend-for-yourself time as you mingled with hundreds of other mad kids from every nutty district in Scouseland.

Once the noise reached a crescendo and 'You'll Never Walk Alone' hit the turntables at five to three, it became a scarf-robbers' paradise. Three o'clock and up went the huge, throaty roar that signalled kick-off. This was rapidly followed by a mass bunk-out of the Boys' Pen; a quick up and over the huge steel fence, followed by a graceful dive into the arms of a swaying Kop. The climb-over, which was a difficult manoeuvre at the best of times, was a lot harder if the bizzies guarded the fence. Then you would have to use the steel framework within the Kop roof, but if you were scared of heights, dithery of foot or not blessed with God-given agility, then you were stuck in the Boys' Pen with a bad view for the full ninety minutes. The bizzies, showing sense more than a lack of agility, would never dare attempt the climb, even if they did fancy putting a stop to the bunk-out, in case it resulted in themselves or one of the youngsters falling. Some of the wilder Scouse monkeys would clamber up onto the Kop roof for the duration of the match, or for part of it, before, point proven, they'd climb back down to join their cheering mates. Sometimes when the match got boring, or we were winning too easily, 25,000 pairs of eyes would be watching one of the more daring performing his circus act, and to this day, I find it hard to believe that nobody ever died from falling. Who knows? Maybe it was because Scousers were always great climbers; I mean, look at that Jimmy Tarbuck (as one docker said, he was the best joke he'd ever heard), but he still climbed to the top of the pro-celebrity golf world with shit jokes, and that Cilla Black (White Cliffs of Dover teeth with a voice like a fork on a plate), but she still used those teeth as a mountaineering hook to clamber to the very top of the showbiz world, and then you've got that Edwina Currie (proof that any moose can have a sex life). Those three combined, climbed right to the top of Mount Tory with ease. And that Edwina bird even got as far as the Prime Minister's bed, now that's what you call real climbing agility.

Later on, I realised that the non-match-going, much gentler hippy firm in our school had also been listening to our passionate songs and fervent noise, when somebody gave me a copy of the Pink Floyd album *Meddle*. If you listen carefully to the Kop in full voice, you'll hear a young boy cry out somewhere in the middle of the chanting sequence; well that's me, getting scarf strangled by some bigger skin from the Scotland Road or Breck Road area. Play it, you'll see.

We never got into that arty, progressive rock, stay in your bedroom and listen intently kind of shite, like a number of other kids at the time. As they'd be listening to concept albums in the bedroom, on a lot of those 'cap-sleeved and bell-bottomed nights', we might squeeze in the odd Slade single, K-Tel compilation or a Kop choir album on our two-tone kecks and Ben Sherman nights, especially if no one had a ball to kick around in yer monkey-boots (ox-blood and yellow laces) – still too little for Air Wair, you see – or nobody fancied going egging (looking for birds' eggs to collect) a few miles out in the country. No animal rights hippies to hound you in those days, only the odd, big-titted, nympho, woollyback wench to chase the young ones off Daddy's land before returning to milk the eldest of your crew who she had just stashed in the stables. *Lucky bastard!* It was never me, though I'd have swapped all me Liverpool proeys (match programmes) for the chance to walk home with a bundle of hay hanging from the crack of me arse. It was on these egging missions and general bootboy walkabouts that the local sweet factory, Pendletons, and the local dairy, Hansons, would often get screwed; maybe that's why half the estate never seemed to run out of milk, butter and jars of any well-known sweets you could care to mention (Cola Cubes Rule OK). During the six week summer holiday it was definitely 'Schools Out For Summer' by Alice Cooper, and 'Saturday Night's Alright For Fighting' by Elton John for us. If you'd have asked us about Mike Oldfield's 'Tubular Bell' we'd have thought you were talking about some Kirkby bootboy who'd been seen carrying around a specially adapted homemade weapon inside his Crombie coat. Our Mickey Oldfield would have made his tubular bell for walloping invading skins from one of the rival council estates. Mind you, pubs like the Roughwood, the Woodpecker, the Johnny Todd and the Park Brow in Kirkby all had massive mobs of their own, and would often fight among themselves when there was no match on, so I'm sure they could have found a use for a tubular bell without any brave invaders.

You'd see the hippy firm thinking they were dead cool with their ELP, Yes and *Tubular Bells* double LPs tucked under their hairy cap-sleeved armpits, as their pin-striped bags swished in the wind. Those pants were just a little bit wider than Daniela Westbrook's nostrils; main difference being the pants would be joined at the fly. No amount of Charlie could burst that zip. We called those trousers swimming lanes, for obvious reasons, and if anyone was wearing them, we'd say, 'If you take them kecks off and lie them flat, then roll a one-pence piece down the pleat and it stops dead centre between any two lines, then I've won them and you can't have them back.'

Musically, I used to think, *fuck the concept albums and waiting twenty minutes to hear the sound of the devil's voice, or some secret coded message from some charlied-up rock-god divvy.* Give me a three-minute single any day of the week. Once Slade had 'skweezed me and pleezed me', it was straight out into the fresh air with all the other apprentice bootboys, hitching down the motorway with a jar of Cola Cubes or Pineapple Chunks under me arm, on me way to see the Redmen play away. Venturing out to see a little bit of life and how the rest of the scenery looked always did appeal to the true travelling footy fan. Anyway, if you spent your time walking the streets of Kirkby, a place absolutely overflowing with bootboys, seeing as it was one of the biggest new council estates in Europe, then you stood a far greater chance of getting your head kicked in than if you toddled off to one of these so-called tough away grounds. For a basic, early, toughening up instance, I'd like to share a typical memory. It went something like this.

* * *

The old currant bun dazzles and shines full-on, like it always seemed to during your childhood. Maybe it's just a case of me looking through the old rose-tinted glasses. Those self-same glasses can play havoc on yer memory because as I drift back to an early 1970s summer, I could swear I'm trying to dodge puddles on my new Raleigh Chopper bike. Our kid's close behind, catching my spray, but he doesn't care, he's too busy singing that funny Alice Cooper song, 'SCHOOLS OUT FOR SUMMER, SCHOOLS BEEN BLOWN TO PIECES,' and he's bellowing it out to the hilt.

'Change the song will yer,' I'm shouting, 'That song didn't come out till about 1972/73 and it's only March '71, Liverpool are playing Everton today in the semi-final of the FA Cup, don't spoil it for me.'

Drifting deeper now and the sun seems as bright as those huge rock star stage lights and I feel a lovely warm glow as it shines directly on me. I feel like the new cycling star of the moment. An orange Chopper always beat a yellow version; I drummed that into our kid so many times that I think he still slyly believes it today. The big silver handlebars made it feel like I was riding on a mini Harley Davidson, out in front of my own little chapter of junior Hell's Angels; Born to be Wild, Get your motor running, head out on the highway . . . sorry, got a little carried away there. The highway in my Raleigh Chopper days was the fresh concrete of Kirkby New Town, and my nasty traffic cop was one Terence McCaffrey esquire, a Roland Rat look-alike and local bully to boot. This miniature Ken Dodd was bound to put a spanner in me chain, a load of tin-tacks in me tyres or his tickling stick over the back of me neck if I wasn't careful. The little shit was a few years older than me, an ardent Evertonian and always after me bike, but Charles Bronson on steroids would've had a serious battle on his hands to take it away from me. Anyway, me da had made me aware from the start of my early Chopper-owning days that this little gem had cost a tidy few quid. He'd been working permanent nights down at the A.C. Delco car parts factory to pay for my trusty steed, and any loss or damage would result in his size nine Dr Martens being instantly dispatched to the arse of my beige, bell-bottomed cords.

Oops! Steady there boy, nearly fell of the bike then. It doesn't matter how many times I have my lovely 1970s bike ride dream, the face of the Rat still startles me, and I suppose that's one of the reasons why it's become such an abiding memory. Yer see, every time I reach the little smashed-in air-raid shelter at the top of our local footy field, Terence fuck-face McCaffrey always blasts his goofy teeth into my shiny, happy scene.

'Give me the bike' he's shouting. 'Give me the fucking bike now.'

Trust Billy Bob the bully to pop-up just as me and our kid are buzzing. Little Connor Mac is running around with his ma's radio telling everyone the news that 'the Redmen have just knocked the Blue Shite out of the FA Cup,' and not even rat-features is going to spoil that 'we're on our way to Wembley' feeling. I think of me da for a moment. He'll be dancing his legs off inside Old Trafford now.

'Hey you, give me the fucking bike, dickhead.'

The Rat has got his arms out with a large stick on show, while young Connor stops to watch. I'm getting closer; I can't turn around as the dirt path is way too narrow and those bastard nettles are growing everywhere. Shit, I don't fancy that stick over the head.

'Give me the bike, Kopite gobshite.'

Oh I see, so Terence knows the score as well does he.

'Come on tithead, come to daddy, come to daddy.'

It's that last daddy that does it for me. There's no way I'm stopping now, in fact I pedal faster looking for maximum impact. I'm aiming for the gap between those two big goofy gravestones that are always hanging over his bottom lip. WALLOP. I run straight over him, only to crash into the ground a few yards on because my corduroy bell-bottoms had caught up in the chain.

As I get up, I notice the huge Birds Eye fish finger factory where me ma used to work; it's looming high over me, and in the after-tangle I realise that I'm now half man, half bike. With hardly a squeak from Roland the Evertonian rat, a quick backward glance tells me he looks like he's been in with Rocky 1, 2, 3, and 4, all at the same time.

There was no retribution to pay that day and rodent features never really bothered me again. Apparently he thought I was a bit of a psycho, and it's a fact of life that you can get away with absolute murder when you're labelled a psycho. It's something I admit I played up to over the years.

I spent the last few hours of sunlight on our local footy field dreaming I was Alun Evans, one of the semi-final scorers and my first real footballing idol. Once it became too dark I was back on the streets: here I was Brian Hall, the other derby day hero, as I wove my way around the dimly lit lampposts before smacking the ball for the umpteenth time past the invisible Everton goalie. The lanky bastard had no chance as usual, as I imagined him rooted to the spot down at the delirious Stretford End. My street of dreams was

Quernmore Road and it usually doubled up as Anfield, but today it was Old Trafford, the venue for the semi. The spot, or the lanky Everton goalie, was a fat blob of white paint and I think he was called Andy Rankin on the day – 'Handy Wankin' to us. The blob lay somewhere in the middle of goalposts that had been messily painted on the power station wall by the first kid to move here. My footy dreams briefly let me forget about the state of my appearance and my bike, till eventually all the other kids returned indoors and I nervously struggled home on my half-wrecked Chopper. I stopped at the gate. My clothes gave me the look of a car mechanic who had just finished overtime, and the only thing I lacked to complete the grease monkey effect was a pair of industrial boots, which my father duly supplied to my oily rear end at the doorstep of our house. He had eventually noticed me standing outside the front-door window after I'd failed for roughly the tenth time to get the bottle up to lift and then drop the door knocker.

'But da, da, what about the Reds?' I intervened.

'Never mind the Reds, what's wrong with that bike? Get it in here now.'

The semi-final intervention blag hadn't worked one iota, as I still got walloped. But it was all worth it in the end, as it paved the way for a smoother ride through childhood. Goodbye 1980s; Roland Rat-face, keep out of my sunny 1970s. Ha ha, the mind plays tricks, eh.

I love remembering back to that day in '71; it sort of felt like my first day in battle for the Reds. Daft, I know, but as you grow older you realise just how much of a role Liverpool FC and the footy in general have played in your life so far. At a press conference after the 1971 semi-final, Bill Shankly had asked the reporters where Harry Catterick, the Everton manager was. They told Shanks that Harry had been kept away by a little illness, and had had to miss the game. Shankly replied, 'You what? Sickness kept him away? My god, if I'd have been dead, I'd have made them bring the coffin to the ground, prop it up in the stands and cut a hole in the lid where my head was.'

When I heard that man speak I wanted to be part of Shankly's Red Army, so from the Rat incident onwards, I was the kid who'd always be clocking the Crombied-up bootboys that knocked about round our way. They were forever telling tales of football fisticuffs up and down the country, and of how Shankly was their King. You'd catch snippets as they chinwagged on the local holler (waste ground), near to the power station goal with the white blob, before one of them would gave you the proverbial 'fuck off kid' or a tasty, sprayed-red Air Wair boot up the ringpiece. Me, I couldn't wait to travel. Maybe I might meet some Cockney, Brummie, or Yorkshire rats who had the same ugly set of railings as Terry McCaffrey; if they did then I was getting stuck right in with the other Liverpool skins, no messing. Ha, you'd better watch out Britain, 'cos here comes the Annie Road's answer to Danny DeVito, four foot and a bit of serious Scouse attitude. Not yet left school, but dying to hit the M6.

The DeVito Kid didn't have to wait too long, when me da took me and me brother to Leeds a year or so later. We sneaked off for half an hour and tried to view the bootboys in action. We saw the big Liverpool mob, with those Kirkby skins in close attendance, and an even bigger Leeds mob, who put the shits up us because we thought they'd suss us two little titchy Scousers and do us in, but we didn't come across any skirmishes, and quickly returned to where me da and his mates were standing.

A few months later, as Danny DeVito grew into Joe Pesci I was given a free ticket for a home game at Anfield against Newcastle. The Geordies had signed a new star called Tony Green, and being the young footballer that I was, I badly wanted to see him play. Liverpool, with the electric Keegan in the middle, walloped Newcastle 5–0, and as I left the ground Newcastle had a firm of about 200 men – not boys, men. They had black and white scarves tied under their chins and were mostly wearing denim jackets and Crombies. As they got to the Arkles pub on the corner of Stanley Park, thousands of boys and men came running down from the Kop End and steamed straight into them, I'm thinking, *fucksake there's thousands of them*, and naturally, the Geordie men started to run, as most people would have. Then all of a sudden thirty or so of these Geordie fellas turned to fight. Now they were utterly outnumbered but had decided to make a stand, so eventually they got pummelled to the ground as AirWair boot met feather-cut with true 1970s elegance. Think of that 'Oops Upside Your Head' song, but with these words:

> You'll gerra boot wrapped round yer head,
> You'll gerra boot wrapped round yer head.

And that's what time of the day it was. The fact that they took a bit of a hiding was down to weight of numbers, and a better, truer fight would've been thirty or forty of Liverpool's top skins against this Geordie firm, no holds barred, in Stanley Park, with no Plod Squad about. Liverpool's hardest boys back then were called 'Kings of the Kop'. I don't know the name of the Newcastle equivalent, maybe it was the Gallowgate Giants. Now that would've been a real tasty quarrel for a kid to watch, not one of those WWF tag-match fuckabouts that the kids seem to love today. Mind you, thirty hard Scousers are bound to batter thirty hard Geordies. Simple give-him-a-dig sense will tell you that it's bound to be harder to throw right-handers when your arms are weighed down with all those 'Elvis', 'Cut Here XXXXX' and 'Mam and Dad' tattoos. Remember the old-saying, 'Clean arms means cleaner digs.'

As I tagged along, not far from the middle of the mob, most of these older skins ignored me. I had a distinct feeling that I'd been planted in the middle of that fight scene just to take it all in; as I looked at the faces in the crowd, they seemed to look right through me, as if I wasn't even there. Perhaps it was because I was only Joe Pesci-high. Eventually the plod arrived and broke the crowds up, and as the thirty Geordies, dust-up over, dusted themselves down, they were treated like heroes by the massive Liverpool mob. Every one of them was first clapped, then cheered, then clapped again down the road. The bizzies, in true *Blockbuster* style, didn't have a clue what to do. It was surreal.

The huge mob of Liverpool skins and bootboys continued to clap the Geordie boys all the way to their coach, and it came as no surprise that the non-runners were all on the same bus and not part of the rest of the Newcastle crowd that had just acted the Brendan Foster, by giving it platforms and army boots up the street. Even though some of them were cut and bruised, they were smiling and waving like returning war heroes. It looked dead funny but it was totally weird, and I followed the clapping Kopites, clapping myself, all the way to the doors of the charabanc. I was a young pretender, as a lot of young fans are among a huge, violent football crowd. The North-East away-day bus must have been run by the Newcastle No-Leggers company, because these fellas were walkers, not runners.

Liverpool at Anfield was a fearsome fixture for any rowdy away fan in the early Seventies, so much so that hardly anybody paid a visit. If a mob did arrive it was like Christmas had come early for the thousands of up and coming hardcases who roamed the Anfield streets. Massive tenement blocks like Gerard and Fontenoy Gardens, along with the myriad of streets that ran off Scotland Road (Scotty) and Great Homer Street (Greaty), were main ambush points on the route to or from Lime Street Station. The tenement landings and back jiggers (alleys) would be full of marauding skinheads and bootboys every time Liverpool played a reputable team. Both of the tenement blocks were a concrete maze if you didn't know the layout, and the bizzies had an impossible task of clearing the gangs on matchday. Me ma and da both had large families who all lived in Gerard Gardens and Gerard Crescent, and as a youngster I'd often walk around all the nooks and crannies reading the football graffiti on the walls. By the age ten or eleven I knew the place back to front, from the Wash-house, Bishop Goss School and the Pontack pub to Cassons, Johnny Ginelli's chippy and the walls of the Museum. Come Saturday, so did the older bootboys.

At home, the Liverpool supporters were widely acknowledged as the fairest in the league and would clap the opposition team off the field if they played brilliantly, but the same friendly hands that clapped classy, opposing footballers would hand out severe beatings to any opposing fans they might find outside the ground.

Nearer to our stadium – which we called the Shrine – Stanley Park separated the hallowed turf from Goodison. It was often referred to as the away fans' graveyard. Coaches from out of town would be smashed up outside the park gates or further down the East Lancashire Road as they passed

Norris Green or Kirkby. One ruthless mob of boys known as the Kirkby Kidnappers would often leave ammo massed up in a trench near a main crossing, especially when Liverpool were playing a hated rival team like Man U. On a couple of occasions, coaches too wrecked to continue their journey had fans pulled from their seats to be beaten up in the nearby fields. Some were stripped naked before being released somewhere in the centre of the huge council estate. This wasn't clobber robbing; this was naked humiliation for the fun of it.

I was sitting with a gang of kids on the Kirkby market stalls one Saturday night when two men walked past us in the buff. One was still wearing his platform shoes and socks, which made him look like a right weirdo. They were holding discarded fruit boxes over their privates and asked us where the police station was. Their accents and appearance cracked us up; they stood out so much in the empty market place. We realised they were Man United fans that had been to Anfield for that day's game. A lot of coach companies were soon crossing Liverpool off the list as a future destination. Throughout the Sixties and Seventies, Anfield was a rocking, passionate, wall of sound, but sometimes I think the 'best behaved' tag that we got came from the fact that hardly any away fans came to Anfield.

Instead we were going to take ourselves and our new-found fashion sense out to the country and beyond.

CHAPTER THREE

Smoothies R Us

BY THE TIME punk music had blown a hole in the boring progressive rock scene, around late 1976, we had become truly experienced hitchers who were absolutely dying to leave school. We were never really interested in pulling our thumbs out in school to try to pass a few GCSEs towards a place in university, or a better job on the nearby industrial estate, but if the Reds were playing away we'd pull our thumbs out all day long to get a lift to the match. We started hitching because we never had the money for trains or coaches, and the older skins were always regaling us with the tales of motorway battles and robberies. As the motorway was only a few miles down the road from our new council house, it was time to get on board, jump a lift and join the crew.

We never seemed to worry about pervert pick-ups or paedophiles in the mid-Seventies, although some fat, greasy lorry driver did come the beast one day on the way to West Brom, only to receive a large green 'yocker' straight between the eyes as we jumped from the wagon's cab. I'd love to see him now, then he could say hello to a nice tubular bell right across the temple, the greasy fat fuck of a lowlife. Me ma and da meanwhile, thought we were out playing footy on the local fields or in one of our mates' houses listening to some sounds. If they'd have known about our monthly motorway shenanigans, or the story of the HGV beast they'd have battered us and locked us in the bedroom during away games for the next six weeks, and seeing as me da had a bigger wedding ring than all of Joan Collins's and Elizabeth Taylor's stuck together, our heads would have been well and truly dinted in. The bedroom sentence would have also resulted in me getting splinters off the woodchip as I continually butted the bedroom wall in frustration before finally crying my eyes out as I thought about Stevie Heighway on the wing, or King Kenny curling one in somewhere 100 down the M6.

This song, sung to the tune of 'The Fields of Athenry' and later re-worded by Gary Fergo up in Huyton, simply told the story:

> Outside the Shankly Gates, I heard a Kopite calling
> Shankly they have taken you away
> But you left a great eleven, before you died and went
>   to heaven
> Now it's glory round the fields of Anfield Road
>
> (Chorus)
> All round the fields of Anfield Road
> Where once we watched the King Kenny play
> With Stevie Heighway on the wing
> We had dreams and songs to sing
> About the glory
> Around the fields of Anfield Road

A lot of young friendships were made at these away games. A shared interest in punk bands like the Clash and the Jam, alongside our obsession with football and clothes, saw these juvenile Scousers meet up at places like the famous Eric's nightclub in town. The punks and other Eric's regulars were quite elitist and talked as though they had sole control of the establishment; they were not prepared to admit just how many Scouse urchins were in among that crowd, especially when the decent bands came to town. I was always there if someone like The Clash, The Jam or the Damned were on, but if it was shite like The Adverts or the early Siouxsie and her bastard Banshees, then forget it. I'd be there with me trainees or suedies (Clarks suede boots) on, pogoing at the front with all the steelies and DMs, and if that doesn't go down too well with some forty-year-old ex-punk, then tough shit. Some of the other bands I went to see at the time were The Lurkers, Stiff Little Fingers, Magazine, Wire and Madness.

Me and me two mates, Dean and Tommy, loved this band called Deaf School; I must've loved them, because I even bought the albums. The lead singer had one of the biggest wedge-headed quiffs you've ever seen; it was nearly as big as Dean's, who fancied himself as the street version of the singer. His stage name was Enrico Cadillac and despite the long fringe and bad stage name this cool-arse wore nylon Hawaiian shirts and cool sandals just like we did. For about two years, Enrico, Bette Bright (later the wife of Suggs from Madness) and the rest of the Deaf School crew were our cream of Liverpool. We simply loved them, and thought Betty was God's gift to Scousers. We'd go to see them whenever they were on, and one time at the Mountford Hall (Liverpool University) they had this single out called 'What a Way to End it All' and we all thought this was going to be the big hit, but it wasn't to be; better in the end really, then you can always keep that good thing to yourselves. Once those good, working-class street trends in music and clobber get sussed by the bad money-heads and then the masses, they end up absolutely fucked, don't they? It's the Terry's

Chocolate Orange syndrome: they tap it, unwrap it and then gobble it all up. And those executives in the silver suits – don't they just love to hammer the living fucking daylights out of it till they've squeezed every last pound note from its original meaning? We were glad Deaf School didn't hit pay dirt.

If a full night on the tiles was in operation, then me and me mates would be there togged up in Deaf School-type Hawaiian shirts, oul fellas' straight-leg suit pants from the charity shops and sandals or suedies with no socks; always more Enrico than Sid from the Pistols. We were never into the gollying (spitting) or cutting yourself up, or putting on the big act that you were some kind of social fuck-up. We just wanted to see the bands, be different and dig the new breed. Some punk rockers were ordinary council estate boys, but I thought most of them were middle-class kids who would jump the train into town at the weekend to act the part. They looked tough in chains and leathers but scratch the surface and they bled custard, a bit like their spokesperson Johnny Rotten, a true sell-out if ever there was one. I remember him saying, 'Never trust a hippy.' Maybe it should now read, 'Never trust a punk.'

Music has always been a common denominator for young people, whether it be confined to the bedroom concept albums or screaming at the DJ for your favourite new punk single in a boozer in town. And when we hit the town, we not only had music and clobber in common, we also had a cocky Scouse attitude on board. The flared Levis were getting narrower all the time and soon I was asking me ma to take the seams in on all me kecks. Adidas Kick or suedies and frayed-leg Levis had become Adidas Samba and straight-leg Levis by the spring of 77. We started to wear those blue sailor pumps with the white sole and oul fellas' cord shoes from Timpson's in the summer. Then we started buying or hoisting Hawaiian-style shirts from secondhand shops like Ann Twacky's and 81a; not the loud *Loveboat* coloured ones, I might add, only the plain or slightly patterned darker ones (fuck them muzzied-up *Magnum* shirts). Crew neck lambs' wool jumpers and cotton sweatshirts took over from v-neck Slazenger and Puma jumpers; in fact, it was funny just how much oul fellas' clothing we had started to wear. Even some of me da's oul 1960s tiny-collared shirts started to look okay in his wardrobe, and before you knew it, I was starting to wear a couple for the odd Friday/Saturday night bevvy in town. I'd skitted and taken the piss out of me da's clobber big time for the past few years; now here I was sneaking some of his older 1960s gear out of his wardrobe just so he wouldn't clock me.

Some of the boys noticing would go, 'Tremendous shirt that Nicky, where's that from?'

'Me uncle sends them over from Paris for me.'

'Yer kiddin'? Can he send me some then?'

'I'm only joking, soft lad, it's from me oul fella's Beatle collection.'

'Is it? Fucksake, it's a whopper shirt, that. D'yer reckon he might have one for me as well?'

A Dave Bowie and Roxy Music/Bryan Ferry scene started to unfold at clubs like the Checkmate, and later a punk club called the Swinging Apple. Now although this probably happened in other cities, I don't think those kinds of music scene people elsewhere were really into football, whereas in Liverpool you couldn't avoid it. Even most of the Scouse grandmas could always tell you who wore the number seven or eight for Liverpool or Everton, and a lot of the young Bowie freaks would have a Red or Blue allegiance even if they didn't go the match. These Roxy/Bowie boys and girls had always been clothes innovators, so a natural progression occurred where we basically took it onto the terraces, only this time it got trainee'd-up. Head to the waist, you'd look just like a Bowie/ Ferry freak, but from the waist down it was trainees and jeans instead of pants and pointy shoes. I suppose some people wanted to dance and sing along at the clubs while others wanted to run and sing along at the match.

With us dressing and talking so differently from other teams' supporters and from lads in the surrounding satellite towns, we got more and more full of ourselves. 'Mushrooms', some of the woollybacks fifteen miles out used to call us: 'All got big heads and live in shit.' Plus, with the fact that some Liverpool people had started to move out to those woollyback suburbs and quickly multiplied, they'd be giving it the mushroom one again, as in, 'Once one of them pops up and grows, next thing there's fucking hundreds of them.' I'm sorry to disappoint you sheep, but the fact is them woollyback girls always loved a Scouser, that's why they dropped their drawers in Spain and Greece every summer before having baby mushrooms in the local woollyback hospitals. I think a lot of the girls loved it when Liverpool lads would buy them drinks and have them giggling out loud, and I suppose the accent not belonging to their own small town meant nobody was going to find out when they had a bit of fun. You know what they say about those small town girls once they've been let of the leash. Simple fact is, woollyback men don't get the ale in. Another pointer towards good sexual relations might be to stop the ferrets from jumping on the poor girl's tits every time you brought her home.

The mushroom jibes came direct from the land of fifty pence vest and undie advertisements. These adverts are legendary in Liverpool. They appeared in local papers like the *Liverpool Echo* and lads would sit there sussing them out before erupting with laughter. Things like: 'School string vest, heel of lead singer's platform boot, one sock, and stained undies with no elastic. Price 89 pence the lot. Phone Wigan 123:1234.' Or: 'Blazer with one arm, laces from size 14 Air Wair, plus tea-stained photo of rare pigeon at rugby ground. Price £1.47, all in. Phone Warrington 234:3456.' When you're surrounded by the thrifty mingebag mentality of that kind of woollyback, no wonder you feel aloof and start to form a superiority complex. Ask any Scouser and he'll tell you, most of them woollies have got Fort Knox wallets. They're the only fellas who won't buy a girl a drink after she's only just promised to share his straw bed, and even then they'll ask her to pay half for the taxi fare home; now that's a door-hinge supreme. Most of the men of wool can make a Welsh Rod Stewart look generous. Sometimes on the way to an away game, one of us would have last night's *Echo* and the classified vest-and-undie adverts would have us in absolute pleats.

For home games, we started to meet in the Anfield Road End of the ground. With a cocky attitude abounding and a rapidly growing crew, some of the Annie Road End boys, including myself, even began to think that we were 'the boys' in town. I have to say 'think' because there are that many firms of scallies around Liverpool at the weekend that it can resemble cowboy country, with snazzy cars instead of horses and carts, gangs of outlaws wearing tasty clobber instead of Buffalo Bill jackets and snakeskin stack heels, and a host of wise-arses drinking in saloon bars all waiting to shoot you down if you get too big for your Rockport boots. Don't let the businessman on the podium fool you about our city needing more parks and gardens. Most of the Scousers I've ever known want to party, go out, see a show, get on the juice and dance till they drop, especially once they've earned some decent dough. Even the lads I know with stiff legs and no rhythm always end up having a good jig after a few bottles. Liverpool has always been a bit of a Wild West capital of Britain, where bevvying and partying for the weekend is a must. The town itself is one fantastic place to go on a bender, with 1001 boozers brimmed-up with those fast-talking scallywagesses; if you're shy, get there, they'll blag you. But if you start getting too cocky, or wearing any ten-gallon hats proclaiming you're the hardest, it's one place you're bound to meet up with a mad fill-yer-in mob sooner rather than later. No one gang has ever ruled the roost like they do in some other towns, so yer see, it's deffo cowboy country. 'Every dog has its day' and 'what goes around comes around' are two well overused sayings in Liverpool, and even the so-called biggest and toughest are bound to get their comeuppance if they start getting way above their station. Cowboy Town, what can I say?

Away matches for the Road End boys, meanwhile, were a whole different proposition than Liverpool city centre. For a few years, 1977–80, we walked around football grounds like we were God's gift to the terraces. It all sounds so fucking contrived now, but that's where we were at. And with most grounds juiced up and dying to give the 'weird dressers' a bit of a hiding every Saturday, you had to permanently have your wits about you. We soon forgot about Betty Bright and Deaf School come match day, as some Birmo'd up ponce would be trying to lamp you one. Once the 1977 season started, it took only a couple of months to realise just how different we were. We were getting called 'queers' and 'pufters' most weeks, which was absolutely hilarious at a time when there was neither sight nor sound of fascist homosexuals like Peter Tatchell, ramming that heterophobic diatribe down people's throats. Telling us our kids need to be taught in school about the love life of Jack and Pedro, in other words, the Kama Sutra according to Johnny Vegas and Bernard Manning. Join the real world skeleton cheeks. I didn't need to be taught that stuff in school; I was learning it across the fence at places like Leeds, Newcastle and Man U every other Saturday.

When I look back at those brief moments, early doors '77, I know that we were the absolute beginners in the travel breaks and clobber stakes. We got about two years of being totally different from all the other supporters we'd see around the country, before the penny finally dropped for the masses. Everton at the same time had a much smaller but just as game Park End mob, and a few of my mates were part of that crew, but the thing is, they never had the team to follow to Timbuktu like us, so they never really developed along the same lines numbers-wise and travel-wise. It's one of the reasons quite a few of those lads travelled away with Liverpool, Scousers only, mind you; fuck-all was watered down with woollybacks in those days.

Once that style hit the terraces during the late summer of '77, the Road End boys were sporting Dave Bowie and Bryan Ferry-type fringes that hung over one eye, plus their own staple diet clothing of straight-leg jeans, Adidas trainees, button-down Ben Shermans or Fred Perry tee-shirts, Benetton lamb's wool crew-neck jumpers (Marksy's if you hadn't been abroad), with a snorkel parka, cagoule, or a high-neck, Harrington-type jacket. That more or less sums up the whole Scouse rig-out and things have developed from that line of clothing right down to this day. I still wear more or less the same things, and probably always will. If I reach a good old age, I can just see myself walking along the prom as an oul man, dressed in me Samba, straight-leg jeans, Fred, and this nice New Man jacket that I just can't wear out, and some young kid walking past and saying to his mates, 'Look at that oul cunt, he's on the ball with the gear, isn't he?' And his daft mate going, 'Nah, he hasn't got no hair to dye blond, and they're not Prada them boxing shorts hanging out of the top of his kecks.'

Compared to the way our firm started wearing different clothes, the main difference today is about attitude and the fact that they're all label mad, with the dearer the better seeming to be the norm. That false load of crap reminds me of that Harry Enfield character, the Brummie beaut, when he says, *I've got considerably more money than you*. The originals were never about Prada, Versace or any other daft, fashion-victim, rip-off label, like some of the knobhead pop stars and footballers wore. Take those Kicker boots that arrived a few months later; they were worn because you could traipse round half of Europe before they fell apart and they also looked half-tidy with a good pair of jeans. In other words, they were simply good boots. The original lads were about being different and wanting to be clued-up streetwise about things like travel, music, footy, clobber and who the biggest knobhead of the day was.

A good Scouse example: say some yuppie whopper is wearing a small metal Arsenal badge while walking down Kings Road with a few grand hanging out of his D&G back-bin. The whopper is searching for some 200-nicker t-shirt to impress the wine bar crowd tonight. He also thinks he knows the score on the football, the footy firms, and who's who at the match. Deffo a full-on 'phoney stormer' in my book, but most of today's top beauts have probably got him down as a well-sussed lad. I can just hear them now: 'Oh he's rather custy that Cecil, wears all the gear,' and 'Cecil's a boss supporter, he took two of the lads to Newcastle in his new silver BM last week, apparently he's well in with Robert Pires.' Wakey, wakey, whoppers, where's your nous? The sons of Maggie eh, always impressed by money and not the man instantly comes to mind. Learn your lesson lads, it's not about wanting to get into the VIP lounge at the Hippodrome, it's about laughing at the dickheads who frequent those hangers-on yards.

It's a bit like me oul mate Joey knowing the score after dragging himself up by his own bootlaces, while his nineteen-year-old son hasn't got an igloo when it comes to street smarts and thinks people like Eminem are well in the know when it comes down to what's happening today. Sad eh? Listen up, it's like this: Joey O, who has a bit of pull when it comes to getting into the nightclubs and up-market bars of Liverpool, is always getting bugged by Christy to sort out passes or door admissions for club opening nights when some half-arsed celebrity turns up to cut the ribbon. Christy's a bit of a ligger, he'd be the first to admit it, yer know, easily impressed by some phoney pop star, soap star or footballer being in his own breathing space. The lad often goes out of his way to hang out where they hang out.

Well after bugging his dad Joey non-stop for a week, about getting him door-passes for the new 'cool dude' club opening, Joey finally goes, 'Stop going on, will yer? Can't you shut up about celebrities and opening nights?'

And Christy, his lad, goes, 'But you'll still sort it for me, won't yer?'

Joey O, realising he's a lost cause, decides to have a bit of fun, and goes, 'Haven't you heard that Liverpool's been named the Capital of Culture?'

'Yeah, of course I have.'

'Well stop acting like a Manc then, soft lad.'

When you mix a little bit of Scouse nous and that original timeless rig-out with European away games and success on the

football field, as in new trainees from Switzerland, T-shirts and
jeans lifted abroad in France and Germany, and new tops and
coats from Portugal, Spain and Belgium, all ragged at pre-
season tours and European Cup games, then new gear would
appear every few weeks on the Road End terraces. The staple
rig-out though, has always remained the same. The main
difference now is that you can buy it on every British high
street, and that's the reason it's worn by every Tom, Dick and
Harry from Alaska to the Arndale.

But for now it was the summer of '77 and for one group of
young football trendsetters things would never be the same
again. For the Annie Road End crew, the bootboys had had
their day. With the rest of the country yet to twig what was
happening, the early Annie Roaders' battles were always a case
of scallies onto bootboys, and a lot of the time it was young
lads onto older fellas. I can remember this big Man U fan, who
looked like Chubby Brown with a fair-haired Keegan-perm (in
our terms, one lost-in-space spaceman), attacking me on the
patch of land outside the Scoreboard End at Old Trafford in a
long leather and a pair of half-mast pants. This was one mixed-
up thirty-five-year-old Northern Soulboy – sorry, I should say
Soul*man* – whose just-over-the-knee kecks could have sailed
across the Atlantic all by themselves. He couldn't get near me
as I squirted tomato sauce over his leather while other young
lads laughing nearby were telling him to fuck off home to his
wife and kids. I told him to fuck off to Wigan Casino and the
dopey bastard told me he wasn't from Wigan. The laughing
and squirting only stopped when Officer Manc eventually got
involved. By the time he'd cleaned all the sauce off, Wigan
Casino had probably closed down. The hot-dog-sauce-on-your-
clobber routine was one of our favourite match day stunts, and
I can still see that black long leather as we tried to dye it red.

We soon had our infamous 'darts team', who could hit a treble-twenty, fucked-up barnet from a good fifty yards. The Jockey Wilson firm were constantly darting around grounds looking for opposition targets and the newspapers printed pictures every time they hit a lacquered-up centre part bullseye.

We also had our feather-cut burners, who became notorious around the woollyback grounds for setting those lovely sweeping feather-cut hairstyles alight. Sounds mad now, but at one time an away match wouldn't go by without a couple of hairdos going up in flames. Today the little firm who used to make bonfires out of barnets would probably be looking at ten years each, even longer if the fella's star jumper and penny-round shirt caught fire too. Man City across the fence in 1978 comes to mind, when one Rod Stewart-type Manc, or should I say Paul Calf-type, who was mouthing off big-time, had his gorgeous locks set ablaze. One minute it was 'Scouse bastard this, Scouse Bastard the other', the next minute, a struck match and his rug was aglow. Every Scouser in the vicinity burst out laughing as he furiously patted out his own fire, and strangely, a few young Mancs across the fence were giggling too. He had instantly turned from a top terrace bootboy into a plucked pheasant with a head like a flattened cat.

I know it sounds crazy with the barnet burners, but it was only young lads letting off steam in their own warped way. I've no doubt the social shrinks came up with their own detailed analysis, along the lines of, 'Tommy's parents smoked throughout the pregnancy, and were forever lighting the little coal fire in their living room once Thomas was born. This had a lasting psychological effect on young Thomas, who decided to re-enact his parents' smoking and coal-fire actions by lighting other supporters' heads on fire at the match.' Or some other load of triple X bollocks. With the young Road Enders being confronted by gangs of older bootboys most Saturdays, the clash of training shoe and clumpy boot often brought a huge contrast in and around the nation's football grounds.

There were lads I grew up with who thought we were bananas when we persistently got on one. But if I'd stayed in the house listening to those concept albums, I'd have missed out on the real life. Plenty did miss the boat: it pulled out of Dover for Ostend in 1977. You still had a good chance of catching it in 1979 when the Mancs jumped on board, or 1980/81 when the Cockneys went all Pringley. And if you're sitting in each night on your Crazy Georges three-piece suite pondering how things might've been, don't worry; there might be reincarnation for Scousers once you've popped your clogs. But be wary, be very wary, you might just come back as a Burberryed-up Brummie and then you're truly fucked. Sarcasm aside, if all you stick in the muds who used to wonder why we loved and followed the footy so much are more or less happy with your lot, are not that bothered about missing any boats and are quite enjoying being a loss adjuster for the Halifax claims department, then that's okay; just stay in and get into your old sounds, or act young and foolish by getting into your daughter's Westlife and Kylie albums. But if you thought like me in those just-left-school days, then you'd have been thinking, *why stay in the house and listen when you can bounce off the nightclub walls and sing along?* So one night we took ourselves into town and that's exactly what we did.

We started asking the DJs for the same songs every week, which most of them wouldn't go near, never mind play. One lad loved his music so much that he'd often bring a few singles out with him, mainly reggae and punk stuff, but them disco DJs were having none of it, until one night this DJ in a club called Scamps (now the 051) in Mount Pleasant put on a couple of Pistols and Stranglers singles 'as a request for the Road End boys, who are always on my case every weekend'. That was it: it went off big-time, with the club furniture and display pictures getting wrecked by the pogoing, Adidas/snorkel mob. A few people got annoyed with drink spillages and whatnot, so the disco, soul and funk freaks ganged up and a large battle commenced. We never went back again, not for fear of reprisals, but because of the thought of having to face up to a disco damages bill, plus the fact that there were a few casualties. I learned later that the black DJ got severely reprimanded by the owners for granting our request. One lad in our company called Joey (a popular name in Liverpool) pogo'd his way through so many disco display boards in the club that he was like a snorkelled-up version of the Hulk.

Lads who were starting to get into the same clothing and music as us struggled to hear their favourite music, unless, as I've said, they went to Eric's or some other small, underground punk club. But these places were few and far between and would always be full of crap birds, plus a lot of the fellas in there were the ones you used to boot up the arse in school for being bad suckholes. Good music/crap tarts, we used to say, and those steelies never did look quite right with tatty fishnet suzzies. And fuck that black nail varnish and black lippy for a lark.

By mid-1978 we were requesting songs like 'White Man in Hammersmith Palais', by the Clash, 'In The City', 'Down in a Tube Station' or basically anything by the Jam – and getting absolutely nowhere in the process, unless we ventured over to Michelle Claire's or the Swinging Apple, but in these places you had virtually no chance of copping off in our clobber. Acting the dirty ticket by getting a quick bunk-up in the bogs, yes, bagging-off, no, and there were no smoochy slowies at the end of the night. All the birds we liked – and there were quite a few female dressers in the early days in Liverpool – went to soul/disco clubs, so if you wanted to bag off it had to be a Barry White night. And let's face it, most disco music is pure drivel, end of story.

A lot of those punk birds did their shagging on the stairs or in the bogs inside the Swinging Apple, while Iggy Pop went on about being 'The Passenger' or the Talking Heads sang about some 'Psycho Killer'. Other frequently requested songs were Elvis Costello's 'Oliver's Army', Stiff Little Fingers' 'Alternative Ulster', Sham 69's 'Angels With Dirty Faces', and anything that you could chant or sing along to in the boozer. Other groups who were well liked were the Beat, Teardrop Explodes, the Stranglers, and later on, the Las, Talk Talk, Big Audio Dynamite, the Waterboys, the Smiths, New Order, the Bunnymen and local heroes Groundpig, but asking for them to be played in your average drinking den was usually a waste of time, and the match lads never really had, or took over, a nightclub of their own.

Probably the closest they got was when The State opened up years later. Along with Cindy's (clobber, necking and slowies) in the late Seventies and a club called Gatsby's (clobber, pot-smoking and slowies) in the Eighties, The State was about as good as it got for the young smoothies – when we were younger that's what we called anyone who dressed that way at the match or out in town. Smoothie sounds daft and dated now, but that's what we called like-minded lads who'd thrown away the AirWair. It was never a label like 'casuals', for instance, more of a loose term you would use, like you might say:

'He's a smart lad; he's a bit of a smoothie isn't he?' Or, 'Sound pair of trainees on him, he knows the score that kid. Deffo a bit of a smoothie.' I suppose it eventually turned into scally.

The main reason the clubs would not play our type of music was because they were petrified of a Scamps-like situation arising. They were scared that it might go off large-scale and the place would get wrecked. 'White Riot' by the Clash was never going to keep the peace in the midst of a young, half-drunken club clientele, and when push comes to shove, the early Road End lads were nearly all boozer boys at heart anyway. You could always fill the pub jukebox with Van Morrison, Dylan, Simon and Garfunkel and the Beatles, who were all staple music alongside the punk New Wave, and as long as the boozers could take your cash they didn't seem to mind what you sang along to. The usual late-on bevvies and stay-behinds could end in thirty lads being shown the door at half three in the morning as the words to 'Billy Hunt' by the Jam or 'Stay Free' by the Clash rang out around the empty streets. If it was bagging off time, with thoughts of doing your press-ups, then you'd be off to one of the Saturday Night Fever discos like Scamps, Annabel's, Flintlocks, or the Hollywood. Here the night would often end with a Commodores slowie, where your chin could be tiredly drooped so far over the girl's shoulder that you'd end up with a bigger jaw line than Lionel Richie.

I remember that song at the end of the night, 'Once, Twice, Three Times A Lady', and my mate Dean and I both wanted to dance with this lovely girl, and nobody could beat Dean in a race for a bird, so as I'm watching them wrestle on the Babbaloo dance floor, scratching the balls of my Lois jumbo cords, I'm thinking, *fuck you stallion, you're not leaving me on me own*. So I go in search of another Scouse cutie-pie. Found her: gorgeous, baggy white blouse, tight Levis and Kicker boots – I can just make out the Kicker tags in the dark. It's looking all right to me. Tap her on the shoulder and away we go. Little sovereign earrings and a wedge haircut and quiff frame her lovely face.

Here I am, I'm Susan George'd-up to death. It's feeling good, but I step on her toes and completely lose me rhythm. I'm dancing wonky but I carry on, hoping it's going to get better. Her perfume smells nice, and ski-slope jawed Lionel's starting to sound real smoochy, so I take a chance and rub my cords against her jeans, and just as I'm getting into it, *BASTARD*, I clock her in the mirror on the other side of the dance floor. She's throwing wanking signs and knobhead gestures to her mates because I'm dancing like a sumo wrestler in a pair of stack-heeled Pod. *Cheeky cow*. I'm devastated: just when I was giving it me best Bryan Ferry smoothie routine she goes and kicks me in the plums. I'm thinking, *hard-faced, Kickered-up moose, I'll show you*.

So I break-off mid-slowie and say, 'Ta-ra girl, I'm off.'

She looks at me quizzically, so I know I've got my own back a little. By burning her off this way, it's like I'm not interested. As I march towards the stairs, I shout to Dean, 'I'm off the Swinging Apple, I'll see you later if you make it.'

Apple entered, better off in here. They don't give two fucks, these punk birds. Ten minutes later, Dean walks in.

'She was hard graft that bird, so a jibbed her.'

Twenty minutes later, my other mate Tommy walks in with a couple of lads. That's it, get the Clash on, we're sorted. 'White riot, I wanna riot, white riot, a riot of my own.' And that's how an average Saturday bag-off went. In other words, most weeks we didn't get a snifter. You'd look for the girls in the natty threads, that understated Sixties hippy look, sovereign'd and quiffed-up to go, before making your move. But these birds weren't quick to drop their scanties, while punk birds would wallop you there and then, then cop for some Welsh Johnny Rotten later on. Nicely dressed, wise-arse girls you wanted to go with, but sex-wise, some of those punk girls could be worse than the fellas. Take your pick. So you see, clobber even came into play when the ladies popped up, so don't let any fourth-rate hardcase hooligan try to tell you that clobber wasn't essentially important, because it essentially was.

Dress sense around this time sorted out all the wised-up, know the score brigade from the platform and star-jumper, know fuck-all brigade. Today every knobhead from Aberdeen to Ipswich wears the same rig-out, but in the early punk days things were so diverse that what you wore actually did matter. People who we called knobheads then for wearing things like Gola trainers, leg-warmers and white Cockney socks with loafers are probably the same older, none-the-wiser knobheads who now pay fortunes for labels and still miss the point, Davinia Beckham-style; he would have deffo worn leg-warmers with his gold Lois cords twenty years ago, that whopper. From the skinheads to the punks, rockabillies to teddy boys, hippies to smoothies, all clobber on the terraces, or around town, made a statement. Whereas today they're all trying to look like they've got a few quid; walking around hardcase style, acting like they know the score. Most of the young pretenders wouldn't haven't a Mr Magoo how to fuck off abroad with a fiver and no pazzy without screaming for mammy and daddy on their brand-new two-ton mobiles every couple of minutes. No individuality is what I'm on about. You know, the people who buck the trend and don't give two fucks, and I don't mean your fashion victims in £500 ripped jeans and silver DKNY undies. Walking golf balls like the gobshite England captain are labelled style gurus by some of the clueless media. Pull the other one. When Birmingham, Leeds and London footy fans all dress the same, plus a lot of other European hoolies are almost the same, then we've definitely reached the Sheepsville stage.

During the summer of 1977, when things started to kick

off and kick in, I wouldn't have been seen dead walking down the road with someone in a Charlie Chaplin jumper, pinstripe Birmos and shoes the height of wedding cakes. Nah, not without wearing some kind of Frankenstein mask purchased from the Wizard's Den (a Liverpool joke shop) or some other mad disguise, just so nobody would get on me walking and talking with the woollies. Fellas with daft chains or studs through their noses, or bad dragon-style tattoos all over the show, got well blanked. It's a funny one that, because we'd only have ourselves to talk to today, when you consider that chains, rings and bad tatts seem to be all the rage. Take them big Chinese designs across the base of your back that are supposed to have inner meanings like peace, love, and curried ring-piece on fire below. What's all that about? Fucksake! I've no doubt I'll soon see some fella that'll have a Chinese spine tatt that means, 'We took the Shed in 1985 using Kung Fu stars and chopsticks, and had a char sui foo yung just after it.'

CHAPTER FOUR

The Boys From

the Annie Road End

THE ROAD END mob and Liverpool's travelling crew were made up of a number of smaller mobs from all over the city. By late '77, early '78, there were boys like the Huyton Baddies, with Fergos, Bennos, Joey Robbos and the Fullos all coming from the Dovecot and Huyton area, along with Homer, Cooper and Barney. It was watch out time if all the 'O's were on your case. Here was a ruthless bunch of young tear-arses with one eye on a quick earner and the other on handing out a quick beating to any would-be Farmer Giles invaders. If you were wearing your star jumper near Anfield and happened to bump into these boys, it was time for you and your star jumper to blend in with the Milky Way.

There were the Kensington boys, with your Garragosses, yer Willsies, yer Barrys, yer Rockys and yer Russells always in attendance, a large Red firm just by themselves, with fifty younger urchins, like your 'Ant Hill Mob' Boydies, your 'Jimmy Page' Metcalfes and your size-twelve-Pod Dickies all buzzing in and around the Holt boozer before and after match days. This firm were mainly out-and-out Liverpool hoolies who basically couldn't give two fucks about the earners as long as they kicked some away fans' arses right into touch. If any kids were born shitting red instead of yellow, it was this crew. They never produced any young Red sprogs as they were always jumping off at Edge Hill (it's a local joke, so look in one of those 'teach yerself Scouse' books if you are not with me), but they were the best firm ever at pulling the emergency cord to jump the train early doors.

Then there was a south end of the city firm, with Jimbo, Gilly, Heron, big Sean and Fat Eddie all looking to do severe damage. Further to the south you had firms from Speke, Garston and Netherley, and probably the biggest south-end firm of all, the Halewood chains, still active today and one of Liverpool's biggest and maddest partying crews; if you didn't find them dancing at their local Leather Bottle hangout, it was only because they were dancing around somewhere else in Europe, or after some home fans on an away ground car park. The Leather Bottle in Halewood could well be one of the finest venues available to host the all-new version of *Come Dancing*. Gargan, Mono and Geoff were three of their founder members, ably accompanied by Jam, Gram and a plate of boiled ham. For anyone looking to learn the Bootwalk, the Mr Gargan fella can still be found giving the odd dance lesson in the Sandon boozer every Saturday night. That crew have done more dancing than Lionel Blair on home leave, after he was suspected of smuggling charlie inside his Cuban heels.

There were zappers (pickpockets), or dipping teams, from Kirkby, Croxteth and Scotland Road. They mainly operated at away grounds but would have no problem with dragging your sheepskin coat halfway round Stanley Park till it eventually fell off or came free of its collar somewhere by Goodison. One day, as we were beating Tottenham 7–0 at Anfield early in the '78 season, a few of them were operating on the other side of the fence, among a small Spurs donkey-jacket mob that looked even worse off than us. One of the Road End lads called them the YMCA firm. When asked what he meant, he replied that they were, 'Young Men Who Caress Arse.' Somebody said, 'Shut up dickhead, that's YMWCA.' And he said, 'So fucking what, there's one of them as well.' Dizzy, dizzy, dizzy. But no two ways about it, some of these fellas might well have been mistaken as the first gay away crew, seeing as they were always feeling other fellas' arses in and around the ground, just to see if they were carrying.

You always had your pure bevvying crew at the away games, and some of the best Liverpool fans you could ever wish to meet could be found amid these Scouse Vikings. People like Sully and Potter, and the via-Llandudno Wilcox crew, mostly from the Scotland Road area. This latter firm could normally be counted on to be carrying train tickets to the southern end of Europe, so anywhere en route in the UK was no problem. There were characters with two or three names like Smigger from Kirkby, alias Lumpy, alias Davie Johnson Face, and Jaffa, alias Cigar, alias Guinness – different name every week, these lads. Other strange names included Marty the Firebobby, Ribena Skull, Barney Cuckoo, James Cagney, Donkey Dick, Griffo Two-Tone, Cockney Matt, Lend's Yer Odds, Bonk, Snorkel Juice and Manhead. What an absolute mouthful of lads. Then you had Hally and Mick Mc from the Bootle brigade, and the Miles gang from Vauxhall. The Milesies had a bigger crew in one family than Southampton had in their whole ground. It would've been brilliant if they'd been a hooligan family for a few weeks, then you might've seen them being first family to take an away end.

The Jester boozer on Scotland Road was a main ambush point for away fans and people like Sconch, Burkey and Jimmy

Bolo knew all the best jiggers and hiding specks around that area. The Liverpool firm would be hidden among the Scottie nooks and crannies, before appearing into the light like a bunch of Scouse Zulus wearing Samba and Freds. Young scouts of the day, like your Boylos, your Lloydies and your Lackeys, would keep the older lads informed about the enemy's position, and whether or not Officer Dibble was on the beat. Those Scouse bizzies were always wise, and were giving escorts out to the away fans long before you could expect the same civil treatment at other grounds. Without your friendly Scouse bizzie escort, a whole lot more of you away fans would have been laid to rest outside the doors of the Jester, so all you forty-year-old ex-hoolies should send your thank you notes to Merseyside Police. I lost count of the number of times I saw that Scouse urchin mob come running down the Jester hill. The well-known boozer closed a good few years ago, only to re-open as a funeral parlour; quite apt when you consider how many away fans bit the dust at the foot of that hill. While it was closed, there was talk that an older Road Ender who'd made a few bob for himself was thinking of re-opening the premises as a nightclub called The Sheepshaggers' Graveyard, but apparently he couldn't 'get planning'. Shame really, it was always a good speck for a bevvy.

Early Road End days, I jumped the coach to a few games from the Park Brow laundrette in Kirkby (Smigger's Tours) and some of those lads went on to be the most fervent Rednecks you could ever wish to meet. Lads like Joey McCulloch, Danny Johno, Murphy (red-arse) Shieldsy, Boyt and Gilly Stewart. This part of Kirkby was heaving with scallies, so much so that when we played Derby in the FA Cup, three coachloads of these lads chased Derby's mob all over the place. I know it was only Derby, but this was just one small district of Kirkby, never mind Liverpool. It went off outside the Rolls-Royce factory and the boys of Derbyshire were soon ramming their way through the streets when they saw the strength of this crew. We had invaded the pitch at full-time and half of us were covered in mud, so maybe our rag-taggle gypsy look frightened them off.

The same firm burgled Wembley after the Southampton Charity Shield game and loaded the coach up with ale for the long journey north. The older lads had waited for the coach park to empty and for dark to fall, before pulling open a door to lift out the crates full of beer. Some lads went one further and entered the stadium, till someone shouted, 'Dixie, it's the pigs,' and everyone jumped aboard the two departing coaches, only to find it was a false alarm that had been raised by the on-board bevvying crew. I was still at school at the time and the lads aboard my coach ended up so pissed (including the driver) that they left me behind on Keele Services. By this time I had a thumb that knew the M6 as well as any lorry driver and it soon got me home.

Probably the most ruthless bunch of young tear-arses in the Road End mob around this time were the Breck Road firm. This crowd came from the nearby Anfield area and could take on whole away crews by themselves. These L4 pirates were always looking to rob you and your clobber; only problem was, not many people were in the market for buying those second-hand long leathers or bloodstained sheepies. The Breck Road boys included lads like Disley, Willie D, Dave S, Gatter, Mickey M, Freddie Thommo and that loveable young Road End rogue, Colonel Anthony Hogan: this was only the quiff-fringe of a huge, violent mob of young scallies who could be strictly grafters one day and strictly right-hook merchants the next. It all depended on the venue and the opposition. It felt good to be older and on the same side as these lads, as a few years earlier these were the fellas who'd beat you up in the bus stop and rob your scarf.

One lad from this bunch of local loons tried to sell a stolen sports car he'd brought back from a Leicester away game. It was on open offer to the highest bidder on the terraces the following week at Anfield, but the surrounding boys thought it was iffy when he tried to convince some Road Ender that it really was his by starting the bidding at thirty quid. *Thirty quid! Yeah, alright mate, pull the other one.* He said it belonged to Keith Weller, who used to play for Leicester in tights and gloves. Are you out there Keith? If you are and it was yours, have a look in yer loft under yer oul tights for the log book if you don't mind.

There was the early-doors Crocky firm, with Marty Mullen, John Coolly and Phil Brown all Samba'd-up and ready to go. There was another Bootle and Netherton firm that included my old mate Dodge City Razor, the bunch of grapes-fringed Foley brothers with Bootle Tom and his John Lennon kipper, and Marty Bannon, who had a better bushy muzzy when he was six than Freddie Mercury had when he was the Killer Queen. Most of these were half-Irish leprechauns, as in the usual Paddy name plus the fact that they could crawl in and out of your pocket before you could shout, 'Marksy's in Bootle New Strand's bang on top.' Further north up the Mersey coastline were the Waterloo lads, with Mick and Brian Duffy, Ged 'the Belt' Thomas, little Clarky and Rimmer the Mexican among their motley, well-dressed crew. On their day, this was another huge gang of lads. Middle Liverpool, you had McCartney, Jonesey and Vinny Steptoe from the Runcorn-Tuebrook connection and Stuey from the younger Urchins firm; these were Red boys through and through, all still growing up and under strict starters orders before the three o'clock Saturday dance.

These were firms within a firm, and by the end of the season they all knew each other well. This in due course meant they were all shit-scared to run away from trouble in case they got clocked by one of the other crews while giving it toes. If that happened, you'd be leathered for being a shitbag. If you were totally outnumbered, my mates and I often were because we always arrived too early, then that was acceptable, but if the odds weren't too bad, say fifty of you and 100 of them, and you got chased, you would have to live with the shame and face up to a whole load of stick at the next game.

By the time the Annie Road End mob was starting to burst the barriers at that end of 'the Shrine', a few little ditties had begun to ring around, especially when it happened to be a suss-the-woolly moment. If it was, and you listened intently, you might hear this sound whispering through the cobbled streets outside the ground at full-time.

There's a woolly over there,
And he's wearing brown Air Wair,
With a three-star jumper halfway up his back
He's a fucking woollyback.

Or maybe the more simplistic night game song,

Ten past nine is stabbing time, doo-dah, doo-dah
Ten past nine is stabbing time, doo-dah doo-dah day.

It might have been just a tiny bit spooky for any away fans to hear that right-to-the-point little ditty. I can just imagine being at, say, Tottenham in a night game, and 4,000 Tottenham boys singing the same song down to you from way above in the Shelf. I reckon I'd have stayed inside White Hart Lane till ten past ten (just kidding), but it deffo would have made things extra scary before you took that long walk up to the Seven Sisters – and that long walk, on its day, could be about as scary as things got. There was never much humour in those stabbing songs, and even though most Scousers never carried a Stanley, a lot still did, so I can only imagine how that used to sound to some away supporter as it hung in the air with five minutes to go.

Clobber-robbing became an in-thing for a lot of young Road End boys. Sheepskins and leather coats, or the odd pair of decent trainees or jewellery, were the usual targets but you didn't see any away fans sporting the good gear till about 1980, so most lads were only in it for a 'laugh' or because a half-decent coat could be passed up to an older brother or sold when they were skint. This problem got so bad that Liverpudlians became known as notorious clobber-robbers among other football supporters, and a police clampdown saw quite a few young lads get borstal sentences or a few months DC (detention centre). I remember visiting me oul mate Jimmy Bolo, who got nicked on Scotland Road for mugging some West Brom fans when they were near the top of the league, and on the Sunday visit to the DC at Hindley, near Wigan, we found that the place was chock-a-block with young Scousers. In among the Scouse lads were other Annie Road End boys being detained for the same kind of offence. Yet it was nothing new; if you check the old local newspapers and police reports, Liverpool's clobber-robbers had been offering their free tour guide services for years, leading the away fans on the long walk towards the ground from as early as 1964 – leading them astray, that is, to local tenement blocks like Gerard Gardens and the Bullring. Here the lost supporters would be told to drop their kecks, before shaking their ballbags all the way back to Lime Street to duly perform the first streaks seen in the city since the days of Spring-Heeled Jack.

If there was no footy on, then any of the firms above plus a host of others might be found in far-off places like Berlin, Vienna, or the old favourite, Switzerland. It's no surprise that once the initial buzz with the clobber and attitude wore off, some of these fellas settled in Los Angeles, Aussie and the States, and also places like Germany because of the well-paid building work that always seemed to be near a good Eros Centre, if you know what I mean. The Fatherland to the lads was what you could call a 'pay day, lay day' kind of place. One young Road End lad, who we used to call Paddy Press-ups, spent so much time in those German brothels that he thought you couldn't change deutschmarks back into sterling on your way home, because you could only use marks to pay for 'your nuts'. Press-ups was a right dirty ticket. Sex case, sex case, hang him, hang him, hang him.

Jersey, Bournemouth and Eastbourne also got a big fix of Scouse scallies, as some lads noticed that these Tory strongholds were a lot more free and easy with the pound notes, legal work-wise or illegal work-wise. I know one rag-arse who went to Brighton the first time we played them and decided to jump coach. We thought he'd be back home in two weeks but he's still there twenty years later, with a nice little building business to boot. Good on yer, Terry lad. All of those South Coast havens contain a Scouse millionaire or two, the ones who got off their arses in the dole days and did good for themselves, usually in the building trade or by rising to the top of a company after finding a job they would never have found at home.

Some of the closer away games like Stoke, Burnley, Bolton and Blackburn would see grounds and towns almost taken over for the day. Places like Stoke, Burnley and Derby had a reputation among Scousers for being full of women and a lot of lads actively went out of their way to have a bird at every away game. It was similar to the sailors' mentality of a girl in every port. Some developed serious relationships with girls they'd met at football matches and one time at Stoke's Victoria Gound – where we'd usually have half the stadium – it seemed like there were ladies galore standing about with the lads. One fella called Dover laughed out loud as we battled for a space in the ladies' bogs, while his new bird performed a strip inside one of the cubicles. That kiss-curled Dover fella used to have a different girl at every match. I suppose he was what you'd call a footy stud while the other lads were a load of Scouse charmers.

* * *

One of the first times I skedaddled over to Switzer and Austria on a non-footy, clobber-finding mission, I returned in a pair of Ciao jeans, Benetton sweatshirt and Puma strap-over trainees – the first pair in Liverpool, by the way. Next thing is, lads everywhere were after them. Now trying to be original or different was never a bad thing for a young kid in my opinion, as it usually showed a little initiative. Underneath my sweatshirt I was wearing this Marco Polo, Paisley-type shirt I'd found; it had loads of little Beatles (the group) heads all over it and a small button-across strap at the top in place of a normal top button. It was the best shirt I've ever had and I wore it till it fell off my back. Lads were always asking me where it came from, and fifteen years later, on holiday in Innsbruck, I was amazed to find the same shop and, to me it seemed, the same owner from all those years ago. And guess what I found lying there on the shelf? Nah, no Beatles-head shirt, only a load of Gary 'nonce' Glitter boots and a few fuck-off Liberace outfits, due to some new Austrian dance craze that involved lederhosen and acid. I tried to tell the owner that in 1978 he'd had some good gear, but his friendly, English-speaking wife told me they had gone to live in England for a few years in 1979 after her husband had had a skiing accident followed by a nervous breakdown, so he couldn't remember much before that year. I really should have known that the fella's brain had pranged then twanged without her telling me, from the moment I noticed his skin-tight leopard skin drainpipes, being worn with red Kicker boots. I presumed from the way he was dressed he'd been living in Yorkshire, either that or the breakdown had made him think he was the Max Wall of the mountains.

I've made the pilgrimage back to most of our old favourite haunts, places like Zurich, Dusseldorf and Innsbruck, but it's never the same when you go back, is it? Especially when the streets used to seem as though they were paved with gold and tasty clobber; now they're teeming with 'tinfoil terrors' (skagheads) and weighed down with shops selling skin-tight turquoise shirts for Swiss woollybacks and disco dancers. The return to old European stomping grounds like Zurich ended up leaving me with a cold, empty feeling, as I began to wonder if half of Wigan had moved there.

I was a bit of an innovator clothes-wise and hoffman-wise, as were quite a few of my brethren, and although it sounds daft when you're older, it was a big thing at the time. I would get a custy buzz from lads saying, 'Boss trainees mate, where d'you get them?' Or even the right-to-the-point, madder ones, who'd say, 'Switzer? Name the strasse and shop, cheers Nicky mate, I'm off there with me boys tomorrow, Trans-Alpino me up Scotty.' This really used to happen, though it sounds so mad now: all the way to Salzburg for a pair of trainees and a little bit extra. We were all trying to outdo each other in the wise-arse stakes and the clothes and attitude department. You had to use your noggin, not your ma's purse, and loads of conniving went into sussing your way round Europe. What we were looking for was not available for 100 nicker in JJB Sports or some other outlet down the road, so a little more homework and headwork had to be done.

Serious spacemen from places like Rhyl, with gobs like Mickey Thomas on the waltzers and sporting kecks as wide as the River Mersey, were not welcome anywhere near the new Annie Road End firm. Neither were 'Mars Bars' from Yorkshire, the likes of your Mel Sterlands, who usually had feather cuts or fucked-up Michael Bolton-style horse heads like Chris Waddle after a shady LSD trip. It was said that when the gorgeous winger teamed up with England, they had to have his own specially adapted pillow lying on top of his bed at the training-ground hotel. It consisted of a wooden pillow for his head, with two vices at the side to strapback the long part behind his ears; this in turn would get it to flow like a maypole at the back so he could awake with that Knight of the Round Table look every morning before training. I think that oul England centre-half Dave Watson was the first dashing knight in white to gallop around Wembley, and I think he too was from Sunderland. Good singers, eh, but with bad barnets. Sunderland and those other North East sausage factories always were adept at spewing out those fucked-up hairdos. Even around 1974, Malcolm MacDonald was walking around with two dead ferrets strapped to the side of his face, and Peter Beardsley, even though brilliant, had a head like a junior school case-ball with a bad *Thunderbirds* wig stuck on top. Peter always seemed to be a jovial fella, and I think that must've run in the family, when you think how happy his step-brother, the comedian Frank Sidebottom, always was. When you get down to the nitty-gritty, Liverpool even had their own Australian Lifeguard Head of the Year in bad barnet Barry Venison – and where was he from? Yeah, the North-East again. Our own Versace'd-up Barry Venison, the first real Angel of the North.

Even the majority of dahn sarf boys, who usually think they're dead cool and onto something first, were all in donkey jackets or flying jackets at the time. West Ham fans sported more earrings and tatts than your average gipsy camp. I used to think that the pollution and smog in London dyed your hair a blondish colour; how else could you explain all those bleached blond rugs with shitty black roots? I clearly remember battling with some huge ear-ringed Roger Daltrey lookalike, sorry, Frank McAvennie lookalike, outside Upton Park around 1981. He had a dyed-blond poodle on his head and a flying jacket that could have kept the water hot in five different immersion heaters, all at the same time. The man was an absolute grock, and so were most of his firm, but I'll tell you this, we only walked straight into them because we thought they were Status Quo roadies.

I suppose that's one of the greatest things about what they now call the casual scene, yer know, the fact that it started in the North, in Liverpool, and not dahn the Old Kent Road, to then be churned out Carnaby Street-style to the masses. Being the capital, where they've supposedly got everything sussed, they have to claim to be the first at everything, I mean, even though we've always lived on fantastic fish and chips in the North, once the statisticians came up with the fact that the first chippy opened up in Mossley, Lancashire, in 1863, instantly some Cockney glory-hunters claimed that a Mr Joseph Malin opened a chippy in the East End in 1860. Fucksake, is nothing sacred!

Yeah, glory hunters sounds about right. How else do you explain all those Cockney Reds, Blues, Celts and Gers leaving Euston on matchday, when I've yet to hear of 200 Tottenham boys pulling out of Lime Street station or Manchester Victoria on a Saturday morning to go to White Hart Lane. Maybe Cockneys were the first Mods, skins and punks, but we were well ahead of the game by '77/78, due mainly to our living in a port and dockland setting where you get more than your fair share of wise-arses and off the back of a lorry merchants. Put that alongside our European travelling shenanigans, our on-the-dole headworking, and the fact that we had by far the most successful football team to follow, year in, year out, and we'd basically thrown a double six to start the terrace togs game.

I have been to and worked in the Millwall area and that south-east part of London has got nearly as many boys as Liverpool. The place is full of wise-arses, and when you consider that Liverpool's a city by itself, that is one huge mob of lads south of the Thames. But even they weren't on the 'chara' in those early trainee days. I've met quite a few Millwall boys who were honest enough to admit this. Sorry boys, we all know you missed the hovercraft over for that one, and another bunch of northern boys were well ahead of you.

The first ones after the Road End Liverpool boys to realise that stack-heels fucked your ankle ligaments up, flares got caught in your bike chain and feather cuts belonged on Bondi Beach were, I hate to say it, a few Manc lads, about a year and a half to two years later. They were never numbered-up like us and still had a few bad biker tattoos and bog-seat earrings in among their firm, mind you. They were the City Cool Cats mob, and the Salford and Man U boys who chased me around half of Manchester (thank God it wasn't the Arndale Centre, I never could find my way around that drab fucking place) before the 1979 FA Cup semi-final against United at Maine Road.

It happened when me, Eddie and Joey O hilariously approached fifty of them outside Victoria Station. We would often be up on our toes, mooching about waiting for the serious numbers to arrive. This was usually down to the fact that we'd arrived so early, due to our habit of bunking the crack-of-dawn trains, but it meant we could often walk straight into home mobs when there was just three or four of us. Sometimes we'd battle if the odds were, say, only two or three to one, but if it was ten or twenty to one with a few bad grocks on your case, it was time to skedaddle. Later on, lads with Stanleys could hold off, or chase, huge mobs when massively outnumbered, and that for me was the main reason why the Road End boys started the Stanley knife trend. The oul Stanley paranoia, as we used to call it, saved many a young Scouser's arse when he found himself trapped in Shady Lane. A quick fiddle in the pocket could see big away mobs giving it toes, and the young Scouse kid was probably only twiddling his knob half the time.

From a distance we thought these fifty Mancs were Scousers, with a lot of them wearing Fred Perry. I've found out since that they were called the Perry Boys. Anyway, those Salford boys always sounded half-Scouse from a distance, and with the old Irish/English ancestry abounding, some even had gobs like us. We were briefly taken in by the clobber, but as soon as we got close and noticed their earrings, iffy tatts and not a friendly Scouse kipper in sight, we knew it was time to scarper, and me oul mate Speedy Gonzales again took over. *Bastards! Now we're not the only ones*, I'm thinking. More than anything, it was always the old earring giveaway that let a wised-up Scouser know the score. In our book, the only men who wore earrings were sailors and guitarists.

We eventually got legged as far as Oxford Street station –

and that is one long legger – only to be rescued bang on time by the advancing Scouse cavalry, who were dossing around the station due to their train arriving ten minutes earlier. When they arrived en masse at half-nine in the morning, the Road End boys would usually wait about until one of the big-time head workers finally came up with a half-decent idea, as in tom shop, clobber shop or battle stations, for our next move. Any of the Manc lads who were chasing us that day would well remember the strange scenario as me, Eddie and Joey O first got chased for yonks, then swiftly did an about turn on sighting the Road End cavalry and started to leg the Septics (septic tanks = Mancs) back through the streets of Manny. A few of them got collared and walloped but it wasn't anything severe.

That night, back in the boozers of Scouseland after a 2–2 draw, we still couldn't believe that somebody had a little crew that resembled our fucking big crew, and I knew theirs was bound to grow like ours had. From small amounts of straight-leg jeans and trainees sprout thousands of pairs of straight-leg jeans and trainees. In bed that night I thought it was a dream, but when I awoke, *bastard*, it was all true; I watched the highlights on telly the next day and noticed a well-dressed Man U lad in his Fred standing by the Kippax fence. He was still standing next to thousands of sheep in long leathers, with their blow-waved hair flapping in the Moss Side breeze, but shit, I knew it was the beginning of the end. Somebody had finally sprinkled some Fred Perry seeds on Manchester, or maybe some Scouser's Fred badge had fallen off his shirt on a Huyton washing line and the little seeds had worked themselves loose before floating thirty miles up the East Lancs on a cool breeze. We were twatted up the Mersey without a Lois paddle and there was no going back.

Now Scousers can sell anything, so my own view is that

some Scouse renegade, money hungry and up for a few quid, had robbed one of the lifeboats off the Royal Iris ferry, filled it with the decent clobber of the time – Kickers, Samba, Lois and Freds – and paddled his way up the Manchester Ship Canal into Salford dock before selling his wares and his soul for 100 gold sovereigns to the Manchester Indians. And if we ever catch that Kirkby Cowboy, we'll fucking kill him!

Terrace chic, as it was later labelled, ran strong for a few more years, though it never reached the mass-market, Sheepsville state that it has today. In essence, it was all over by around 1985, and maybe even a bit earlier, when those New Romantic teds popped up. It never did look right trying to dress up like one of the Three Musketeers when you lived in Cantril Farm or Kirkdale, and the music was pure Cockney cack anyway. Adam Ant for instance, I mean, fer fucksake, enough said. Spandau Ballet Dancers thought they were dead cool wearing kilts; heavens above, you could have tried harder than that; the young Scouse Mary-Ellens had us all perved-up in the late Seventies when they started wearing them – and we wanted to know what *they* wore under theirs. When those Watford beauts from Wham kicked in with their Frankie McAvennie blow-waves, three-for-a-pound white socks and shuttle-cocked undies, it was the final nail in me oul Kicker boots. Sheepsville was on the horizon.

* * *

Once I'd left comprehensive school, and seeing as I had a membership for Eric's, the legendary punk club, I would often stay out all night if Liverpool were playing in London or someplace else that was a decent ride away. In the early days of the Road End crew it would be Cindy's or Eric's for us – Eric's for music and Cindy's for copping off. We sometimes showed up at the Checkmate on a Sunday, but only the odd Saturday, because they were always hard to cop for, those Bowie birds, seeing as half the time they'd be eyeing up the other girls as much as the fellas, or they'd be looking for some anorexic cheek-boned, David Bowie lookalike (a look that was hard to find in chips 'n' scouse Liverpool). But ordinary Scouse birds can out-blag the lads and are simply the greatest ladies on earth for having a good laugh with, so the music or copping off dilemma would rear its head every weekend. Whenever copping off became more urgent than seeing a band, a few weekends visiting those Debbie-and-Dave discos would become part of our itinerary. I hated that disco music, Oops Upside Your Head and all that crap, but needs must. Club-wise, the choice could be best summed up like this: disco dollies, punk shagbags or Bowie bisexuals. If you went for the first option, you wanted to cop for a decent bird; second option, you wanted to empty your walnuts; third option, you were in a weird mood and wanted to experiment a little.

If the Redmen were playing and we were on one or it was hoffman time and we were catching a choo-choo later that night, then a punk place was better, because if you were lucky enough to cop off with some disco dolly, it would only get in the way of the hoffman. So sometimes we would deliberately avoid the girlie places, as not many young tanked up men can turn down the gamble or chance of getting their half-hundred weight (slang for 'to mate' – or nooky), even though it usually ended in a taxi ride for only a bit of brief bare-tit.

Eric's would finish at the normal throwing-out time, so we would go on to clubs that opened until five or six o'clock in the morning; after-hours drinking dens like the Night Owl, the Babbaloo and the Other Place. Once they had thrown us out onto the street, we would waltz over to Limey (Lime Street station). There we would climb down the safety ladder at the side of the station building, which was no mean feat, considering we would be tanked up with ale and it was about six storeys up from ground level. If we were too bevvied to attempt the ladder, we'd try to dodge past the British Rail guard at the platform gate. If that failed, as a last resort we would buy an underage half-price ticket on the bright and early train that left for London just after six, but that didn't happen too often.

If we had to knock about for a little while before a train departed to some foreign country like Newcastle or Southampton, we would wait in the all-night taxi drivers' café not far from Lime Street at the top of London Road. Many a time fights would break out between drunken young scallies and the fed-up, at-graft cabbies, so the owners, who wanted our tea and toast business and didn't really want to ban us, started to leave a bouncer-cum-ageing-bootboy on the door. Anyone who was in too much of a drunken state, or was a known kick-off merchant, would not be admitted. It was hard being on your best behaviour when you were pissed, tired and seventeen, but we needed this place more than they needed us. Sometimes it would be like that scene from *Quadrophenia* where Jimmy the main Mod kicks off on one of his boys and the owner throws them out; yeah, similar but on a much larger scale, as in bigger café and more scallies. I got thrown out by the ageing bootboy a few times. I remember on one occasion, at about four o'clock in the morning, catching my reflection in a rain-spattered window and thinking, *get home, yer fuckin' low-life, if yer da could see you now it'd be a size nine AirWair boot right up the arsehole all the way back to Kirkby for you, soft-shite.*

Once the word went up that it was time to catch the train, the Road End boys would leave en masse, and it was always a strange sight to see a gang of young tear-arses roaming the empty city streets at half five in the morning, with only the odd lone milkman to hound or terrorise. Any decent clobber shop window would have us stopping to inspect the gear and if everything was looking custy; it could easily be bricks away, with a change of jeans for everyone who made the train. If you were a slowcoach then the rest of the day could be spent in a Cheapside cell with the rest of the weekend plonkies, after you'd been nabbed by some Johnny-on-the-Spot bizzie. Getting nabbed after the smash and change routine was bad news for any young Road Ender, as trying to find out the half-time scores in a cell while some paraffin lamp farted in the background was not a pleasurable way to spend your Saturday afternoon, especially when the rest of your mates were on one, and if the desk sergeant happened to be an Evertonian or a woollyback plod, early release was not an option. Being wound up all afternoon about the result and what your mates were up to, was all par for the course.

One shop called the Westerner in St John's Precinct had the windows so brimmed up with jeans that lads would go out of their way to stash scaffold bars early doors for a spot of window jousting later on in the evening. Raiding this type of establishment before the getaway train left became a favourite stunt in away-game town centres, so earliest departures were the Annie Road boys' usual mode of transport. This Westerner place would be stocked up with Levi jeans and clip-button shirts, staple clobber for the lads. But sadly, littered among the good stuff, would be the dreaded 'cowie' (cowboys) boots. These were the height of ridicule for any up and coming scally, and labelled as strictly Man U or woollyback footwear. So with this in mind, one early season away game in '77/78, some of the lads catching the train decided to cop for the lot.

On boarding the bright and early, half the lads put on these stolen John Wayne boots and declared themselves 'the Rochdale Cowboy Stretford Enders'. A mock fight ensued between the cowboys and the Scousers, which ended up in absolute hysterics as every Stretford End cowboy was first brought to his knees, then stripped of his cowie boots before having them thrown out of the window somewhere on the way to Runcorn, a satellite town twenty minutes down the tracks. I'd have loved to have seen the faces on the British Rail maintenance men when they found a brand-new snakeskin cowboy boot every few miles down the line from Lime Street to Runcorn. Come to think of it, it was a good job the Man U and Leeds bootboys didn't take up the cowie boot fashion in serious numbers, as a kick up the arse from those Clint Eastwood specials and you could end up with six arseholes, or a face like Charlie Magri after a championship bout. I mean, at least those Stretford End platforms and Yorkshire boxing boots hit you with a dull thud.

Once we were used to bunking the train, hitching became a thing of the past; while some supporters carried on using that method, the Road End boys started to think we were above all that. We no longer thought it was cool to be on the motorway with your fringe sticking up in the wind, begging for a lift off some fat lorry driver with a giant stash of nudie books under the passenger seat, showing pictures of other lorry drivers' lonely wives fingering themselves while their husbands drove up and down the country all night long. *Fiesta*'s Readers' Wives page should've been called Lorry Drivers' Wives. Anyway, those middle-aged motorway widows helped me pass a couple of minutes on many a long London train journey, but you had to time it right, by finishing your five knuckle shuffle just as the

guard entered the next carriage, and so enabling you to return
to your seat. If only I had a fiver for every time I've heard,
'Quick here's the guard, where's the nudie books'. Sixties mod
band The Who called their hit single 'Pictures of Lilly'; we
called our little diversion the 'bunkers' wank'. Same kind of
scenario, if yer get me drift.

Shops like Jonathan Silver in town would sometimes get an
early call from the travelling lads, maybe ten minutes before
whatever train they were catching left Lime Street. Twenty lads
at ten past nine, trying twenty different jumpers or coats on;
the shop assistants wouldn't know where to turn before the
hoffman bell sounded. Five minutes later, twenty lads sitting
aboard the train, next-stop Villa.

For the first game of that 1977/78 season, against
Middlesbrough, we all travelled by football special train to see
King Kenny make his debut. The special always left from the
old platform nine, and you started to see some of the sharper
lads standing in little cool-arse gangs among the ordinary
supporters. Once the ordinary lads noticed the new dress mode,
the little cool-arse gangs soon became the whole mob. I hated
the specials, as more often than not I would end up locked in
the cages situated halfway up the train. These cattle trucks
would be manned by over-zealous British Transport plod and
stewards who thought that by being a good oul Scouser who
snitched on or jumped on any would-be troublemakers, they
would set themselves up nicely for a job at Anfield cleaning out
the khazis in the Kemlyn Road stand. These are the fellas you
see in the blazers in and around the ground today. Headlock
heroes, we used to call them. Any stealing from the buffet – ha,
as if pork pies, crisps, Mars Bars and Fanta amount to a buffet
– and it would be straight down the cages, where the rest of
your journey would be spent alone. There you'd be stared at by

the other travelling supporters (anything from 500–1000) as though you were the Elephant Man in a hooded snorkel with a welly on your head. I've sat in that monkey cage for thousands of miles with the Transport plod as zoo keepers and I've still yet to receive any rail-mile travel vouchers.

The reason for going by special to this first game was simple: if you went by ordinary train you'd have to be mob-handed, because Boro was simply the worst ground in the league, apart from Liverpool, for getting sussed and having your trainees or sovereign rings robbed. It was so rowdy we started to call their ground Ayrsome Trouble. Our dress sense and accent stood out a mile in Middlesbrough, and it was undoubtedly the numero uno worst ground for having your snorkel hood pulled over your head and receiving a size-twelve Chelsea boot (the ones with the elastic in the side) right up the arse of your new Lois cords. Those big Boro boys always seemed to wear those Chelsea boots, so much so that years later, when they became the fashion, we referred to them as 'Boro boots'. One of the reasons Middlesbrough was such a naughty yard was that, on leaving the train, you had to walk through a narrow city centre shopping street while trying to blend in. Sounds simple, eh, but nothing could be further from the truth if you were wearing straight leg jeans, oul fellas' cord shoes, suedies or Adidas, with a snorkel coat or Harrington. Then you stood out like Liberace on a picket line, and before you knew what had hit you – because you couldn't blag that half-Yorkie, half-Geordie dialect – you would be jumped on by twenty feather-cutted star jumper wearers, all shouting, 'Kill the queer!'

Those bastions of British high street fashion were the worst places on earth for a young Scouse trendsetter to strut his stuff. Middlesbrough's boys were always the clear favourites to lift the title, though Leeds would give them a run for their money by coming a close second: the title I'm referring to was, of course, The Land That Time Forgot, a championship often won by the width of a trouser leg or the height of a heel, with the best players being able to land a platform shoe straight down the middle of a bouncy John Travolta bonce. Oh yeah, and the last UEFA Cup place normally went down to a play-off between Birmingham and the Dinosaurs. Later that season at second-placed Leeds United's ground, it looked funny standing next to the fence inside the ground, as it acted as a sort of time barrier. On one side you had a couple of thousand Liverpool boys, all laughing and joking about the morning's events, and across the great divide you had hundreds of Brian Connolly (lead singer in Sweet) lookalikes, all platformed and Air Wair'd up to go, trying to get at the 'Bowie freaks', as they called us that day. A few years later, once they'd decided to lose twelve inches off the width of each trouser leg, eight inches of the length of their Brian Connolly barnets and two inches off the sole of each shoe, I had to laugh when I thought of all of those Sweet and Gary Glitter albums lying half-burned in the fireplaces of 1,000 Leeds back-to-back terraced houses.

That day in '77 we sang, 'Sheepshaggers, la, la, la, sheep-shaggers, la, la, la,' and made loud farmyard noises throughout the match, as in, 'Baaa, baaa.'

They sang, 'Quee-ers, quee-ers, quee-ers,' and, 'You're just a bunch of pufters.'

I wish I'd have had a portable tape recorder at the time. Those Yorkies were just a bunch of trouser-phobic fascists. So who eventually gave them the right to wear our gear, especially after giving us so much stick? Let's face it, Leeds always looked the part in Birmingham bags and stack heels as they made their way over the hills to Elland Road, and they should never have been allowed to wear our kind of kecks. I could just imagine one of those Leeds lads a few years on, slowly making his way home from the match after another defeat, sitting down to watch *Dr Who* in his new straight leg jeans, and his dad saying, 'I've told you before lad, you want to stick to your own.'

'But I am. I'm marrying a white lass, dad.'

'No, I mean your fucking pants, you soft bastard.'

By the middle of that same 1977/78 season, the first Road End boys to leave their dads and mates behind on the Kop had been joined by much larger numbers of young scallies. The Road End chant was now being heard as loud and as frequently at the home games as it had been heard at the new season's away games. This in turn led to much heavier policing at the Anfield Road end of the ground. We played Middlesbrough in the New Year and they brought a small band of bootboys with them. They always had a loyal hardcore following with a few tasty grocks on board, and seeing as they'd normally give you a hard time up at Ayresome Park, we thought we'd return the favour with interest.

Hundreds of lads were soon bopping along the fence telling the Boro boys they'd made a big mistake and their first New Year's resolution should've been not to come to Liverpool. The bizzies could see that all these young lads were up for climbing the barrier after twenty or so jumped into the away end. Before long, seventy or eighty had sneaked over unnoticed into their section. We ended up fighting at the tea bar at half time and no matter what the police did, more and more Road Enders kept making their way across the narrow divide. Small scuffles kept breaking out among the more boisterous supporters, but what the bizzies didn't know was that most of the lads were keeping a low profile till the final whistle went. It was retribution time and when those Liverpool boys are up for revenge it is similar to having a monkey on your back that wouldn't go away. The Kop were singing, 'There's only one way out,' and although the seven or eight thousand singers at the centre of the huge home end were normally indifferent to any hoolie shenanigans, today they were up for it.

As the final whistle went, people streamed away from the ground in the dark. Boro's mob were guided towards their coaches by a few stray plod, and once Stanley Park showed up, all hell broke loose. Pre-match stashed ammo, in the form of sticks and bottles, was instantly smashed over Boro heads. The few big grocks they had were systematically dragged to the floor before receiving a severe hiding. The lads generally attacked the biggest or the leaders to begin with, then the rest would either scatter or drop like skittles. Donkey jackets were getting slung all over the place as Adidas trainees met foreheads full flush. With no bizzies in the vicinity the beating went on unabated. One lad who kept going on about the hard time he'd had up at Boro's ground was dragging people out of the way before smashing bottles he'd stashed in a crate directly over donkey-jacketed heads. Some grievous bodily harm was given out after that game, I can tell you. Hundreds of Kopites eventually came swarming into the park, only to find that the job was already done.

When the massive Kop firm came around the ground for a fight you could tell they were not from the Road End: a few of them were still in semi-flares and the seven or eight hundred strong Annie Road End crew were all dressed to the nines, and even if you didn't already know somebody by face, you knew which side he was on by the way he was turned out. It was easy to tell who was who, even in poor light, as nobody was dressing like us and the away fans just couldn't do the accent. Even though the policing had become much heavier, it was still nowhere near strong enough to curb the growing young mob from handing out beatings to crews of visiting hoolies. Get me – hoolies, not ordinary supporters with dads and kids wearing scarves.

A small West Ham firm paid a visit and soon enough the snorkel jackets and wedge haircuts were bopping along the perimeter fence to have a shufti. From the moment the final whistle sounded and the corner exit doors opened, they were kicked from pillar to post. Thirty or forty of them ended up hiding behind gravestones in Anfield Cemetery. It was like an army manoeuvre as the cemetery was swept for Cockneys, who were rounded up one by one and badly beaten. Some of the fellas found hiding tried to do the Scouse accent for a get out clause and were swiftly pulverised for the worst impersonations of the Liverpool lingo since Nerys Hughes in *The Liver Birds*. They didn't come back with a better impression for a good few years after that.

Aston Villa, who were doing quite well at the time, brought a crowd who paid dearly in Stanley Park and I don't think they came again. Chelsea, Man U and Man City meanwhile, just didn't turn up. Every time we played at their grounds, the chant would go up, 'You never come to Anfield.' The message travelled and so Arsenal brought half of London with them for a League Cup semi-final, which resulted in probably the worst violence ever seen at Anfield. Battles erupted and complete bedlam ensued. They were followed the next day by a host of newspaper reports trying to get to the cause of the problem. I could've summed up those reports in two words – Road End. The following season you'd have been lucky to find ten Arsenal fans inside the ground at the same Liverpool fixture.

If anyone from London did show up for a few years on the trot, it was a smallish Tottenham crew. They always seemed to have the best London firm of hoolies, with quite a few black lads among their number. But once they met this new Road End firm, backed by a violent mob of Kopites, they seemed to dwindle after the 1978 7–0 defeat. I don't know if it was down to the fact that they got chased and hounded nearly all the way back to Lime Street Station, when quite a few of them got badly beaten up on Scotland Road, or whether it was simply down to the fact that their team used to get tonked every time they played the Redmen. Whatever it was, any mob they had in the late Seventies soon resembled the mob they had in the early Seventies – almost non-existent. Only they know the real reasons for not fancying the trip.

Liverpool at this time was undoubtedly on-top central. Wise away fans, like Arsenal's after the League Cup semi, didn't bother to turn up for the next few years. I include the Mancs (both teams), Leeds, Chelsea, West Ham, Newcastle and Birmingham among the mobs who just didn't fancy the trip to Liverpool. They knew the dance, and they didn't want to dance anywhere near Anfield, that's for sure. If there were no away fans to goad, taunt or batter, which was normally the case seeing as Liverpool was such an on-top place to visit, then the Kopites and Road Enders would deride each other, especially if the game got boring – and as Liverpool were wiping the floor with the opposition most Saturdays, then derision between the two sets of home supporters became the norm.

The 100 or so boys that had first shown their faces and their clobber at the 1977 FA Cup Final at Wembley (the young ones stood out that day as all the older ones had fucked off to Rome early) had now grown into a massive mob of sixteen to twenty-five-year-olds; if you were older than that, then forget it, you were an old man, and old men never did look quite right in straight-leg jeans, Fred Perry, Stan Smith or Samba trainees and a short snorkel jacket that you could bounce around in as you joked about with your mates. Liverpool used to win so easily that often the only time you'd clock the football match in progress was when someone scored or something unusual happened. Ordinary songs from the Sixties and Seventies Kop repertoire were hardly ever sung on the Road End terrace, as most lads were too busy gabbing about music, clobber, or who'd copped for a good few quid lately. One typical song went something like this, to the tune of Sham 69's 'Hurry Up Harry':

> Come on, come on, hurry up West Ham come on
> Come on, come on, hurry up West Ham come on
> You'll never reach the pub

This was sung to the small travelling band of East Enders in the Annie Road End before they ended up hiding in the cemetery. Other songs would be improvised to suit the club or chart song of the day, usually with threatening or mickey-taking overtones involved in the lyrics.

Once the more cut-throat hardcases of Liverpool got involved, this rapidly became the only football mob I'd ever seen or heard of that talked about making a few quid in and around the game more often than about the game itself. By the end of May 1978, it had grown into one massive violent crew of young wolves in smart clobber, and other fans who were really in the know and were bored shitless by the old bootboy image had begun to sit up and take note.

CHAPTER FIVE

On The Ordinary

THE FIRST BIZZIES to patrol the fences separating the two sets of supporters down at the Anfield Road End became well-known characters themselves. The main two were Blackbeard and Flatnose. Their nicknames are self-explanatory really. Blackbeard was an out and out hooligan in a plod uniform. He would get stuck right into the home or away fans; it all depended on who was kicking off the most on any given Saturday. Ask an Annie Road Ender about any old faces from those seasons and he'll put Blackbeard right in the mix, as this cop would smack anyone who so much as looked at him for too long. He looked like that other well-known muscleman copper, Geoff Capes, only with a hairier face. And whereas Capes would often be seen tossing the caber in one of those strongman contests on television, Blackbeard could usually be found tossing supporters over the dividing fences every match day at Anfield. There was nothing politically correct about this copper, but boy did he get the job done.

Flatnose and Blackbeard would take absolutely no shit from the away fans. When a crew arrived at Anfield, usually for an end of season game when they were trying to avoid relegation, I've seen those two bizzies beat up whole away mobs with their truncheons – when you actually saw a mob, that is. Whereas today people sue hospitals, the bizzies, dentists, cigarette companies, school teachers, and even their own parents for putting a nappy on with the safety pin showing, there was no such blame culture in Blackbeard's day. Left unhindered, with his back-up troop in waiting, he would sort out any terrace tantrums in no time at all. Because of the leather-gloved control they exerted inside the ground throughout the game, most violence kicked off in the streets before and after the match. It's probably one of the main reasons why there was never a serious riot inside Anfield. At some games, it was as though Blackbeard and Flatnose were softening up the away fans before the Kopites and Road Enders waiting in Stanley Park finished the job, although I'm sure the two bizzies in question never felt that way.

As I say, the Liverpool boys were not used to seeing many away fans at Anfield in the mid to late Seventies, so if a mob did turn up it was a bit of a novelty. Crystal Palace in the FA Cup early in 1977 were one of the first teams to bring a half-decent mob. Perhaps they were a bit naïve, with them being in the Second Division at the time, or maybe they were just 'up for the cup'.

The first big mob to arrive en masse was, surprisingly, Coventry City. In November 1977, for whatever reason, the boys of Cov brought a huge mob for the League Cup fourth round. The League Cup was important to teams like Coventry at the time, so Liverpool gave them about 8,000 tickets. I'm telling you this for three reasons: firstly, it was the biggest mob at Anfield since maybe Celtic in 1966; secondly, Coventry were never renowned for any big away support; and thirdly, and most importantly, it seemed like half their fans were wearing sheepskin coats for the cold November night match. Who knows, maybe in Coventry that week they had a two-for-one offer on sheepies; either that or you got a free one with every season ticket you bought – they had to find a crowd from somewhere. You might be wondering why this third point was the most important. Let me explain.

Liverpool played West Ham a few days later, and West Ham had brought a little mob of 3–400 fans. A lot of them were punks, skins and just ordinary supporters. They weren't dressed like us; they were mainly Air Wair and donkey jacket boys. I knew a couple of these West Ham lads, Brett (little Hammers earring) and Felman (fair-haired kid), and a couple of their mates kept commenting on why so many Liverpool boys were wearing brand new sheepies. Get me drift? Coventry's fans had been followed down the back streets and jiggers of Anfield by hundreds of young scallies, before being jumped on, with restrained violence I might add (no need to damage the sheepies, and Cov were never a bad enemy), before being relieved of their coats and whatever they contained. It was a sort of mass mugging, and at this next home game against the East End's finest – which we won easily, as usual – I was in among the Hammers fans speaking to a few lads who thought it was a carry-on from the old skinhead tradition of wearing sheepskin coats to the match. But it wasn't; it was because Coventry's fans had been daft enough to wear their nice, new coats on a cold rainy Anfield evening, with thousands of shirt-wearing scallywags standing in wait. It turned into a bad case of, 'Fuck the League cup for a lark, I wanna sheepie.'

Any time a new team arrived on the scene, our little firm and the Road End big firm would look forward to the expedition with eager anticipation. This season's new boys, in our terms, were Bristol City. The cider drinkers had already been in the First Division for a year, but on our previous visit we'd travelled down as normal footy fans; now we'd changed, so for the Road End boys it was treated as a fresh adventure.

With the ordinary train bunked, via Brummieland, we set about trying to find Bristol's cider-drinking mob but found the shops instead. We were surprised to find that the first sports shop we entered stocked the trainees on the shelves in pairs, and lo and behold, wasn't the shelf weighed down with our own fave rave, the oul Adidas Samba?

'Any size eights there, bollocks?'

'Gerrout the way, them nines are mine.'

'Any six-and-a-halves for a little fella?'

Once the shelves were Samba-less, any other half-decent trainee would do. Joey O who was late getting inside, later described it like this, 'I kept picking up these trainees to look for me size but they were all shitty old pairs. The two lads who were shop staff were just standing there, staring at the display. There was at least ten pairs of shitty oul trainees lying on the shelf, in place of the new ones they'd all cut off with. I looked at the two of them, shrugged me shoulders and walked out. Bastard, I tell yer. I was never late again.'

Joey O was always late.

At the time, these rally jackets were well up our list of required garments, so, shop found, similar scenario: oul jackets left on hangers, then off to the game. At half-time inside Ashton Gate you could see all these young lads walking about in brand new rally jackets and spotless Adidas trainees. One lad got tugged over by the bizzies to be questioned, which in turn gave our little firm the signal that it was time to depart. Me and Joey O kept laughing at Eddie, who'd copped for the last pair on the shelf. They were a ten, while soft lad was only an eight. He looked like the Adidas court jester, with his toes already starting to curl up at the end, so his nickname until they were worn out became the Adidas Banana. Fastened-too-tight, turned-up, boomerang trainees never did look the part.

Fifteen minutes after the first lad got tugged we left the match, it was five minutes into the second half and 100 other lads were soon in tow. They all thought we were leaving for a battle, or about to embark on another clobber finding expedition, but we just knew when it was hoffman time and had no plans whatsoever. We walked out into a lovely sunny Bristol afternoon with our new rally jackets slung over one shoulder. Fred Perry's at away-games would be left outside your jeans, just to hide the ugly, fat, studded leather belts a lot of us wore in case of any trouble, and as was usually the case, we found it.

On reaching the city centre, we were confronted by a gang of Bristol Rovers fans, who approached us to join them and to lie in wait for their 'hated enemy', the City fans. *Fuck that for a lark*, we're all thinking, *we only want a laugh, or some new gear probably wouldn't go amiss, so do one, you cider-drinking weirdoes*. But no, they weren't listening so we were having it. A beating for the Rovers boys ensued, with many a leather belt finding its mark. Following the brief skirmish, we reached the station by following a girl in tight white pants, clearly showing black suzzies underneath; weird, I know, but she loved wriggling her arse in our direction, so we wriggled right behind. At the station we ran down the platform to catch a departing Birmingham train back home. Nobody knew the match score, as the game was still in progress. Once we'd boarded the train, which was empty except for us, it went a bit like this: quiet train, buffet car burgled as there was no one about, free lager, sarnies and crisps to Birmingham, the Road End party in full swing, guard shows up, guard assaulted, gets on the blower, bizzies waiting for noisy partygoers at New Street Station, hundreds of us legging across the tracks in all directions, no peace for the wicked nor for the bunkers, party ends, later train home after two hours in beautiful Brummieland, away game draws to a close, see youse all next week.

The point of the story is: take no notice of these so-called 'top boys' with their organised kick-offs and so forth, because most of these things happened purely by accident and true mass battles occurred every blue moon. When I say mass battles, I mean massive, hand-to-hand tag-wrestling matches that went on for ages. Chance skirmishes with quite a few digs thrown happened at every ground up and down the country almost every Saturday afternoon, but serious violence comes and goes in short spurts. I mean, come on, even Norwich City had a mob in them days, so big fucking deal about who's the hardest and all that shite. 'We're the hardest, they're the hardest, we legged them, they legged us . . .' Give it a rest. It's all in the eye of the beholder, and it's only worth telling if there's a funny reason or moral to the story. Take that Carl Lewis fella, he could out-leg anyone – yeah, until Ben Johnson went on the gear and turned into a Ferrari on stegs. And I mean, Mike Tyson was always the hardest an' all that – till he got well and truly walloped by that Cockney Canadian, Lennox Lewis. I must have seen no more than ten true mass battles in thirty footy seasons.

If I had to pull one from the bobble hat, it would have to be Man U in the FA Cup semi-final at Goodison in 1985. If they hated us before that game, they fucking despised us after it. It was the game that ended up all over the papers for the levels of violence, and golf balls with nails hammered into the surface were pictured on the front of the Sunday papers the following morning. Before the game, vans were tipped up all around Everton's ground, pubs were smashed to smithereens if they contained any Man U, and ambulances were zooming about all over the place carrying the woollyback casualties. Some pubs were smashed up so badly that their owners got the insurance firms to quickly do the necessary repairs before selling on to people who made the first decent offer. They'd reached the end of their tether after seeing the levels of barbarity reach an all-time high. During the game Scouse firms were diving into the Man U end as though they were on kamikaze missions and throughout the full ninety minutes battles continually kicked off in the Paddock and Park End. At the end of the drawn game, the United fans wouldn't come out onto the street, as a reception committee of thousands lay in wait. The nailed-up golf balls were being thrown into the doorways and bricks were hammering against the exit doors as the bizzies tried to push them out, while endeavouring to quell and move on the massive waiting mob. Gangs slid off to Stanley Park only to return when the Mancs left the ground, and attacks and hidings were instantly going off all over the park and ground circumference.

Over the years lads had been telling tales about getting vultured (picked off in a small number, or alone) at Old Trafford and if you weren't with the Road End boys there was always a good chance of this happening, so revenge had been the motive for a lot of the ferocity shown on semi-final day. By Saturday evening the savage onslaught was over and, with the build-up to the midweek replay at Maine Road already underway, the Liverpool boys were talking of nothing else but more violence for the visit to Manchester. The word travels fast on the away mob grapevine, and soon enough an early evening train containing 300 Liverpool boys had its emergency cord pulled a mile or so before its normal destination – a stunt often used to avoid the expected waiting Dibble. With no police about, the mob of lads were soon rampaging through the streets of Manny before chasing a firm of 200 septics into the doors of Victoria

Street Station. They ended up running into the hands of the bizzies they'd tried to avoid.

Moments before Officer Plodrington turned up, it looked like things were about to run out of control, with Stanley knives getting openly brandished in the mild evening air, but a massive police presence put paid to any thoughts of continuing the weekend's onslaught and hundreds were stopped or nicked for going equipped. People were dropping weapons outside the ground while in the queue, as the police set up a large-scale stop and search. Against the wall of the stadium lay hammers, blades, the same golf balls, darts, knuckledusters, small iron bars and even a crossbow.

Man U won and the Liverpool supporters rioted all the way back to the city centre. I walked back to town with a 500-strong mob who couldn't find any Man U to have a battle with, maybe due to them winning, because if they'd have been up for it you might've been looking at the biggest football battle of all time. You could almost smell the violence in the air; sometimes it was that bad. Houses around Maine Road were smashed up; buses were wrecked and cars were overturned as the rivalry between the two teams escalated onto the streets, which was par for the course when these two teams met. It's unlikely the violence will ever reach those levels again.

* * *

By the spring of 1978, the Annie Road End in true Scouse tradition had mushroomed and even a few tidy girls had started showing up, but I could never name them, as they're probably married with kids now. So my lips are sealed. No need to embarrass the children of a footy-loving ma, but if I can just hint at what I'm getting at, without naming names, I'd say it like this. One lad who was quite happy to catch the special train instead of the ordinary was my Annie Road mate Burkey. Now Burkey, who had a knob like a Blackpool donkey, used to catch the special in search of that 'special nosh'. He didn't give a shite whether Liverpool won 2–1 or 7–1, but if he got his Swiss roll chewed, then he'd had a right result, roughly about eight inches to nil.

We never had any leaders, which was always the way coming from cowboy town. Some fellas were more violent than others and some lads were bigger carners and grafters, but nobody would look up to a leader, it wasn't in the Liverpool make-up. Sometimes a certain crew would whisper the message that we were going in the home end next week and you'd hear nothing till you were standing there waiting for the crew to arrive. West Brom, Sheff U, Arsenal's Northbank and the Stretford End all got a visit from the Road End crew.

Another adventure we looked forward to that season was Chelsea away. The fashionable West End club had been promoted from the Second Division, and stories abounded about mobs of punk rockers and hooligans who could strike fear into any firm of boys who fancied paying the Bridge a visit. Hmm, I'd heard that one before. While other, more worried fans would take up the Elvis Costello stance and declare, 'I don't want to go to Chelsea,' our lads couldn't wait.

Months before the game, the Road End boys were talking about how they were looking forward to the fixture. It was pencilled in for March 4, but fate intervened by drawing the two sides together on January 7 for the third round of the FA Cup. A huge firm of boys travelled down for the tie, and as usual, we stayed out all night before bunking the bright 'n' early train just after six in the morning. This time things were different, as hundreds of lads climbed down the fire escape ladder, instead of the normal thirty or so. I suppose most young lads could never keep a good scam to themselves for long. Hitching was by now losing its thumb, and even though the Haydock bizzies and garages were glad to see the back of us, I don't think the Lime Street transport dibble were too happy, seeing as the problem of controlling hundreds of marauding scallies was now almost solely theirs.

When we arrived at Euston Station, instead of departing the normal way by walking out of the gate at the top of sloping platform, we'd often go into the British Rail subsidised canteen underneath the station concourse. We used to look funny queuing up with the British Rail workers, twenty snorkels and Harringtons alongside all the dark navy uniforms. We'd generally have a laugh over our cheap full English breakfasts with what was by now a predominantly West Indian and Asian workforce. Now and again, the odd Asian jobsworth would complain about our presence in the canteen, but the moaners in question would be quickly scolded by the other workers, who probably realised we were on the bones of our arses. I mean, I used to have a fiver in my pocket on a good day; many other games I wouldn't have two ha'pennies to throw at the home mob. We had to be on our best behaviour in the rail canteen and were careful not to let the rest of the Road End crew know about our cheap brekkie stunt. We got a good few seasons out of that one. If we'd have gone in mobbed-up, the cheap morning nosebag would've been over before the first sausage was bitten. A lot of us were not used to seeing so many immigrants, and the Bernard Manning type jokes would soon be flying about, but one overheard racial quip or comment and it was bound to be 'bang goes the bangers', so it was the one place we always behaved, as nobody fancied a cold sausage roll in Euston Gardens with the pigeons and the paraffin lamps.

The mainline London station must have seen 1,000 snorkels that day, as Liverpool's firm for the game was basically awesome. We had about five different mobs of 2–300 boys in each mob, and after the game everyone had a different story to tell, so I'll tell you mine. We got twatted out of the cup 4–2 by the West End poseurs. Off the field, battles were kicking off everywhere. Chelsea's fans came on the pitch at the end to celebrate, which almost turned into a full-scale riot when we tried to get over the fence at them. The bizzies were somewhere in the middle of all this as missiles rained down on the pitch. There were little fights breaking out all over the ground, including the Shed, and I remember our firm all huddled together, saying, 'It's a funny oul place this Chelsea, isn't it?' Which translated as, 'Fuck the FA Cup, we're thoroughly enjoying ourselves.'

They kept us behind after the game, but Chelsea still ambushed us outside. I'd never seen that many punk rockers looking for a battle outside a concert, never mind a togger match. But a lot of people's aggression at matches is controlled by the result, and we'd lost, so today we weren't running, which meant Chelsea had to. The Liverpool boys knew that to run today would mean you'd be slated in the Road End next week. Everyone was bouncing towards that Tube station and we were seriously mob-handed. My abiding memory was of a skinny Sid Vicious lookalike getting pulverised as his pink leopard skin shirt was ripped from his back when he got caught with the other Chelsea stragglers. I'm sure it was his bondage kecks that slowed him down as he tried to do one. As the old tooth-braced punkette Poly Styrene had sung, 'Oh bondage, up yours,' Sidney lad.

A couple of months later, we played them in the league. Now this was a whole different story. A lot of supporters knew that Chelsea was bound to be rough, so only a couple of thousand Reds turned up, but that included 6–700 Road End boys which, split into two mobs, was just about right for looking after yourself. We got hammered 3–1 in the footy, a tonking for Liverpool in those days, as we hardly ever got beat. And come the end of the game, it was bang on top outside. At first Chelsea got chased by a solid mob of about 500 on their way to Fulham Broadway, only to return with a motley crew of punks, skins, rockabillies and other hoolies. There seemed to be thousands of them, and as numbers often do, they mingled in at first before scattering the Liverpool mob all over the place. We got chased right past the Fulham Broadway station entrance and ended up half a mile further before stopping. Nobody could catch the Speedy Gonzales crew at this time; we were always trainee'd up and ready to go, and those clumpy steel toe-caps were no match for our turbo Adidas in the running stakes.

Everybody had been split up by the vast crowd leaving Stamford Bridge; it was always a major mistake if you didn't stick closely together at a rough ground. Once me and Joey O had stopped to ponder which direction to head into, we noticed this fellow Scouser over the road whose face we knew from travelling away. To us, he looked obviously out of place. For a start, his Adidas Samba almost jumped off the kerb at you, while his regimental snorkel parka, topped off with a massive quiff, were a dead giveaway. But what slightly confused us was the fact that he was carrying a bag of spuds and a loaf.

'Alright Macca lad,' says Joey, 'what's with the loaf and spuds? Have you got a flat down here now?'

'Nah, I've just been chased by a load of punks and skins.'

So I go, 'Yeah, but what's that got to do with cooking a load of chip butties?'

'No, this oul Liverpool skin put me onto this one, it's for

when it's on top. What you do is, you go in the first grocers or sweetie on the road and buy something that makes you look like you live local. So I bought these, and they never had no milk, or I'd have bought that too.'

With the tension and everything we just burst out laughing.

We eventually came to Parsons Green station, where we jumped the Tube back to Victoria before changing for Euston. On the Tube journey we were surrounded by Chelsea skins who were nearly all booted, earringed and tattooed up. As I've said, this was always a telltale sign of a non-Scouser, even more so later on, when loads started to dress like us; the earrings and shitty tatts would forever remain a giveaway. With this Chelsea mob aboard the train though, the clobber was enough. As we looked about the seats we could see a few other Scousers mingled with the Chelsea hordes, and every time I looked at the floor and clocked the loaf and spuds tucked between Macca's Samba, I broke into a nervous laugh. After my second or third laugh, this big, hairy-arse, Chelsea half-punk, who must've been paranoid, goes,

'You got a problem mate?'

So in something resembling a Cockney accent, I go, 'Nah, not me mate.'

'Only I thought you and your mates were havin' a pop.'

Joey O, who could sense getting sussed out a mile off, spouts up in his own heavy Cockney twang, 'Nah, not us mate, the only trouble we're looking for is with them Scarse cants.' It wasn't a bad impersonation, but there was definitely a bit of Australian arse-bandit in there somewhere.

'Likewise mate, likewise, give us a shout if you spot any of the norvern cants.'

Joey O's crap Alf Garnett accent had worked. 'Will do mate, will do,' he added. Don't push it Joey lad.

My Tube chuckles had been brought to an abrupt halt and, as my arse began to twitch all the way back to Euston, I was thinking, *I'll tell that big soft cunt I'm laughing at his toilet seat ear-rings when I get off this choo-choo, but no more leggers please, I've had no kip since Thursday*. At the time, a common nightmare for a young, every-game lad like myself was the thought of being cornered by a weaponed-up mob on the Tube. If you lived and breathed football like I did, it was a nightmare you were bound to dream sometime. When things were tense, especially in a confined space like on an Underground train, I would seriously struggle with the chuckle-button, as I was always one of those burst out laughing merchants during a moment of tension. And if there was ever one thing in my make-up that was going to make that nightmare come true, it was sniggering at the wrong time. To keep the giggles under wraps, I had to concentrate all the way to Euston on some granny sitting with her legs akimbo. Why oh why do they have to spread them so wide? She was squashed in a corner seat with her flowery oul bloomers on show, and the mere thought of what was underneath provided me with just enough queasiness to keep the smile off my face. But if I'd turned the other way and caught the tiniest glimpse of those spuds, that was it, we were gonna get twatted in the next station, which I think was called Shit Street.

Back at Euston, you'd see the Annie Road End boys lounging around telling their own individual stories. You'd quickly get to know the blaggers, the fibbers and the exaggerators from the hard-cases, the wise-arses and the absolute nutters. Every football crew contained this first bunch among their ranks, and a lot of them seem to have gone on and written books, claiming we did this first, not second, or we legged them, they never legged us. But the real strength of any match mob would always be determined by how many of the second bunch you could count on turning up every Saturday. Well, the Road End spawned a whole host of different characters, some of them of the slash your arse variety, some of the slash your arse then rob your wallet variety and some who were slightly different, who were among football's best head workers and grafters long before every man and his Burberryed-up dog jumped aboard. They grew and multiplied in the Annie Road End from the 1977 season onward, into what became labelled 'the casuals' – a label that means nothing in my home town by the way, the place where it all started.

I would be the first to admit that other Scousers had been bunking and conniving at football matches way before my time, and that's a story for someone older than me, but never with our attitude, style and frequency had they been able to travel about so freely. It's a nailed-on fact that not many could afford to watch footy abroad on a regular basis before I started. And if they could, they must have been middle-class Reds, and you know what they say about them, they're the same as middle-class Mods, who buy all the accessories, like new scooters and parkas, or in the Reds' case executive season tickets and luxury breaks to European games. But, and it's another Yozzer Hughes of a butt – neither of them ever get up to fuck-all. All sing together after three: 'What a waste of money.'

When it was time to sack the bootboy image by trying to be different, there wasn't much on offer when you couldn't get further than your average Brisish high street for your clobber, and even though the basic rig-out was always straight jeans, lambswool crew-neck and button-down shirt, rounded off with Samba or Kickers, you couldn't start acquiring Daniel Hechter version shirts, Ball version jeans, Benetton version crew-necks, Matinique version coats, rounded off with mad versions of

Adidas, by going to Sunderland on the special. No, the basic rig-out spin-offs could normally only be obtained if you crossed the English Channel. Once they were obtained, a regulation cocky Scouse attitude, the spirit of youth and wanting to better yourself, gave you the first real scallies at the football, and what some people would like to call the first casuals to walk the walk.

CHAPTER SIX

Up On Yer Toes, it's the

Confrontation Station

LIVERPOOL ARE PLAYING the Mancs on Boxing Day 1980 at Old Trafford. We'd played them two years earlier on the same date and 1,000 lads had run amok around the ground, especially at the back of the Stretford End, as Liverpool won easily 3–0. But for this Chrimbo special, British Rail had decided that they were not going to run any trains to a game that had always been in the highest category for a potential soccer scrap. For the last few seasons the Annie Road boys had arrived early in big numbers, and for a few years the Mancs couldn't get near us. It was our heyday as a firm goes, and any Man U sheep who tried to intervene would be chased, pulverised or arse-ripped. We'd congregate outside, quietly, on the far corner of the Scoreboard End of the ground, and as soon as the main Liverpool mob arrived, we'd quickly walk around the ground before any bizzie intervention, then kick off around the back of the Stretford End.

For a few years I was well up for it. Especially when one year at the end of the Seventies, the Man U fans who were queuing up started hilariously diving over the turnstiles to avoid getting a dig. Quick learners eh; we'd recently been trying to teach them how to dress and now we were teaching them how to jib in. Anyway, here I am, never one to miss a bunking opportunity, so I dived over with them. Funny thing is, the second year, it happened again, only this time, the Man U woollybacks who I dived over with, quickly realised I was a Liverpool fan and fronted me. I can still see them shouting, 'He's one of that lot outside, he's a bloody Scouser' in their grim up North, Neville voices. It was a case of stay inside with twenty mill-town sheep on your tail or jump back out to safety and 300 friendly Road End faces. The fellas who fronted me were divvies, and I knew it, so I wasn't climbing back out unless it was an emergency or it was way too early. As soon as a few more Liverpool boys joined me on the inside of the great trouser divide, they backed off pronto.

Liverpool had one ruthless, massive firm of young scallies, but from Heysel onwards, in a kicking-off sense, the young Road End firm would never be as angry, or as continually numerous as this again. In fact it was only in 1989, when a sort of Annie Road End reunion took place for a fourth round FA Cup tie at Millwall that a seriously naughty crew that more than matched the old one arrived in town with the Reds.

But here we are, in the last few shopping days before Chrimbo 1980, it's the run-up to a boxing-on-Boxing Day clash with 'Unarted' and, with no choo-choos readily available, for this take-your-selection-boxes-to-the-match day, coaches and cars have to be swiftly organised. Now if you and yer turkey sarnies didn't want to get a hard time at Old Trafford, then you went mob-handed, with the boys, usually by train. It was always the worst ground for getting vultured or picked off if you were alone. If you happened to be in a small group, with say, two or three other Scousers in a car, then it was on top.

Nah that was a definite no-no as far as visiting Manc-land was concerned. Those septic tanks were never clued-up in the clobber stakes, but were exceptionally clued-up, probably top of the division, when it came to sussing out a lone Scouser. Clobber-wise, you stood out like a sore thumb; accent-wise, another sore thumb; and hatred-wise, you were absolutely despised, which had something to do with our cocky attitude and the serious success we were enjoying, so basically it was another sore thumb, in fact, it was the only place on the planet where a Scouser could have three sore thumbs.

Being a bunch of oul-arses, a few well-travelled lads got their heads together and booked a couple of 'in the know' coaches. You only found out about, or were allowed to book aboard these two bedlam buses, if you were a well and truly signed-up young scally. To be signed-up for the Chara, you had to be a lad who firstly, was not of the 'plop in yer pants' variety, if a kick in the plums was being threatened, secondly, you were a well-known face at the away games, and thirdly, you could usually be counted on to laugh in the face of adversity if things were about to turn plum ugly.

Boxing Day comes, arrive in Manny early, nowhere open. Eventually our scallied-up driver finds this huge, round boozer, shaped like a drum; I think it was called the Drum but I could be wrong. It was on the main road into Old Trafford and was apparently playing host to the Irish and Dewsbury Red Devils' supporters' Chrimbo buffets. The landlord kindly decides to serve the ninety or so lads who have just walked in, on the pretence that we'll all happily leave once the Man U Paddies arrive from the land of Blarney, or the Yorkshire renegades arrive from the land of stack-heel and mullet. They've never been too shy to earn an extra crust, our jovial landlords, have they? Otherwise, he'd have given our rowdy crew a serious once-over, thought for a second, then given us an even more serious knockback.

Bevvies start getting supped, songs abound, and that Christmassy feel starts to take over. But what's this? Our plonky-nosed, money-grabbing landlord tells us we'll all have to leave soon, as the Paddy-and-Mick United party are about to arrive. The buffet is in the next room, and our host is asked bluntly what about the Christmas spirit, yer know, and goodwill to all men, and all that?

'Nah,' he goes, 'I want you out, and I want you out now.'

'Well fuck you, you Manc Scrooge, we're not moving.'

Someone eventually gives him a dig, and half the buffet goes west. A lot of the lads in there were jokingly going, 'Well, loads of our nanas and granddads were Irish, so the scoff's probably for us.'

We didn't leave that boozer until an hour before kick-off, arranging for the drivers to pick us up outside the ground at the end of the match, and you just knew that a full-scale rumpus was about to take place. The Dewsbury branch of biker Man U eventually arrived, only to be greeted at the door with some serious right hooks, so the greedy manager complained and received a pint glass to the head, for which one Scouse lad eventually received five years' jug. It was jug for jug and getting raucous. Here you had 100 or so of Liverpool's maddest scallywags, and as we walked up the road, it became evident that the reception committee had been pre-warned about our imminent arrival. There were fucking thousands of them. It was like an advert for that grandmas' knitting supplies shop, Wool-lovers and Pullovers. They were climbing on railings, up drainpipes and lampposts, in *Planet of the Apes* jumpers, presenting a sea of cheap white socks, their gorgeous Stuart Pearson centre-parts blowing in the wind. Others were scrambling for any vantage point in a whole host of hand-me-down Norman Wisdom jumpers, all trying to get a look at the firm who'd just ruined the Irish–Yorkie buffet, and who they were about to make pay for their Chrimbo naughtiness. *Uh uh, Chongo, it's looking shady.*

Everybody realised that no plod intervention was forthcoming, and a couple of the craziest, oldest lads, who were probably in their late twenties by now, were saying, 'No infiltrators, no fucking infiltrators.' And another lad close to me, who had this huge mad smile, was going, 'Now this is what you want, no-one fucking run, these're all sheep-shaggers, run at them as a mob and they'll all just go.'

He looked fucking nuts and I badly wanted to believe him. I looked around, and I was half-bevvied, but I laughed; it was like the Alamo, and I always laughed when it was bango. Most of the huge, baying crowd seemed to be locked in the Seventies, the usual Birmo'd-up beauts with the odd Manc scally dotted here and there. A second look at our mob told me we'd deffo reached the confrontation station, and you just knew the boys were thinking, *now we'll see who's got any bottle when it's no retreat time*. It was about to erupt large-scale, as I knew that none of these lads would run in front of each other. Quite a few blades came out of pockets. I've never carried a blade, never would. I always thought, and still think, that weapons were like a magnet for trouble; blunt instruments like bats and bars, then maybe, but as the Stanleys came out, and with no Christmas turkeys to carve up, the reality that arses were about to be slashed in number fully hit me.

Punches and digs were thrown on the edge of the tightly bunched crew and one Man U scarf-wearer who got a little too close got severely knocked out. Anyone who overstepped the mark was instantly jumped on by five or six Scousers, and quite a few of the frontline boys were boxers, the same ten or so lads who were always up for a little extra sparring. When this firm was about, one-punch knockouts were well on the agenda. You could sense the crowd getting closer and more and more out of control as we made our way through to the ground. It wasn't through bravery that they were getting nearer, it was that mob mentality taking over, where the majority of the shitbags at the back of the crowd push the others to the front. Meanwhile the ones at the front had seen a few glints of steel and were doing anything to get to the back.

I saw only one brave Man United fan (if you can call him brave with that mob of jumpers behind him) appear from that massive crowd on street-boxing day. He had a big woolly head and looked like Joe Jordan, and he was wearing a Man U jersey when hardly any supporters wore those football tops. So Toothless Joe he was, and to this day that's always been his name to the lads who were there. He made his move and was downed by three or four scallies, one huge uppercut putting an end to his bravery. I looked at his fucked-up face; he was on planet Absolutely Twatted, with blood coming from his nose and mouth. The real Joe Jordan was a frightening sight for the knobhead footballers on the field, but out on the street it was a different kettle of fish; on the pavement this guy was just another gormless, gummy bastard who didn't scare anybody, except maybe a few plastic footy skins who hid in the crowd. My last glimpse of Toothless Joe showed a swarm of Annie Road ants surrounding a head that looked like Joe Royle's and Sam Allardyce's stuck together. Porn Chairman Sullivan seems to love Arthur Mullard — sorry Steve Bruce — as manager, giving him a new five-year contract to help keep the Burberry boys in the Premiership. It got me wondering if it was because the board finally felt sorry for him all those years after taking a slab of concrete full in the mush at the above game. Is that true? *Yus, my dear*.

Nobody else was making a move once big Joe bit the dust, and I didn't wait around to see if he got his regulation Man U army stripes. It was one of those time-stands-still moments when you start to wonder, *well come on, what's the next move?* The brain-teaser was quickly answered when the young Annie Road firm charged at the huge crowd as that Lou Macari chippy came into view. At first, a few of them tried to stand, but as the stampede mentality took over, thousands started to flee. It might've been 1,000 but it looked like thousands compared to our small mob. I've never seen a mob that big all trying to give it toes at the same time; they were literally falling over each other and pushing each other out of the way in their haste to escape. Every lad there that day called it Custer's Last Stand, and it just went to prove that if you had the right set of boys around you, on any given day, then it was hard to come to harm. Most football fights look miles worse than they really are, but this one really could have been a lot worse.

As the huge crowd ran away, the stragglers were tripped and beaten. The bizzies eventually put in an appearance as we turned left into the Scoreboard End, and I got nicked just as I was clouting some daft Welsh prick who had been shouting 'You Scouse bastard' only a minute or so before. I think he had to be north Welsh, because he had that waltzer spinner from Rhyl look about him. Never did like those north Welsh, Man U, suck-holing nuggets anyway. Give me a Welsh-club-supporting Welsh Nationalist any day of the week. Some of those Welsh coastal whoppers have got a serious chip with Scousers, and all because our granddads and uncles have been causing mayhem at Gareth's and Emlyn's caravan sites for years. Twenty minutes later, the bizzies let me out of the van, something you wouldn't see today. Apparently no clapping-in took place on the way into the Scoreboard for the shit-hot 100. Well, what could you expect? They were always bad losers those Man U.

Years later, I was talking to this lad from Salford in a bar in Tenerife, and he told me about this mad Scouse 100 who should have got battered at Old Trafford on Boxing Day 1980 but ended up chasing after a huge home mob.

'They'd have got battered if everybody would have turned around.'

And he laughed when I said, 'I know mate, I was there.'

We had a few good bevvies on that holiday; he was an okay kid. I saw him a few times at the games later on, and he'd always say to his mates, 'This fella was one of the Scouse one hundred.'

He had me smiling at how funny it is, the way things work out. He made me realise that not all Mancs were jealous of, and hated Scousers. And some of the wiser lads I've known over the years from Manny had no real hatred at all. It's daft, isn't it? Especially when you think I, like hundreds of other young Liverpudlians, never had any real hatred for Man U, not until I realised just how much they hated us.

* * *

In the March of that same year, Liverpool had their biggest on-top of all time when they played Spurs at White Hart Lane in the quarter-final of the FA Cup. That Goal of the Season machine, Terence McDermott, scored as good a volley as you're ever likely to see to send Liverpool's travelling army into raptures and Tottenham's massive home crew on a final-whistle suicide mission. The Goal of the Season ended up causing the biggest on-top of the season; trust a Kirkby fella, eh.

Before the game, the kids in the know had 'made a meet' at Euston Station, so the main lads would all be together for that long, dodgy trek down the Seven Sisters Road. The meet was organised for a little later than normal to allow the shoppers in the crew their usual jaunt around the West End, where places like Bond Street, South Molton Street, Lillywhites sports shop in Piccadilly and Harrods and Beauchamp Place around the corner were always on the early morning itinerary.

Once the early arrivals were all back at Euston, the main ordinary train arrived as planned and a few hundred boys bounced off in fine fettle. Whenever this Scouse crew turned up away from home, the first chant would always be, 'The Road End, ch, ch, ch. Oh we're the barmy Annie Road army, tra la la la la la.' Then, on entering the Tube station, where all big crews would find their voice with that acoustic Tubeway echo, the Clash's 'English Civil War' would go up: 'When Johnny comes marching home again, hurrah,' but we'd just 'la la la' the tune, not the words, as the mass Tube jib bounced onto that Victoria Line northbound train for the short journey to the Seven Sisters. For years nobody bought a ticket, and whenever I'm in London I automatically go to board the train without paying, before realising that these days I've got the money and I'm not with the boys anymore. On leaving the station we would run past the guards, and fellas who have now grown up and got coin in pocket have told me they instinctively still try to dodge past the clippies. The old habitual bunk dies hard.

Anyone approaching this young Road End crew who looked threatening was jumped on and walloped. A few boozers were attacked on the way to the ground and a few Tottenham boys got leathered. Some scuffles broke out with the local black population, who were not too happy to see this mob of 500 northern urchins running wild down their shopping street. Now this main crew of Road End lads were not usually up for acting the hoolie for no reason. Being hostile and kicking off generally meant we were on a revenge mission or we were at a ground where trouble was par for the course. Some of the older Liverpool supporters had told a few of the younger lads about the hard time you could get at the Seven Sisters, so Tottenham's reputation had gone a bit before them. First and foremost, this mob chasing and walloping anything in its way was a show-of-strength crew.

Some lads, on checking the strength of the firm, were clocking for tom shops or anything else on offer, but that High Road that leads to White Hart Lane is never going to be New Bond Street. At the time, it had more in common with Petticoat Lane, with bric-a-brac places, small record shops and the odd supermarket thrown in the mix. I walked past one large supermarket and was shocked at how many black and Asian faces were inside. When I was younger, it always surprised me when an area was full of black or Asian people, like it did a lot of other Scousers. I hadn't grown up in multi-cultural Liverpool 8, and it took a few years for the penny to drop that this was the way things were in some other cities. It was a type of ignorance that some people confuse with racism. Don't get me wrong, we had our racists, but on the whole they were lads who had only ever been taught white history, yer know, kings and queens and all that la-di-da stuff, and how gout-riddled Henry the Eighth started a new religion so he could shag loads of birds. Hardly any of us had been taught about the different types of people who lived in Britain's cities. If you think it's a racist thing to be surprised or totally ignorant about the number of black people in certain parts of the country, blame the British education system. I mean, nobody told me about Abdul and Mohammed from Tottenham, or Isaiah and West Indian Neville from Handsworth just up the road from the Villa. But once Terry McDermott scored that classic volley, some young lads were about to get a full lesson in multi-cultural mob attacks, as the Cockney firm outside was huge, of every colour, and most importantly, they were all baying for our blood.

A taste of what was to come showed up in the form of hundreds of coins being constantly thrown down from the Spurs home end, nicknamed the Shelf. Half the time, with no close-up camera security about, you could throw what the fuck you liked at these games, and one Scouser came up trumps when he threw a leg of lamb over the fence separating the two sets of fans. It was soon followed by sausages, pork chops and a couple of huge sirloin steaks that had just been lifted from a local butcher's. For a few minutes a meat battle ensued, as the home fans threw the stuff back, before eventually fizzling out as the meat became mince. The small crew who had raided the butcher's huddled closely around each other, before rising as one to deliver half a dozen eggs, which couldn't miss their Cockney targets. Fellas were pointing up at Spurs fans who had been hit, as they vigorously wiped their heads and faces using scarves, tissues or anything else resembling a cloth. A number of Liverpool fans were taken for treatment for coin-inflicted head wounds as skirmishes broke out all over the ground.

From the moment the final whistle sounded, White Hart Lane became On Top Central. You could sense it as you left the ground, as the London Old Bill kept nobody behind and busily shoved supporters out of the ground. It was as though they'd just about had enough of the terrace tantrums themselves. It was obvious when you hit daylight that half of London's hoolies had turned out. The walk up to the Seven Sisters became the longest some Liverpool fans have ever taken, as attack after attack was launched, while the London dibble played their part by offering no protection, being heavy-handed with any Liverpool counter-attacks, and basically standing by as one Cockney crew after another tried to land punches or kicks on the Liverpool mob, which was basically too big for its own good. Being too big was always a problem for a crew; smaller numbers of hardened Annie Road End scallies usually meant a safer day all round.

Tottenham had been knocked out of the cup, and a bad result could have a major bearing on the likelihood and severity of attack. Well, Tottenhams skins, and any other teams' fans who were there that day, gave us the worst time we've ever had at a British football ground. One well-known lad was put through a supermarket window. I, with about seventy others, tried to fight all the way back to the Tube station, totally on the back foot. It was hopeless; every time you fought back, the London bizzies would give you a slap. If you tried to mingle, it was even worse. Any previous chase to the station or shady battle concerning Liverpool was put firmly in its place that day. Ask any real Red about Spurs in the cup and he'll tell you the same story.

When we did finally reach a seat on the Tube, fellas all around were breathing sighs of relief, and saying things like, 'Fucksake, that was a bit iffy'. Me and Joey O used to laugh a lot during an on-top situation, especially when supporters who didn't usually travel were startled at the home fans' behaviour. We sat down for the Tube ride back to Euston and couldn't stop laughing about the shocked look on some of the normal fans' faces. On our usual 'ordinary' train home – Cockneys, along with some other mobs, called them inter-city trains but we always called them ordinary trains – the Liverpool team hopped on board to a tumultuous welcome, and as the lads who'd been shopping sold their swag to the players, they regaled them with the tales of just how daunting our trip back to Euston had been.

Because of what happened at that game, only 1,000 Liverpool fans turned up for the league game three weeks later, of which, 6–700 were the Road End's finest. And yeah, you've guessed it, Tottenham were nowhere, and we chased their mob all over the place. Maybe the fact that they won 2–0 had something to do with it. As that brilliant old Tottenham favourite, Greavsie, would say, 'Football, it's a funny old game,' and a good or bad result could make some people act even funnier.

* * *

The year before, just after we'd won the European Cup, Birmingham's St Andrews stadium played host to another memorable battle. Their ground looked like it had been nailed together. It was crumbling outside and falling apart at the seams inside. Everywhere you turned you could see the place was littered with ammo. From the moment I entered the terracing I just knew a large bout of target practice was about to kick off. On one side of the fence you had a huge Blue mob of skinheads, punks and Brummie car mechanics (we always thought that Brummies looked like car mechanics, for some heavy metal, biker reason), and on our side you had an even bigger mob of young Red scallies, wedged-up, and traineed to go. Liverpool walloped the Blue Shite 3–0 and one end of the ground turned into a concrete battle as fans tore lumps of the decaying terraces up to hurl at each other. Punks and skins to the left, scallies and urchins to the right; take your place for the 1978 Midland Concrete Slingers Final. Old stanchions, parts of the roof and an old tea bar were being ripped out and the battle raged on and on and on. For so long, in fact, that you were terrified to watch the game in case you caught a slab of concrete in the neck. They never did fit well, those concrete polo-necks, especially when thrown by some Johnny Rotten lookalike with a Noddy Holder accent, who spent half of his life welding 'ringers' together. Outside, we chased them all over the place, as usual. They won't like hearing that, as today they think they're dead hard. Ha! Their ground was always a doddle; in fact, I think they only got into football after Led Zeppelin split up, either that or their mob fell to bits when Ozzy Osbourne fucked off to the States.

At least most of the Brummies playing a part in that slingers' final were skins and punks. I mean, how many Burberry'd up Brummies does it take to shout Burberry out loud, before even their own porno chairman finally gets wind of the beige chequered onslaught. And being the 'fanny-entrepreneur' that he is, will he then decide to start selling Burberry dildos from the pages of Asian Babes, Brummie Bush, The Walsall Wank, or any other of his Brum-City-owned tasty-tit mags. Simple soccer economics tells you that more chequered dildo sales equals more money for quality players. Just shouting Burberry in a Brummie accent reminds me of that story about the world's greatest nuclear scientist, who happened to be from West Bromwich, and when he introduced himself likewise, nobody would believe him, as the accent just doesn't ring true for someone 'so brainy'. Just try saying it. 'I'm the world's greatest nuclear . . .', go on, in Brummie. Oh yeah, and the feather-cut burners were back in town for that scallies versus punks day, as a couple of Sex Pistols yellow spiky tops got turned into char-grilled foo yung. Now I bet you've never heard of that Midland delicacy. That old woollyback morning call that went *cocka doodle doo*, that he'd woken up to at the crack of dawn, had been replaced by the tweet tweet of a few trainee'd-up Scouse budgies. Joe should've thrown his AirWair boot at the noisy cock and stayed in the flock all day.

The end of the same season took us to Leeds, where Liverpool, title in the bag, had to score a couple of goals to reach eighty-four – two goals per game in a forty-two-game season – to win prize money of £50,000 on offer from the Sun-Coral betting organisation. One of the finest, if not *the* finest, Liverpool teams ever assembled had managed to concede only sixteen goals all through that Championship-winning year and now, last game, they had to score two more to reach that prize-winning target against those oul blow-waved Yorkshire smoothies. So what did they do? They went and scored three, and outside those Men of Wool decided enough was enough. It was Zulu Dawn all over again as the boys of bell-bottom came over the hills in their legions.

Before the game the first Liverpool boys to arrive by train in Leeds were singing the songs that only piss-taking champions sing, and as they stormed out of the station they were greeted by the sight of Old Crinkly Dick standing his ground and blocking the way. I don't know how the oldest copper in Liverpool got the escort job that day, or on a lot of previous days, because he had to be the most ancient-looking codger copper this side of an un-ironed pair of Levis. He looked like a prune in a police uniform, and with his reflexes not being what they were, Crinkly Dick was run straight over as though he was a bridge into Leeds city centre. I never did see him again, though we'd gotten used to him over the previous few years. Mind you, things would have been different if Flatnose and

Blackbeard had been waiting at Leeds station, a fucking big heavy black glove different.

It was a warm sunny evening and the Leeds fans must've still been milking the cows, as none were about before the game. Little did we know it was only the calm before the cow's fart. After the game those three goals acted like the bull who said, 'Hey watch where tha's putting tha hands lad, that be ma wedding tackle you've just touched, that there's no udder.' Which meant that the farm-hands were bully-up for it? The Liverpool boys were well prepared for any Leeds attacks. We knew they'd be bitter and twisted, and they were suitably chased back over the hills to their stables time after time. But like a gang of Yorkshire yo-yos they kept coming back for more. Now I'm getting cocky by this time, and I'm openly, with others, starting to laugh at the Leeds mob, who can't stop playing the yo-yo game. We're giving it the, 'Come on you gang of woolly-headed shitbags' routine, and, 'Get home to your wife and kids, you daft oul sheepshaggers.'

By this time, I'm also having my own little cat and mouse game with this six-foot AirWair wearer, when suddenly, fed up with my constant derision, he runs at me with a house brick. *Fuck that*, I'm thinking, *I don't want to leave me lovely Scouse railings on these rabbit-shit-infested Yorkshire moors*. As he raises the brick to hit me in the face, I instinctively raise my hands to cover up, but as I do, the bushy blond slams the brick right into my bag of walnuts. I know right away from the pain that this set of walnuts are totally fucking whipped. That's it, game over, I'm done in. His troop of ageing bootboys, noticing my plight, start to jump all over me with their bouncy soles. All of a sudden I've gone from a piss-taking young urchin to a Scouse bouncy castle, in town for just one day, rented out for an AirWair anniversary party.

Eventually Willsie from the Kensington-cavalry part of the Road End came to my aid by using a fence ripped off the front wall of a nearby house-cum-stable. Was Leeds the only place that converted houses back to barns? Do property developers actively pursue house-to-barn conversions? Lash out the carpets and curtains, smash all the ornaments, throw down the straw and put a little lamb by the fire. In my case, they had a knack of turning up at the right time, those boys from Capaldi's café – me oul band Deaf School even wrote a song about that famous café on Kensington. Willsie's fence had got the Leeds yo-yo firm back on their stack-heels again, only this time they were chased out of sight, and after a bit, 6–700 of us took the long walk back to the station in a joyous mood with not a pair of flares in sight. The boys who were too lazy to go on foot had a bonfire celebration by setting a bus alight just for the devilment; naughty, naughty. It was a fine day all round, because although I'm having a bit of a pop at Leeds for being the Land That Time Forgot and all that, and it fucking well was by the way, if you got a good result outside Elland Road then it was deffo a right result, because it was always one of the worst grounds in the league for a soccer squabble. Saying that, as a young, clobbered-up Road Ender, there were not many finer sights than seeing hundreds of Leeds wools giving it toes over the hills with their penny-round collars and Rupert the Bear kecks flapping away in the wind. I've seen that sight a few times and it looked custy to me, a bit similar to those Bay City Rollers birds chasing after Les the lead singer as he left the stage door. There you go, *Shanga-fucken-lang* to Leeds.

The few times I've been chased at football matches seem to etch their way into your memory a whole lot clearer and sharper than the times spent running after other firms. The young

Annie Road End crew, due mainly to shame and having a firm of boys that was almost too big for its trainees, never really gave it toes en masse when all the boys were together, so most football firms provided a bit of a brief skirmish before giving it toes when they realised the full strength of the mob. If somebody at the front was flashing a blade, or quite a few were producing their Stanleys, then basically it was goodnight Vienna, confrontation station over.

The bad thing about those decorators' daggers was obviously the thousands of stitches they gave out, and the only thing in their favour, if you can understand where I'm coming from, is that they nipped a lot of foot-brawls in the bud. Not many gangs carried on fighting when they got a glimpse of a lad introducing Stanley to the crowd, and blade paranoia saved many a lone Scouser's arse from getting kicked when he either produced the said weapon or kidded on that he was carrying one. It was a trick that worked for a good few years, till everyone was onto it. Blade paranoia saved my bacon on a couple of occasions, when I reached inside my kecks for the non-existent carpet slicer, before chasing off my shit-scared would-be assailants. It found its way onto the terraces through Scouse grafting crews, who having found themselves compromised at a number of football games, decided that, with these mobs of vulture-type hooligans continually looking for prey and often sussing out their small Scouse earning crew, they'd start carrying the arse-rippers as a form of insurance or deterrent. People like the dipping firms (pickpockets) were the first to carry Stanleys, as they'd usually be dipping among the other team's well-to-do fans or at an important neutral game that didn't involve Liverpool. Other lads quickly noticed how much of a deterrent the little 'yellow handles' were, and before too long, quite a large chunk of the Road End mob were regularly lifting them from DIY stores, before tucking them down their undies to take to the away grounds.

* * *

Improved transport and communication networks meant Europe and the rest of the world was getting closer by the day. Some lads had the money to travel but still wouldn't go; loads of others were unemployed, had got used to being skint and thought that that was the end of it. But after Rome '77, a new Liverpool mob had come hurtling down the M6, and they seemed to be saying: 'Get out of the way, you're not stopping me.' These are the fellas I'm talking about, and they fiddled their way around the Seven Seas simply to follow their team. Big silver cups apart, anything else brought to the party was a bonus. And while some fellas gave in too easily to being skint and stayed in bed, wanking over Fiona from Darlington, or plucking on guitar strings till they could strum 'Dark Side of the Moon' backwards, others got up off their arses, pulled on a pair of trainees and a thinking cap and headed for the White Cliffs of Dover to help push the boat out across the Channel. Fellas like for instance your jibbers and your bunkers. It's a Trans-Alpino rub out baby, take me there. Double-clicks away, here we go.

PART TWO

The Bunkers' Society

CHAPTER SEVEN

Yer Jibbers and Yer Bunkers

AT THE END of the 1975/76 season, Liverpool needed to beat Wolves at Molyneux to win the First Division Championship. If they did, they would also send the famous Midland gold shirts into the Second Division. It was the only league game where I have seen more than 40,000 away fans inside a ground. My lasting memory of that title decider was not of Liverpool's players securing another championship but of the thousands of fans who got into the ground without paying, by using whatever methods they had to, on a balmy, cup-gathering night in the gorgeous Midlands.

Me da picked me and my brother up from school in a minibus with about ten of his workmates, so at least we didn't have to work our thumbs at Haydock roundabout like we usually did. Our happiness at having a lift there and back was short-lived, because as we arrived in Wolverhampton at about six o'clock, thousands of Liverpool supporters were walking and driving away from the ground, shouting things like, 'Don't bother mate, it's totally full,' and, 'The gates are locked and there's thousands outside, you're best getting off.'

Undeterred, me da carried on with his mates towards the ground. Some of his younger mates seemed totally unfazed by the locked-out signals we were getting, as they happily whistled at the Black Country ladies that walked on by. With no sexism rants being rammed down people's throats by the fascist lesbian firm in those days, the wolf whistles were greeted with sparkly eyes and a nice smile, instead of a tut, a grunt and a beady eye. As the young guns whistled, however, I felt like crying, thinking that I wasn't going to get in. Me oul fella, sensing my apprehension, goes, 'Don't worry son, we're just gonna have a little look for ourselves.' Thousands of Kopites were streaming away from Molyneux, but he kept walking towards the floodlights, keeping the two of us by his side so as not to lose us among the vast, rapidly departing crowd.

Eventually we reached the locked gates. Suddenly we were looking at a different crowd altogether. They were like an inner ring of supporters, all mad busy devising ways to get inside the closed stadium with its full-up signs. One gang was ramming a heavy wooden double door with what looked to me like a totem pole, but I realise now was a telegraph pole. Heaven knows where they found that. Another mob was pulling bricks from the high wall, like men trying to break out of a prison cell. I'm thinking, *the match'll be over before they get anyone inside*.

A human ladder, a bit like a circus act, was being formed by another gang, and they seemed to be getting results more quickly as man after man stepped onto the top guy's shoulders before disappearing over the wall. The tank of a man who was the bottom rung in the ladder had stuffed newspapers into the shoulders of his jacket. Liverpool's answer to the padded-shouldered New Romantics, working till he was musclebound, was hoisting fellas over the wall so quickly that me da was about to throw us into the queue. He then thought better of it, shouting his mates over so they could build their own ladder. As they prepared for the climb-up onto each other's shoulders, his mind changed once again when a large round hole appeared in front of one of the brick-scraping gangs. Jimmy Boyle of Glasgow's Gorbals became famous for performing the same trick inside Barlinnie Prison, when he removed the bricks from a wall that separated his cell from his mate's next door.

Next on the scene was a gang of fellas all dressed in black, looking like they'd been to a funeral. They all seemed to be six foot twelve to me and the front one, who looked like an Irish navvy on steroids, was carrying a huge sledgehammer as though it was a child's toy. Bish! Bang! Wallop! Mr Demolition in a black suit took over, and before you knew it a hole as big as Elton John's arsehole appeared; in other words, about the size of a large tractor tyre. Next, the gate-ramming gang was moved aside and a crowbar appeared. Bish! Bang! Wallop! Open sesame and the ground sucked everyone in.

Me da had to drag me in, because although I'd bunked into grounds on many occasions already, I'd never seen a mass bunk-in like this. I was standing there mesmerised, just taking it all in. I remember thinking how prepared that demolition firm had been, with sledgies and crowbars and whatnot. *Be prepared and no ground can keep you out*: that's what I kept thinking, and I carried that same thought with me every second Saturday and into Europe for years.

It is unlikely – make that impossible – that you will ever see a mob of over 40,000 away fans in a ground for a league match again, not with ID cards, memberships, cameras and so many home supporters owning season tickets. Plus the local plod would be sure to scupper any massive-crew ideas that some supporters might entertain, especially if they still keep police records about nights like Wolves v Liverpool, 4 May 1976. It later transpired that even the players had opened the changing room doors to let hundreds of Scousers into the ground. The grateful supporters quickly wished them good luck before walking straight through to the pitch and onto the terraces. Different days, mate, different days. They weren't overpaid pop stars, they were just the football boot part of us. I loved those players and always will. We beat Wolves 3–1 that night and the celebrations went on till dick-docks, especially the big party on the M6 all the way home. Alas, poor old Wolves were duly relegated. But stored somewhere up top, in among 1,000 recollections, lies my own abiding memory, and that will always be of the mass bunk-in that opened my eyes to the lengths some Scousers would go to, all to see their beloved boys in red.

Earlier that season we'd been to Derby County for an FA Cup tie, and a similar but much smaller-scale bunk-out, not bunk-in, took place. Now at Derby's Baseball Ground you could always pay or jib into the boys' pen, situated down at the opposing home end of the antique stadium. Due to its easier bunk-in gates and the small ticket allocation we always received, you'd see Scousers nudging thirty with half-shaven beards entering this children's area. Every year that I went there, from the mid-Seventies onward, it would be a quick double-click taken care of, then we'd all move to the front of the fence by the corner flag. There we'd sort of lie in wait, and once those red shirts came trotting down the tunnel, the cavalry call would go up and the charge would take place. Me mates and I, in true cavalry style, would roll up our stolen programmes to make bugle horns before loudly sounding the charge. All hell would break loose as it became every man for himself in battling for a place to clamber over the pen fence. The Liverpool visitors' section was on the other side of the ground at the far end of the paddock. We'd be running across the pitch laughing and shouting abuse at each other while slip-sliding in the usual Derby sand and mud.

At this cup game, I ran straight up to one of my heroes of

the time, the springy-skulled Kevin Keegan, and shouted, 'Wahey Kevin, how are yer mate?'

And he goes, in this bad Yorkie accent, 'Alright lad, now come on, gerroff the pitch will you.'

'Fuck you, you curly-headed Yorkshire twat.'

Everyone in earshot started laughing. I mean, he might've been a player we loved but he wasn't a Scouser, so he sounded like some kind of schoolteacher to my ears, a bit like that bossy sports teacher in the movie *Kes*. Maybe I would have listened if it had been Bob Paisley or Tommy Smith, but nah, not some bad perm from Doncaster. A few years earlier I'd shaken hands with Keegan in the Anfield car park and wouldn't wash them for a week afterwards, such is a kid's devotion to a football star. I thought he walked on water, but as you grow up – and I was growing up fast – you realise it's a two-way thing, this adulation you give to a certain player or manager. Shankly, Joey Jones and a few others will have it till the day I die, but Keegan later proved to be nothing but an absolute mercenary, so I'm glad I told him to get to fuck.

Once we got to the away end we had to dodge the Derby dibble, and as I dived over the wall into our end, thinking, as usual, that some big Scouser was going to break my fall, the crowd parted and I ended up diving headlong onto a barrier, which I met with a dull thud. It was one of those slow-motion moments where you can see you are about to get clattered, but are helpless to change direction. Like a character from a *Tom and Jerry* cartoon, I slid slowly to the floor. It felt like I had half-killed myself.

As I looked up from the floor, everyone was in stitches, but my arm felt like it was broken, so I shouted, 'What are you fucking laughing at, yer gang of knobheads.' This only made the lads laugh louder. *Mr Bad Perm Keegan would be chuffed if he could see me now,* I thought. I only found out years later, after another match accident followed by an x-ray, that my arm had indeed been bust at Derby but had healed naturally over a period of time. I suppose no doctors or hospitals were needed in those days of running on pure adrenalin.

Coventry was another strange jib. Each year we used to bunk into Highfield Road and sit with the handicapped supporters in these little dugouts by the side of the pitch. Loads of those Del-boy three-wheelers would be parked up around the perimeter of the pitch and I'm sure they all used to be sky blue. We used to call them 'referees' whistles' because that's what they looked like. You could be sure two of those whistles parked out on the driveway wouldn't go down too well with the nosey neighbours on a snobby new estate. After a few years of entering through the disabled gates, I got to know a couple of these handicapped Coventry supporters. One in particular looked like Tony Blair, only this fella was a much better comedian. This one year it was rainy and miserable, and Liverpool and Cov were playing just as miserably. Coventry were on the attack, with a player called Tom English in possession, and as the future prime minister in a wheelchair starts pouring us a cuppa from his flask, English is tackled and goes to take the throw-in. This English fella wasn't very good, and this disabled guy, who I thought was hilarious, was constantly giving him the bird, or 'bad stick' as we call it.

The ball had gone out just in front of us and as the English fella lifted his arms back to take the throw-in, this guy in the wheelchair, who had small thalidomide arms, shouted out in this Midlands accent, 'Give us the ball English, I could throw it better with these fucking things.' Me and the lad Vinny, who was sitting alongside me, spat tea all over each other. Tom English looked over, so this wheelchair comedian shouted,

'That's right English, I'm a fucking spazzy in a wheelchair, but I could do a whole lot better than you. I could mark you out of the game sitting in this thing, even if it had two burst tyres.' Well, we were in pleats. This fella was a nutter, and the three of us laughed our way through the rest of the match. The dire weather and game had been given a lot more colour by our new-found friend. I went back to look for the Wheelchair Wonder a few years later but was struggling to find him, before some jobsworth steward eventually poked his nose in and told me to get back onto the terraces before he got the plod involved.

In those early independence days away from me da, I'd started to case the grounds by walking around them before kick-off to get a general lay-out drawn up in my mind. I'd often go on walkabouts around two o'clock and Eddie or Joey O, or whoever was with me, would be asking the same question most Saturdays, as in, 'Where the fuck have you just disappeared to? We've been looking for you for ages.'

'Just doing the rounds for future reference, that's all.'

By 1980, there was hardly a ground that I didn't have a basic mental diagram of, as throughout the 1970s I had steadily filed away details in my brain. They were logged under a heading that read, 'Football stadiums and their best entrance points.' Some people did this kind of thing for terrorist reasons or to maybe mastermind a robbery, or perhaps they were disgruntled season ticket holders, who after another poor start to the season, wanted to set the ground alight to save themselves from any further misery. I did it for no other reason than to make sure that I'd be sitting or standing inside that ground every time Liverpool paid a visit. I hardly had an away ticket for almost twenty-five years of footy, but once those red jerseys were in town, you could rest assured that I'd be one of the more fervent heads inside the arena. Lockouts were never a problem for me, or a good few of my mates for that matter. If you did a survey of all the stewards and gatemen around the country asking who the biggest bunkers were, year in, year out, I'm sure ninety-nine per cent of them would say Liverpool.

It has virtually faded out now, and is not something I'm bragging about or proud of, but then again, nor am I ashamed of it. When you were born in a rough and ready part of Liverpool, you learned to work your head and make the most of whatever circumstances you found yourself in. Other people around the country had tough upbringings within tough districts, but as Bill Shankly had said when leaving Huddersfield for Liverpool, 'I'm going to a place where they live, eat, sleep and drink football, and that's my place.' Twin that with the rebellious Liverpool mentality, quite unique in England, and you're looking at a city teeming with passionate football fanatics. Football and legends like Shankly were always our sunshine.

The basis of this rebellion lay in the fact that Liverpool has always been an immigrant city, where the population only grew to any substantial size during the Irish potato famine. Once these poor Irish immigrants had found their place in Liverpool society, along with thousands of poor Welshmen who also settled within the city boundaries, a rebellious, mainly Celtic city began to grow on the banks of the Mersey. A sprinkling of Italians and Chinese helped along the cosmopolitan dockside flavour.

Once Thatcher and her Tory cronies seized power just as I left school, and bang on cue began to dismantle most of the industry within the city and its docks, some would say because of its Bolshie left-wing history (not enough yes-men), and apparently it was on the wrong coast, which meant it wasn't 'dahn sarf' money-wise, a siege mentality, a feeling of defiance and a sense of being an outsider in my own country grew strongly within me and has stayed with me and thousands like me to this day. If you know your real history and that your forefathers had to fight for every penny earned and for trade union rights and working solidarity just to gain a foothold on the bottom rung of the ladder of British society, then along comes the skeleton-faced, shopkeeper's bitch of a daughter to dismantle everything they'd fought for, then not conforming to the rolling green fields of England theory comes as natural as day. It's one of the main reasons quite a lot of the Liverpool and Everton supporters don't follow the fortunes of the national team, and why many of the older supporters refer to the national team as London FC.

Bottom line, Liverpool people were mainly from the Shankly school of thought. They were left-wing socialists. The South in general came from the Thatcher school of thought; they were right-wing capitalists. The London Government had the power, so they tried to push us out to sea. It was an us-and-them mentality, a kind of Liverpool FC versus London FC for the Politics Cup. Weird, eh?

I'm sure the social shrinks or some soccer shrink (I'm sure they've got them now, as they have one for everything else) could come up with a reason for our bunking into football grounds all over Europe for twenty-five years, just as they probably could to explain the feather-cut burners and arse slashers, but them fellas have never been legged at West Ham, been to Europe with no passport and fifteen pence to their name, or had twenty sixteen-stone Geordies trying to catch them as they toed it round the Eldon Square shopping precinct at ten o'clock in the morning, all because the Likely Lads had sussed them spending too long trying to read their tattoos. A fella can sit behind a desk for six months and learn everything about how to plaster a ceiling, the ins, the outs, the tools to use and so forth, but until the day he finally leaves his desk, pulls on his boots and gets out on site, trowel in hand, on a freezing cold Monday morning, he'll never be able to plaster a fucking ceiling. So why listen to the degreed-up so-called social experts? Money for old rope. Those fellas will charge you £30 an hour to tell whether you should eat a pot noodle with a fork or spoon, or which way to pour your cornflakes in the morning so you don't suffer from depression.

I don't need any shrink to tell me that it was about wanting to see a bit of life and not wanting to be held down or held back by your social background; being absolutely determined not to let a lack of cash tie you to the job centre lifestyle that successive Tory governments were trying to impose on you. Some of those prominent Tories of the past had said ordinary people should never have been given the vote, and labelled them cannon fodder, then factory fodder. Well the factories were all closing down as I left school and I didn't fancy getting left behind on the scrapheap with the rest of the factory fodder, nah that wasn't for me. So there you have it: it's rebellion, or it was for me anyway. Don't buy into that psychobabble shit; the only true experts on any subject are the ones who live the life and walk the walk, in whatever capacity that may be. Oh yeah, and if anyone wants any bunking, self-help or soccer psychology lessons, meet me in the sacked dockers' pub, the Casa Bar, Hope Street, Liverpool, any Monday evening after work and I'll sort that out, only £35 an hour.

When I'd just left school and finally worn me thumbs out, I'd get up on a Saturday morning and bunk the train to wherever the Reds were playing. When I got there – and I always did – it'd be a quick once-over of the ground, sussing out my entrance point, before doing a bit of shopping, scallying or bevvying. Then, and only then, I'd think about entering the stadium, after half past two. On the dot I'd be straight over to my chosen entrance, whether it be a turnstile gate, ticket collection office, players' entrance, first-aid door, plod door, vehicle entrance gate, BBC or ITV camera crew entrance, climb-over or whatever seemed the best option on any given day. I've walked into grounds alongside a sheep-skinned John Motson on numerous occasions, but he probably never noticed me, even though I've let on to him about five times. If he got on me at all, he must've thought, *oh there's that cameraman who always wears the Adidas, always gives me a decent let on, that fella.* There was no major plan going on, and apart from my general mental sketch of each ground, it was all off the cuff. Once I knew the basic layout of the other teams' stadiums, it really became a cheap day out. It was a habit I grew into, and by the time I was roughly twenty-one, it was all second nature to me.

Most of these clubs were too tight to improve their stadiums, as supporters came low-down in their list of spending priorities and still do, so they rarely changed from year to year. On the odd occasion that some of the mingebag directors did spend a few quid on improving or changing the ground, improvisation would take over. It is only in the past few years that many stadiums have been updated or rebuilt, but you can still jib in easy enough if the need arises. Most of the young kids now are either wedged up or are so useless that the first thing they'd do if they were locked outside a game would be to phone their oul fella, asking them to bring more dough down the ground for a touted ticket, or to get his arse down there immediately to provide a lift home, as he was feeling a little cold outside. What a cynic I'm turning into.

Some football grounds, season in, season out, were easy for

the jibberoony – most London games, for instance. Those Cockney coliseums probably weren't used to people trying to save a few quid by bunking in, as a lot of their fans, especially in the seats, seemed to be glamour boys and hangers-on, you know, hanging around the players or onto their shirt-tails and their every word. My God, there's thousands of that type now. I wouldn't count West Ham or Millwall when they were in the top division among the easy bunk-in grounds, and maybe that was because a lot of their fans seemed to be rag-arses like us. Either that or you were too busy watching your tail for any would-be South or East London flying jacket attack. It was a good thing when we got a gateman sorted at Millwall, as it meant you didn't have to wander round that shady ground looking for an easy jib. Meanwhile, places like Tottenham, Chelsea and Arsenal always seemed to be pop-starred up, with loads of them Mick Hucknall-type characters who all of a sudden found football in the Nineties, once they had a few quid and thought it was glamorous and cool to spend some of it down at the match. Fuck them curly red perms; no Annies in the Annie Road End. If I was one of those loyal Man U boys who'd been going the match religiously through all those years of Liverpool domination and I saw him swanning into the ground, I'd be tempted to sing his own song back to him, as in, 'Holding Back the Ears' before giving him a quick kick up the arse of his 300 nicker pants. There's loads of them phoneys today; it's like Bob Hoskins said in that film *The Short Good Saturday*, 'Celebrity football fans, ha, I've shit 'em.'

Any bunkers you might see hanging around the turnstiles today are probably only trying to jib in because the game they're at is a lock-out, whereas when we started jibbing our way around Europe it was because we didn't have two bob in our arse pockets. For instance, I travelled to Highbury to watch

Liverpool play Arsenal in a league match in December 1978 with no money whatsoever.

Our usual Friday bevvy had become the usual Saturday morning bevvy, and dotted around town that night were quite a few John Travolta-type Yankee sailors. You'd often see them out and about and they stood out in the crowd because of their well-ironed flared pants (tight at the top, swishing away at the bottom), Cuban heel dancing shoes (like Prince used to wear), brightly coloured silky shirts and these fuck-off extra-white teeth that you could see coming towards you half a mile off in the dark. With those railings anyone of them could've played the Joker in Batman; I used to wonder how you got your hands on that MacLean's Shotblast Toothpaste. I'm sure that before leaving the ship for a little spot of Night Fever they Tippexed their teeth one last time to dazzle the Liverpool ladies with that sweet sailor smile. These Yankee sailor whoppers were all bang-on *Saturday Night Fever* boys with Donny Osmond teeth and we had them down as one funny bunch of all-dancing beauts. But don't let that fool you, because you would never cause any trouble with this set of YMCA macho men. They all seemed to be six-foot musclemen who stood together in packs, admiring each other's tightly strapped ball sacks. I realise now that their height must have been exaggerated by those tins of Heinz beans they had for heels, and their boxing-glove-size bags of ollies were only sticking out so much because those tight kecks they wore could make even the littlest-knobbed fella look like John Holmes in a *Debbie Does Dingle* porn film. But credit where it's due, the disco deckhands were always up for a one-on-one straightener with any would-be trouble causer, and these guys would take nooooo shit.

We were still enjoying ourselves at around 2:30 inside this stay-behind club called the Night Owl when, from the entrance

at the top of the dark, dingy stairs, this team of young Croxteth
ladies turns up out of the blue. The drinks soon start flowing
and 'copping off' procedures begin. Before you could shake a
leg at two Marvin Gaye slowies, the night/morning had almost
drawn to a close and me and me mate Eddie had taken a shine
to two of the young scallywagesses. We quickly decided that
we're on our way to Croxteth and we shall not be moved. Only
thing is, on arriving at the Croxteth abodes and parking our
bums on the necking settees, being young Scouse Catholics,
the girls' drawers shall not be moved. A brief 'bare tit' and two
hours later we were on our way back to Lime Street. As I went
to pay the taxi driver, I reached into the inside pocket of my
Harrington, only to find malted milk biscuit crumbs instead of
any dough. *Strange*, I'm thinking, *I could have sworn that's
where my small reel was* – by small reel, I meant two fivers
scrunched together. So I start whispering urgently, 'Eddie, get
your dough out, I can't find mine.'

Eddie was trying to grow his curly black hair into a Bryan
Ferry wedge, but it was just too springy. If he'd tried for a Leo
Sayer perm he'd have had a good one, but a Ferry quiff, no. But
he persisted, so it ended up looking like a bunch of grapes
hanging over one eye. As grape-fringe searched his pockets, the
realisation set in that those good oul Catholic girls of Crocky
had probably stopped us from getting our hands down their
scanties because our own money was already stuffed down the
front. They'd dipped us. I was so skint around this time that
she must've been surmising the pound in my pocket might be
worth two in her bush.

'Listen mate, you'll have to drive to the Bullring [a notorious
block of tenements just up the hill from Lime Street Station]
first to pick me mate up.'

'Okay lads, no problem.'

Thank God he was a trusting fella. I was elbowing dozy Eddie to be quiet, as he still hadn't worked out what was going on.

'Shush dickhead, and be on yer toes.'

'Why where are we going?'

'The Bullring, soft shite, so what does that tell yer?'

'I don't know, you tell me. Now where are we going?'

'Oh never fucking mind, just be under starters.'

We arrived outside the tenement block and the driver goes. 'Tell me when lads.'

'Alright, here'll do mate.'

The moment he pulled up to a halt, we were off out the passenger-side door.

'Come back yer pair of little cunts.'

The guy was shouting at the top of his voice, probably trying to wake up the locals to help him capture us. But this was the Bullring, the 'Bully' in local lingo, and they were used to people making noise at strange hours, with it being on the route home for a lot of weekend drinkers and also one of the favourite destinations for taxi-runners like us. It's hard to drive straight through those tenements and few drivers would leave their cabs alone for two minutes around there to chase you on foot. We ran straight up the stairs and hid on one of the landings for ten minutes. We could hear the cabbie beeping his horn and shouting a string of F's and B's and a host of other obscenities that were hard to fathom out.

As we sat on the landing floor, an old lady came out and said, 'What are youse two up to?'

'The oul-arse cab driver was trying to rip us off love, so we done a runner and we're just hiding from him.'

'Alright, but don't make no noise, yer pair of devils.'

'No, norra sound love, honest, you won't hear a peep.'

Me and Eddie started to quietly discuss what had happened

and came to the conclusion that the girls were a team of dippers, seeing as they were out so late in a little mob. They had probably had the kecks off a couple of Yankee sailors they said they'd been drinking with earlier that night. And believe you me, they would've had to have had their kecks off, as there was no way you could've gotten your hands into any of the pockets attached to those sprayed-on sailor strides. At the top, they were like those tight Falmers grey pants some woollies used to wear; 'ball stranglers', we called them. They always looked like they would melt on your legs if you stood by the fire.

As soon as the taxi engine could be heard driving off into the distance, we walked down the stairs of the tenements and straight down the hill into Lime Street Station. There we caught a train just after seven o'clock to London, got into the Arsenal game via the 'envelope' trick (see next chapter), then headed straight to Victoria Station to catch the train to Dover for the Saturday night boat to Oostende. Boat bunked, next it was a train to Brussels for the Super Cup Final against Anderlecht on the Monday night. We had no money, no passports, and one day to kill before the Anderlecht match. Hot dogs were snatched for food from a couple of those all-night takeaway wagons that offer you mayonnaise on your chips – yak, no thanks – plus we did a couple of the usual shady restaurant runners. Sleep was taken on a hotel room floor, kindly offered to us by other Liverpool supporters. We'd tried getting our heads down in a car park lift, seeing as none of the hotels would give us a room for the night without paying up front (wise-arses). We walked into the match no problem, Liverpool got beat 3–1, took a train back to the boat, walked right around the Ostend terminal building, avoiding passport control and any Belgian clippies, before climbing up over the side of the cross-Channel ferry. Boat bunked, train to Victoria jibbed, Tube to Euston walked on, train back to Lime Street jibbed, we finally arrived back home the following afternoon, none the worse for wear, with only one thing on our minds: *just wait until we see them Crocky birds*. Those dippers with tits were always hard to suss out.

The early-doors European games like Moenchengladbach in the 1978 BIG CUP semi-final were usually the easiest and best of the lot, as this was pre-Heysel and hardly any European teams had a mob of skins (hoolies) in those days of slightly more innocence, shall we say. So a nice, leisurely bunk was usually assured. Not like today, where you can bump into a fired-up mob of nazis quite easily at such football outposts as Slovan Liberec in the Czech Republic, fucksake, I didn't expect that one, never mind those Continental cowboys at places like Cologne, Paris St Germain, Lazio and Galatasaray, among many. Nah, bollocks to throwing chairs at foreigners, our drill went a bit like this: no watching your back, nice bit of clobber in your sports bag, then off to the match with the sound of klaxon horns guiding you to the stadium. That's the way I always liked it. The European away games and hoffman trips abroad were that good that I'll tell you all about them a little later. For now, let's concentrate on this side of the Channel; yer absolute bread and butter, and to kick things off we'll start *Sesame Street* style with an A.

CHAPTER EIGHT

Dirt Cheap Football

and the Access Envelope

A IS FOR the Arsenal, and the old 'tick tock, we are the Clock' instantly comes to mind. Each year we'd bounce out of Arsenal Tube station and head straight for the match-day collections window. If we were mob-handed, it was near kick-off and it was going off big time outside, then we'd sometimes dive over the 'turnies'. Providing it was late enough I was straight in. Earlier than half two and I simply wasn't having it: no bored shitless, empty ground stuff for us. I'd learned that jibbing in ahead of schedule had me twiddling me thumbs for an hour, leading to a bored stiff bunk-out, which only meant I'd have to bunk in again. I did it three times once at Chelsea and me mates were calling me the Turnstile Yo-yo.

As far as jibbing-in goes, Highbury was always an 'envelope' ground, and the envelope trick went something like this. First, one of us would walk up to the collections window and say to the person (usually a female) handing the tickets out, 'Any tickets been left by the Liverpool players yet love?' It was either this, or you'd name a certain player from either the home or the away team. It was only idle banter to bide your time, while the proverbial eyes on springs would be busy darting about, trying to memorise any companies or individual names from the list that usually lay on the counter in front of her. Once you had a name clocked, you'd go over to your mates and give them the name. Any other information obtained, like who had left the tickets for whom, normally meant you were assured of getting your hands on the free match tickets within the envelopes behind the counter. Your mates would go to the window and ask for them using the proper name. If you couldn't read the list effectively, then you'd invent the name of a company, like this: 'Any tickets for Joey O's Fried Chicken, or the Liverpool Fred Perry Society?'

As she was checking through the list, you'd either get a definite reading or she'd inadvertently tell you one herself, by going, 'Did you say Ben and Jerry's Ice Cream Society?'

And you would quickly reply, 'Yeah, yeah, that's the one.'

Local accents only at all times; one sniff of the old Scouse twang and it was a definite no-show. If the accent was finely tuned, at this point she would usually hand you the envelope full of tickets, especially if there was a large, impatient queue waiting behind you, leaving her with less time to check you out. If she didn't come up with a name from the list for you, and simply replied that no tickets had been left under that name, you could either repeat another imaginary company that the tickets might have been left under, just to give you more time to read the list, or simply walk away if you'd already managed to gather the required information. If the names were quite easy to attain then you'd memorise two or three to be on the safe side, or in case someone else wanted to try their luck.

Me and my Bunkers' Elite mate Frank once enjoyed a fine beverage with Peter Cook, Dudley Moore's old comedy sidekick, in the lounge at Arsenal. Frank could get you into the Savoy for a free fifty quid brekkie, the main Wembley ticket office for cup final briefs and the Albert Hall changing rooms to meet Mike Tyson all on the same day if he put his mind to it. So as you can see, we had a good few things in common. We regaled Peter with some of our freebie tales and how we got into the lounge, as he seemed to be a friendly enough fella, and as he entertained us with some showbiz gossip, he surprised us by saying that he was born in Devon, not London, and was a Tottenham fan, not Arsenal. I can only surmise that he was in the hated rival ground to see the Reds; I never found out whether he was a glamour supporter like Pringle Tarbuck or Mick Hucknall, or a real, dyed-in-the-wool fan like me and Frank. We nearly missed the train home that night, as we were having such a good laugh with this fella of dryer-than-dry humour that we never clocked the time and almost ended up diverting to a sweaty Kings Cross B & B. But I'd rather hear the tooting of the train leaving Euston than the tooting of the scabby-arsed prostitutes you'd see walking the streets of Kings Cross.

Some grounds eventually tightened up security on their match day collection windows after a few years of repeatedly falling for the envelope trick, so we started to get to the ground a little earlier and wait for people like footballers to drop off their complimentary tickets. As they handed them over, they'd give the staff member instructions about who they were for and who they were from. We'd be earwigging the player's instructions before bouncing up to the hatch to ask for the tickets in question. This happened on hundreds of occasions, but the one that sticks in my mind happened at QPR's Loftus Road ground.

Liverpool's team coach arrives and, as the fans clap them in, Bruce Grobbelaar runs over to the collections office. Frank and I pin back our lugholes as Brucey says, 'Now listen darling, I've been leaving these tickets for Mr Blah-blah each week, but some bloody Scouser keeps giving his name in every time we play away, so I'm getting stung for my tickets at every ground. Now could you please leave these tickets for Mr Blah-blah under the name of, say, Mr Da Silva instead, and state that they've been left by Mr Bruce Bung and not Mr Bruce Grobbelaar, just so these scallywags won't get their hands on my tickets?'

And the lady goes, 'Yes Mr Bung, I understand perfectly.'

They both start to laugh, before she adds, 'We've had this problem before with the Liverpool supporters, so I know exactly what you're on about Bruce, you just leave it with me sweetie.' I'm thinking, *sounds like another footballer's bootlicker to me.*

Frank and I hear all of this, so I go, 'Give it a few minutes, then I'll front it.'

I walk away and borrow a hat from one of the lads who was looking for tickets same as us. It was a double measure of caution, in case the lady had seen my face snooping about.

A few minutes later, I approach the collections window, and using a London accent, I say to the same lady, 'Have any tickets been left for Mr Da Silva please?'

She gives me the once-over before replying, 'And whom have these tickets been left by?'

'Oh yes, it should be a Mr Bung.'

The lady gives me a nice wink, smiles as if to say, 'It's good this secret code game, isn't it?' and hands me the envelope. From the moment I walk over to Frank, who is standing about twenty yards away, we get the giggles. *What's with all this secret name business?* Outside the same window, Phil Collins turns up and some of the lads are ready with the Genesis blag, but no one has the heart to cop for his tickets when he seemed amiable enough after a natter. Frank even gets him to sign on the dotted line; mind you, me oul mate Frank always was a bit of an autograph hunter.

Another memorable envelope day was the Terry Venables comeback game, when he returned to British football to manage Tottenham after a brief stint as Barcelona manager. As usual we'd had our free early morning Harrods brekkie (we had moved on from the Euston railway gaff by now), bounced up to the ground and claimed our free envelope. We got tickets for six of us in the Tottenham directors' box, and didn't realise that they were Mrs Venables's seats (wife of Terry) until she came into the match five or ten minutes after the kick-off. She was really nice about it, as she thought we'd bought duplicate tickets from a tout – because that's what we'd told her – and insisted that the stewards take us to different seats. This got right up their noses, because they were dying to throw us out. It was the usual suspects: Frank, Joey O, Eddie and a couple of other members of the Bunkers' Society, all being treated with kid gloves by the irritated stewards. Their mindset told them that with six Scouse scallywags sitting in the directors' box some shenanigans had gone on, and they were quite correct, but Mrs Venables, I can only say you were a lady, and the way you stuck up for us told me a lot about the kind of person you must be (you've gorra good 'un there, Terry me old china). I say this because the stuck-up, snooty Tottenham directors (especially one) were looking at us as if to say, 'How dare you raggedy-arsed football supporters come and sit in our posh seats.' As I was escorted from the select seating area, one blotchy skinned, hound-dog face was staring at me as though I'd beamed down from Planet Bog-brush. When he looked down his nose at me for the third or fourth time, I risked getting thrown out by fronting the Clement Freud lookalike, 'Who the fuck are you looking at, you cocker-spaniel-faced Tory twat?' To which I got no reply. For us, politics, life and football were always intertwined.

Another good ticket provider was Johnny Giles, the old Leeds United player who became a sports columnist. We had his envelope at Chelsea a few times, good seats too. Ah well, he deserved some retribution for getting Keegan sent off in the Charity Shield years before. Newspaper reporters and photographers were always fair game and their passes or tickets were continually up for grabs at every football ground. Duplicate passes would usually be handed out if the originals had been copped for, or else the gatemen and security would know the newspaper mens' faces and let them in anyway, so that was always more preferable than taking an individual's tickets, but if you were desperate to see the boys in red then needs must and being choosy soon left the arena.

Photographers' passes were picked up the same way as players' tickets, but if you didn't want the hassle of finding out where they were being handed out, you could become a 'freelance' at the weekend. One time on the London train, on my way to Crystal Palace, I found an old photographers' camera, which duly got me into Selhurst Park. After adding an orange five-a-side football bib to my normal Saturday attire, I walked into the next seven or eight games, no problem. I eventually left the camera on the train at Lime Street after a drunken London away-game party. Carrying it around was starting to bug me anyway, but if a big game came up with no tickets on the horizon, I always had the bib and camera blag stashed away in me locker.

A lot of the time the envelope trick would involve tickets left for press members by the daily newspapers, but just as frequently it could be some big name footballer leaving freebies or comps for his pop star or TV personality acquaintances, and we didn't give a hoot about making it hard for these people to get into the ground or about making life more difficult for what to a large extent were people with well-paid jobs or your basic hangers-on. For the football-unwise, a hanger-on is someone who tries to hang around footballers just so he can pick up freebies or impress business colleagues by saying things like, 'Oh yes, I'm very good friends with Kenny Dalglish, he's just signed all the cricket ball-bag protectors in my new sports shop,' or, 'That Ian Rush is a fantastic guy, he's coming to open my new cake shop next week, we've called it Pinocchio's Éclairs after Ian. You'll notice the large plastic conk over the doorway with three ring donuts thrown over the nose.' I've seen loads of these fellas come and go over the years; usually they had a few quid too. You'd see them hanging around the players' entrance every Saturday, waiting for the players, acting the big fan in their nice kecks, waiting for their envelopes to be dropped off. Then as soon as their football friend had been transferred and the freebies dried up, were they going to buy a ticket? Were they fuck. The mingebags were all terrified of paying a tenner to watch a game of footy, whereas our little firm didn't have two megs to rub together, not until later on that is, once we'd learned a few ways to line our own pockets. I suppose criticism for the football liggers sounds a bit rich coming from me but I was never a hanger-on. I would rather bunk in any day than kiss arse.

* * *

At Spurs a few years later, we noticed they were keeping a vigilant eye over envelope proceedings, but as one form of easy access closed, another opened to take me and the rest of the Bunkers' Society in for free. Tottenham had recently finished a lot of building work on their stadium and for first-aid reasons an ambulance would normally be parked in the same corner each year where the main stand met the visitors' section. Me and Frank decided to have a look around the back and not only did we find an open door with nobody in attendance, but inside that door was a lift that took you to God knows where. We looked at each other for a moment, before Joe Strummer whispered in my ear, 'Elevator, goooing up.'

Not being shy, we stepped into the lift with three other ticket-less terrors in tow. Strangely, the doors opened to reveal a hundred starving supporters with money in their hands all wanting to be served NOW. We'd come up behind the burger bar counter in our end of the ground, a great result. The staff looked at us as though we were the caterers who'd forgotten the pies. We were starting to get cheeky, because some of the staff could hardly speak any English, and the rest looked like exchange students from some far-off foreign shore. Not a Cockney server in sight; no wonder they all looked so clueless. Eddie started to laugh and serve some guy who wanted a hamburger, we all started to laugh and think about serving, now it was bound to come on top. See, difference was, they had the hats and we didn't, and some of the queuing supporters were starting to recognise us. Now if our little firm could've just gotten their hands on a few of those 'munchie-serving rig-outs', I'm sure the other staff wouldn't have minded if we'd made a few bob selling Tottenham tucker to the other Scousers across the counter. We looked, they looked, then we looked once more, here we go, it was Mexican stand-off time again, till an educated voice said, 'It's a good "inman" [way to get in] this one, and it will be for a few seasons if we get over the counter right now before the Spurs stewards get involved.' He sounded about right to me, so we vaulted the food counter while the staff stared in confusion, oblivious to what was going on.

One lad turned directly on his heels to face the counter he'd just vaulted to place his order. Somebody instantly said, 'But you could've had whatever you wanted from the other side.'

'Nah, I don't mind paying for my food, and I'll be back next year, so no need for on tops.'

He was spot-on, and we returned for a few seasons, till one day the ambulance was still in place but the hidden door was locked. Oh well, the lift-up was good while it lasted; now where's that steward? Ah there he is. 'Scuse me mate, where's that new ticket collections office?'

Another club that usually provided a good envelope system for the innocent Road End scallies to take advantage of was Aston Villa. As the ticket collections window was situated right at the heart of the away fans' turnstiles, you didn't have to wander around the ground in search of it. Villa Park was one of the first grounds where I took up the offer of a free bevvy in the players' lounge after the game, and the first where I took up their decent offer of a free seat in one of those corporate glass boxes: nice dinner, but a shitty view with no atmosphere. I hated those corporate boxes in the late Eighties, and I still hate them now; it's usually where you'll find most of the phoneys. The reason I decided to take up the offer of a few free bevvies after the game was because a lot of these envelopes contained match tickets accompanied by lounge tickets. Now seeing as we were usually in a hurry to get back to the train, coach or car, just so we could beat traffic or catch an early choo-choo, we didn't always take up the home clubs' offer of a few free drinks with the players after the game. Villa being a bad ground for traffic and train congestion, we decided to take things easy by taking a leisurely stroll around to the players' lounge, situated quite nicely in the corner of the away end (Witton Lane). As we entered the gate, a doorman asked for our lounge tickets, which we duly produced.

Ale drunk, programmes signed, we decided it was departure time. But on leaving the gate, a little tipsy I may add, I was approached by these young autograph hunters who insisted that I was Gary Shaw, a one-time Villa hero. Now I didn't want to disappoint the youngsters, so I started signing away. Next minute, pen in hand, up pops Daddy Villa, who looks Pakistani but speaks in a heavier Brummie accent than Ozzy Osbourne on speed. He clocks me signing, then says in front of the kids, 'Well, tell me which player this is then?'

And this little Pakistani kid goes, 'It's Gary Shaw dad.'

And daddy says bluntly, 'That's no fucking Gary Shaw. It might be Steve Staunton of Liverpool, but I'm telling you, that's no fucking Gary Shaw, matey.'

Steve Staunton? I'm thinking, *yer blind Brummie beaut, Stevie Staunton looks like his face has been flattened in a Breville toaster.* But being in a happy mood after yet another Red victory, I go, 'You're right mate, didn't wanna upset the kids, so I just signed.'

'Well that's out of order matey, my boy's waited ages for those bloody autographs.'

I started to walk away but this fella starts following me, and he's repeating, 'You're no fucking Gary Shaw matey, that's fucking out of order, Gary fucking Shaw my arse, Gary Shaw, no don't think so . . . blah blah Gary fucking Shaw blah blah.'

Could this fella rabbit. As soon as we were way out of earshot of the kids, I turned around to confront Villa's Asian supporter of the year, as everybody had stopped laughing, and the way this guy was mouthing off, Officer Dibble was bound to turn up on the scene, duly turning what I thought was a very humorous moment into something more serious.

'Listen soft shite, how old is yer kid?'

'He's eleven. Why, what's that got to do with it?'

'Well, I'll tell yer why. Hang on, don't stand so close, garlic breath. When I was five or six, I knew exactly who *my* Liverpool heroes were, so if your lad thought I was Gary Shaw, big fucking deal. Now get to fuck, you miserable Brummie twat.'

With that I went to boot him up the arse. He realised I was semi-serious and took off, but it went to show you how one person's sense of humour could be so different to another's. He needed to find his chuckle button, fast. And some toothpaste.

A few years on and we had a fine beverage in the Villa players' lounge with that bevvier of bevviers, Paul McGrath. The Irish fella was a great centre-half, who also came across as a decent fella. We asked him to settle a bet on how you pronounce McGrath, to which he gave the best answer to a daft question by getting the ale in.

Birmingham's St Andrews ground, not far up the road from the Villa, gave me a funny experience in the mid-Eighties when I arrived late one time for the match. I quickly legged it over to a disabled entrance, which was being guarded by this big Frank Bruno type of a guy, and said in my best Noddy Holder voice, 'Alright mate, I've just driven the disabled bus away from the ground, remember me, I was speaking to you as I left?'

I'd noticed it was a wheelchair access entrance, so I just took my chance, but this big black fella goes, 'Nah, don't remember that mate, are you sure it was me?'

So giving it my last shot, I go, 'Yeah, definitely you, how would I forget a big fella like yourself, we were having a laugh, remember?'

And he replied, 'Oh I remember now, yeah, we were having a good laugh about twenty minutes ago, about the footy.'

'Yeah, that's me, glad you can recall me, I know you see loads of people and that.'

'No, I'm sorry about that guvnor, you were one of the more cheerful ones, yeah we 'ad right good laugh. Best get in, you're going to be late.'

'Cheers lad, see you later.'

And I was off to me seat. Smiling to myself later as the game was in progress, I realised I was that convincing that even the steward wanted to believe we'd spoken earlier. Either that or my twin had gone in ten minutes before me. The powers of persuasion, I think they call it.

Chelsea was another ground where we took up the offer of a complimentary tipple, and at no time before or since has there been a better tipple on the house than the time we beat Chelsea in 1986 to win the League title. Celebrity envelope acquired, match seen, League won, joy abounding, I walked out onto the pitch after a brief sojourn in the Ken Bates-sponsored freebie lounge, and then went back through the tunnel towards the changing rooms. As I opened the away team door, fully expecting to be told to fuck off, I was greeted by clouds of steam, with not a single player in sight. I made my way through the changing room and a table laden with food appeared like magic before my eyes. As I looked down the full length of the scoff on offer, who did I see happily chomping away on some of the nosh that was partly hidden by the steam? Why it was none other than Liverpool's very own midfield chicken drumstick, Jan Molby. Jan looked at me, I looked at Jan. My god, I was starving.

'Is it all right to have a sarnie, Jan?'

'Yeah, of course it is, get in there, mate.'

Fucksake, he was more Scouse than me; it was just like getting served in the chippy back home.

'Is it for anyone, this buffet then?'

'Why, where have you come from mate?'

Bastard! It was probably the most dreaded question for any true bunker.

'I sneaked in Jan. I'm just a mad Lib'pool fan who wandered in from the ground. You won't blow me up will yer?'

'Nah, tuck in mate, it's celebration time.'

'Cheers Jan.'

What a man. Sixteen stone of classy Danish bacon and one of the best footballers I have ever seen. I've seen him in that Sky TV indoor football tournament in the past few years and even though he's now twenty stone and forty years of age, he's still brilliant. As I started to eat anything in front of me, players appeared through the clearing steam. I could see Craig Johnston with a dead cat on his head, Ian Rush waving his big Welsh tool around, and at last the man himself, King Kenny, who had just scored the winner to deny arch-rivals Everton the title. I waited for somebody to tell me to piss off, but they were all just as happy as me as the wine started to flow. Here I was, chicken leg in one hand, champers in the other, title in the bag, King Kenny to one side and Ronnie Whelan and Stevie Nicol to the next. *Glory Hallelujah!*

Elton Welsby, a local radio and TV presenter, was trying to interview the players, who were all too busy celebrating, so I cheekily got a little bit closer so as to offer myself up for an interview. He looked at me in a puzzled manner, as if to say, 'Are you one of the reserves or something? Cos I don't know who the fuck you are.' Besides, I think Elton was too busy clocking Rushie's tool to bother with me. I moved back to the buffet table for some more scoff, thinking how these footy players were spoilt soft: little game of footy on a Saturday, nice shower, food and ale laid on, luxury party coach all the way home. Meanwhile me and my buddies would be joining the wide-awake club all the way back to Euston; watching out for some brain-dead Chelsea skin who was dying to send his steelies into your plums just because his team had lost. Different ball game this one, son, different ball game altogether. It was like Armani suits and salmon sarnies compared to cheap trainees that ran all day on even cheaper British Rail brekkies.

When I eventually got back to Euston and told me mates where I'd been, they were calling me the proverbial jammy bastard, while others looked on more cynically, as if to say, 'There is no way you can get up to that shit without getting caught.' All I'm thinking is, *it takes a bunker to know what another bunker can get up to, know what I mean boys*. You could only tell your story in the right company, because a lot of fellas who never had the front or bottle to do what we did often found it hard to digest or take in, especially if they rarely travelled away or were true 'Saturday's Kids' like Paul Weller sang about. These were fellas who were ruled by their wives and girlfriends and never got further than the betty (betting office), the shops or the local boozer every weekend. Either that or they were just shit scared of life. *Don't go here, don't go there, don't go any fucking where*. It was like me da used to say, 'They've got no get up and go.' Sometimes I'd see more in a month than they'd see in ten years.

When I say that there haven't been many better complimentary tipples than the one above, I'm referring to the fact that the ale was on the Tory Wolfman himself, Ken Bates, and the fact that he seems to be one self-righteous, full-of-himself Tory to boot. A few years after that championship-winning game, a few of us got into the Chelsea main stand before entering the main players' lounge at half-time. We got talking to the Wolfman, who hadn't twigged that we were on a freebie, and started to wind him up gently about Chelsea being crap. The next thing you know, he's trying to impersonate Harry Enfield's plasterer character by giving it the 'loadsamoney wads of dosh' signs all over the entrance to the lounge. He'd risen to the wind-up really quickly, and one Chelsea steward, who seemed a little intimidated in hairy Ken's presence, said, 'I'd be careful if I was you Scouse, he'll have you out on your ear in no time at all.'

'Arr, we're only having a laugh mate, don't worry about him.'

In the meantime, the loopy wolfman was waving an imaginary wad in the air and shouting 'loadsamoney' at the four of us. We thought it was hilarious and that maybe he was drunk, but then, it was his ground, and I suppose he thought he could do what he liked, but he couldn't stop us from having a free one, or two, or three on him, could you Ken? Have a decent shave on the Russian you took for a tidy few quid, you hairy Cockney spaceman. Never trust a Tory with a beard.

On the morning before the game, me and Frank were enjoying a stroll down New Bond Street when up pops the old plastic Braveheart himself, Mel Gibson. Now Frank's wife, like millions of other women, kinda likes Mel, so Frank bounces over on her behalf and asks him to sign on the dotted line. Mel, who I thought had starred in *Home Alone* as Macaulay Culkin's younger brother, seeing as he's about four foot six, gives Frank a very cold and abrupt 'no'. Frank thinks midget Mel's misheard him, so he asks again, only to receive the same blunt reply from the Australian Jimmy Cranky. Well, that was it, the old red mist flew straight out of Frankie's nostrils, and even though Frank was no giant the Australian actor standing up close made him look like Jack Charlton on stilts. As the miserable Aussie walks away, Frank's calling him all the short-arsed bastards under the sun. Miserable Mel, realising he's about to get more than a mouthful, quickly makes haste up the fashionable west London street with his six-foot girlfriend in tow. I could tell by the look on her face that the lanky lovely didn't have an igloo what language we were speaking.

* * *

By the time me and the lads had traded in our old Raleigh Choppers for the fast-wheel option of travelling, we were on the road to becoming the Adidas football gypsies. Personally, I wish I still had that Chopper, because although you needed calf muscles like two Christmas turkeys to ride in third gear, they were always classic bikes. But they never could help you get a job down South, plus there are not many earners to be had on a pedal bike, I mean, what can you do with hands full of handlebars? By the time European Cup finals started to pop up every couple of years, free hands were what you really needed to pay for fast trains and boats. And as the red machine strolled into Brighton for the first time in yonks, one particular lad had a novel deals-on-wheels idea on his mind, an idea that he reckoned might help him pay his way.

Tony Mac was an original head-working Road Ender from Fazakerley who had noticed a gap in the travel market, as those Lawrensons, Home James, Crown and Wingate coaches seemed to be making a bucket from ferrying the lads about. Tony, in true Yosser Hughes style, starts thinking, gizza go, go on, *gizza go, I can do that.* Now Tony had travelled down to Brighton with a wise 100 Road End crew, in two St Trinians-style coaches. They left from the Holt boozer in the Kensington district of Liverpool on the Friday midnight before the game. The rag-arse charabancs departed with some of the drunken scallies standing on board. They wanted to see this Brighton place at their own leisure and not with the escorted supporters from the football special or the well-organised club-affiliated coaches. The Who were playing in Brighton after the Liverpool game, and if the drivers were given a decent dropsy, there might be time to bunk in for the encore and hear them belt out that 'Magic Bus' song they'd written about Scousers; written because things kept appearing from under the seats. *What a weekend*, thought Tony, *the Reds down in Brighton, followed by the fantastic Who, I'm having some of that. By Jove, book me on there, Macca lad.* Before the coach drives off, I have to stress this was an age before another old hero, Pete Townsend, joined Gary Glitter in 'D'ya wanna be in my gang' land. The social experts labelled him an emotionally distressed rock star; in other words, he was another pop star nonce.

The coaches got lost in London at about three in the morning: dozy fucking driver as usual, in this case a fat fella with the navigational skills of Mr Magoo. Quite a few London nightclub revellers were pummelled in those dark dizzy streets; they were a part of this impenetrable foggy maze, and someone had to take the blame for us getting lost. The pebbly beach of Brighton and the whiteness of the Grand Hotel finally came into view at around half six, and bang on cue those mirrored-up scooters were already prominently parked on the prom. *Fuck me*, I'm thinking, as me head bounced off the window and me lager went all over me jeans; *we've just arrived on the cover of a Mod album*. What a lovely day for a football match. It was Vespa and Lambretta heaven, with the choppy English Channel as a backdrop. And today, for one day only, 100 northern urchins were starring in *Fifty Quidrophenia* the mod movie with a Scouse twang.

The coaches are parked and suddenly loads of drunken

scallies appear from the two charabancs. They instantly strip down to their boxer shorts and shiver and laugh as they begin to feel the full brunt of the bracing seaside wind. The brave ones dive straight into the freezing cold, frothy sea and pulling their boxies down thigh high, they start performing the 'white whale' (bottoms out of the water only). Those less inclined have a bit of a paddle, while the least inclined look on at the paddlers and swimmers as if to say, 'Rather you than me mate; don't fancy any of that salty sea water up the crack of me arse.'

I was straight in. I didn't have to shed me underwear, as I didn't wear any anyway. A hot Spanish holiday had seen me remove my socks and undies for good, and it became the norm for a lot of young fellas in Liverpool not to bother with them. After the initial tight jeans were first worn, now everything had to fit a little loose, not baggy, maybe just one size up to let yer balls and tits breathe. One good mate was even called Tommy No Socks. I think we all liked that fresh-air feeling, and if yer bollocks were loose, then you were loose, no need for any tight skiddies to cramp yer style. It was only years later that I got into wearing undies again, after a brief stint on a freezing German building site.

Once I'd shot-blasted me ring-piece and me nipples were like two spring rolls, I came up for air, spat out the salt water and took a good look around me. From leaving the coach in a semi-drunken haze, I'd instantly gone to feeling like a cocky, Scouse superman in two minutes flat. Bring on the Mods, Mockers, Plods, Dockers, Fockers and even your Clockers, I was ready for fucking anyone. *Come on seagulls, come and have a go if you think you're hard enough*. For a brief moment we stared at each other as we resurfaced. With salty water dripping off our eyelids it looked as though we were about to have an on-beach mock-battle. Realising this, a lad called Vinny stood up in the surf.

'Aye, aye, first things first, I thought you were supposed to find prawns in the sea. The only prawn round here is the one in me undies. Come on, let's do one.'

Joey O looking down at himself, turned to me and said, 'He's right yer know, me balls look like two sui mais that have been in the freezer for four years.'

And Eddie butted in with, 'Fucksake, state of me knob, it looks like an ant wearing a polo-neck jumper.'

Another lad called Tommo didn't seem too keen on getting out of the water. As he sat hunched over with the waves lapping against his belly, Joey O said, 'Come on soft lad, it's time to depart. Don't tell me, you're one of those water babies.'

'Nah, not really Joe, me doctor said that salt water was good for thrush, so I'm just giving me bell-end a good scrub.'

And that's exactly what he did. After a minute or so, he got out of the water and Joey O goes, 'Bit of the old sea-water relief, eh Tommo?'

'Yeah I suppose so. It's like a nice ripe tomato now.'

Tommo had discovered natural sea-water exfoliation for your bobby's helmet; now I bet they don't sell that in the Body Shop.

Not many brekkie yards were open on Brighton seafront that morning, but we eventually found one just off the prom. As I took my place at the Formica-covered table, Eddie turned to me and said, 'You've heard of birds with those inverted nipples, haven't you. Well after going in that sea, I think I've got an inverted cock.'

'Don't worry about that Eddie,' said Billy Big Tool. 'Your sausages have just arrived first, yer jammy bastard.'

With that, Eddie turns round to see Billy's King Eddie of a knob dolloped down on a plate in front of him. It looked horrible lying there on the plate, so Eddie stuck his fork into it, only a bit too hard. That was it: tomato sauce was squeezed all over Eddie and a tomato and brown sauce fight broke out. Some fellas just couldn't resist firing that sauce. The lady informed us that the Brighton Bobbies were on their way, so we hastily departed to our coach. It was another one of those 'stuck in the middle of nowhere, with just a set of minty clothes on your skin' kind of mornings. And with maybe two or three quid to your name, something had to snap. Shops, shops, where art thou shops? But the shops were not open for an hour, so somebody came up with the bright idea that we should jump a load of Mods and demand that they hand over their parkas.

So at eight o'clock in the morning, twenty Scousers were hiding behind Brighton Pier waiting intently for the next crew of Mods to show up. Here they come, about ten of them, oblivious to the sauce-covered scally mob waiting ahead. First pair of suede desert-boots crosses the line, that's it, it's off. They tried to scatter, but in the end every last one of them got nabbed.

'Get out of your parkas or you're dead.' That sounded naughty, I must say.

They didn't put up much of a fight, and I think they might have been a set of middle-class Mods, as their lack of punch and indifferent attitude towards losing their original fish-tail parkas made me question if they weren't just weekend wonders down to see the Who, then back to pushing pens around the office come Monday. They must have had us down as Scouse beachcombers who lived under Brighton Pier on cockles, mussels and a few bars of rock that kids dropped through the cracks in the pier floor. Maybe we were down-and-out gypsies from the north; dressed up in clothes that looked like they were covered in blood. Whatever, we put the frighteners on them on first sight. Once they were all de-coated, they were told to fuck off pronto, which they obediently did, and before Officer Beach Patrol could appear on the scene, we made haste back to our coaches. They were parked discreetly out of the way, and as we boarded we told the driver to put his foot on the gas. The mob who ran onto the coach looked weird, with an assortment of long fishtail parkas that had The Who, The Jam, and those red, white and blue targets painted on the back. Some had even copped for pork pie hats, but at the bottom of those parkas and hats were 100% Adidas. I thought they looked good, and as we clocked each other we couldn't help but laugh. It was tough on the posh Mod firm, but at the time we just thought it was a big joke; it's only with hindsight that you begin to think of them freezing as they walked into the distance thinking, *they were a strange bunch of rockers, who the fuck were they?* By three o'clock that afternoon, I bet every last one of them knew who we were.

Later on that day, one of the same parka-wearing scallies happened to make a few quid by sneaking a travel agent's cashbox. He only produced three tenners, but people knew he'd copped for a few bob more than £30. He was forced to turn out his pockets and had his arse felt, but adamantly refuted any claims that he was 'sticking down' on the other four lads he was with. It was a big thing, this sticking down, as fellas copping for a few quid were often reluctant to evenly share the spoils with lads who had basically only kept 'dixie', or lookout. After his shoes and socks were removed they had still only found £30 of his ill-gotten gains. It only came out years later that the wise-arse sneak-thief had kept the other few hundred quid tucked inside the lining of the pork pie hat he'd robbed that morning. He hadn't succumbed to the older lads rattling his cage, and for a seventeen-year-old had shown coolness beyond his years. Not surprisingly the same fella is now mansion'd-up in the leafy north coast suburbs after becoming a successful entrepreneur. Let's face it; they were always the biggest robbers, those budding businessmen.

As I've said, Tony Mac was part of that crowd in Brighton that day, and somewhere along the road to the south coast the up-and-coming young gun told the rest of the lads he had a cunning plan. Tony had seen at first hand the lengths some lads would go to, all to follow their beloved men in red. Knowing a thing or two about fifty-seater coaches, he reckoned that the next time we all travelled away it would be a much better trip if he was the driver. He said that if he was the jockey we could stay out till dick-docks, return home whenever we wanted and basically party on board non-stop without any middle-aged, moaning Magoo of a driver putting his oar in.

'But Tony, the driver's not bad fella.'

'Yeah maybe, but he's not one of us.'

The match as it goes was garbage. We drew 2–2 against the Hove Albion, had a few brief scuffles along the road, before, unbelievably, lovely oul Brighton popped up with a serious firm. Now this was unexpected. A fair old battle commenced, and as the Road End boys finally chased the seaside sand crabs away, up turned the Brighton bizzies. A couple of sweet shops had been ransacked during the melee and their tills had been rifled, with one being carried down the road in the direction of the Who concert. Instead of making the usual enquiries or scrutinising the mob for whom to nick, the Beach Patrol in Blue rounded up the first fifty Scousers on offer and herded them by meat wagon to the nearest station for questioning.

Lots of questions were asked about the missing till but the

lads who'd been pulled in knew the drill and all kept schtum. Beach Patrol then decided to split the fifty up, to ask some further one-on-one questions, but before the split-up came, a final query was put to the group as a whole.

'Right, who out of you lot has got a police record?'

'Yeah I have, it's called "Message in a Bottle",' came the instant reply.

'Don't be funny with me sonny. Do you have a job?'

'Yeah, I'm a freelance tattoo artist, officer.'

'Right, lock funny boy in a cell by himself, now!'

The questioning went nowhere and the scallywag split-up proved fruitless. As we trundled out of the station we didn't have an igloo where the coaches were parked, so we all headed for the prom and hopefully our entrance to the Who concert. *People try to put us down, talkin' about my gen . . .*

The drivers knew that most of the lads had been lifted and had parked near to the concert hall on the promenade. While this had been going on, Tony Mac esquire had left the match early, made his way down to the prom coach park and, on noticing this lovely, brand new, fifty-seater, top-of-the-range design – the complete opposite to our coach – he entered, started up, then drove the blighter all the way back home to Kirkby. I could just picture the cunning little conniver silently creeping about, clocking chara after chara, while we bopped about noisily on the terraces

Two years later and the scoundrel was still doing his own day-trips to the Lakes, plus weekends in Wales for the oul ones, with the odd away match thrown in, but only when he thought a trouble-free trip was assured. Tony Mac Tours was in town and the little head-worker hardly ever went the match again; too busy becoming a travel agent. As I've said, they were always the biggest robbers, those little budding businessmen.

CHAPTER NINE

The Trans-Alpino Rubout

SOMETIMES WE WENT abroad right off the cuff. If we planned an overseas hoffman, then Trans-Alpino train tickets were a must. Thing is, you only had to pay to Bruges or Ostende, which cost about twenty quid, and could then rub out the destination and put in whatever place you wanted to go to. We'd often bump into other Scouse firms that were on one and we'd always be comparing rubouts. I was a big rubout merchant and had the technique off to a fine art. Trans-Alpino Rail was conceived as cheap European train travel for the under-twenty-sixes: even cheaper if you had the right colouring-in kit. When the Trans-Alpino office by Liverpool University finally closed down I was distraught.

Our little firm, through the advent of wearing lambswool socks, had gotten itchy feet one week, so we decided to hop over to Switzerland to see the mountain snow and how the other half lived, among other things. We had it all mapped out. Small bag, pazzy, twenty quid, Trans-Alpino ticket rubout to Interlaken and we'll take it from there. But on getting to the Trans-Alpino office, it was closed down. *Fuck it*, we thought, *we'll bunk-it all the way to Zurich instead, and if we still fancy Interlaken, then so be it*. But it was hard to bunk the boat from England across the Channel; the other way around was easy. So we toddled off down Mount Pleasant to Lime Street and enquired at the European travel desk about a fare to Zurich, which went a bit like this.

'How much to Zurich? . . . HOW MUCH? . . . Er, okay, what about Antwerp in Belgium then? . . . YER WHAT! HOW MUCH? FUCKSAKE . . . Erm, what about just a boat ticket to Ostende? . . . Oh I see, you buy them at the terminal in Dover. Cheers love.'

The tickets to us at the time seemed to cost brewsters. Also, I'd recently been collared bunking the train in Austria and been locked up for nearly four days, till they found out that I really was the man on me passport. Four days for jibbing the train, *mein Gott!* Mind you, you know what they say about strict Bavarians in them tight shorts, and if all rail networks were staffed by similar workers, with their efficiency and ruthlessness, our bunking shenanigans would have been jack-booted into touch almost overnight. Anyway, my experience had put us off bunking the whole journey, as you had to have eyes on springs for every minute spent aboard the train, and there's no fun in that. One of the greatest things about train travel was being able to relax and look out the window at the changing landscape, but on these trips you didn't have to avoid just the ticket clippies, you also had to contend with border control and the occasional passport police looking for illegal immigrants and stowaways. So bunking all the way to Switzerland was no simple trip to the land of cuckoo clocks. With no football on, we were making this trip purely by choice and didn't fancy bunking the boat: it was a goer but it was never easy, and getting the knock-back at Dover was a right pain in the arse when you were looking forward to getting abroad. It had happened before, and once those boat fellas are on your case there's no going back to try again. I remember them saying, 'Not you Scouse bunkers again,' when we got collared. It was the law of averages that it was going to happen, especially with us and other Scousers going abroad so often.

After thinking about how pricey the cost of a normal ticket was, we decided, *fuck it*, went straight to the nearest betting office and threw our money on that wrinkly oul piece of bacon Lester Piggott. He lost, but guess what? We still skedaddled abroad. But this time we had virtually no money between us, and once the train and boat were bunked, we only got as far as Antwerp before finally returning home. It wasn't what we'd planned, but we still returned with the oul Adidas bag in hand, happy that we'd seen the White Cliffs and heard the foreign lingo. With the Stan Smith, Trim-Trab and Kickers displayed in the shops in matching pairs, just waiting to be lifted, Scousers going abroad had found their own little footwear heaven.

If I came home skint, then the next Anfield home game could see me enter at the players' entrance, which, once the steward was distracted, would lead you straight onto the halfway line. From there, you could immediately bounce into the paddock or the Kop. I never got up to this one much though, as you know what they say about shitting on yer own doorstep. But if I was on the bones of me arse, somebody would always look down from above and sing the words to 'Let It Be': 'If I find myself in times of trouble, Mother Mary come to me, speaking words of wisdom, LET HIM IN.' And the ground would open up and in I'd go.

I suppose some habits refuse to leave your Levis, and I carried on jibbing in till I was well into my thirties. Its funny to see all of these ex-jibbers now season-ticketed up, walking into cup finals with £60 seats, glancing over in my direction and saying, 'Fucksake Nicky, times are changing', and I'm thinking, *yeah, you're not kidding*.

By the mid to late Eighties, we had stewards or gatemen

sorted at Man U, Man City, Millwall (for the few years they were up) and Middlesbrough. When I say sorted, I mean they didn't kick off when we bunked in. It was a weird coincidence that all these games began with an 'M' and we started to think it was some kind of divine 'letter M' intervention from above, but once again, it was just the way the cookie crumbled. What I did know was that a few free gifts were dropped off along the way, things like the odd bottle of Moet or the odd 'ten spot', but most of these guys would have let us in for free because they knew we loved the footy just like they did. We were like-minded in thinking that most of the clubs they worked for were out and out money-making machines, run by snooty directors with Mercs, mansions and fat wallets, who left hundreds of freebie tickets at the door every Saturday for their business associates and golfing partners. I mean, come on your lords and ladyships of football, an ordinary man's gorra do what an ordinary man's gorra do, so fuck you and yer personalised number plates, we're here to follow the shirts.

Grounds that were more difficult to bunk into could sometimes send us to the bigger openings or larger gates, where they would usually have vehicular access for things like catering vans, ambulances and wheelchairs. Places like Oxford and Luton were sometimes more difficult to enter than most of the big stadiums, due mainly to the fact that smaller grounds meant fewer jibbing opportunities. They'd operate a lot fewer turnstiles, partly for cost-cutting but mainly because they were old, hemmed-in grounds with not enough space, and were just not geared up for the Big League. At the time they were yo-yo clubs – up, down, up, down. Well, in 1982 Luton had yo-yoed themselves up into the top flight and soon the Liverpool boys were back in town.

By this time we'd reached the stage where we wouldn't even

bother to try and get tickets — maybe for a semi-final or final, if they were on offer, but we didn't worry about it at all, and I mean *at all*. Not like other good supporters, who would have sleepless nights before big games wondering if that precious little permit was going to turn up. I'd seen the grief that that could bring at first hand when, in 1974, some Liverpool supporters were painting their houses in red and white stripes or were willing to go a few rounds with a local boxing champion to try to win an FA Cup final ticket in a local newspaper competition. All kinds of hare-brained schemes were being undertaken to get the required little piece of paper that would let you enter Wembley to watch Liverpool play Newcastle. Maybe when I was younger I would have entered one of those competitions, but by the time I was sixteen I'd been reared on stories of fellas stealing steam-rollers from nearby building sites to try to smash through the Wembley wall before the 1965 FA Cup final, and other fellas who had climbed into the ground the night before, only to be found in the toilets the next morning. Apparently they were only caught because the stewards always carried out a stadium sweep on the morning of the final. Some wise-arse fellas, though, had gone prepared by taking stolen Wembley stewards' outfits, complete with dodgy, drawn-up passes. They apparently gained entry no problem. That was the one that stuck in my mind when the older Kopites would tell you their stories.

Places like Oxford and Luton, compared to Wembley and Rome, were Kirkby to Kensington High Street apart, but nonetheless they were harder to bunk into. Once Luton came around in the early Eighties, the ground was a bit of an unknown quantity — and also something of a mystery when we almost couldn't find the place, due to it being hidden by the surrounding houses. Now, after a couple of hooligan incidents and a few years down the line, Luton had banned all away fans and ran a members-only scheme for their own supporters to stop infiltration by away fans. That was it: we hated Luton. How dare they stop us from going to watch our beloved Redmen. Some lads were trying to get their hands on home members' passes, forged tickets, anything that might get them into the shabby old stadium. Our firm decided to do nothing except rely on our usual jibberoony tactics. Up popped Luton and down we travelled.

As three o'clock approached, people started getting edgy, as this Luton place was proving to be no pushover. On making our third or fourth appearance at the players' entrance, after lapping and eyeing-up the stadium a few times, I noticed that the Bunkers' Society was basically mob-handed, and realised we could've taken the Stretford End with the ticketless mob we had outside. Bizzies' truncheons were drawn and things were starting to look dodgy when suddenly a minibus full of disabled supporters arrived. Some were Liverpool fans and some were Luton, so over we go for a brief inspection, just to check the tyre pressure of the wheelchairs in waiting. Noticing my motives and the lack of able-bodied people willing to help push these young fans through the opening gates, my mate Eddie sidles up. We automatically tap these two youngsters on the shoulder and start to talk about the game. As the conversation picks up, we both wheel the two young fans through the gate and straight into the ground. Before anyone can ask, 'Who the fuck are you?' we say our goodbyes to the two lads, who give us the thumbs up as they realise what has just gone on. Straight onto the all-weather pitch, right into the corner flag, foot on the wall, into the Luton home end, then it's shut yer gob time until three o'clock.

The disabled gate was usually a last resort, as it could be

slightly embarrassing if you got collared trying to walk in, either alongside any group of disabled people, or especially with your hands gripped around the wheelchair handles. This happened to me once at Oxford, when a guy in uniform asked me where I thought I was going with the wheelchair I was hastily trying to push through the gate.

'I always take young James here into the game.'

I thought that young James's name tag had saved the day, only to receive an electric current straight to the brain when he looks up over his shoulder and goes, 'You fucking don't, I've never seen you before in my fucking life.'

Disgraceful language on young Jimmy, I'm thinking, but that was me snookered. With nothing left to say I beat a hasty retreat with me tail between me legs. It wasn't a frequently used technique, because you could be taken for a weirdo, and if it came on top you could end up looking like some kind of disabled-person kidnapper, and who wants to be labelled one of them?

Back at the Luton game, the Reds were not doing so well, so a bit of banter ensued with the home fans. Me and Eddie, gobs fully open, were having a good laugh with some of them, especially these two naughty old ladies, like the two from Harry Enfield's 'young man' sketch. Only thing is, a few voices of discontent can be heard jangling about in the background, probably too scared to come right upfront. As the naughty jokes start flying about, this big Irish nugget sticks his fridge-freezer-size head over the old ladies' shoulders and asks, 'How did you two get into our end? And what are you doing inside the ground anyway?'

He looked like Jethro out of the *Beverly Hillbillies* and was clearly trying to intimidate us with his size, but that doesn't really work if you come from where I'm from, so I go, 'We're watching the footy, that's what we're doing. Anyway what's it got to do with you? Are you an Irish Garda off duty, or what?'

'No I'm certainly not, but I've got a season ticket for here and I don't want you lot in here.'

One of the two ladies said, 'We're only having a laugh and a joke, it's okay.'

'No, they shouldn't be in here, and I want them out.'

So I say, 'Take it easy, Jethro lad. Anyway, where are you from mate?'

'Tipperary in Southern Ireland, but I don't see what that has to do with anything, and I still want you Scousers out.'

Jethro, whose head close up looks like two taxis welded together with the bonnets open, won't leave it alone, so I go, 'I had ancestry in Tipperary, but I hope they weren't like you, you gormless, fat-headed culchie bastard.' (Culchie was Irish for woollyback; me ma told me that.)

I thought he was going to come at us, so I stood me ground and prepared for battle, but he ran off in the other direction, pushing his way past people. I'm thinking, *fucking hell, his bottle went quick*. We started joking with the two ladies again while continuing to watch the game, but other moaners had begun to complain about our presence. I'm still thinking, *ah well, at least that big shithouse has moved away*. Five minutes later, that same shithouse returned with four Luton plod and a couple of stewards. Eddie elbowed me in the ribs and we quickly made our way to the front, but more bizzies came from behind the goal area, shouting instructions into their walkie-talkies. That was it, we were up and running; Speedy Gonzales was back in town. We jumped over the wall and onto the pitch with at least ten bizzies and stewards after us. We started laughing our heads off; by now it was farcical, given the fact that we had nowhere to run to. If it had been a bigger stadium with larger terraces like the Kop we'd have stood a half-chance of losing ourselves in the crowd, but this was Luton and we were bound to get nabbed in a Subbuteo stadium.

Before we legged it down the touchline, the two of us were shouting back up at Jethro, 'Go on you big shithouse, fuck off back to Tipperary with all the other brogue-wearers.' And as we ran, we were going, 'Hey fridge-head, Jethro, yer fucking big bungalow brain,' like a pair of demented kids.

We made it to the wall at the opposite end of the ground and jumped in. It was like the football Grand National as we hurdled over seats and flew up the stairs, before charging back down again as we were surrounded. I could even see some Liverpool players looking over hands on hips as if they were saying, 'Oh no, not those scallies again.' It was a Keystone Cops caper, with no hooliganism involved, but next day the newspapers, overboard as usual, said there was a large disturbance in the crowd. It also showed the contrasting attitudes you could find in two different sets of supporters. We were two young footy fans who had travelled 200 miles to see our team play on Saturday afternoon, we caused no trouble, and yet those so-called Luton fans did nothing but moan to get us chucked out. Get a life. If the tables had turned and two or more Luton fans had been standing in the Kop having a good laugh, everyone to a man would have made them feel welcome, and the only way the welcome mat would be tugged from under your feet was if, (a) you were causing trouble, (b) were in a big mob, or (c) were shouting way too loudly for a hated rival team. All you Luton supporters, and any other jobsworth, humourless, strait-laced Jethros out there, you know what you need don't you? You need educating just like Rita, yer gang of stiff pricks.

Another good way of getting into an away game fixture was

to keep the previous year's ticket stub, as often teams would not change their ticket layout from year to year. A lot of lads from the Bunkers' Society kept a box or drawer at home full of old stubs, and where they'd tear the small piece from the end of a ticket as you entered, you could make a new admission piece up from an old stub, so keeping a few from each ground was a good idea. I used to, till the clutter from one too many seasons became too much, causing me to throw the lot out. Sometimes lads would sneak the small admission piece from out of the turnstile operator's opening, and if you acted like you had torn it from what, in effect, was last year's stub, you were normally in. On other occasions I've also seen lads put their hands through the small opening and snatch bundles of ticket stubs when things were looking a little desperate and it was getting close to three o'clock. This duly turned into snatching the cash from behind the 'turny' and I'll tell you about that later, but it hardly ever happens anymore, as most matches today are ticket-only. Once the head stewards sent the message about turnstile fiddles upstairs, and the money-hungry directors realised that some of the gatemen were getting a little cash on the side at the cash-only turnies, another old earner for what was always a badly paid job was bound to bite the dust.

When tickets were extra scarce, like big cup games or title deciders, a few of the Liverpool boys would sometimes buy, say, two tickets between maybe a mob of ten. The two lads with the 'briefs' (tickets) would enter the stadium, taking any double-clickers inside with them. Once in, one of lads would ask a doorway steward to help him in some way, say over by the pie counter, or maybe to point them to the first aid or, the best of all, say that they knew where some supporters were bunking in. This would always get the steward's full attention. Once the distraction had been organised and the doorway was left

Liverpool fans at the Olympic Stadium in Rome to see us lift the European Cup for the first time in 1977. One or two of these faces became well-known Road Enders – you know who you are!

Anfield in the Eighties and fashions had changed. No more sideburns or frizzy mullets – but the passion was the same.

Fighting on the terraces at Chelsea, always a lively ground to visit. By the Eighties I was more concerned with bunking in and having a mooch than running around the terraces like a loon. Ask Ken Bates.

Celebrations come in different guises: this bus was set alight at Leeds after we won the league title with perhaps the best-ever Liverpool side. The Yorkshire cavemen attacked us outside the ground but came unstuck.

Urchins trying to get at Newcastle hooligans on the pitch at a Friday night match. Fighting at a Liverpool game often had an underlying factor – in this case a revenge mission for some Scousers being beaten up.

A line of coppers await us off the ferry returning from Moenchengladbach in 1978. Some enterprising Scouse pirates had lowered the ship's flag and raised a Liverpool one instead. And the duty free, as ever, got a good going over.

Happy days: some of the lads from the Halewood Chains celebrate in Rome in 1984 when we lifted the Big Cup for the fourth time.

Young Annie Road End lads in Rome: Mono (fourth from right) with his out-of-step perm and caterpillar tash must have been the geezer Harry Enfield modelled his Scousers on.

A typical picture of me in Europe: waiting to find an empty seat after bunking in.

Two of the best-known Liverpool flags, from the Kingfisher, a pub in my home of Kirkby, and the Leather Bottle in Halewood. These guys go everywhere.

Coventry 1987 and the lengths some of the lads will go to get the best view during a game. We still had a great team at this time but the wheels would soon come off.

Plastic paddies on the ale at Church Street station in Florida during the 1994 World Cup – one of my best times at football. That's me third from right and Marty Mullen in the shamrock shirt.

The Liverpool Artists' Society on tour: a group including *Brookside* writer Roy Boulter (second from left), former Farm singer Peter Hooton (third from left) and novelist Kevin Sampson (third from right) in the Russian capital before our game against Spartak Moscow.

Get them! The catch phrase of lovable rogue 'Colonel' Anthony Hogan (front) with (left to right) Reds fans Waller, Tommy Taxi and Guy Blundell.

I still get the travel bug every time I look out over the River Mersey. Though the way we've been playing the past few years, I think the ship's almost sunk.

unguarded by the stewards, the bolts would be pulled from their fastenings, doors swung open, hey presto, the other lads would walk in quickly – not run, as you didn't want the bizzies noticing before they were all in and one of you had closed the door. You might have to give it toes through the open gate if one of the decoyed stewards returned too early, or if some wide-awake copper spotted the jib, but he could only nab one of the Bunkers' Society at any given time, so the others would be in. This happened at a lot of the big games, where tickets were like gold dust.

It happened *Monty Python* style at Blackburn in the third round of the FA Cup, in January 1991, in their old wooden main stand. What stood out about that day was that the twenty-five Liverpool supporters involved kept walking or running away from the open gate, before bumping or slamming back into each other. It was like a televised comedy sketch, and it was all due to the fact that the ancient Ewood Park main stand consisted of rickety wooden corridors like an old haunted house. Because the lads didn't know their way around the stand, and with the narrow passageways being full of the Bunkers' Society all getting chased by stewards, it was like the funhouse at Southport fairground. Nobody had a clue where to find an escape route, so everyone kept bumping into each other. As usual, the laughter started to erupt. Soon, some of the more boisterous bunkers were ejected from the ground, probably because they gave themselves away with their constant laughter. The remaining fifteen or so started to mingle in with the Blackburn supporters at the tea bars, but as they clocked each other, it had become such a surreal scenario that the remaining fellas couldn't stop themselves from laughing again. One by one their fits of laughter gave them away and they were either collared by a steward or grassed on by the different sets of home fans, before being ejected by a bizzie. Eventually only seven or eight remained inside the main stand until kick-off, when it was time to step out onto the pitch to take the long, shaky walk into the Liverpool end. Some resisted the urge to watch the match with their mates by finding the odd empty seat amongst the home support, and by keeping a low profile, which was a special skill in itself, especially if you were a passionate supporter.

Another favourite jib could work two ways, as in it could get you into the ground for free if you were outside, or it could get you out of the ground to bring one of your mates back in. It was ridiculously easy, and a technique I often used when I was still hungover and tired from the previous night's bender. If you needed a sure-fire, route-one routine to get yourself inside a football ground, this was the one.

Let's say you've arrived at Southampton after a long, boring journey. You're at the turnstiles and you want to have a quiet drink and a read of the programme inside the ground before kick-off. But there's no spare tickets about and it's a bit on the slow side to double-click, as it's still too early. The lady at the collections window is wise to your yearly Scouse party trick, and won't be handing out any freebie envelopes without you first showing a driver's licence, passport and two utility bills. The first-aid gate is only admitting people who look like Egyptian mummies, or those with life-threatening injuries. There are no disabled people being allowed in today because they always give the players too much stick. The press, TV and newspaper photographers' entrance is being manned by two SAS officers, who only admit people carrying huge cameras with three forms of ID. So how the fuck are you going to get in when it looks like Ronnie O'Sullivan has got you well and truly snookered at the Saints?

Hang on, did that loud speaker just say, 'The fella driving the red Vauxhall Vectra had better move his arse before his car gets towed away, as it's blocking the whole street.' Five minutes later, it's over to the entrance gate you go.

'Excuse me steward, open the gate please, I'm back.'

'Back from where sir?'

'Why, I'm back from parking that bloody Vauxhall Vectra they've just read out over the tannoy. It's okay, I've put it in the club car park now.'

'I don't remember you leaving this gate sir.'

'Oh but I did, you were busy letting those other people through as I went out.'

'Oh I see, in you go, have to check you see.'

'No problem mate.'

Now sometimes with this bunking routine, you didn't even have to hear the tannoy or go to any certain gate, although it always made things easier if a group had just departed from your chosen entry point. Most stewards would never think you had the gall to pull that one and would usually let you walk straight in, no questions asked. We'd often arrive at the ground quite late, walk right up to the gateman or steward and say,

'That was my car outside, and I've moved it now, so I'm coming back in, okay?'

And the answer would normally be something like, 'Err, okay.'

Once inside the stadium you might hear another announcement that one of your friends could use, but even if you didn't, you could walk over to another exit, taking somebody's match stub for extra safety, and tell the steward you were leaving the ground to move a vehicle or get something from your car. Once outside you could send your mate over to the same gate, say five minutes later, wearing your hat if need be, where he would usually be admitted. If not, he could go to a different gate with the stub and use the same blag.

Most officialdom in this country judge people by appearance, and if you are dressed quite smartly and tell the steward that you've had to re-park the Merc, then your average footy steward is letting you in, end of story. According to the stewards around the stadiums of this country, I've owned thirty or forty imaginary Mercs. In reality I would never drive one of those look-at-me cars, not even if I was minted. Gimme an A-to-B motor any day of the week. Loudarses are a pain in the arse, but act like one and you get to see the match.

Meanwhile, if you've left the ground, boxed off your mates and enjoyed a brief sojourn to the car park to have a gab with the other lads, it usually means your timespan on the outside has been used up and it's time to re-enter the stadium at the same entrance/exit point. If the stewards have swapped about a bit, as they often do, then it became even easier. I once watched six people use the same trick, at the same gate, because the steward was a nice, easy-going oul fella. We weren't taking liberties in my book, as nobody got hurt and we were always desperate to see the Reds play. I'm sure the gold-minted footy clubs didn't miss the money. We only used these bunking techniques because we had no money and a religious devotion to all things Liverpool FC. It's the biggest faith in Liverpool, with Catholic and Protestant coming a close second and third. You're talking about the Church of the Urban Football Field, where saints who wear red are bowed down to and adored. Shankly as God, Paisley his right-hand man, and a whole heavenly host of Apostles that include Liddell, Fagan, Hunt, St John, Rush, Dalglish, ending with Owen, and where homage would be duly paid every Saturday afternoon at 3pm. Although quite a few fans have had their ashes buried in the Kop goalmouth, or scattered on the Spion Kop terrace, the ground was labelled 'The Shrine' by the man who'll forever be on the throne, Bill Shankly for more reasons than these alone. I'll let the words of an old Kop classic speak for themselves,

> Oh come all ye faithful
> Joyful and triumphant,
> Oh come ye, oh come ye, to Aaaaanfield
> Come and behold them,
> We're the kings of Europe,
> Oh come let us adore them
> Oh come let us adore them
> Oh come let us adore them
> LIIIIIVERPOOL.

When you're a young lad growing up in Liverpool, and you fervently sing songs like that with 25,000 other Kopites under one roof, it leaves a mark. By the time I was 16, they'd left an indelible mark on me, and soon enough, I had a Liver-bird burning away for life upon my chest. We're not talking about some little football team here, where a lad might spend a few hours on a Saturday afternoon, no, this was a club supported by thousands of passionate, cocky, Scouse fanatics, who ate, slept, and drank football 8 days a week and whose team were simply the best. We're looking at a set of supporters who could never be truly happy till the Big Cup was lifted, and once you'd stood in that Kop, amongst these people, and you'd sang your heart out till your throat was red-raw and your allegiance was to Shankly and the boys, then it was only a matter of another game or two, till it was 'Red till fucking Dead'. The fact that I wanted to display my allegiance took me off on a whole host of travels, and through my determination to not miss out, due to my lack of funds, I now find myself here at Cardiff today for the Worthington Cup Final against the Mancs. I'm 40, I've got a sixty pound seat, and a set of love-handles that won't allow me to double-click anymore, but yer never know, yer just never know.

On a quick one, for those notching up the facts and figures in the old Bunkers log-book, the simplest and hardest bunk-ins come to mind quite easily, considering the years I've waltzed into grounds. The easiest was without doubt the World Cup games in Florida USA 1994, where a cock-up by the authorities on the tickets (as usual) left most games 10,000 short on capacity, and the touts were literally giving the tickets away. But if you didn't want a free ticket, then free entry, via the widest gate entrances you've ever seen, was another dollar-free option. It must've had something to do with the size of those Yankee 'doughnut'n' steak' spectators, because I could've rolled into those grounds side-ways.

The hardest, well it had to be the Italy World Cup in 1990. They had three security gates to go through at the opening match between Argentina and Brazil, in Juventus's new ground, The Stadium of the Alps. Caniggia, that cat-weazledRangers player with the scraggy head scored the winner, in a game the Brazilians dominated under a hot Italian sun. They were always a bunch of sharks those Eyeties, with one line of police – who we called 'the Carbonara', one line of security – 'the match-mafia', and finally, a line of turnstile operators and gate stewards, who were unnamed and paid in small amounts of lire, which basically translated as, if you could get past the first two they were always up for a 'dropsie'. Hard as it was to get in, they still hadn't met up with the Scouse Bunkers' Elite. And once one of us had infiltrated our way around the three security lines, a box of used ticket-stubs was duly lifted from behind the gate entrance. The tickets for every game showed exactly the same printed cover, except for a different match date in one corner. That was it, we were in, and only a couple of knock-backs occurred during the numerous games we attended, before Michael Bolton – sorry, Chris Waddle – eventually missed that penalty against West Germany back at the Stadium of the Alps a couple of weeks later.

While we're on the subject of Italia 90, during and after a nightclub battle in Rimini, a large contingent of England fans were rounded up and sent home via Air Taggitalia, on the first plane readily available. Most were innocent and had paid for one or two weeks hotel and board. Whilst they were being flown home, their belongings and passports remained in Italy at a seaside hotel they'd only just booked into. We knew a few of the lads who'd been deported back to England, so we assumed their identity at the residence and stayed full-board, free for a week. One man's Rimini riot had become another man's Italian holiday, so don't worry lads, it didn't all go to waste when you went back to Blighty. By the time the week or so had ran out, we'd seen O'Leary score a penalty winner for Ireland in Genoa, I'm behind the goal as it hits the net, we'd seen the very average, horse-headed David Platt swivel and volley home against the Belgians, to earn himself mega-transfers, and brewsters galore, then it was on to the Cameroon game in Naples, with nice-guy Gary's two pennos saving the day for England. We actually entered the West Germany semi-final with tickets, once me oul mate Franny swivelled his way past checkpoint after checkpoint, to eventually reach the underground changing-room area where Steve McMahon sorted him out with a few tickets. But it was only after he'd asked Franny 'How the fuck did you get yourself down here?' Good on yer anyway Stevie, those briefs made life a lot easier for the three Scouse scallies outside.

* * *

A final story that encapsulates the Bunkers' Society happened over a period of less than two days during a Home International weekend in London, on another warm sunny day in May. The Reds had just won the 1978/79 title and a lot of the Road End firm didn't want the season, or party, to end, so along with a couple of my old Park End mates, around twenty-five of us decided mid-bevvy on Friday, May 25, to head off down for the England versus Scotland match at Wembley. It was quite normal for two or three Evertonians to be with us. They often went away with our firm because they reckoned it was always a better laugh with the much larger-earning crew, and anyway these lads were my good mates. I would sometimes go away with them, which was never any big deal in those days. Any Scousers who go looking to fight with other Scousers are not the full shilling in my book. This international went down as the Brooking-Keegan one-two game, which England won 3–1, and although that's the main thing most football fans remember about the game, it is not the same reason why me and a few lads recall that sunny May weekend down in the Smoke.

As was the norm, we stayed out on the ale all night and caught the midnight train to London on the eve of the game with not a train or match ticket between us. Every one of us was looking to make some money, as we were all skint, unless one of the lads had some secret stash going on. We'd caught the night train to many London games but never to an international, so we were unprepared for a Manc firm hopping aboard – the 'midnight' at the time was prone to stop at the two northern cities before heading down to Euston. Some fellas were half-dozing as a commotion was heard in the early hours of the morning. On rising, we were greeted by an excited Joey O telling us that there was a 'septic' England firm on the train.

Down we marched through the carriages to find a large firm of Mancs waiting. We expected them to about-face and run but they stood their ground. Without introduction, the punches began to rain in on them. It was strange to see them clambering past each other trying to get away in the narrow corridor. They definitely had more than us, maybe fifty in number, but they could see they'd walked into a kamikaze, non-running firm. We had one of those small firms of boys who wouldn't be legged by any numbers, as the shame would've been too much to take. Only the people at the front were getting hit, and then the front became the back as they tried to leg it through the train. It reached the joke stage after a couple of minutes when our own lads were punching each other in the dark, and when the train entered a pitch-black tunnel everybody started laughing hysterically. It had all the makings of a Scooby Doo moment with all the lads aboard the hooligan ghost train.

Once the train exited the tunnel, there wasn't a Manc in sight – it was like Old Trafford. We started egging each other on, and some fellas were laughing and saying, 'Nah let's leave it, you can't get a proper dig in, and we'll only end up giving each other shiners'. But a few other lads, who happened to have boxed quite a bit, were having none of it, and probably due to the fact that they'd had a wee drink that night or maybe they were looking for some on-train training, they decided to go in search of the septic mob. SCOOBBY DOOBBY DOO.

We went back to our seats and were laughing and joking

like young lads do after a bit of bravado. All of a sudden one of the boxing lads comes pegging down the train shouting, 'Come on, get off your arses, you've got to see this.' As we made our way down the train, everyone was waiting for this big surprise, but all that had happened was that the Manc lads had barricaded themselves in on their side of the train. It did look a bit weird to see the passageway blocked off, and when somebody tried their hardest to open the door and it wouldn't budge, we all started making these daft, spooky noises and shouting silly threats, like, 'You'll be in your coffins by Stafford,' and, 'Watch your back or you'll be on the track.' Everyone was booting the door and making as weird a noise as possible before the joke wore off and we returned to our seats. It was a strange scenario with everything being pitch black and I'm sure those Manc lads remember it as well as we do. It was comical more than anything and I don't think anybody got seriously hurt, though it was a good job it didn't happen a couple of years later in the Stanley days, as God knows what kind of midnight mayhem could have gone on within the confines of the carriages then.

The London night train was always slow and for the rest of the journey lads like me who couldn't sleep for more than five minutes began to play tricks on each other. Wedge haircuts and tidy quiff fringes started to get sliced. Lights were turned out and shouts of 'Here's the Mancs' and 'Unarted, Unarted,' went up before we laid into each other; toy-fights, we used to call them. Light bulbs and anything else you could lay your hands on were constantly being thrown around the carriages, and it became hopeless if you wanted a decent kip. In the end, even the sleep-anywheres gave in to the lads who were always running around on fresh-air speed. You know the type; the lads who were always buzzing for a laugh, always up for a dare or a bit of mischief, the ones who just fucking couldn't keep still; yeah, lads like me. I was your typical Spring-heel Jack, the kind who could only kip in a nice, comfy bed. I always envied those jammy bastards who could nod off on jam-packed trains, rickety oul coaches, concrete station floors, brass-gaff stairs, crates of Budweiser bottles with a mop handle stuck halfway up their noses. So when I was younger I made it my business to keep them awake, as I was doing on the night in question. After a while, with no chance of getting your head down, somebody finally said, 'Fuck the fighting, let's go and have a gab with the Mancs.'

Some of the more hardliners, like you find in every mob, were saying, 'Fuck them. Don't start talking to them sheepshaggers.' But I was never one of them; football fighting was always a big joke to me. You could have as many battles as you liked in Liverpool every weekend, so those footy battles were never any big deal in my eyes. One on one is usually a fight, maybe even five onto six, but 200 onto 300 usually ends up in either a farce, a tangled heap, or a legger for one mob, with only the stragglers being kicked and punched to the ground. It's only every blue moon you'll see a full-scale battle. Anyway, we were bored shitless, so five or six of us made our way up the train with the proverbial olive branch in hand. But the Manc lads were having none of it, as they thought it was a trap and once the barricades came down the fists and trainees would fly.

Eventually the train stopped in the middle of nowhere and peace offerings were made through the windows by two lads who had known each other in borstal. Once two or three of us had crossed the boundary line after the barricade came down, I suddenly realised how vulnerable we were. I could tell that Paddy, a good mate who'd come through with me, had sensed this himself, so remembering the earlier confrontation I said, 'You can only get a few punches in in here, it'll be alright.' I hoped I was right, otherwise we could get pummelled. The septics were alright when we got talking, but you could see the snides in their firm who were thinking about throwing a dig. There was one lad called Beef who was a true Manc rag-arse and later on we got to know a couple of these lads at matches. They were the original Manc boys, like Binnsy with his glasses and his quiff, and this was the first time any mutual gabbing went on. Later that afternoon we would help a couple of them bunk in, along with fifty or so Jocks who got charged for the pleasure.

But the strangest event of the day, one that is still scorched on my memory, came early that morning in Trafalgar Square. It involved a couple of London 'scabby fannies' (prostitutes), a thousand drunken Jocks and a viewing audience of twenty young Scousers, who saw the proceedings like this. Two scantily dressed prozzies came over to the square where hundreds of Jocks were singing and partying, with a profusion of those yellow and red flags and the usual bundles of tartan on show. They began to flaunt themselves provocatively in front of the half-bladdered tartan mob. We were sitting high up on those huge lions, and became intrigued when some older fellas started to fondle, then drag more violently at the two women. At first they were enjoying the attention but you could see things were starting to get out of hand, as too many drunks were trying to get a feel of their tits or trying to throw their hands up the brasses' short skirts. Things started to get ugly and it seemed the women had realised this, as they tried to break free, but by now this was a tartan pack of wolves all hungry to get at the two women for their own little pound of flesh. The women tried to kick or shove any would-be attacker but they were being molested and interfered with by too many men. Each time they made a bid for freedom they were thwarted and held back, till the mob eventually overpowered them. The Jocks were like a pack of wild animals, all wanting their bite of the kill.

A year before, under the watchful gaze of Admiral Nelson's statue, I had run off clutching Jean-Claude's spiv tickets on a sunny, happy day. What I was witnessing now was a whole lot darker and murkier. One of the women saw an opening, and began to kick, scratch and fight her way out from the middle of the pack. She eventually got away but almost all of her clothes were missing; I think only her shoes remained on her feet. As she ran away her bare backside swayed from side to side as though she was performing a streak, but this was no run for fun, this was a stripped-bare sprint for your life. The other woman, by now totally overpowered, had every item of clothing stripped from her body, shoes included, before being held down by at least thirty of the Scottish supporters. I hate to say this, but she reminded me of a freshly plucked chicken. Her shoes and knickers were soon being paraded around Trafalgar Square like the trophies of an invading Viking mob, and one fella placed the knickers over his face like a balaclava, to the absolute merriment of anyone close at hand.

To the left was a naked, running woman, being half-heartedly pursued by five or six drunken men; to the right was a naked, captured woman being held and molested by the pack. From the bowels of the pack you could hear a distant chant; it was one lone man in a gruff Scottish voice. The sound grew louder as the others joined in, and it began to emanate out to the rest of the Square. A slight trickle of rain appeared from the sky, and as the rain became a light drizzle, hundreds of drunken Jocks took up the brutal chant: 'WE WANT A RAPE, WE WANT A RAPE, WE WANT A RAPE.'

It was one of those time stands still moments, as an eerie greyness enveloped the whole scene. We sat there half gob-smacked, and I say half, because in those younger days I think only the appearance of Jesus himself, wearing a pair of Rockport sandals and an Armani tunic, would have dropped our jaws to the floor. We had only just gone past dawn and here we were with the second spooky happening of the day, albeit that this latest one was a whole lot more gruesome than the ghost train incident. The main thing I remember thinking is, *everyone's back home snuggled up in bed, while I'm at one of the shadiest fucking rape scenes that you could ever witness in the so-called civilised world.* Shadiness comes in all shapes and sizes, but what was going on here, out in the open, at the setting of a famous historical monument, didn't get much shadier.

On cue from some beast master, an opening appeared in the pack and the next thing, this oul fella dropped his scruffy, baggy trousers. In true Steptoe style, he took out this big set of false teeth that probably contained half of last night's egg and chips doused in vodka; then making a corridor for himself, he pushed anybody close by aside, before moving between the girl's outstretched legs which were being firmly held down. There, he dropped to his hands and knees to lap like a dog at the girl's gaping pussy.

Joey 0 turned to me and said, 'The . . . dirty . . . stinking . . . Scotch twat!'

The sun had started to seep through the greyness, which only served to highlight the ugly scene even more. The other Jocks were cheering him on and some were slapping his wrinkly old arse. He stood for a moment to strip bollocko, leaving only his shoes and socks on the ends of his bony white legs. Twos and threes were holding onto to the woman's fleshy arms and protruding feet, even though she had totally submitted. It was like watching one of those David Attenborough wildlife programmes, where the little gazelle gets tossed about by the indifferent lions. This little gazelle was a thirtyish, medium-sized woman but she was getting treated in that same disdainful, piece-of-meat way, while the 'lions' were a rag-taggle bunch of Scotch plonkies.

The full realisation of what was going on seemed to snap a few of us to attention, so we started shouting 'POLIS, POLIS' in a Scottish accent, just so the baying crowd would stop. Somebody in our crew said something along the lines of, 'Whatever you think, that's someone's daughter, you know,' so the 'Polis' shout went up again, only this time louder and more urgently.

'POLIS, POLIS, QUICK, POLIS.'

The fellas on the periphery stopped mid-swig and began to look about; most of them were too drunk to realise it was a couple of our lads doing all the shouting. Some of them backed off, leaving a gap between themselves and the naked girl. It was as though they were distancing themselves from the crime in progress, without actually stopping any of the gropers and molesters who were still mauling at her flesh. We carried on with the shout and a couple of lads darted to the other side of the square to holler from a different direction. More and more men were moving away from the woman as they tried to scan the surroundings. Hands were raised to brows against the emerging sun, trying to focus on any approaching plod. The girl looked petrified and was shaking uncontrollably as she let out a piercing scream before managing to break free. She looked like a scared rabbit running for her life, but even as she made her dash for freedom fellas were grabbing at her body and trying to drag her back. She had the appearance of a naked ragdoll, with her white skin contrasting fiercely with the grey, dusky morning and the concrete surroundings.

The police finally appeared, and in her eagerness to latch onto somebody in uniform, the ragdoll figure almost got run over. For her, they were her knights in dark blue uniforms. A coat was placed around her shoulders and she was put inside a police van. Horrible and as cold as it sounds, in her dishevelled and naked state I instantly thought of the term 'meat wagon' for the van, as it seemed appropriate considering she'd been thrown about like a skinned piece of meat. I could only imagine what her thoughts were at that moment; something along the lines of 'safety at last' comes to mind.

I didn't see anybody get arrested. The drunken Jocks just carried on singing that song 'WE FUCKING HATE ENGLAND, WE FUCKING HATE ENGLAND' as if nothing had happened. The bizzies, from what I could tell, seemed to know the girl and she was driven away. That song would have been the last thing she heard as the van doors closed. Eventually more plod arrived on the scene, but I still didn't see anybody get nicked. Mob rule had gone unpunished, as it usually does. I think the other girl, even though near-naked, had kept on running all the way to Watford without stopping. No one, especially when that drunk, worried about Aids or VD in those days, and I can only try to imagine what would have unfolded if the mob had been allowed to continue in the same vein. It was a side of the so-called 'friendly' Tartan Army that the Scottish FA and football's ruling bodies would never tell you about, although anyone 'in the know' would know that the Scotch supporters can be as rowdy as anyone on this earth when the occasion moves them. They are a fantastically noisy mob who can party as good as any set of fans. What I'm saying is, these things went on, and I know because I was there. Tough shit if the truth strikes at the wholesome kilted image of the Tartan Army. If it makes any difference whatsoever, they were all bladdered to a man. Vodka'd-up and whisky'd-to-go, ah thee oul demon drink eh, what can yer say? It is one the weirdest things I have ever witnessed at the footy.

Later that day we copped for a load of match programmes and made a few quid selling them outside to the mainly Scottish crowd. This was in the days before England had any kind of hoolie mob, so you were normally guaranteed a peaceful Wembley day out. A few years down the line, once those freshly labelled 'casuals' started to catch on to the Liverpool way of dressing, Home International games between the two rivals would never be the same again.

The long, strange away day didn't quite end there, as one of the lads opened up a closed, unmanned turnstile door and loads of Jocks quietly queued up for the only cheap pay-in gate at the stadium. After ten minutes of collecting the entrance money, the lad finally left the operating side of the turnstile as too many Jocks had started to realise what was going on. More and more Tartan Terrors had joined the queue and the little scam was drawing too much attention, so sadly, it was time to scarper. Although he knew he was only moments away from getting nicked, he said it was still a wrench to drag himself away from such a fast earner.

England won the game 3–1, with that Brooking-Keegan one-two goal being the highlight, and did the day finally end there? Did it fuck. Part way through the match we'd got talking to this nutty Scouse skinhead called Stevie Binns, who was dressed in full skin mode with boots, braces, button-down shirt and Crombie. He told us he was bucking the trend in trainee'd-up Liverpool by being an old-fashioned skin, because he loved the clobber, the music and everything about the lifestyle. Fair dos, we thought, as we carried on messing about, having a bit of a laugh and joke. We were hardly interested in the game in progress, as international football to us was always boring. The skinhead seemed to think it was even more boring than we did and entertained everybody in the vicinity with his own little reggae dances, before moonstomping while sticking out his massive tongue, a trait that Buster Bloodvessel would later make his own. His tongue looked like a gammon steak without the pineapple in the middle, and briefly reminded me of the dirty oul Scotch fella and the morning's events We started to egg this skinhead on, saying things like, 'If you're so mad and you like bucking the trend, why don't you run on the pitch and stop the game?' and, 'If it's so boring, what d'yer reckon about taking all these Jocks on?' It eventually fizzled out and he wandered off to show someone else his reggae dances and his cow's tongue.

We were sitting on the crush barriers, as we always did, high up in the top Wembley tier, and eventually yawning and international football boredom saw us nodding, as we'd had no sleep since Thursday, yet again. But who's this on the pitch, waking the crowd and us up and stopping the game? Why, for fucksake, it's none other than the all-dancing, Crombie-coated Scouse skinhead. What a funny fella he was to take up the challenge; you've got to admire that kind of bottle, for not giving a shit because he felt like doing something nutty for a giggle. He was all over the Sunday papers the next day, a real character and a half that lad. Hats off to yer, skin. I'll bet he's still got all the clippings in his loft, tucked away inside an old, well-polished Air Wair boot.

Stepping wearily aboard the train home at Euston, I amazingly drifted off to sleep. Now for that to happen I must've been knackered. Accompanied by the sound of the train hurtling back to Scouseland, I dreamed of the Scouse skinhead, the two bare-boned prostitutes, the Tartan Army with the dirty oul man and his false teeth, and the Liverpool turnstile operator who was loved by a couple of hundred Jocks. Oh yeah, and the stagecoach battle with the Manc rag-arses. My thoroughly cabbaged head was so chock-a-block full of mad dreams that I fell into a lovely, deep, over the white cliffs of Dover, dream-inspired kip. And woke up in fucking Carlisle. *Bastard!* I'd jumped the first train out and was supposed to change at Crewe. You'd think I didn't like my own flock back in me bedroom at home the way I was carrying on.

PART THREE

Europe

CHAPTER TEN

DHSS: Dustin Hoffman

Sips 'Shampagne'

IT GOES WITHOUT SAYING that Liverpool and the North in general got the shitty end of the stick under the Thatcher-led Government from 1979 onwards, but I'm saying it again. My God did we get the shitty end of the stick. There you go. Thatcher's Employment Secretary, Norman Tebbit (Baron von Tithead Tebbit to us) told anybody who was listening and who was on the bones of his arse that he'd better get his bony arse on a bike if there was no work to be found where he lived. Well Norman, me oul flower I, like thousands of other young Scousers, understood this statement to be aimed directly at me. Now the thing is, in 1981 when you made your famous quote, I was still the proud owner of a rusty orange Raleigh Chopper; it's bound to be fucking hard to pedal from Liverpool to Chingford on that. Plus, the lolly-ice stick that the kids used to place in the wheel spokes just to get that cool clicking noise would drive you absolutely mental by about . . . Spaghetti Junction . . . no, forget that . . . Knutsford . . . err . . . Warrington . . . ah forget it.

Most Liverpudlians learned from an early age that if you didn't pull yourself up by your own Kicker laces, nobody was going to give you a labouring job in a factory like Fords, or down at the Docks like your da and granda. Nah, those days were well gone, and by the time Tithead Tebbit made his speech, loads of us were already up and running anyway. If you're on the job scrapheap by the age of twenty, what it gives you is the time to think, plot and then travel. So whereas most people were in full-time employment from an early age, a lot of northern kids, Scousers in particular, had the time to gallivant all over Europe following their football team, if they so desired. The question was, if the desire was there, were you ready to face up to the challenge of getting out there, as in, how do you go from A to B without a brass farthing to your name? Some lads locked their doors, plugged in a guitar or a hi-fi and seeing as they were stony broke, they got stoned, but other young doleites would see this giro-life as a challenge; it was a challenge many took up.

By the time the Number 10 latch was getting locked by Thatch the Snatch, Liverpool sailors had been crossing the seas for donkey's years. They'd arrive home laden with exotic gifts and new inventions, so most of their homes already had state of the art electronic goods, modern clothing and the latest perfumes, long before anybody else. Those huge Betamax video machines were brought back from foreign ports like Kobe in Japan, to sit proudly under hundreds of Scouse tellies, years before Barry from Rochdale had one. Snazzy cameras picked up in exotic-sounding ports lay on top of the mantelpieces in plenty of working-class homes built high on the banks of the Mersey. I had an old sailor's 'reefer-style' duffle coat and my imagination let me pretend I'd just arrived back on dry land every time I put it on to walk the streets. American preppy clothing, like college baseball jackets and caps, were brought back from the States and young kids would be running around the local hollers (open space in a built-up area) telling anyone who was interested, 'Hey, look what me Uncle Vinny brought me back from New York.'

Almost every family in Liverpool had a connection with the sea, usually through some sort of relation in the navy, whether it was the Merchant or the Royal, and we were no exception. On leaving school, I tinkered with the idea of joining up myself and often thought of skedaddling down to Gravesend to learn about sailing the seven seas at Merchant Navy College. A few of my schoolmates had already set sail, but for me the oul LFC addiction always got in the way. On looking out from the old Pier Head, you couldn't stop me from visiting 'Cloud Pirate' though, and I always loved being by the sea. When those ferries and boats left for Europe and Ireland, from places like Dover, Harwich and Liverpool itself, I'd be up on the top deck with the wind in my hair, dreaming I was one of those historical adventurers off to find new lands, a real ocean-bound sailor on those tall sail ships; a kind of Adidas Captain Pugwash or Sinbad in trainees and a wind-cheater was probably nearer the truth, but we can all dream. Mc mates would always be in the bar, on the Guinness and lager, but I was strictly top deck. Down below with the on-board drinkers, you couldn't feel the freedom in the wind, plus the smell of those fried eggs from the canteen along with the sound of seasick passengers spewing up in the bogs was bound to scupper any chances you had of drifting off to dream. Top deck, you could be Sir Walter Raleigh, the first man to ride a Chopper in the States; or the famous discoverer Christopher 'did he fuck find America' Columbus, the man who pretended he'd never seen the Irish fellas who'd rowed over there years before himself; or perhaps the man who couldn't bear to take his hand off his wallet, Admiral Armani Nelson, born never to get the ale in, off on some mad salty seafaring adventure round the oceans of the world.

I always hanker after the sea and could never live somewhere far inland; a lot of Liverpool people will tell you the same. Although I don't think I would like to be in the working navy today, as a lot of those kids who joined up on leaving school and who I've bumped into since, have told me all about those Asian ship crews who live off the sniff of an oil-rag and will work for two processed peas and an elastic band to keep their kecks up, day in, day out. Now that's bound to fuck up your pay claim, isn't it?

I had cousins in the navy who brought back all kinds of foreign wares. One of my Uncle Pop's mates, Joey Gamble, used to give me and our kid all of these boss American comics, which half the street would lie in wait for. The bastards never returned half of them and the other half would be read to bits before getting swapped for old Liverpool proeys (football programmes). Sorry Joe. I used to read the adverts in the back of those comics and often wondered how you sent off for some of the gear there, things like college baseball jackets – I'd seen the sons of sailors wearing them – or those X-ray glasses that were supposed to let you see through a woman's clothes. My god! I used to pray to the Lord above in the hope of owning a pair of those X-ray specs. By the time I was twenty I didn't want to send off, I just wanted to go, but seeing as I wasn't in the navy, Liverpool FC for me and a few thousand others became our way out, our travelling companion and our passport to foreign destinations.

Lads had started to come back from Europe with Adidas bags full of clobber, small sweet-paper bags full of 'tom' and back pockets full of weird Monopoly money with strange pictures of colourful kings and queens printed on the note faces, or pictures of Italian binmen if it happened to be lire. The first fellas to cop for lire in Rome in 1977 thought that they were absolutely minted, till they found out that fourteen zillion bought you one used shin-pad, a packet of Juicy Fruit chewies and last week's *Daily Mirror* with the telly page missing. Saying that, it still helped with the bootboy-to-scally transition that summer, as they hit the shops on the lookout for their first pair of straight-leg jeans. We had a saying at the time that basically meant if you didn't get up off your aise, then you were never going to see if the grass was greener elsewhere, and sitting on your bum day after day was the obvious road to nowhere. It's said that DHSS stood for being on the dole to some people, but to the more adventurous it stood for 'Dustin Hoffman Sips Shampagne', which in Scouse gobbledegook translated as, only the lads who travelled would ever taste the champers – albeit spelt with an S instead of a C, but we had to make it fit, didn't we?

My uncle Roy and his mates, like thousands of others, had travelled all the way to Rome by train and returned with a small book full of stories from just that one trip alone. But the one that stuck in my mind was the one that they told me about a mainline train station in Northern Italy, a murder on the tracks, and a stone-cold killer dressed in black (hang on, I'm sure that's a Mungo Jerry song).

Come the end of the 1977 season, we were in two finals, but thousands of Liverpool fans had to miss the FA Cup at Wembley because they couldn't afford two trips in five days. Also, because travelling by plane was still the expensive option, many had already left for the overland journey to Italy when the Saturday game kicked off. The choice wasn't easy: FA Cup Saturday or European Cup Wednesday? They chose Euro, so small bag in hand, off to Lime Street they go.

With most of Northern Europe already covered, Roy and his mates came to a halt in an Italian station. As their train pulled up they noticed a middle-aged woman on the platform bending down to reach into a basket. As she did, a man walked past and, with a slight movement of his hips, nudged the woman onto the railway line. In the moment the Liverpool lads rushed to the window, a train flew past in the opposite direction, and as they stood staring, all they could see was the woman's legs sticking up from under the wheels as the train rattled on by. They said that her legs were shaking violently, and as the train passed quickly through the station, she was gone; all that remained were large traces of blood.

To this day, they've often wondered if it was a contract killing, a lunatic railway murderer on the loose, or maybe a domestic dust-up that had sent one man – and one woman – right over the edge. Typical of young men, they hardly mentioned it for twenty years, as the story of what went on in Rome later that night merited more in their Euro diary than the murder they had witnessed on the tracks.

That evening they found a lovely hotel in Rome – chandeliers, plush room, happy manager – and when they asked how much it was, the manager said it was only a pound or so in English. They nudged each other, as if to say, 'Quick get your cash out, the man's a divvy.' Over the moon with their beddy-boes sorted, they downed their bags in a nicely decorated room containing three double beds and, after a quick swill, they hit the town. Ale drunk, Colosseum viewed, songs sung, they returned in the wee small hours, knackered and ready for a decent kip on the night before Liverpool's biggest ever game. Wearily entering the hotel, they unlocked the door to their kipping quarters, only to find about seventy fellas sleeping in the room who'd all paid the same cheap rate. What a fucking conman. Mind you, they always were a bunch of head-working wise-arses, those Eyeties.

With Liverpool FC starting to make inroads into Europe, the stories and the goods were now not only coming into Liverpool via the seamen and the ships, now they were coming down the motorways, train tracks, ferries and the aeroplanes, via the supporters or a host of rogue gangs who thought, *hey, the Liver Bird's flying to Europe again, come on, jump on board, fuck that dole for a lark, you're never going to the sights with that hard-luck handout.* The rogue gangs included more than a few shoplifting teams, and lads who normally wouldn't steal a packet of Fruit Pastilles were soon getting their whole wardrobe sorted out on the way back from a European jaunt.

Liverpool by the mid-Eighties was both unemployment central and black market central; it depended on what you wanted it to be. It was no wonder that a lot of the shops closed down in main shopping districts like London Road at this time. People could, if they wanted, buy anything they desired, usually from a scallywag fence down at the local pub. Daughter getting married? Engagement and wedding rings from Switzerland. Kids need new clobber? Rig-outs from Germany in the pipeline. Washing machine knackered? Top of the range will be with you in two weeks, Sandra, is that all right love? You could buy anything from a car to a pair of Fruit of the Loom undies. While Peckham had Del Boy, Liverpool had Joey Mac, and believe me, this Joey was fuck-all like that leather-kecked golfball from *Bread*. Plus, the fella wouldn't sell you any old shite like Del Boy would; no, it was more than his life was worth. Joey Mac could get you the whole range, no seconds, no duds.

Come Saturday afternoon, local Yates's Wine Lodges resembled the Argos. You sat down with your Aussie white: put your order in: right shade, right spec, right price, which was usually a third of what was on the ticket, though you could pay up to half-price if something was all the rage. If a boozer in Bootle had wagonloads of Berghaus coats on the Saturday, you could guarantee that by the following Wednesday boozers in Kirkby, Kensington and Scotland Road would all have them hanging up at the back of the bar, to be sold with a pint of lager for yourself in one pocket and a pint of mild for your oul fella in the inside bin (cellophane wrapped, of course). Liverpool, along with that other head-working gaff called London, also became the lorry-hijacking capital around this time. Unemployment always breeds head-working, but big-time unemployment breeds big-time head-working. Get the message, Baron von Tebbit? Dim as a bedsit light bulb with the same shaped head!

Liverpool today it seems is on the up, Capital of Culture and all that bollocks, and those once closed-down shopping districts are now full of new building developments and swanky apartment blocks. Out with the old and in with the new. It is no coincidence, I suppose, that this new dawn kicked in with the Tories being kicked out. I hope one day somebody robs Tebbit's bike and hangs it up outside the Adelphi Hotel, or on the front of one of those new apartment blocks, to act as a memory jogger of hard times gone by. Mind you, it's gonna be hard getting his and Maggie's tandem over those twenty-grand security gates, but it would be sweet if someone did, you know, just to remind us all about his silly little bicycle idea.

* * *

We loved being on those cross-Channel ferries. It let you know that you were on your travels; you were off. At the same time, one of your mates might be toiling away in a factory like Fords or Vauxhalls, bored shitless, spray-painting car wing mirrors or something else that killed your brain cells. I had an apprenticeship at the time, and once my four-year contract was signed, just after leaving school, me da, who was a shop-steward, made sure I couldn't be sacked, as I was nearly always clocking on in Calais at around the time I should've been clocking off in work. The call of the footy was far stronger than the call of the factory siren. They tried to get rid of me a few times, and I had verbal warnings and whatnot, but the two-faced fuckers in suits only lashed the whole workforce of a 100 or so onto the dole anyway, which happened right at the end of my four-year stint in collar. Even then, the bastard bosses tried to blag me out of any redundancy money due, saying that as I was now time-served, they had fulfilled their obligation to train me up and the company owed me nothing. All this from a British Leyland company whose northern operation was well in profit, but who had come to a decision to concentrate all of its fork-lift industry further south in a factory that was losing money. It was just another example of a southern power base saying, 'Fuck those Bolshie cunts up there, let's move everything down here.' It told me from an early age not to let them treat you like factory fodder or all you'll get in the end is a swift boot up the arse, a phoney handshake and a fifty nicker, gold-plated Timex watch.

Some young lads would be staring at the mast of the Royal Iris ferry as it made its way across the Mersey Estuary with them on board. Once the ferry had docked at a landing stage over the water, they would catch a bus to start a working day at Cammell Lairds or Vauxhalls in Birkenhead and Ellesmere Port respectively. At the same time, other lads were busy trying to raise their own flag up a mast, not on a ferry across the Mersey but on one of a host of cross-Channel ferries that could all get you back home, via the train, from the Fatherland, after the 1978 European Cup semi-final against the German Borussia Moenchengladbach team. It was the game that preceded the Liverpool boys going on to lift the big silver cup at Wembley against Bruges in 1978.

It wasn't anything that went on during the German game that stayed with me, but what happened before and after. I'll do things backwards and start with after the game, the reason being that, whilst returning home from the first leg, it happened to be one of the first times, if not *the* first time, that the boat 'went totally west' instead of the normal north-north-west to Folkestone or Dover. Let me explain.

The 2–1 defeat Liverpool had suffered was no problem, in fact, when the European Cup was really the champions cup, a first-leg 2–1 away defeat was quite a good result, and the Liverpool boys were in good spirits on the boat journey back to the shores of Blighty. The way I boarded boats in those days would no doubt have seen me labelled as an asylum-seeker or illegal immigrant if I pulled the same stunt today. Most of the time I would take the long walk around the port buildings and enter through a staff entrance, or climb over the tyres at the side of the ferry if the entrance points looked iffy. Liverpool's young firm was never of the boat or hotel-wrecking variety, more of the Scouse Pirate and climb out the hotel window variety, if you know what I mean. For years Liverpool supporters had been raiding the onboard Duty Free shops, and the boat that day was basically robbed blind.

As we slowly pulled into the White Cliffs of Dover, somebody took down the ship's flag and raised a huge Liverpool flag up the mast. It was all in jest and only a bit of fun, but ship folk can be real touchy about things like flying the flag, especially when the boat has already been ransacked. When these things happened, people would say things like, 'Damn, those robbing Scouse football supporters again'. But another funny thing about that day, was the fact that plenty of long-distance lorry drivers and a few ordinary passengers, noticing the commotion being made by the supporters, entered the shops and helped themselves to a little bit of 'Duty on the free'. The purser's office had been locked after the ship's wages went missing and the staff left the shop unmanned. Soon enough, it had been fully plundered, jewellery and all, leaving only the sweets and postcards behind. That was it: the captain must have blown through to the port authorities that these Scouse Pirates had pilfered all of the goods aboard and were now flying their own colours as the boat came into dock.

A couple of Scouse shipmates (most of those boats had some kind of Liverpool crew) forewarned the lads that a large blue presence was waiting back on terra firma. So as you walked around the floating ship, you could see fellas getting rid of stolen booty, throwing cigarettes and booze overboard. Whisky, vodka, and gifts of all descriptions sank below the water, while ciggies and after-shave bobbed along on the waves. If Terry the Tuna was swimming about looking for a prezzy for Cathy the Carp, he wouldn't have had a problem that night, and if you weren't prepared to get rid, you were promptly nicked. Greedy lorry-drivers arriving on the top deck were asking lads not to throw the stuff away, knowing all too well that they wouldn't be searched, as they were not part of the football crowd and the authorities were bound have their hands full with that motley crew. But the fat lorry drivers (well not many of them are skinny) wouldn't pay for the goods, so hundreds of lads continued to lob the stuff overboard, except for one or two on-board sharks, that is. These were the main jewellery hoisters, and seeing as they couldn't bring themselves to lob the watches and gold to the bottom of the deep blue sea, they hit on the idea of hollowing out a couple of those French bread sarnies – the Vienna type – and after pulling the bread from the crust with a fork, the main bread artist then placed watch-bread-watch-bread back in the empty crust, till it was full and not too heavy. Next, he hollowed out another sarnie for one of his mates to carry through the Customs back on dry land. They then split up just before stepping ashore; no need for too many sussy sarnies all in a row. They coolly got away with the sandwich trick, due mainly to the fact that 2–300 lads had to be searched. Anyone knows you have to be a top bread-worker if you want to get on in this life.

As the lads tiptoed through Customs with their jewellery butties, the lard-arse lorry drivers were driving away smoking four ciggies at a time, while putting after-shave on before their next kerbside wank over a *Fiesta* reader's wife. It made sense; they knew they had to make an effort to smell nice for Vanessa from Scunthorpe. You could guarantee, first phone box, they'd be on the blower to the boss, trying to make sure that he'd booked them in for the long-haul drive to Liverpool's next European adventure. Today, with serious drug problems, those expensive gold and onion rolls would stand out to the Customs like big Frank Bruno tag wrestling in the nude with a load of polar bears, and same as Frank, they would've been duly ripped to bits. A lot of Scouse pirates who simply shoved contraband into bags and coat pockets because they couldn't bear to fling the stuff away, were swiftly lifted the moment their Adidas Samba touched England. That's what you get for being a cling-on.

At previous Liverpool games in Germany, at the likes of Frankfurt and on the way to Dresden, some lads who'd never had two skidmarks to rub together stumbled across a novel way of earning extra cash. It began when the German 'ozzies' (hospitals) started advertising blood donorship. Whereas in England you had to be charitable and thoughtful to give a pint of your red stuff over, in the Fatherland it was a straight business transaction, and you got paid around £15 for giving over ze pint of your own tomato soup to the deckchair robbing doctors and nurses of Deutschland. Well, news travelled fast on the Road End grapevine, and come the Moenchengladbach game we were all having some of that. Once the main group of boys found a blood donor clinic, and the word went up, in the time it takes to say 'Frank Bough wears suzzies underneath the *Grandstand* table' there were 100 young lads in the queue. After giving good Scouse blood over, poor oul Joey O disguised himself and went back to give more, as did quite a few other lads. What a bunch of dickheads. Joey nearly died, all for the sake of about thirty quid. He was on the verge of fainting a few times on the way to the match after giving too much red stuff away to the Kraut transfusion service. Suddenly he'd changed from a healthy young Scouse tear-arse with limbs of steel into the ghost from *Randall and Hopkirk*, with a face like a well-washed Leeds kit and a walk like Pinocchio after a spliff. The daft thing is, it was probably only sucked from his arm in the first place to be pumped into Hitler, who people suspected was living under a false name in a bungalow outside Cologne. It was thought that the keyboard player from a group called Sparks was really an ingeniously disguised Adolf. Meanwhile, his daft bird, that Eva Braun, couldn't blag a decent disguise to save her life; I mean, fancy opening that hairdryer and tongs factory for the whole wide world to see.

Blood transactions and boat piracy trips are the kind of things that open your eyes to the big world outside the chippy, the boozer and the betting office. I mean, how was I to know that when you had a piss in a German swimming pool, all the piss turned bright red on contact with the pool water? We'd bunked into this hotel pool the morning of the game and were enjoying a nice swim in our boxer shorts, till unbeknown to the lads, some of the other swimmers and a couple of beefed-up lifeguards started to look suspiciously in our direction. I quickly realised this, whereas the others were too busy doing belly-flops and playing 'dive underneath' for the one deutschmark we had between us. It was obvious why the Germans had started to have a sussy gander in our direction; you don't get an undied-up Scouse mob in a German swimming pool everyday of the week. Now we were enjoying our dip-cum-bath so much that we became wary of getting out of the water, as it would instantly show our bad cock-flashing undies to all the nosey squareheads, plus the fact that the two muscley Sauerkraut sausages were looking for any excuse whatsoever to lob us out head-first, directly onto the Strasse. Dozy Eddie, typically, then decided to bring the prying eyes of a few more Gerds and Gunters onto our gathering by openly lathering-up his curly wig with the one bar of soap we had between us, the thoughtless whopper. As Eddie rinsed his soapy barnet, I turned to one of the lads and said, 'I'm dying for a burst.'

'So am I,' he says. 'Fuck it, just do it in the water, it'll be all right.'

With that, we turn away and start to have a wee. Uh uh, what's all this then? At first, I thought somebody had snapped their foreskin, while busy having a sly tug over the large-titted fraulein busy doing the breaststroke in the outside lane. Lads being lads, it was instantaneous from the moment she entered the pool that the 'phwooars' and 'wheheys' went up, and she seemed to be enjoying the attention, or maybe that was down to the fact that she was the only one in the water who wasn't giving us the old commandant stares. Anyway, all of this red stuff starts floating in and around our group. Before you know it, the two guards are on their way over. It was over and out for us. Without being told, we walked straight out of the pool, and I'm talking about ten lads here, picked up our neatly piled clothing, walked straight past the reception, then out onto the street. Back on the Strasse we were like ten Burt Lancasters, yer know, in that movie where he dived into all of those garden swimming-pools. We looked like a swimming-pool crew of boys, scanning the horizon for another swimming-pool mob to have a ruck with, a strange sight indeed. We dried the excess water from our skin by simply walking down the street, where the passing German workforce ogled us in confused amusement. The moment one of those McDonald's-type restaurants popped up, it was straight into the boys' and girls' bogs, to first, direct the hand dryers up to dry the hair on yer head, then down, to do yer front rubic-cubes, finally, it was bums-to-the-dryer, to cool off the forest-fire down the crack of yer arse. They were always a lifesaver those Big Mac joints and the food was always a novelty, as back home they still didn't have those pink, E-numbered strawberry milkshakes that you could run around all day on. So milkshakes downed, it was back on the prowl. A couple of hours later and Boris's Bloodsucking Service was busy squeezing those milkshakes through medical tubes instead of straws.

* * *

Around this time, fantastically cheap European package deals were coming thick and fast. And lo and behold, where did Liverpool decide to have a pre-season tour? None other than the old Scouse warehouse that Liverpool supporters used to call 'Christmas come early' and the rest of the country called Switzerland. It was the summer of 1981 and the Road End mob had grown too big. Some people were heading back to the Kop for a bit of peace as the Annie Road End had now been divided into three sections and Officer Blackbeard could easily give you a right hook if you were squashed up against the fence. The lads had gotten fed up with sports gear, and had started to dress down. They looked like a huge mob of English teachers searching for a ruck, or maybe looking to cop for a few tweed jackets, the old-fashioned ones with the patches on the sleeves. This downbeat look had first appeared early in 1977 but got totally swamped by sports gear. Now it was back in town, and soft lad here was bouncing around the grounds in a beige corduroy jacket, oul fella's suedies, jeans and brush-cotton checked shirts, along with a nice short haircut. I must've looked like an Irish school teacher fresh over on the boat, who still didn't know if he was in Cork or Kirkby. We looked brainy, but we weren't; we looked studious, but we only read books with pictures in; we looked skint, and guess what, we fucking well were. But it was changing, oh yeah, it was changing all right. The thing is, every time somebody copped for a few quid at the game, or got a few bob together from work, usually another redundancy pay-off, we'd be acting like Viv 'Spend Spend' Nicholson for a month, till it was back to square one and Europe beckoned again.

Well Europe definitely beckoned for the Annie Road boys as the 1981 pre-season tour approached. Tales of untold riches and of streets paved with Rolexes and golden-soled Samba had abounded for years. They'd emanated from the original travelling lads like our crew, but I'd known these tales were grossly exaggerated since the Zurich semi in '77 and another pre-season trip a year or so later. Those streets were really paved with bog-chain-sized ID bracelets, square sovereign-type rings that looked like coffee tables, and the original golden, toilet-seat-size earrings. *So it was true that the Cockneys had been here before, otherwise, why would they sell them?*

The Zurich Gestapo had definitely been pre-warned, as quite a few urchin crews were instantly escorted back to the train. Gangs of lads were being turned around at the station exits simply for looking like Scousers and for laughing too loud while carrying their Adidas bags instead of backpacks, or for not wearing the obligatory hiking boots (yet). The message from the early arrivals soon found its way back to Scouseland, so over the next few days loads of hush-hush crews arrived in town; they went down in history as the quietest Liverpudlians ever to set foot on the cobbled streets of Switzer. B&Bs were rapidly found as the silent crews settled down for their Alpine break. We had to play FC Zurich and Lausanne within the next few days, so no need to get escorted back to the station before the tom shop shenanigans kicked off.

Fellas who usually sang their hearts out after two wine gums were strangely subdued in and around the streets of Zurich old town. And as mob after mob dreamed of gold and of how even a few hundred quid could soon enrich their lives, the Zurich dibbles began to wonder what all the fuss was about. The thousands of marauding scallies they'd been expecting turned out to be 5–600 nice, quiet English teachers, all here to soak up the crisp Alpine atmosphere while studying hard for their literature degrees. Through their expensive Swiss binoculars they couldn't see that something was bubbling under; these well-behaved Scouse students knew it was always nice to go home before the league fixtures got under way with your

expenses paid and a bit more on top. Well, this Zurich place
was about to come on top.

The night of the big game and the rain came pouring down.
It rained so heavily that the match was hastily rearranged for
the next day. But the thing was, all of these young English
teachers now had nowhere to go, and the grey sky rapidly
turned into the old red mist as a crew of 2–300 departed from
the small friendly stadium and began to make their way back
to the town centre by tram. Squelched, soaked and sodden
plots were instantly hatched as cobble-stoned Zurich town
came into view. From here on in, all I can say is that the locusts
left the trams behind before systematically eating up fifteen to
twenty tom shops; now that's a lot of gold-chomping by
anyone's standards. By the time the levee had broken, so had
every fucking tom shop window within a half-mile radius.
Liverpool that week would look like the city of H. Samuel,
only with a lot less onyx and lot purer gold. The British soldiers
used to do this on behalf of the Royal Family, when pillaged
goods would usually find their way back to yer lords' and
ladyships' cabinets, with the best booty being saved for the
Queen's sideboards. But these were different soldiers. These
were soldiers who were essentially skint, held no allegiance to
the Queen or her sideboards, and basically wanted a nice, new
three-piece-suite and a larder full of food to feed the family on
return.

The next morning and night in Zurich bore resemblance to
a scene from *Mad Max*, or *The Warriors*, as the local council, or
local police, decided to bring in this Hell's Angel security firm
to guard the already smashed-up jewellery and clothes shops.
These big, hairy-arsed, chain and dagger carriers were all over
the show, and you can't stand around in the centre of town
openly brandishing artillery like that without the go-ahead

from somebody in the Establishment. Most shops of distinction were boarded up, and although some still had their display windows intact, they were showing huge diagonal or horizontal cracks. Some of them must've used Everest. I reckon Scouse-proof double-glazing must have been flying off the shelves over the following few days. The shop fronts looked like they'd endured a hurricane.

Anyone from Liverpool who was seen in the area the next day was either chased or beaten by the Bavarian Hell's Angels. Some lads who had missed out tried returning to the scene of the crime, only to receive severe beatings. As usual, quite a few innocent fans wearing colours were pummelled to the ground. The lads who'd been beaten up had only ventured back to 'Tom-shop land', when they found out a few earrings were still on the shelves inside some window displays, but what they hadn't realised was that the lads who'd been there the day before had only left them there for the Cockneys to pick up ten years later. One of the innocents abroad got cornered by a large group of mace-swinging Bavarian bikers, and on cue, he plopped his undies; frightening firm, you see. One man's Mad Max became another man's Bad Slacks. To this day, he's still called Poo-Poo.

As was the case with football-related incidents, the innocent ones would often get the blame. All the bizzies have to do now is spot the Burberry Brigade with England, or the Lacoste trackies at Liverpool and they've usually collared the main culprits. Most of the wise-arses only found out about the Hells Bells security firm at the first home game of the season, as the serious-bracelet-wearers had hit the autobahns and railway tracks as soon as the damage was done. I often wonder if the biker firm were paid in Rolexes or maybe some huge gold bog-chains to use as weapons against any invading Italian Mods.

You never know, maybe they were let off from paying their Alpine parking fines by the ageing Zurich traffic wardens, who themselves carried new identities. They too had once stomped around Europe having Tom-shops off, only difference being, in their robbing days they'd been wearing jackboots and leathers in the name of the Fuhrer. Scousers, meanwhile, wouldn't be seen dead in those jackboots, or follow a leader with a greasy fringe and a Midge Ure muzzy.

One of the craziest things that happened in Zurich over that wild couple of days was when a team of young lads copped for some serious jewellery. It was supposed to have amounted to almost £200,000, a fortune at the time. The lads, who were no big-time robbers and were out for a laugh as much as a few quid, duly put their stolen booty into a left-luggage locker at Zurich train station. On leaving the station, they noticed a couple of small boats bobbing up and down on the river and decided to take one for a spin, so on cue, they start splashing away and making a general nuisance of themselves. In the time it takes to say what a handsome pair of brothers the Nevilles are, they were being pursued by the Zurich Gestapo, and after finally being nabbed and nicked, they were identified as the tom hoisters. The shitty key was found during a search, somewhere around the arsehole area I believe. The stolen booty was recovered and the lads ended up doing a swift three months in a Swiss slammer, where apparently the scoff was so crap that they all came out looking like Steptoe in that episode where he stripped off and had a wash in the sink.

One of the lads, who truly learned his lesson the hard way, was nabbed robbing a Cornish pasty in Lime Street Station on his way to an away game only a year or so later. From £200,000 Rolex heists to 20p burn-yer-lip pasties, what a comedown. He jibbed going to the match altogether a short while later; as he said he was fed up with 'daft nickings'. A lot of fellas who went on to bigger crime, or bigger business, cut their first teeth at these Liverpool pre-season games, and quite a few of them, after getting collared and cuffed one too many times, decided to kick the match into touch. I, like hundreds of others, never did. The footy was in my blood. What can you do?

Over the years a few things can nag at you, and one of my little nags was the fact that I didn't get a silver fucking sixpence that night. I mean, you only get a few chances in life, and when you're young and skint like I was, it would have been nice to find the odd Rolex watch wrapped up in hamburger paper, lying inside an empty Happy Meal box outside the Zurich McDonald's. Freezing me bollocks off on building sites years later, I would often have that Zurich tom-shop scene popping up inside my brain.

My oul mate Mark Murphy, while singing alongside me in Roma as Michael Owen hit two many years later, told me that the same thing had nagged at him down the years. Apparently what had happened to the young Marko was that, at the time of the pre-season, he had a severe case of acne, and his spotty kipper was giving him the jib with the birds. Topex and Clearasil hadn't worked, shaving two layers of his own skin off hadn't worked, and not eating Mars Bars, chips and greasy food made no difference whatsoever; in fact all it did achieve was that, as a Scouser, he ate absolutely fuck-all, leaving him with loose Levis, as he lost weight, not spots. He said that by the time the pre-season tour came around, he was ready to try anything. It was here where he almost had me, when he explained that before that same FC Zurich game he was going to try and climb to the summit of a local mountain, in order to try an old Swiss remedy that said that by rubbing ice cold snow all over your gob, it froze the bollocks off the pimples, before they eventually all fell off. But Marko knew some other kid who had already tried it and he said all he got was cold cheeks.

It was good to see Marko in Rome more than twenty years later, with skin like a young Elvis and a good few quid in his bin. When I cheekily asked how he'd gotten rid of his beans on toast face, or if growing up had just done the job naturally, he replied, 'Nah, nothing natural about it. D'yer remember when we got back into Europe after the Heysel ban and we played FC Tyrol in Innsbruck. Well I took a ride up that Olympic ski-slope, and that's where I sorted it. Yer see, it was that *Austrian* snow you were supposed to rub in.'

I laughed until me kecks almost fell down.

There were other, more famous jewellery heists by Liverpool supporters at the likes of Uttoxeter, when a train broke down and a huge, bored mob jumped off the train at the quiet Staffordshire racecourse town. There was a raid at Chelsea away, when Liverpool won the league title in 1986, somewhere on Kensington High Street, and also closer to home at Ratners, the Arndale Shopping Centre in Manny before a Man U game. Rogue Liverpool supporters were mainly to blame when a jewellery shop was smashed up near Kings Cross in London on a Saturday morning before an Everton-Tottenham game, although I'm sure a few Evertonians went home modelling a new line in slightly scratched sovereigns that day. All in all though, the majority of tom shop windows went in across the Channel.

People have logged things about Brussels when Liverpool played Juventus in the European Cup final at the Heysel Stadium in 1985; yes, logged things about the terrible disaster that happened that night, but nothing about the jewellery shops that were openly looted that afternoon in Brussels city centre. People like to brush things under the carpet and make out that they didn't happen, till one day some lying nugget comes along and tells people a story that's made up; it's one of the reasons I wrote this book, for posterity and for factual truth, not to glorify, revel in or second guess what 'really' happened.

Take that Nick Hornby fella, for instance. In his *Fever Pitch* book, he goes on about Liverpool fans throwing bananas on the pitch during John Barnes's first game for Liverpool at Arsenal. Next thing is, all hands believe it. Well I was there in that shitty corner of Highbury, right at the front of the fence, on a hot sunny August day at the start of the 1987/88 season: 2–1 to us and no bananas went onto the pitch from our corner of the ground during that game, Mr Know-fuck-all. What really happened was, the Liverpool lads had raided a sex shop down in Soho that morning and three or four huge dildos were thrown onto the pitch at the start of the game. The same used to happen at Coventry every year, where a sex shop near Highfield Road would be raided just for the fun of it. I've yet to meet one Liverpool fan who happened to see those opening-day bananas. Opening-day dildos, yes, but I can see where you're coming from: bananas sells books.

We had a big firm of lads in the home end that day and they didn't see any chimp food go on, but then I suppose nobody would throw them from the lovely, non-racist North Bank, would they? Bananas only went onto the pitch at Anfield when John Aldridge threw them back before the derby game, and at Goodison Park in the Cup later on, both times chucked by Evertonians, and I wouldn't say that that was done from a purely racial point of view but probably in a bid to wind up the Liverpool fans; racist to Barnes, maybe, but winding up the

Reds was the main reason. So stick to Arsenal facts, whopper, instead of using us to sell your books.

You get other fellas who go on about the glory of England in Marseille and who's the gamest fighters. Gamest fighters – what's all that shit about? *Newcastle's the hardest, Millwall's the hardest, nah, I think Leeds are the hardest.* Bollocks, bollocks, bollocks. Doesn't it depend on what firm you bump into on the day? I've seen mobs of Chelsea and West Ham giving it serious toes through the street, but then I've had to get on my toes from the same firms, so it all depends on who you bump into, doesn't it?

I remember being at the World Cup in Italia 90 and some loud-arse Cockneys were going on about how wonderful it was to chase twenty margarine-fringed Belgians across the terraces of Bologna's ground, after David Platt scored that late winning volley. I was there, and chasing Belgian hot-dog sellers is laughable, especially when they're wearing kits and scarves. And there's no real glory or joy in chasing twenty Al Pacino lookalikes around Rome as England qualify for another World Cup, even though it's about time those Roman hoolies copped for it. Nor in throwing bottles at the Peter Schmeichel lookalike who has just served you ale all night in Copenhagen. Gamest Fighters, a game you'll find in all good bookshops, but only to be played by the gamest gobshites. The real joy lies in doing something that's original, something that might be hilarious, or something that goes down as legendary. You gang of plazzy hard-cases.

CHAPTER ELEVEN

The Road to Paris

AFTER WINNING THE Big Cup in 1978, we got knocked out early in '79 and '80. It was why I lived by that motto of enjoying it while it lasts. Yer see, we'd already made plans for trips abroad, so once we got knocked out, by first Nottingham 'no strike' Forest and secondly by the brilliant Russians of Dynamo Tbilisi (they throw up a boss team every few years, the oul Russkies), we didn't know what to do with ourselves. Even though a lot of individual Road End firms were constantly hopping abroad anyway, it was always a miles better trip with the footy.

Some of Forest's fans had to pay for our early European exit, so a few of them were lobbed in the Trent that night. It was the mythical 'sploosh' that supposedly awaited every away fan who visited their ground. We had a huge mob of boys for that European Cup game and they dealt out a few firm blows for beating the Reds so early in the competition; a bad result could sometimes do that to you. From a following of 7,000, about 2,000 lads fancied ripping the place up. Hundreds of us went around to the Trent End to see who was going to teach us to swim, but there was no show from them – they were never what you'd call a passionate firm, that Nottingham crowd. They also paid for beating us in the League Cup Final at Old Trafford, when they were given a penalty that was miles outside the box. Liverpool's crew that night went bananas, and I think Forest sensed this because they wouldn't come out of the ground. As rowdy a reception committee as you were likely to see stood outside the gates waiting. Kamikaze crews then launched into the Forest fans, dragging anybody they could get their hands on from the doorways. Here they were walloped. The Liverpool crowd was so incensed that even thirty-five-year-old flagwavers in glasses were fair game. Hot dog stalls were tipped up and buns, sausages and bottles of sauce were thrown into the crowded exits, before being replaced by the heavier ammo of bricks and masonry. Ten minutes after the game, the Manc bizzies had to literally kick them out onto the forecourts. A huge, violent firm then rampaged through the streets of Manny, till hordes of meat wagons eventually restored order. It's funny to think that some of those cockeyed refs have caused more ructions than a top category hooligan.

Continental travel, as in train-boat-train, was our drug of choice and being hooked on Europe then going out early meant football travel withdrawal, which was an absolute killer for us. With the lads going cold turkey, weird trips were organised and different Road End crews could be seen hitting the road for the strangest reasons. With no Liverpool game to follow and the travel bug itching away in our Adidas, a little firm of ours decided to go and watch Dundee United in Belgium at one time. Unprepared for a change in weather, how did we know it was going to be a case of Belgian brass monkeys? Four Scouse Fred Perries with goose-pimpled ball-bags, over to watch Dundee in wintry Belgium, now that is one strange, mad jock of a game to choose for an Aboriginal walkabout. Scouse Aborigines with frozen bollocks meant warm-coat ideas soon kicked in, and this lad called Willie decides he's got to rob a sheepskin coat to keep warm. After disappearing for a short while, Willie re-appears in this Detective McCloud sheepie, the type with the big furry cuffs and massive white collars. Well, we were in tears. He actually thought he looked the bee's knees, but we told him he'd have to cop for a white horse just to finish off the McCloud appearance. We added that, on returning home to his Maaaaaa's, the Animal Rights were sure to come knocking, what with Willie being held responsible for the mass slaughter of 4,000 Flemish lambs? It was pure savagery to slaughter all those innocent fluff-balls just to make the collar for that thing!

That night, Detective Willie McCloud got truly polluted in Dundee's end, as the highly amused Jocks looked on. We were more bemused than amused, when we returned home a day or so later, tired, skint and hungry with a weird Detective on board. And as we parted company in our own taxi cabs at Lime Street Station, this funny question went unanswered, sort of left floating along in the Mersey-air: 'What the fuck did we go there for?' We didn't have a clue why we'd travelled, none of us could fathom out the head-workings of a young Scouse Aborigine. Not even Detective McCloud could work out the riddle. And if you're still about Willie, I was wondering, is it still on the floor in front of the fireplace? Or did you finally knock it out to an Eskimo on one of your seafaring jaunts? Willie was one funny fella, especially in that fur-lined humdinger of a coat.

We travelled to see music groups like UB40 in Belgium and singers like Stevie Wonder in Paris, when the famous soul singer hilariously fell off the stage. I know he's blind but he was laughing himself. We had to be up and running and any excuse would do, but all in all, following the Redmen with thousands of other Scousers was where the real fun was at.

* * *

Though we'd been knocked out of Europe early for two years running, domestically we were still cleaning up. So come the 1980/81 season we were relieved when the Reds strolled past the Finnish part-timers of Oulu and drew the Jock champions of Aberdeen. McCloud's fellow detective, Alex Taggart Ferguson was holding the reigns in the northern Scottish city, and with it being an England v Scotland game, it was billed as usual as the Battle of Britain. And I'm not gonna make a big song and dance about this, but Liverpool fucking hammered them. DOING THE LIB'POOL BOOTWALK, la la la la la la la la la, la la la la la la la, la la la la la la la, DOING THE LIB'POOL BOOTWALK. It's probably the reason why old beans on toast face still hates us.

It was a long, long drive up to Aberdeen but Terry McDermott, that man of perm and sovereigns, who scored class goals galore but pissed on nurses too, scored one of his best ever. It was my favourite goal of all time. As we danced euphorically, we turned to see hundreds of oil-rig Martians staring in disbelief at our appearance. I'm thinking, *I know that look*. Fuck me, it was October 1980 and we'd been dressing this way for more than three years, but the Aberdeen boys were looking at us the same way those Leeds fans had a couple of years before, and by now, even Yorkshire's finest had twigged on. *Fucking hell*, I'm thinking, *it's another land that time forgot*. The red sauce bottles were squeezed across the fence and before they knew what was happening quite a few Anne Robinsons had been added to their numbers. In the return leg, they actually brought a half-decent crew of Scotch cavemen, lots of red hair atop loud, bright sweaters. Even though the tomato sauce stains were long gone they still looked like a load of

Gordon Strachans wearing Ronnie Corbett's cast-off jumpers. They not only got a much-needed lesson in dress sense but their poor oul team also got a lesson in football, as they were tonked 5–0. We never had the heart to go around to their end, even to swap scarves; just kidding, we never wore any. We could have gone round to wish them a safe journey home and all that, but we didn't; a sweet result could sometimes do that to you, straight the ale-house and all that palaver.

Come the semi-final, we were drawn against the champions of the Fatherland in Bayern Munich. It was time to jump on board as the Red Express gathered steam and more clobber on its way into Bavaria. First things first: the opening leg was at Anfield, and it ended in a 0–0 stalemate. The important thing here was what was said next by the Bayern Munich captain, Herr, sorry Hair Paul Breitner, who looked like Rory McGrath; you know the fellas, the ones who when they're shampooing their springy bonces in the bath, end up thinking, *ah fuck it, I'll just shampoo me whole head and face, it's all the same.* Well fluffy face said Liverpool would get walloped in the second leg by the Kaiser's finest, and so the rest of Munich presumed we'd be returning home with nothing more than the usual Adidas bags full of duty free. Whoa, slow down there, you cheeky, pube-headed, Kraut Leo Sayer, what about some clobber, and especially a couple of pairs of those smooth, Bavarian bib 'n' brace cut straight from a reindeer's arse? Now they were bound to look custy with a nice pair of Pod. He had spoken way too soon, and with the fabled German professionalism thrown right out the bierkeller window, we were in with a definite shout. And even when we got there, the hard-faced Munchen travel agents had jumped the gun, as pre-match they were walking around the ground giving out leaflets to the locals, offering travel and directions to Gay Paree for the final. *Hang on*, I'm thinking, *isn't this supposed to be a game of two halves?* Right, let the jousting commence.

On the afternoon before kick-off, one Scouse urchin, walking around the centre of Munich without a penny to his name, happened across a history museum that contained a set of Adolf Hitler's cufflinks. The lad in question told the other Liverpool boys ensconced in the bierkellers of Munchen that he was thinking of having the cufflinks away. Most of the supporters were enjoying the local beer too much to take any notice, so off he went. Apparently old Adolf had been involved in a bit of a ruck in Munchen when he overthrew the Bavarian government while storm-trooping his way to power. It was later called the Munich Beer Hall Putsch and for all we knew they could've been dropped in a pre-war melee inside the boozer we were now in. Who were we to disbelieve? Hitler and his caterpillar tash had emigrated across the border from Austria to Munich in 1913, and he spent most of his time in the Bavarian capital before becoming Der Fuhrer, so if he had dropped a set of cufflinks through the floorboards, there was as good a chance as any that it was here.

An hour or so later, the lad returned with a couple of his mates, cufflinks in hand. He was ready to strike up a deal on the spot; it was name your price time. Others vouched for the lad; he was no 'blowse'. If he said he'd copped for the little Nazi's cuff-fasteners, then that's exactly what they were. Fucking hell! How do you put a price on a piece of Nazi memorabilia like this? Some fellas, whose heads were already half-kettled with Gunter's special brew, refused to believe that the links were genuine. Others, who knew this lad to be a paid up member of Paisley's Panzer Division, couldn't even begin to name a price; fucksake, this was an Annie Road football firm, not Sotheby's auctioneers. In the end no deal was struck and the lad returned to Liverpool with Hitler's cufflinks in his coin pocket. Later that week, he was spotted trying to sell the afore-mentioned items in the boozers of Huyton, but still nobody believed that they could really end up in a Scouser's bin. I don't know what happened to the lad in question or the cufflinks, but I'm quite sure it was a genuine sale. In hard times a desperate salesman will sell for anything, and that's probably the reason why no one would believe him. If he had hung on for a few years, with the emergence of the internet and whatnot, he could've named his price to anyone from a BNP member to an England No-Surrender boy; especially the day after that 5–0 tonking was handed out to the great-grandsons of Adolf's old Gestapo friends. What happened to those cufflinks? I'd love to know.

Sir Robert Paisley decided to give local Toxteth scally Howard Gayle a run-out in the Olympic Stadium against Munich, and what a run-out it was. Nobody can catch them Toxteth kids when they're in the mood to give it toes. Gayle was brilliant, but he had to be subbed late on when it looked like he was about to chin a few Germans who were constantly trying to kick him. He kept his cool long enough to do the damage, whereas somebody like me would've been tempted to boot the fuckers right up the arse in the first fifteen minutes, resulting in man sent off, game lost. Big Ray Kennedy scored a late goal to give us a 1–1 draw, so we were through to the final on the away goals rule. Paul Breitner, alias the Frankfurt foghorn, you opened your big German gob too early; we were on our way to Paris to play Real-Deal-Madrid. *Ain't no stopping us now, we're on the move. Auf Wiedersehen Curly.*

At the end of the game, hundreds of young Road Enders converged on the pitch, and if you watch the old video of the highlights from that game, you can see me and all the other boys as we got on, or tried to get on, to celebrate and congratulate the Reds on their magnificent performance. Some were too drunk and couldn't run, someone was carrying a set of cuff-links he couldn't sell, some were wearing new trainees that got covered in mud, and nobody cared. We were on our way to Paris and we would not be moved.

By the time the next home game came around, one of the main stories from the trip that was getting bandied about the Anfield Road terraces was of one of the Scouse dippers, who had apparently lifted a German businessman's wallet that contained no less than £4000, a tidy tank to a rag-arse footy fan in 1981. The lad in question generously bought plane tickets for his buddies to fly home. Now that's an ideal way to hit Europe, overland for laughs before the game and fast plane home when it's all done and dusted. Mickey the Shyster, a Road End fly-by-night who dreamed of marrying a rich girl, wouldn't have bought plane tickets for the lads; he'd have put up a three-grand deposit against a house in Formby. The other grand he'd have spent down the singles clubs, looking for a fresh-out-of-court, rich divorcee, hard-up head-worker that he was.

* * *

The city was buzzing for the final. Liverpool versus Real Madrid, for the vase and a half they call the European Cup, in Paris. It still sounds sweet. Tickets, as usual, were as few and far between as Shane McGowan's teeth. Our mob didn't worry though; we were off, and no French riot bizzies were gonna keep us locked up on top of the Eiffel Tower with just a pair of fuzzy binoculars between us while the game was in progress. Not a fucking chance, Pierre. It was the same in 1977, in

Rome, and again in 1978 against Bruges at Wembley; the headlines read, 'Don't bother going to the final without a ticket. It will be like Fort Knox to get in.' Yeah, I'd heard that one before. It was obvious it was aimed at the Scouse Bunkers' Elite, but by 1981 we were the jibbers supreme, with a few years' European experience under our belts. We'd see about the Fort Knox bit.

When we got down to the lovely oul White Cliffs, we found out from the tannoy announcement that the boat taking final passengers on board, and just about to leave, was departing for Ostende, not Calais. Being impatient to leave the country, we hopped aboard. Was it impatience that sent us off in the wrong direction, or was it because the authorities would have an eye out for any Scouse boat-bunkers on the French crossings? All I can say is, we didn't care what direction we headed in, as long as we eventually ended up in the town where the Reds were playing. Preferably we would arrive the night before or the morning of the match and, if an unfamiliar path took you there, then so be it; it usually meant you were having fun.

From the moment we finally arrived via Brussels (strange route) in the famous old city of Paris, it was as though somebody had splashed bright red paint all over the shitty brown hovel. Good job it was Scoused-up to death, as the City for Lovers was an ooh-la-la of a shithole. Why is it that when you hear about how good a place is, it hardly ever matches up to the hype? Gay Paree was one big letdown. It was minty, the hotels and streets were minty and it was an absolute minty rip-off as far as a simple glass of lager went. Chic, kerbside cafés selling cups of coffee as dear as ten sausage dinners in our chippy, and for what? To drink minty French lager that tasted like it came from the River Seine, while staring at the miserable passers-by. And if you didn't have ten grand to blow in the fancy boutiques, or you didn't want to visit the art galleries, like the Louvre, with the boring lady painting, see the bell-ringer's house at Notre Dame, or the bigger version of Blackpool Tower, then it was just another messy, over-rated gaff. Liverpool's own Anglican cathedral made Quasimodo's gaff at Notre Dame look like a gangster's house in Southport, and the Eiffel Tower was selling miniature Eiffels at shop base; at least the shop at the base of Blackpool Tower sells chips and candyfloss. The Parisians themselves looked like they were still suffering with a guilt complex for caving in after a couple of Germans threw sausages at them in the Second World War. The hotel I stayed in was in the Gare du Nord Station area, and guess what? Yep, it was absolutely fucking minty.

The day before the game we happened upon a couple of the sights and ended up getting rat-arsed somewhere by the Moulin Rouge. Nicole Kidman and Ewan McGregor went on to make a daft musical about the setting, but we could've made a better film on a much tighter budget and called it *The Reds On Rouge* because the Liverpool boys were coming out with superior lines, much funnier jokes, and were performing drunken jigs that were more in line with the scabby-arsed place. In the meantime, Madrid's supporters must have been getting the paella ready because there wasn't the slightest sniff of a thin Spanish muzzy knocking about in those Parisian streets. Real Madrid's boys? Ultras? Who made that one up? Swansea, who have also been known to wear the all-white, would've had a better mob than Madrid, serious. Oh well, another mob myth bites the dust.

I got back to the hotel about three in the morning and realised that getting some kip was going to be a big problem, seeing as a few Goldi-grocks were already lying in my bed. We had two big scruffy flocks, with five fellas in each. It was a joke.

If you tried to pull your plums out from between your thighs, somebody else would fall out of the bed, so a strict no-movement rule was hastily put in place. After trying the dead body routine for an hour, we finally gave in. *Fuck it, come on let's have a laugh*. At first we started to wake half the crumbling hotel up, then, stupid I know, we started to walk along the foot-wide ledge on the outside of the building. What is this fascination that young fellas have with foreign hotel ledges? We were four floors up, so it was plainly a daft thing to do, but it became even worse when three of us stopped outside this open window. Looking in, we became aware of a strange-looking Frenchman who was busy having a wank – with a toothbrush rammed halfway up his arse! He was tugging away on this puny little French knob that was about the same size as a Lacoste croc. We were in stitches, and even though he clocked that somebody was at the window, he just carried on five-knuckle-shuffling. We knew he was French because he kept making these bizarre 'ooh la la' grunting noises, while the toothbrush was steadily getting jerked in and out. You could just about make out the brush head as the rest disappeared up trap two. It was funny but also disgusting, so I shouted, 'Pack it in, you French beast.' He just carried on with the strange grunting noises, regardless. Tommy, a lad who was with me, went to climb into the room to give him a good kick up the arse, and only when he noticed a leg pushing through the curtains did both he and toothbrush see the light. For the next few years, what with me being impressionable and all that, I thought it was a French-only trick, which they used when the old French loaf wasn't lying about. What is it with all this arrogant 'don't dare touch me' attitude that you see with the likes of Desailly, Petit, Henry, Cantona, and Le Beaut, the baldy ex-Chelsea centre-half? What've they got to be so standoffish about; maybe they're scared of the French toothbrush trick becoming common knowledge? *Bastard, I've just remembered Gerard Houllier's nationality.*

Pissed and knackered, we ended up getting a little shut-eye around seven o'clock in the morning, but even those few hours were interspersed with some loud, nutty farts and snores. I eventually awoke thinking *never again* to the sound of wailing cop cars. As I looked out of the window, the sight that greeted me was surreal. Over the road from the hotel stood twenty Scousers, most of whom I knew. They were screaming up at me, 'Get the fuck out of it, do one now, disappear down the fire escape, anything, just get on one.' In the middle of the road were four cop cars, with a traffic jam full of loud beeping horns. Surrounding the police cars were couches, beds, chairs and all kinds of furniture that'd been thrown from our hotel building. The contents of maybe thirty rooms were lying strewn across the road. Yet our room still looked like the same pit it had always been. *Anyway, questions later – I'm off.* I went up the stairs instead of down, because from the moment I left the room I became aware of the uniformed French fuzz down at the reception as I looked down the gap of the wide spiral staircase. I reached the roof via the fire door and was confronted with two or three other lads standing shakily at the top of this rickety old fire escape ladder, waiting for the first person to make a move. I told one of the lads to throw my bag down when, or if, I reached the bottom. The lad was quaking and looked frightened to death.

'Be careful mate, there's no fucking way I'm going down there.'

'But you'll have to, otherwise you're nicked and you'll miss the final.'

'I don't give a shit. I'd rather be nicked than dead.'

'Thanks for the vote of confidence, sunshine.'

'Nah, I'm terrified of heights, mate, and I'm still pissed from last night; DTs and all that. You'll be alright.'

He was shaking so much I threw my small sports bag down myself. As it hit the alleyway floor, a load of shitty-arsed pigeons flew up and landed on the opposite roof. They were looking over at me as if to say, 'Go on, you nearly killed one of us then, now let's see if you fall.' Even the stinking Paris pigeons had an air of arrogance about them. I began to pretend that I was bunking the train in Lime Street Station, via the old London ladder route. It was time for mind over matter if I wanted to watch the European Cup final and not the cell bars all day. The hard part was getting on the ladder by turning your back to the drop over the building, before trying to gain a footing as you stepped on. Once I was on, I virtually skipped down the seven or eight-storey building; grabbed me bag, didn't shout ta-ra, didn't look back up; and skedaddled off away from the hotel down a stinking Paris jigger that came out somewhere in the middle of the traffic jam. My boys were still standing there, so I quietly sidled up and sat a few yards away on a couch that had probably come from the first floor, judging by how heavy it looked and the decent condition it was in. Everything else was broken or smashed to bits.

Eddie's going, 'He's gonna get nicked, the dickhead.'

I'm thinking, *who're you calling a dickhead?*

And Joey O goes, 'Keep it down, knob-rot. If them bizzies gerron where we're from, we'll all be nicked.'

It was funny looking at them looking for me, but I could see them getting impatient, and like me, when there was any waiting around to be done, they weren't doing it. As their impatience grew, Eddie finally noticed me.

'How long have you been there?'

'Ten, fifteen minutes now.'

'You lying bastard. Come on, we're on one.'

As we walked away from the scene, I said to Joey, 'Never had any of the lads down as hotel wreckers. What happened?'

'Somebody pulled a chandelier down from the hall ceiling, so the manager decided no one was gonna get brekkie. When everyone complained, these strange Turkish-looking fellas came out of the kitchen tooled-up and started to fancy themselves, so it kicked off. Loads of lads went back to the rooms and threw all the furniture out. Serves him right, it was a fucking doss-house.'

'Too right mate. I wouldn't have wanted brekkie from that yard anyway.'

That afternoon the Champs Elysées was ours, the Arc de Triomphe, commemorating Napoleon's victories abroad, was ours, the bottom of the Eiffel Tower was decked in red and white banners, and even though it wasn't as good as Blackpool Tower, it was still ours. As the Liverpool urchins hit the snazzy shops, all I was thinking was, *Real Madrid versus the Reds, wahey, it just keeps getting better*. Later that afternoon we took time out at a bar full of drunken Liverpool supporters, and in between the Gay Paree songs we could hear Stevie Winwood's *Arc of a Diver* album at full tilt. I'm thinking, *the Arc de Triomphe with the Arc of a Diver, this can't be bad*. It was perfect sunny-weather music to head off to the Parc De Princes stadium: football here we come. 'Arc of a diver, effortlessly . . .'

The Madrid fans had been non-existent the night before, and on the day they were a big let-down. No noise, no numbers and no sharp Spanish scallies. The only supporters they did have seemed to be old fellas who'd just woken up from their siestas in white bowler hats. They were busy hanging onto their tickets for dear life as young Scouse snatch mobs tried to cajole them into showing those priceless little pieces of paper. Small gangs of lads were approaching the Madrid fans, asking for directions and insisting that they point things out from the face of the ticket. It was only a ruse so it could be snatched the moment it hit fresh air. By the way, to all the healthy-lifestyle experts, wrong again, it was never the fish diet that made these Mediterranean boys live longer than us, it was the fact that over an average lifespan, they slept ten years longer. While the Liverpool supporters were singing and dancing in the streets, the Madrid fans were still half-asleep. Want to live to be a 100? Have a siesta. Take Terry Daly, alias Terry Ten-Franc, a great Liverpudlian who has sailed everywhere on the good ship rag-arse while all the time looking a whole lot younger than his real age. This fella knows exactly what I'm on about. Terry Ten-Franc has slept right through jail sentences, whole European trips, and might be the only heterosexual man alive who could be trusted to sleep through an Anglo-American lesbian porn-film starring Britney Spears and Kelly Brook. Even though Terry is well into his forties, he's had at least a good ten years knocked off for sleepy behaviour.

Outside the Parisian stadium, you had a sharp contrast: old Spanish guys dressed in black (who live till they're 100) over-whelmed by young Liverpool guys dressed in tee-shirts and jeans (who'll still be wearing that same gear if they're lucky enough to reach seventy-five). Some of those Spanish oul fellas probably tasted their first little bit of ticker strain in Paris that day, courtesy of the young Liverpudlians who wanted their tickets. I suppose with suffering the Paris-palpitations, they'll be the Madrid fans who only live till they are eighty-five. As the different crews of LFC boys ran about looking for that precious little piece of paper, I looked at the mainly elderly

Spaniards and hoped that the Real Madrid players started the match in the same sleepy manner as their fans had the day.

As kick-off approached, hundreds of ticketless lads were trying all kinds of tricks to gain entry and, following a brief spurt of bunking activity, the French riot plod were finally called in. Hundreds of them arrived by the wagonload before filing into order. Once they were given the signal, their mass ranks charged at the Liverpool fans, but no one moved. They advanced a little further, under the orders of their big-nosed captain, who had a loudhailer not much bigger than his beak. Again, no one moved. The police, dressed like that Darth Vader fella from *Star Wars*, stopped about twenty yards in front of the ticketless Reds. They stared, we stared, it was a Mexican stand-off. Then the fans' command was given, and it went like this: 'GET THEEEM!' Weird, for police who looked so imposing, standing there in those black, shoulder-padded rig-outs, carrying heavy batons and wearing huge crash helmets, they sure took a powder quickly. Some of the retreating riot police dropped shields and sticks in the melee and young scallies were soon waving them high in the air. Next, two drunken lads walked by laughing through the visors of the black crash helmets they were wearing.

While the riot cops were running away, some lads saw their chance amid the commotion and took it, piercing through the security line of stewards and zooming directly through the main gate and into the stadium. I was one of those chancers, and I was in. The organisers would've shown a lot more insight by employing a load of those *Big Issue* sellers from outside any W.H.Smiths, as there is absolutely no fucking way you can get past them.

I ended up in the so-called Madrid end, which was virtually another Liverpool end. I thought about getting down to the supposedly red side of the ground, to try to find me mates, but just before kick-off the Liverpool supporters started singing 'You'll Never Walk Alone' and almost all of the Real Madrid end was drenched in red, so I decided to stay put. The game, as European Cup finals often are, was shizer, but when Alan Kennedy buried the ball in the back of the onion bag, nobody gave a shit about the state of play, and the stadium almost collapsed with the noise as we sang the Redmen home. It was another glorious night and Paris was duly soaked in Scouse. Could things get any better? Well, with this team you just never knew. *Make the most of it while it lasts, keep with the motto, let the dancing commence.*

For the life of me, I cannot remember anything about the night after that match, where I went, where I slept, nothing. It's a shame really, but it's just one big blank. The next day I returned home with my head hanging out of the window from Paris to Calais, before finding my usual top-deck spec to try to take it all in. Liverpool 1, Real Madrid 0. For the third time in five years we were the Champions of Europe. The red flags were blowing in the cross-Channel breeze, the supporters were euphoric and I was top deck, happy as Larry. No boat shenanigans today. Peace on earth to all good boats and all who sail in them. A good result could sometimes make you feel that way.

CHAPTER TWELVE

Earners, Learners and
Tin-Foil Burners

MICKEY THE SHYSTER was an original and anyone who knew him, whether they liked or disliked him, could tell you a story about Mickey. He was an early Annie Roader who grafted and connived his way around Europe, but the head-working characteristic that made him stand out from other young Scouse terriers was the fact that everywhere he went with LFC, whether it was a league game or a European away tie, he would be constantly on the lookout for a lifetime meal ticket, in other words, a wife who was loaded. Yer see, Mickey had been chucked by his childhood sweetheart, who left him for a fella who had better clobber than him, a bigger wad than him and happened to look like a young Robert Redford, only he lived in a mansion up in Formby – and I mean, how the fuck do you compete with that? It left a big dint in Mickey-boy's brain and someone was going to have to pay.

Mickey became so cynical about the ladies, boring us with his woeful tales of all the money he used to spend on Julie. Well now it was this twenty-one-year-old's time for revenge, and the women of Europe were all fair game. Mickey, it seemed, was determined to pluck his own little gold-ringed pheasant from the sky. With his incessant banter and charm, he set about looking for his own slice of Formby at Oulou Palloseura of Finland, in the first European away-tie of the 1981/82 season. We'd been drawn against the same team the year before, in another early round, on the way to winning the BIG cup in Paris, and as usual we were all up for the long Viking expedition. Today it's a one or two-hour plane journey, instead of the massive trek through Northern Europe that we made. It was such a long trip that a 100 or so lads decided to stop at Hamburg on the way over, for the Beatles history and the pull of the Reeperbahn, or getting pulled off in the Reeperbahn, however you want to put it.

First night, one of the lads who was badly gassed took himself inside the door of one of these Hamburg fanny frauleins but was 'too drunk to fuck', so the cat-o-nine-tails was jokingly applied to his red arse. The stinging effect caused him to puke up all over Madame Bratwurst's bed, so with the carrots from Monday's pan of Scouse all over the mattress, he'd well and truly fucked up her business for the night. He soon sobered up though, as she applied the whip to the area around his half-pulled-up Lois jeans, then his face, then anywhere else she or any of her newly informed, baggy-fannied sisters could land a blow. They attacked him brass-en-masse as he tried to give it toes up the Reeperbahn.

These things became par for the course when you took to the road, and while other supporters were going to places like Bury in the League Cup, our firm was traipsing round Europe with their kecks hanging down singing 'Walk On'. And if you think Scousers are always trying to be different, well you're fucking right we are mate; fact is, you end up with a whole different mentality when you spend a large chunk of your early life meandering round Europe, instead of forging out to buzz-

a-minute places like Walsall and Oldham for some daft
Kentucky Fried Cup. You know the ones; you've all been in
them.

Mickey, meanwhile, had confided in me on the long rail-
ferry-rail journey over that Finland was full of blonde
bombshells with skin as smooth as snow, and everywhere that
Mickey went that . . . sorry, you see once Mickey got on your
case, you believed, or wanted to believe, anything he said. So if
the fellas were having it, what chance did the ladies stand of
resisting his gift of the gab? Mickey was the gabber supreme;
sneak thieves would often use him to blag shop assistants while
they rifled the till, the storeroom or the displays. Yet all he was
after was a woman who would shower him with a load of
dough, and the more she had stamped on her meal ticket, the
merrier. He reckoned women were always having the kecks off
fellas, but once he fished around Europe and caught his own
little golden trout, then he was gonna give them a taste of their
own medicine.

'Europe's where I'll find one,' he'd say, and then add, 'Those
Scouse birds aren't the answer. All dollies who are too wise for
their own good.'

Cockney birds? 'Nah, they're all sharks, only looking for a
Porsche or Merc macho man.'

Manc birds? 'Nah, all rag-arses like us.'

Geordie birds? 'Can't understand a fucking word they're
saying.'

Nice Irish colleen? 'Fuck that, take you two years to get
your bare-tit.'

Nice Scottish lassie? 'Fuck that, they're more penniless than
us.'

Brummie babe? 'You'd never get a hard-on with that accent.'

And so on. He had an opinion on the whole range of ladies

he might meet, and with him nurturing solid gold dreams, Liverpool being drawn against Monte Carlo Rovers or Dubai Bromwich Albion meant he'd get the chance to visit the rich divorcee clubs of those places the night before the match. With the Finland trip complete, he'd returned home with some Lapland dosh, a few trinkets, but no fair-skinned beauty in tow.

Next up was AZ 67 Alkmaar of Holland. The stadium at the small coastal town was too small, so the first leg was moved to Ajax of Amsterdam. As the game approached, the lads talked about whether or not we'd get through easily, and whether or not Amsterdam was up for any earners. All Mickey went on about was finding a nice brothel-owning madam who would be only too happy to wrap him up in Dutch guilders for life. As far as satisfying any Dutch dubber's sexual needs was concerned, he'd have had to wrap about a million dollars around his little todger before it even touched the sides. If he tried to make a Pamela Anderson, Tommy T-Bone-style video, called *Mickey Meets the Madame*, it would go down as the cheapest skin-flick ever made. All the director would have to do was film himself throwing a jelly-bean into a bucket a few times; hence, it's a wrap. How do I know? Well I saw drop his kecks around the bars of Europe enough times and put it this way, he was never gonna be Big Mickey in the Y-front department. He was dreaming big-time if he thought any brothel-owning brass would become his meal-ticket to the high life. They always were top head-workers, those fanny foremen.

We set off overland on trains to Harwich and then boats to the Hook of Holland; all were duly bunked in the normal quiet, efficient manner. On arriving in Amsterdam, the young Road Enders were surprised to see that the place was almost as security conscious as Liverpool and that even the Mars Bars and Wrigleys had security tags on. The crew rapidly organised and decided to do what they had done in Paris before the European Cup Final against Madrid, when they had literally run through the streets hoisting gear. Against such numbers, the shop staff were helpless. Lads were soon darting in and out of the finer clothing establishments, even though it was only nine o'clock in the morning. Before half an hour was up, half of the sixty or seventy lads were nicked – and as Amsterdam's street police began to round up the raiding party, it finally sank in that the Dutch dibble were definitely not wearing clogs as part of their uniform. In the meantime, Mickey-boy had given up on bumping into Madam Meal Ticket and had found a lovely little Scouse bird travelling around with her mates. She had all the right credentials and came from Liverpool's very own land of BMWs, Mercs and posh dosh: Formby.

That night, the match was stopped for five or ten minutes as Liverpool led 2–0. The whole of Ajax's stadium had sold out, but due to heavy rain and an announcement that the match would be televised, hardly any clog-wearers turned up. There was a small crowd scattered about the terraces, and with a number of baldy Ajax hooligans mobbed up and spread around different parts of the ground, fights started to break out all over the place. Next thing, this tidy Liverpool firm that had gone into the home end started to chase the Dutch mob onto the pitch. Souness, Dalglish and Co. stared impatiently as the battle raged on. I was clocking this huge Dutch skinhead, and as I weighed up what to do with the baldy Japp Stam lookalike already starting to glare back at me, a huge whisky bottle smashed over his head and a little scally who was almost the same size as the bottle did a runner before he bumped into any foreign cops. The Ajax bonehead fell in a heap and that seemed to be the green light for the rest of the lads. One moment things were looking friendly as Dutch skinheads mingled in with the scallies, the next it was going off big-time and the baldies were getting head-butted, punched and bottled to the ground. The fella who'd been clocking me was knocked flat out on the terrace steps with blood streaming from his temple. The toe of an Adidas training shoe volleyed his shaven head like it was a caseball lying on the penalty spot. Two-nil and he was out of it.

As the brawling continued on the terraces, the Road End firm on the pitch legged the mob they were fighting with right up into our battlezone, so suddenly there was no way out. The empty spaces on the terracing allowed the fight to continue unabated; it was skinheads onto scallies with the skins getting pummelled. By the time order was restored four or five minutes later (quite a duration for an in-stadium scrap), boots and braces had been dragged all over the steps, the Dutch skins had been walloped and the game had recommenced. AZ 67 swiftly scored two goals and the game finished 2–2. Souness, he of the perm, muzzy and *Sun* articles, said in the papers a few days later that the fans were to blame, causing the players to lose concentration during the riot. Because we were winning 2–0, I think Souey had started combing his Yosser Hughes-type muzzy on the halfway line. Let's face it, even though he was one of the greatest midfielders of all time, he always did fancy himself as Champagne Charlie.

Mickey had a couple of days swanning around the Dam, playing the lovable charmer with his new Formby filly in tow while the rest of us got on with our usual European doo-dahs. Six months later, things were not looking too good for our Michael when his girl started to realise she was being used by the philandering shyster. Liverpool, it seemed, were going to win the league once again, so off on our travels we go. Poor

Mickey, who was trying to impress the little rich girl, returned from a 3–2 defeat at Southampton in a luxurious, but stolen, car. It was an old Road End trick to come home from an away game in a nice shiny motor. You'd see documentaries at the time about how bad Liverpool was for car thieves, and other places would gloat over it. Now the roles are reversed and car robbers are like a rash all over these so-called nice towns. Anyway, it was people like Michael who were to blame for rising car insurance, and here he was in April 1982, pushing up the premiums while trying to look the part in this souped-up Capri. The fly-by-night wanted this Lisa lady to be by his side during the time of celebrations, as the title was about to be lifted for the umpteenth time. After a few skirmishes, however, she finally dumped him for good. Her wisearse builder dad had also warned her off after a three-second conversation and a two-second look at Mickey.

Now Mickey, being the conman lover-boy that he is, tries desperately to woo his green-backed goddess back, to no avail. After a week or two of lonely, money-less contemplation, Mickey drives his snazzy Capri to a busy shopping street in Bootle and crashes into a wall. The driver's door flies open and the Shyster hangs out of the car and half on the floor. People run to help. An old lady tries to comfort him as he struggles to hand over a photograph he is clutching in his hand.

'Is this your girl then?' asks the lady. 'Ah, poor lad.'

Mickey, who looks like he's dying, says, 'Don't let them move me till she turns up. Please, please phone her, she only works down the road in the Girobank, her number's on the back.'

'Of course I will love, you hang on.'

The old lady goes to the phone and calls this Lisa. She pleads to her on his behalf: please hurry; get down to the sad scene a.s.a.p. Lisa gives the old lady a few knockbacks until finally she relents; she's on her way. Meanwhile, a large crowd has gathered around and an ambulance appears.

'Don't let them move me till Lisa arrives,' wails Mickey.

The old lady, with some other romantically inclined old ladies, tell the ambulance men, 'She'll be here in a mo', listen to his plea.'

The crowd is growing by the minute as people jostle to get a blimp of the dying man. The ambulance crew see that things need to move on, so they go to lift Mickey, who cries out that he won't be moved till his loved one appears. The romantic old ladies tell the ambulance guys to have a heart and let him be till his beloved arrives.

Finally Lisa appears and starts to push her way through to the front. The old ladies and other bystanders start to make way, telling the hospital boys, 'See, see, she's here, now let them speak.'

Mickey by now looks as though he's about to pop his clogs. He looks up from the floor and goes, 'Lisa, Lisa, I knew you'd come.'

The ladies sigh and watch in loving anticipation of their moment of embrace. Lisa looks down at him. He looks up. Nothing happens. So Mickey pleads, 'Lisa, Lisa, what is it?'

'I know your little conman games.'

'What, what d'you mean?'

'It's you, yer phoney bastard,' and she kicks him full in the head. People gasp in amazement, while others whisper about what could make the young girl so heartless and cruel.

'Lisa, Lisa.'

She volleys him again, this time in the stomach, and says, 'Get up off the floor, you phoney little shit.'

'But Lisa, I'm done in, help me.'

She kicks him again, so somebody in the crowd goes to

restrain her. She takes a good look at the surrounding people and the man holding onto her arm, and mutters, 'Youse haven't got a frigging clue,' and stalks off through the crowd.

Mickey wails in anguish, 'Lisa, Lisa, come back Lisa.'

On cue, Mickey-boy realises that she's not coming back and that it's over. He jumps to his feet, pushes his way through the ambulance men and the crowd and once he blimps daylight, performs his own impression of the roadrunner by steaming off into the distance.

Mickey was always off on his own tangent, and was still edgy and jumpy when I bumped into him twenty years later in Barcelona for a UEFA Cup tie. As we sat down for a bevvy near that Christopher Columbus statue at the bottom of La Ramblas, he told me he'd eventually found the woman of his dreams or, as I put it to him, his 'chick with the change'. He laughed and went on to tell me that he'd finally married this dreamy lady, they'd happily raised a couple of bin-lids and now lived in Portugal with all the escudos he'd ever wished for. He was rat-arsed later that night, after the Reds got a good result, and confided in me that he was minted.

'I always knew you would be,' I said. 'You always wanted it bad enough. But fuck the money, are you really happy? That's the main thing. Dosh means sweet FA if it doesn't put a smile on yer face each morning.'

And he said, 'Nah, it's shit really. Those rich tarts can't make a roast dinner like your ma. And the oul days, when we first started wearing the gear in the Annie Road End and all that, that's when you're really happy.'

I was thinking, *you've got a point about the old days, but yer talking shite reminiscing about the roast dinners and back home*. I told him this in a roundabout way but he wasn't having it. Speaking personally, I'd rather have me swimming cozzy full of escudos than a Stanley Park Sunday dinner. I knew where he was coming from, but I mean, that's the problem with a lot of fellas who make a decent life: they just don't know when they've won.

* * *

With the lads now addicted to European travel, and always ready for a fix, a lot of them carried on from Paris to Basle to see the World Cup qualifier between England and Switzerland. Stabbings and battles kicked off during that game as I watched it at home on telly. Even though I've been to a few World Cup tournaments, I was never one for pushing the boat out to see England, as I was always too absorbed in following Liverpool, who were busy clocking up a whole load more cup-winning mileage than any national team.

After beating AZ Alkmaar of Holland during Mickey the Shyster's 1981/82 season, Liverpool got knocked out of the European Cup by CSKA Sofia, whom we'd beaten on the way to winning the trophy the year before. Only a few hundred made the trip to Communist Bulgaria, as the last time we'd played them lads had returned with stories of widespread poverty and people who wore the same undies and vests for six months. The city had some nicer parts, but the shops were like Greaty Market in Liverpool on a Saturday; in other words, they sold Marks and Spencer seconds, like trousers with one leg shorter than the other, which was alright if your name was Long John Toshack, and scruffy, baggy pants for fellas with ball bags like two basketballs lodged in a fisherman's net. Shirts, coats and foodstuff were from trenches in the First World War, along with toiletries like 'tracing paper' bog rolls that tore your hoop to shreds. *Best sit that one out*, I reckoned.

Apparently, the Greek Orthodox Church near the ground nearly had its roof stolen when a crew of lads climbed to the top after finding out that it was made of gold. The Bulgarian bizzies chased the rag-arse roof rogues back down the ladder and rope, but only after the lads were spotted trying to pull chunks away from the eaves. Now you tell me, how do you get parts of a gold roof back through Customs? Whatever the answer, it was all in vain: we were out. It was the champions-only cup then, so you only played against the best team from each country, and one off-day and you were back home with the 'no passport needed' crew. Not like today's farcical Euro and Pound-note Cup – the new money-oriented tournament with five or six off-days for the winner and a whole pot of dosh guaranteed whether you win, lose or draw (still love to win by the way).

After we got knocked out that season, Aston Villa went on to win it with half a team of Scousers wearing the claret and blue. Loads of Liverpool boys went over for the final just to keep up with our May tradition. It's something you wouldn't see nowadays, and it happened again when Arsenal were beaten on pens by Valencia in the Cup Winners Cup final, when gorgeous Graeme Rix missed the vital spot-kick for the Gunners in that shitty crumbling stadium they called Heysel. So quite a few Liverpudlians had already been to the Brussels dump way before the fateful trip of 1985. More than anything, we loved a football adventure, and loads of the boys also went over to Tokyo in December for the World Club Championship, where Liverpool lost to the South American Flamengo team (it was those pink long legs that did the damage). It wrecked my head that I couldn't get the dough together to go over to Japan, and I didn't fancy trying to bunk the plane that far, as they were always the hardest mode of transport to jib. Don't get me wrong, we managed to do it quite a few times later on, but only when 2–300 supporters were all together on the one plane. Jibbing the plane was not as hard as you may think, as often the airport officials would march the supporters straight onto the plane, especially if they were acting rowdy or getting out of control. Realising this, some Road End boys would openly cause a disturbance to enable their ticketless and often passportless mates to board unhindered. Once the stewardess would walk through the plane for the passenger count, the stowaways would be hidden away under their friends' legs, seats or carry-on bags.

By the time Mickey had been chucked again, Pope John Paul II had paid a visit to Liverpool after we'd beaten Tottenham 3–1 at home to secure the 1982 First Division Championship. Tottenham had also been beaten 3–1 at Wembley to secure the League Cup, and during the Pope's visit on a warm sunny afternoon in May things couldn't have been much better as we already looked forward to next season. The fixtures would only be over two weeks and I'd be twiddling my thumbs wondering what to do with myself.

A lot of the original Annie Road boys had caught a ruthless travel bug, so if the Reds weren't playing away, some other team or sporting event would do. Hundreds decided to go to the Spain World Cup in 1982, not long after the Pope's visit, and a large contingent travelled to Mexico in 1986, after Liverpool had just completed their first Double, wearing tee-shirts that read 'D.H.S.S. Scousers on Tour'. It made headline news back in Blighty and they ended up all over the daily newspapers, with people taking offence at the fact that here was a bunch of freeloaders using state benefits to get to the beaches of Acapulco. It doesn't take a genius to realise that there's no way you can get to South America, when plane fares were relatively a lot higher than now, on breadline unemployment handouts. Some knobheads will believe anything they read in the *Daily Full of Shites*.

With all this travelling and trophy-lifting almost assured, we predictably became a little blasé about games like Fulham away in the League Cup, or Norwich away in the League. I know it sounds big-headed, but one of the trappings of success is that, as a fan, you can start to take these smaller games for granted. Now if the players start to do likewise, it's the surefire slippery slope to Doomsville. It tends to go a bit like this: players blasé in certain games – big-name signings to try to change things around – big wages – big contracts – lazy, fat-cat players – poor results – lower crowds – slippery slope – Second Division. It happened to Derby County with the daft, ram-brained directors hiring John Gregory to reverse the trend. Now that's what you call jumping from the fat into the fire, useless twat of a manager that he is. He's long been sacked, but he was always going to be more interested in dying his hair, making a few quid, then spending it on more hair dye and more Bruce Springsteen albums, than of ever grafting his bollocks off to turn things round. Next thing, he's getting backed for another top job by super-agent Pini Zahavi – once the investigations into transfer irregularities are over. There you have it, super-fucking-agent, that's the name of the game for today's top blaggers. With his football knowledge, his signings and his hair dye, you might as well hire someone who was 'Born In The USA', and if you really wanted to bring back the 'Glory Days' then hiring him was like 'Dancing in the Dark', because here was a fella who always wore a 'Brilliant Disguise'.

Still, the fact that Liverpool relentlessly beat teams year in, year out, was a fantastic achievement in itself, never mind the trophies and medals that accompanied those victories. And while this was going on, hundreds of lads like myself were hanging onto the rails of this football rollercoaster and were determined to see the whole ride through, no matter what the cost, job-wise, personal life-wise and no matter what damage occurred along on the way.

A couple of crews from Huyton and Kirkby had discovered their own fruity little way of hanging onto the rails and of making things pay in the process. These lads took to unloading the money from slot, sweet and drink machines all over the country. The fruit machines, which carried the most money, were the main target. Emptying them involved a trick where you blew a straw full of liquid into the coin slot and held in the button until it eventually caused a continuous jackpot. The machine manufacturers have put a stop to it now with new technology, but at the time it was jackpot heaven to coin a phrase, every time the Reds played away.

These fellas started going away tooled up in a van. Once the machines were emptied, the large bags of coins had to be transported back to home base, but only after the Ten-Bob Gang had been to the match. One of the machine crews took things a little further when they began to carry off some of the fancier machines and take them home after the match. I wish they could've got me one of those Space Invader machines when I was younger, that would have saved me a right few quid I can tell you. They would set off to an away game before parking where an establishment housed a number of coin-operated machines. When the game was finished, they'd wait for the right moment before unplugging the 'electric cash boxes', cutting any security chains with bolt cutters and loading the booty into the van. Back in Scouseland, a deal would be struck with a bent pub manager or owner, who would site a machine on his premises, wait for the customers to fill it with silver, then split the proceeds fifty-fifty with the Ten-Bob Gang. No ground rent, no machine rent and no overheads; it cut out the middleman big-time. I believe that the lads involved got so good at learning the different machine mechanisms that they even offered their own quick service back-up system to any customers having a little mechanical difficulty with their newly sited machine. It was a sort of Scouse lifetime guarantee with no monthly instalments.

Monkeying around with machines reared its head years later when Liverpool played Carlisle in the third round of the FA Cup, on the way to beating Everton, yet again, in the 1989 final. On the way up to Carlisle, a few cars sidetracked to the Lake District and hunted down quiz machines located in boozers. The lads went in and out of local pubs, steadily clearing out the appliances in a legitimate way, because for some reason, most of the machines were still spewing out the old questions that had appeared in the Liverpool boozers an age ago. It wasn't a big earner, but it was a funny one. And some of the lads found that they enjoyed answering the questions and emptying the machines so much that they decided to stay in the Lake District getting tanked-up all day. A lot of Liverpool's rogue gangs would have 'sod the football' days out if earners were looking up. I'm sure the company involved changed its machine programming soon after, just so it could never happen again.

Other firms of scallies noticed the huge market in selling club colours outside stadiums and hopped aboard the merchandise bus. They originally jumped on board, with one Kirkby firm in particular at the fore, when Liverpool played Crystal Palace at Selhurst Park, in the 1979/80 season. Up until then, it was mainly businessmen from the South who sold the colours outside the Liverpool games, but things were about to change. Marty was up to his old tricks as he sprayed the Palace singing mob with tomato sauce from the seats above, but the thing that surprised me was seeing all the Road End boys sporting Liverpool colours. Now usually you wouldn't find a tatty scarf between them, but they had scarves, hats and even the odd banner in tow, which looked funny at a normal league game. On approaching some of the lads, I'm thinking, *maybe they're all bladdered,* but close-up I realised they were all all perky as Kylie's tush, which was the norm for the Annie Road wide-awake club.

'What's with all the scarves and hats?'

Seven or eight of them proceeded to tell me that they'd 'had the scarf sellers off' outside the ground, and they were going to 'have them off' every week until they finally stopped coming to Liverpool games and stuck to London or southern teams only. It was a parochial, insular way to think, that only Scousers should be selling to other Scousers, but there you go, that's where those lads were at. It was an extension of the tout-bashing or spiv-walloping that Liverpool fans had always been noted for. For donkey's years, any tout spotted near a big Liverpool game, especially at Wembley, would receive a severe hiding. Today touting has become an acceptable way of earning a few quid, and to a large extent has been hi-jacked by some of those same scallies at Crystal Palace twenty-odd years ago. Once that group of young lads realised that mixing business with pleasure was an excellent way of earning a crust, then people like Fat Stan Flashman were no longer going to have the sole franchise rights in the touting game. It was a natural progression to think, *if you love and follow the footy, why not make money at it?*

From that day forward, you started to see a lot of young scarf sellers coming onto the scene, and the shout of, 'Hats, caps, scarves or a badge' became synonymous with the Liverpool merchandise grafters who work outside the ground to this day. Anybody who goes to Anfield on a regular basis knows that shout, and Anfield wouldn't be the same without it. I often wonder if those same Liverpool scarf grafters are aware of the footings that were dug by the young Annie Road boys that day at Palace and over the following few weeks. The fervour fellas must have made a right bag of bunce on those half-Liverpool, half-Celtic bobble-hats alone, and good luck to them, but before they buy a bobble-hat castle in Spain, just remember who paved the way for them to ride up to the ground with a horse and cart full of colours, to shout, 'Hats, caps, scarves or a badge.'

It was a natural progression for some Liverpool supporters to become ticket touts (spivs), travel arrangers, alcohol and tobacco sellers, arse slashers, moochers and the above mentioned merchandise grafters. I also have no doubt that travelling abroad with Liverpool brought some people into contact with drugs a lot earlier than most, especially in places like Amsterdam. That was a side to the football thing that I'm honest enough to say I didn't like, as most of the real grief I've seen in life has been drug associated, but there you go. Liverpool may well be the drug capital of Britain, outside of or even including London, but it's something I've never used or abused. People make their own choices on these things don't they?

I've seen a lot of young, smart-looking, charismatic kids standing among the Annie Road End crowd during the late Seventies, then bumped into a few of those same lads ten or fifteen years later to sadly find them to be hooked on 'the brown', barely alive, grief-ridden and characterless. Instead of looking smart, they now resembled an empty tube of toothpaste, squeezed dry, toothless and fucked-up. When I think of real grief, it makes me think of smackheads tearing their families and communities apart; mothers racked with remorse as their 'little Joey' burgles yet another friendly neighbour's house; and the slow ride to death that the bagheads jumped on, as their fathers and mothers paid the full fare over and over again. I know of seven lads who were part of that original Road End crew who have since died through drugs-related incidents.

A huge slogan painted across a Liverpool wall in the Eighties read, 'Thatcher's answer to unemployment – Cheap Smack.' Whether it was true or not, we all read into things in our own way, and when I first saw that neat bit of graffiti, I instantly thought, *right, those Tory bastards are not having me.*

Considering all those people and their stories, the one that left the biggest imprint on me began while I was still young, on a patch of grass we called Little Wembley, not far from our house. It was the summer of 1974 and Liverpool had recently walloped Newcastle 3–0 in the FA Cup final. We had just made our homemade flag on a living room floor inside a mate's house, and the Liverpool FC slogan we'd spray-painted in red onto a white bed sheet had seeped right through the thin cotton. *Shit*, now it read Liverpool FC on his ma's new carpet. We were in big trouble and once the turps didn't work we decided that the best thing for it was to scarper for a game of footy.

There we were, playing on the school field at the back of our house, with the sun shining down gloriously – didn't it always? – with me busy doing my Kevin Keegan impressions. As I dribbled and swerved, a young kid about nine years of age walked onto the field. His fantastic smile instantly made everybody feel happy. His nickname was Bambi and he was the youngest brother of my Evertonian mate Dean, who'd just gone in goal because he wasn't that good at being Bob Latchford. This little sparkly-eyed kid walked straight onto the pitch, making everyone within range automatically light up; you know the kind, the kid with the smiler's smile who everyone's happy to see. He was a little uncut diamond, with those big oval *Thunderbirds* eyes.

Five years later, I'm standing in a bar in town doing my best Bryan Ferry impression. Young Scousers all around are looking sharp and most are clobbered-up to the nines. This lad called Cardo from Walton walks in. He's a year or two older than me, with a wicked rebellious streak, proven by the fact that as people like myself are 'trying' to act cool, this fella walks in with his hair dyed bright green, in full punk rig-out, chains, boots, the lot. Now this takes balls: we're talking about a place that is chock full of so-called smoothies, pretend cool-arse, scallywag lads and laddesses, plus quite a few plazzy-gangsters giving it their best hard-case walk on the way to the bar – you know the type, walking like a carpet carrier with a roll under each arm, and acting like they've got chewy in their gobs when they haven't. But Cardo is about as *really* cool as you're ever going to get, having the bottle to walk into this kind of yard wearing that kind of get-up. It was a memorably different thing to do.

Five or six years further down the line and I'm working in London. Me and my mates bump into Cardo and Bambi on Oxford Street, near to Oxford Circus tube station. Greetings and pleasantries are quickly exchanged, but the diamond sparkly-eyes and the hint of rebellion have gone. As they spoke, no real eye contact was made. Sparkly-eyes looked tired and jaded and the hint of rebellion had turned into a hint of menace, as both sought out their next earner on the road to nowhere. Cardo summed up the downbeat meeting when he said, 'Only one wish left. Just get me to Pakistan, give me the pure gear and let me blow meself away.'

It was a real eye-opener for somebody like me at the time, because early to mid-Eighties I was quite drug-naïve. I never was from that day forward. If anything good came from what he said that day, it was the fact that me and my buddies fully clicked just how miserable drugs and the drug life really are. I dislike everything to do with it, and always will. The two kids in question are no longer with us; my condolences go out to their families, because for a brief moment in time, if it means anything at all, I saw those kids shine.

* * *

At the same time that Liverpool's young Road End rogues had decided that no out-of-towners were going to sell *their* club's colours outside the game, another bunch of head-workers arrived on the scene. These were the opportunist thieves, the Johnny-on-the-Spot robbers. One of the first times this crew showed up was for an end of season game at Ayrsome Trouble, Middlesbrough. One of the main lads in this crew was called Marty, and this kid basically couldn't keep still, so if boredom set in then everyone was getting it, usually with the fire extinguishers, his favourite party piece.

Liverpool always seemed to end the season with a night game at Boro, usually with the championship, yet again, in Bob Paisley's red Gola bag. Once this game had finished, about 200 Road End boys got together in the open corner of Ayresome Park, then slowly walked all the way back through that dodgy shopping precinct before landing back at the main station. Once all the boys started sticking together, it was never as bad at the Boro, but if you detoured, or headed off in your own direction, those Boro boys with their built-in Scouse radar scanners, were bound to find you. With it being a lot smaller than Liverpool, it was as though they all knew each other, and if your face, clothes or accent didn't fit, you were heading for a Teesside toe-ending. That night though, all the boys were together, and when that happened, we were always custy.

Things had been quiet all evening and an outlet for some fun was needed, but how can you find a laugh in Middlesbrough, let alone Middlesbrough train station, at ten o'clock on a midweek night? The lads badly needed some activity or something funny to happen, just to make the journey more worthwhile; it gave them something to have a natter about when they got home. We were so used to winning the League that some fellas started saying they would rather win the FA Cup, as at least you'd have a few more days out, with a big day in May at the end. I never felt the same and I suppose only another set of supporters whose team has tasted success over a long period of time would know where those lads were coming from.

As the White Man in Hammersmith Palais said, we were only looking for fun, so a few lads left the station to see if there were any Boro boys knocking about, but they must've been tucked up in bed, nude except for a pair of AirWair, flicking through a copy of Middlesbrough's best-selling, weekly wank mag, *Baggy Fannied Boro Babes*. The lads mooched about all over the desolate station, to no avail. A chocolate-vending machine was visited by everyone on the platform before we decided to go for a walk. But the Boro bizzies were having none of it, so we had to dodge our way out. After a spooky walk around the Precinct of Death, with its gorgeous clobber shops, we resigned ourselves to no fun and walked back. Some lads found a boozer and an off licence, so kitties were swiftly paid into before a few boys went for the ale. Six or seven cans were all you needed, and probably all you could afford. Oh gee mom, times were so tough in those days.

Unbeknown to us, the Johnny-on-the-Spot crew had noticed the train being loaded with mailbags, and before the train had even left the buffers, the story doing the rounds through the carriages said that the first men to open those bags would no doubt find jewellery abounding. Rolexes, Longines and other watches of fine repute were apparently being carried aboard the choo-choo, and this travelling crew were determined to not let the consignment reach the shops. It made me think of the fire that had burned through St John's Precinct in Liverpool at the time, when some of the firemen were known to be wearing sovereigns and gold watches only a few weeks later, you know, when the heat was off in more ways than one.

The sacks containing the booty lay at the far end of the train, where the clippy and a mail carriage had to be negotiated before they could be ripped open. It looked like Marty's fire extinguisher trick wouldn't be needed to get the party proceedings underway. Half an hour into the journey and the whole train seemed to know about the treasure on board, and listening up, it seemed like everybody was talking about getting their own little end of season timepiece. Soon enough a Johnny-on-the-spot runner came hurtling through the carriages to tell everyone the coast was clear: the clippy was busy with his crossword and flask, and shouldn't see anybody passing as long as you kept quiet. It was the green light for gold as the rest of the crew set about bringing the mailbags to the safe confines of the scally carriages, where they could be ripped apart in peace.

The first couple of sacks were dragged through the carriages, and judging by the huffing and puffing it looked like they weighed a ton. The draggers reckoned it was a good sign, and the main Mailbag Expert was convinced that the labelling was the same as other jewellery bags he'd recently seen to at a Spurs in London away game. This further fuelled the expectancy of the mob aboard; it was gold fever again. From the boredom on the platform earlier on, the atmosphere was now charged with electricity as people crowded around, gagging to open the sacks and have a dip. The two bags seemed to give way at the same time, and many hands started to rummage around the lucky bags, each lad hoping that he'd be the one to find the most exquisite piece of tomfoolery.

At first some bubble-wrap envelopes appeared, and the Expert said, 'They're the ones boys, bubbled-up for no breakages, this is the tom lads.'

The first well-padded envelope was ripped open.

'Aye aye, what the fuck's this then?'

And as he spoke, he held up, then stretched, a leopard-skin G-string till it almost snapped. Next up came a black leather thong, which was ripped apart by one frustrated lad. Then someone pulled out a red pair of frillies, duly torn to shreds. By now, I was clocking this little fella who had burrowed his way to the front. From the corner of my eye I could see as he dipped deep into the bag before burrowing his way back to a seat. He seemed more than happy with the large brown parcel he was tearing at, so I thought he knew more than he was letting on. He'd had such a good rummage that I thought he'd had more than an average lucky dip. All of a sudden he leapt from the seat holding a basque and shouted, 'Jewellery? Bollocks. This is a knickerbocker package.'

'No,' insisted the on-board Expert, 'I know these mail sacks and these are carrying tom.'

More and more young lads started to pull packages and envelopes from Santa's saucy sacks but nearly all of them contained samples of knickers and bras. Undeterred, a few of the Johnny-on-the-spot crew headed off to the end of the train to retrieve another couple of sacks. The rest of the lads were shouting daft things to send them on their way.

'No more undies please, we don't wear any anyway.'

'Never mind the crotches, bring back the watches.'

Moments later, you could hear a commotion further up the train, and as it got closer people were shouting, 'Make way, make way.' The doors of each carriage were held back and this lad came riding through on a racing bike he'd found and unwrapped. Things were definitely starting to look up, entertainment-wise. The ale started to flow as we toasted his riding prowess. He kept whacking into the tables but showed decent balance as he tried to ride back to the Boro. Next to come through were the returning Johnny-on-the-Spot crew, singing in true Elvis style, 'Return to sender, address unknown, no such undies, are ever coming home.'

Everybody was laughing as the new sacks were ripped open, and as the first packages were torn to shreds, guess what they contained? Yeah, more scanties. The train was starting to resemble an Ann Summers party without the dildos and the women — in other words, no party at all. But as always, we made the most of it. As a pair of ugly male undies revealed themselves, the kid who'd opened the package shouted, 'Ah what the fuck are these? I was thinking about a nice timepiece, not me ring-piece.'

Eventually every sack was ripped open. A hundred silent jewellery prayers went unanswered as package after package spilled its contents, to reveal nothing but knickers, knickers, knickers. Well, that's not strictly true, because there were a few pairs of woollen willy warmers and some peek-a-boo bras in among those triangles of love. Les Dawson could have summed up the booty when he said, 'Knickers, knackers, knockers.'

One lad explained to another about willy warmers, and the listener said, 'You must be a fucking weirdo if you have to wear a jumper on your cock.'

'Nah, yer knobhead, they're worn for a laugh.'

Me mate Eddy spoke up and said, 'These are Boro bras that have been worn.'

'Yeah, how do you know that?'

'Cos there's some black hair in the nipple parts.'

'And what's that got to do with Middlesbrough?'

'Cos there's loads of birds with hairy nipples in Middlesbrough.'

Everyone laughed, but we never had a fucking clue what he was on about.

With no more mailbags to open, a conga was formed, with everyone in line putting their own favourite pair of drawers over their jeans. Some lads went one further by removing their kecks and undies, before pulling on a nice pair of black frillies or the odd leopard skin G-string (deffo the pervs and big knobs), and even though the ale ran out quite quickly, almost all the way back to Lime Street the underwear party raged on. We had a ball-strangler of a time. If it sounds mad or daft, it was mad and daft. But young lads need to have a bit of a giggle, and that night at the Boro was one that brought tears to your eyes, and that's never a bad thing when you can wipe them away with a nice pair of scanties.

The British Transport dibble jumped aboard somewhere near the end of the line, and hundreds of pairs of drawers were lashed from the windows, a bit like the cowboy boot situation a season or two before. I thought of one of those track maintenance men coming across a saucy black G-string on his walk back to Lime Street the next day. He'd dart into the rail canteen to re-package the item in one of those red British Rail buffet-bags, being careful to place the drawers on top of a box of Milk Tray, before going home to present the wife with a sexy little gift she'd have to wriggle into the moment she caught the glint in his eye. The guard on the train must have finally alerted the bizzies to the missing mailbags, as they were out in force when we departed at Limey. Though lads were getting tugged and searched, I didn't see anybody get nicked, and the laughter continued to echo around the station as the whole mob joked about their underwear escapades. The bizzies looked on sternly but the laughter carried on all the way to the taxi rank. I suppose the only consolation for anyone nicked that night was that if it appeared in the papers the next day, at least it wouldn't say that they'd swiped the knickers from a backyard washing line. Mind you, it was still scanty-consolation for a night spent in a cold cell, where the only warm part of your body was your bum, because of the four pairs of frillies you were still wearing.

* * *

Night games would see small crews of young lads arriving at the town where Liverpool were playing just as the shops were about to close. These were the night-safe boys, or 'nitty crews', as they were known locally. These firms were also the back-slang kings, back-slang being an impenetrable street dialogue spoken when you didn't want outsiders to understand what you were saying. The nitty crews would lie in wait for a shopkeeper to deposit the day's takings, before snatching the enveloped bundle or small satchel from his or her hands. Nitties, 'birdies' and 'zaps' were all terms for wallets, bags, and purses full of money; you don't hear these sayings with kids nowadays, but then again, most of the kids at football matches today have already got their hands on daddy's little zap. Anybody acting the lunatic or trying to be a football hooligan, or even attempting some of the old Annie Road antics today, is better off playing Monopoly; you've got less chance of going straight to jail. The Road End boys I knew used to laugh about certain clubs with hardcase reputations, and most of the stuff the lads got up to outside the football was also a big joke, but those big joke antics are likely to get you a fat, ten-year sentence today.

Jumping back on the Euro wagon after the highs of Gay Paree saw the Reds get knocked out early the following season, in the round after the AZ 67 Amsterdan riot, by CSKA Sofia, and we went out again in the third round the year after that, in 1983, to Widzew Lodz, the champions of Poland. It was bad news when the Redmen departed from Europe early, as a lot of lads booked their holidays around the quarter and semi-final dates. For the lads in collar (with jobs), if Liverpool got through those games, then booking holidays for the final didn't really matter, you were going full-stop, and if the boss didn't like it or was a jealous Evertonian, then you were getting your cards. When Liverpool were stomping around Europe, hundreds of working lads lost their jobs and a lot of them never regained working status, due to the local job shortage. It was the making or breaking of some fellas and one of the reasons why Liverpool always had by far the biggest grafting mob ever associated with any team.

By the mid-Eighties, half the original Annie Road mob were scattered from pillar to post, with jobbed-up places like Jersey, Bournemouth, Torquay, Eastbourne and London all having large Scouse colonies that grew daily. Grafting, living off your wits, 'screwing the soesh' (Social Security), moving out of

Liverpool to work away, or going on 'the big trip' (emigrating): these were the stark choices for thousands of men and boys that naturally became a case of needs must once your livelihood had drifted down the Mersey on a Tory pirate ship, before it finally disappeared clean out of sight to continue on its journey right up the fucking Swannee.

After going out of Europe early in those two seasons, you could usually take it as read that Liverpool would win the League, and yet again they failed to disappoint. In fact they won it again in 1983/84, to make it three on the bounce, and during that third season a new back-pocket friend started to appear in the hands of Euro-trekking Scousers in the form of a neat piece of square plastic that could pay for your hotel bill in Finland, your brass bill in a German Eros centre and your train ticket first-class, all the way, to somewhere like . . . oooh now, let me see . . . Bilbao in Spain.

I carried on playing safe, by bunking and dodging my way around half of Europe. Old habits would not lie down and die, and swerving clippies, leaving train stations and boat terminals via my own exit, and generally travelling and entering grounds for free, had become my normal way of going the match. At times, being one of the supreme bunkers of the Bunkers' Elite could make each away game seem like my own private *Groundhog Day*. Getting caught without a ticket usually only curtailed your journey for a short time, while getting nabbed in possession of dodgy credit cards or dodgy dough usually resulted in a short, sharp shock of a jail sentence, administered by the collaring country before deportation. So far, the longest I'd been held abroad was for four days, and that was by the over-keen Austrian Railway Nazis.

They say that a lot of good lessons can be learned by those who are willing to laugh in the face of adversity, and I don't regret anything about doing a full bunker's apprenticeship before joining the Bunkers' Elite. I would rather do that all over again than face the four-year factory engineering apprenticeship that I blagged my way through on leaving school. Those heavy industry jobs left the port of Liverpool on the Bad Ship Thatcher years ago, and I know without a shadow that if I ever lost all my money on the gaming tables of Las Vegas, which apprenticeship would feed and get me all the way home.

At the time those credit cards were getting sorted by a few dodgy postmen who knew how to feel up the arse-end of an envelope, or were being passed on by some of the Scouse dippers, Sir Bob finally announced his retirement as manager. His decision to step down came after ten triumphant seasons that had seen Liverpool reach a level of footballing success that all the other clubs could only dream about, and it is doubtful if any one club side in the UK will attain that level of greatness again. For the whole of his ten seasons in charge we were absolutely glorious, and it was one of the main reasons why people like me were hooked. It remained to be seen if Scouse Joe Fagan could keep us on the winning track, and if ever there was a hard act to follow, it was Sir Bob. Some people talked about the party being over, so to turn it into a stay-behind what did old Joe do? Why, the wily old tactician only went and won three big shiny pots to give us a fat nutty Treble. Wahey! Climb aboard rag-arses, the red choo-choo is about to leave Limey again.

CHAPTER THIRTEEN

A Treble High to a

Tragic Low

IT STARTED WITH the champions of Denmark in Odense. They were snotted easily, both legs. Next it was the champions of Spain, the shady northern cigar smokers of Bilbao. Phew, they were good; but after a 0–0 home game and a tight 1–0 win in the second leg, we squeezed through. Some lads had thought about taking a boat ride to northern Spain, which I think left from Portsmouth, but fuck that for a lark, you were on the boat that long you might as well get a job as a deck-hand on board. The drive or train through France became the choice of most. Next up were the champions of Portugal, the famous Benfica. It was iffy when we only won 1–0 in the first leg at home. But trust those red shirts to come up trumps when all around were in doubt. Didn't they go and just wallop Benfica 4–1 in the Stadium of Light? Too good brother, just too good. Some of the newspapers and ex-footballers took the Carlsberg stance by declaring, 'We are probably the greatest team in the world – bar none.'

We were now in the semis against Dinamo Bucharest, and just to show how determined we were to beat the Romanian champions, our captain Champagne Souey went and broke the jaw of their so-called hard man. Hard man my arse; Souness was from a tough part of Edinburgh, and throughout the cold early months of 1984 you'd find the bushy muzzy frozen on his top lip was a mile harder than that Romanian.

We were in the final in Rome once again, and little did we know that although we'd had a relatively peaceful ride to the final (there'd been a few kick-offs in Bilbao), it was only the calm before the storm. Having reached the final by beating champions after champions, we were unfairly paired in the final with Roma, who were going to play the European Cup final in their own backyard, the Stadio Olympico. They should have changed the venue immediately, but then again, Rome had been good for the Redmen in the past, and a few swift prayers in the Vatican that morning and we should be alright. The majority of Scouse urchins I knew were Catholics, not that that held any significance, but I knew we would be down on our knees on the morning of the match, saying twenty Our Fathers and twenty Hail Marys, and for what? I'll tell you what for, it was for Liverpool's Proddy Jocks, Hansen, Souness, and Dalglish, to stomp all over those Roman tossers, and bring the BIG CUP back to Scouseland. Sectarianism wasn't part of our vocabulary. We never knew the religion of our other Jock player, Steve Nicol, though he was thought to be a Mormon because he liked the Osmonds. Silence in church.

> Hail Mary full of grace,
> The lord is with thee,
> Please let Kenny burst the onion,
> And I'll never rob the duty free.

And,

> Our Father who art in heaven,
> Hallowed be thy name
> Please let Souey score the winner
> And I'll never bunk the boat again.

You may laugh, but it's not far from the truth.

The journey over was pure enjoyment. We'd beaten Everton – again – in the Milk/League Cup final, and the championship was assured after the second to last league game, away to Notts County. It was a game where we had almost the whole ground, a bit like Wolves years before. At Dover, the boats were mob-handed, with a lot of Scousers on the lookout for a few bob to spend at the final. Once all the roads had run out at Rome, everybody took in the sights, the Colosseum, the Trevi Fountain, and finally the Vatican, for prayers to be offered up by hundreds of Catholic scallywags for their Protestant heroes to do the business. The Proddy Reds, meanwhile, wouldn't go near the place. It's weird, religion, innit?

Before the game, the Romans seemed to think it a formality that their team would win. Flags and bunting hanging up all over the city read, 'Roma European Champions 1984'. It was 'Campioni' in Italian but it was obvious what the banners meant. That'll do me; they were counting their chicken parmigiana, Paul Breitner-style. *Come on you boys in red, stand up and be counted, let Julius Caesar's boys know the new barbarians are here.* Where the fuck's that Spartacus fella when you need him?

The ground erupted when the teams came out and the noise was deafening. Flares and fireworks lit up the early evening sky as klaxon horns went off all over the place. Thousands of banners and flags were being waved hysterically by the supporters as the teams broke to their respective ends.

The game, yet again, was one of those two good sides cancelling each other out occasions, and it went down to pens after a 1–1 draw. After Brucey McBung did his jelly-legs routine to put the Italian players off, Barney Rubble coolly put away the winner and the Liverpool end exploded. I mean EXPLODED. We bounced up and down for the longest goal celebrations you're ever likely to see. When that stopped, when most fellas' legs had caved in, it was time once again to let the real dancing commence. Joe Fagan's Reds had done the Treble. We would've won the four that year, only we'd sold Jimmy 'Cannonball' Case at least five years too early to Brighton, who duly knocked us out of the FA Cup, with Jimbo being their main man. It was the only mistake I remember Liverpool making during that period; Jimbo should've been our captain after Graeme Souness.

In the meantime, bottles of olive oil (Italian piss) were coming over, and Roma flags were being burned in disgust all around the stadium. It was a truly beautiful sight. This was great stuff. *Where's yer Campioni flags now, you ice-cream-selling beauts?* Now the reason I'm telling you this is because of how what went on outside the ground that night affected the Liverpool boys, and how that influenced the next season's Euro campaign and indeed all of European football. The Treble by Fagan's men was fantastic, but the European trips were becoming nastier and the years of running around as we felt like were fast running out for the Road End boys.

The huge cup was lifted and celebrated and the Reds fans left the stadium some thirty minutes later. Everybody was in a party mood, so no stick-together mobs were organised before leaving the Olympic Stadium. All of a sudden, the party mood turned into a 'where's me German helmet mood' as bricks and masonry rained down. Liverpool and its fans had hijacked the party once again, and the Roman spaghetti-inventors just couldn't swallow the pasta and the fact that we'd beaten and out-sung them in their own scruffy, shitty city. Let's face it, the place is a pit, a complete shithole; apart from some old buildings like the Pantheon and the Colosseum, give me the clean and modern streets of Austria, Switzer, and Deutschland with their tasty boozers, spotless train stations, and well-stocked boutiques any day of the week. Your history and your culture, nah, I've tasted it with the boys and it's well over-rated. Athens, Paris and Rome, been there, seen there with the Reds, but I never once bought the smelly t-shirt. The Ronny Raviolis, Larry Lasagnes and Tony Tagliatelles were throwing every spare rock in Rome down on us, and I mean fucking big chariot-wheel rocks, while we were stuck in our thousands inside this long, hemmed-in, subway-type path. The bastards, we were sitting ducks – yeah, but European Champion sitting ducks.

Young lads were running about trying to get a firm together, but it's never that easy when you're in among big numbers. Eventually, a 'when in Rome' attitude seemed to spread among the Liverpool fans and we began to gang up. As baser instincts took over, 100 or so started to fight and throw stuff back. The 100 rapidly grew into 3–400, and at last, the Italians started to see some casualties on their own side. In the dark it was hard to tell who was who, so some lads who were more accustomed to football violence began to shout others to the front of the escort while constantly on the lookout for flying missiles. Fifty to sixty Scousers ran at the Italians, and typically, hundreds of them fled. It was the usual Roman scenario. The ones at the back were getting hit full in the face with bricks or flagpoles and for five minutes Julius Caesar's boys were getting ambushed and cut. The Big Cup victory was momentarily forgotten as vengeance against the stone throwers ruled the roost.

With the Roma fans on the back foot, a mob of Lazio

hoolies – their arch-enemies – appeared from nowhere, singing 'Forza Liverpool', before swiftly joining in with the assault on their rival Roman hooligans. This all took place under a continual bombardment of rocks. The Scouse lads had gathered a massive chasing mob but were soon getting hit and pushed back by the local police, who hadn't budged till the counter-attacks kicked off, but who pulled out the sticks once they saw the fightback gathering steam. The bizzies chose to keep the thousands of jubilant Reds supporters in line instead of confronting their own Roman stone-throwers; it was Liverpool people who paid for that poor decision. The Lazio fans went on to honour the defeat of their hated rivals by painting Forza Liverpool all around the stadium. Those Mussolini boys must've had a deep grievance with their city rivals, as they'd attacked the opposition supporters almost as strongly as their Scouse counterparts.

It was a rough night, and a lot of people received head wounds, while quite a few others were vultured (picked off on their own) and stabbed. It was the kind of thing that made the Annie Road End boys stick together at away games, and when some old-style Liverpool fan went on about how much he hated violence at the football and how it had no place in and around Anfield, it was usually because he didn't travel away or had never been legged or beaten up by opposing supporters. The days of waving a hanky or a cap in the air after a goal, with handshakes all round at the final whistle, had long gone. For perceptive fans who normally didn't travel, this was concrete proof of the reality of violence when travelling away in the 1980s. The Road End lads knew this Roma scenario and they didn't need any reality check. They had seen it all before at other grounds, and revenge missions were often the reason visiting hooligans got beaten up or were stabbed and slashed outside Anfield. More often than not, these attacks would be carried out by the lads who continually hit the road to watch the Reds. It was the same with most clubs' supporters: the lads who were permanently on one to away grounds were usually the big-hitters, the main boys. So a lot of the time, it was tit-for-tat on the violence-go-round, with not an olive branch or a peace offering in sight.

Thousands of lads got stuck on this violence-go-round and made it a lifestyle, and a lot didn't jump off unless love and marriage, a heavy nicking or a jail sentence brought them to heel. It's the main reason why there are so many thirty, forty and even fifty-year-old ex-hoolies. If you leave out the fines and prison terms, maybe most of them just got too old in the end. We always called it the wife and kids syndrome. The funny thing is, I've noticed some of those granddad hooligans returning to their old ways in the past few years. Could it be a divorce? Or trying to recapture their youth? Or maybe they're trying to get in that book, *Terrace Hard-cases?* Who knows? Soon we're going to have hoolies with Alzheimer's and walking frames going to the match in slippers and cardies, then forgetting which mob they're supposed to be getting stuck into.

The thing about the Roma final is that if it had been the other way around, with Roma's supporters getting attacked en masse in Liverpool, or at an England international, a ban or huge penalties would have quickly transpired. It was hypocritical, with one rule for the nice Johnny Foreigners and one rule for the 'wild Scousers' or the 'crazy English'. Something similar but on a much smaller scale happened when we played Roma in 2001. Liverpool beat them in their own shithole again and a large number of Liverpool fans got slashed across the legs by scooter-riding greaseballs, resulting in zilch penalties for the club. Now if ten or fifteen Roma fans got their arses ripped at Anfield, you could imagine the outcry. Contact between some Lazio and Liverpool fans was made and a friendly alliance grew, until a few lads cottoned onto their right-wing tendencies. They were Mussolini lovers, and let's face it, anyone who wants to follow Alexei Sayle around can't be the full shilling.

* * *

The European Champions began their defence of the trophy in 1984/85 by knocking out Lech Poznan, the Polish champs. Many people at the time paraded 'Frankie says this' and 'Frankie says that' t-shirts, except maybe in Liverpool, where Frankie Goes to Hollywood were actually from. Now, if Holly Johnson told you to put your six-inch bone up his three-inch Scouse flute, would you? Nah, thought not, so why wear the daft t-shirts? The charts were full of similar 'Gay Englanders' at the time and music had bitten the dust again. It almost seemed as though punk hadn't happened. Liverpool lads instead had gone full circle, as everybody started to get into their big brother's Dylan, Floyd, early Genesis and Van the Man albums. A new generation of pot smokers was building up, and staying in. Me, I just carried on going out, fresh-air merchant you see. Old Levi jackets, brushed cotton check shirts, faded Levi jeans and suedies were all back in town, as the English teacher/pot smoker look told you exactly what Liverpool thought of Maggie's Gweat Bwitain (a lot of those snotty Tories couldn't pronounce their R's, so that's exactly how it sounded to me). Anyway, fuck her and all who sail in her, I was off to Benfica again; anything to avoid her shrivelled-up gob on the *News at Ten*.

With the Portuguese truly snotted, the quarter-final draw paired us with the snowy Alpine champions FK Austria Memphis. On hearing the news, this lad called Dave Kirby informs me that they were only named this way due to their founder boss's utter adulation for all things Elvis. Apparently he skied in a white Elvis suit with a huge black collar turned up to the snow, and often sent presents of mohair bib-and-brace shorts over to Graceland and Alaska, because he was one of those who believed that Elvis was still alive. The reason for the two addresses being, if he didn't come out of the wardrobe in Graceland when the postman knocked, it was because he was living under a false name with a sexy Eskimo bird, in an ice-carved rock 'n' roll igloo up in Alaska. This Austria Memphis boss, along with a few enlightened others, concluded that the King of Rock 'n' Roll had only faked his death and had probably moved to the snowy wilderness just to get his head together and to stay off the cakes. Other people knew that Elvis had died a cakehead, but the Memphis boss, ignoring the ignorant, sent the lederhosen package addressed to:

Elvis 'still alive in the snow' Presley
The Rock 'n' Roll Igloo
Just outside the Anchorage Wal-Mart
Alaska.
P.S. turn left at the snowy bit.

That Dave Kirby fella had one wicked imagination, but I liked the story anyway. He told me that the managing director led the team out dressed as Elvis as 'All Shook Up' rang out over the tannoy. I was looking forward to this.

Train to Dover bunked, boat to Ostende bunked, train to Vienna bunked and I'm standing in the ground waiting for the teams to come out. Here they come. Hang on, what happened to 'All Shook Up' and where's the Elvis-loving boss? I turn to dozy Eddie.

'Where the fuck's Elvis?'

'What Elvis?'

'Austria Memphis Elvis.'

'Oh that Elvis. That Elvis has apparently left the building.'

'Wait a minute . . .'

The lying bastard! And the guy leading them out looks like Freddie Starr, and the song on the tannoy is being played by some Bavarian oompah band.

Elvis the owner not showing up was my second disappointment of the night. My first had come up outside the ground, before the 1–1 draw had even kicked off, when the Memphis boys amazingly had a kick-off crew – a fucking big kick-off crew. Now getting attacked by these snowbound skinheads wasn't part of the quarter-final script.

The lads got ambushed by the Memphis boys on the local train as it arrived at the stadium. We were so shocked by the attack that no real response was made to the few minutes of mayhem, but we were trapped on board the train anyway, so there wasn't much you could do. All in all, it was a bit of a laugh, but it went down as one out of the ordinary and taught all of us to never count your frost-bound chickens. There we where, planning on building a huge snowman from the snow that lay around the ground. Forget it; I guess some snowmen just weren't meant to be. Second-leg here we come. But the Austrian bizzies raised a hand and said 'notenzie yet you don't, you vobbing Scouse dumkoffs.' A number of Liverpool coaches were impounded inside a large empty warehouse, where the occupants were informed they would not be returning home until the goods that had gone missing from Vienna's shops that day were brought into the open to be reclaimed. Therein a stand-off occurred.

Time passed slowly as the Austrian cops wouldn't budge and the Hoisters R Us firm refused to give back the booty. People became restless as hundreds of Liverpool fans milled about wondering how to break the deadlock. Lads who'd earned a tidy reel didn't fancy the idea of making a jewel pool on the warehouse floor and some slipped quietly off into the Austrian night, before making their own way back to the White Cliffs. Still a stand-off ensued, till one lad, thinking, *sod it, I don't wanna miss Corrie tomorrow*, walked onto one of the coaches and walked back out with a carrier bag full of antiques. He was followed by a few others, who slowly strode to the centre of the warehouse to put leather jackets and various trinkets on the floor. One lad appeared from a coach holding a large grandfather clock, and this was how it went until a large pile of goodies lay heaped in front of the cops. When nobody else made a move, an officer gave the signal and a quick search of the coaches took place. Once a few other gadgets like cameras and cassette players turned up, the lads were sent packing into the night. As the escort of coaches headed out of the warehouse a lone policeman stood over the pile of goods as though he was the main prize-winner in the *Generation Game*. The coaches hit the autobahns, but one was suddenly stopped by a frantic young Scouser who had hidden in the bushes a mile or two up the road. Some of those cling-ons will do anything to hang onto a nice fat bracelet. Two weeks later, with the *Generation Game* just a distant memory, we walloped the Austrians 4–1. Semi-final here we come.

The draw took us to Greece, against Panathinaikos. Hardly anybody, including myself, travelled over. Apart from the fact that a lot of us were becoming a little blasé about Europe (sad, eh?), nobody could really afford to throw a grand into the wind for a game that was virtually dead and buried after Liverpool won the first leg 4–0. The Greek champs and Athens itself were not high on the Road End roster as far as earners were concerned and the team's name ended with kos, which sounded like summer holidays, not footy. Greece was another of those southern European destinations where two-bob was like a tenner and the swarthy locals walked around in mountain goat leathers, Jesus sandals and shit-stained undies for a week. In the land of Telly Savalas sausage dinners and doner kebabs, freebies and pay-as-you-go techniques were strictly no-no. Train-boat-train was a heck of a slog and I wasn't up for bunking the plane, as I had recently been caught trying in an earlier round and they'd kept me locked up in an airport holding cell all day long. I didn't fancy risking a repeat performance with a 4–0 lead already in the bag. I eventually got to Athens when we played Olympiakos years later, which only made me glad I'd saved a grand by not travelling the first time. It came under the same heading as Rome and Paris: shithole. It was dusty; it stank, so much so in fact, that if one of the lads farted, you couldn't smell a thing. Forget all the historical hype, check the streets for yourself, they smell like poo.

In 1985, most lads still couldn't afford to whistle at a grand, whereas now, 3–4,000 would still fancy making the trip over to a semi that was practically finished off at Anfield; 7–8,000, if it was in the balance. Just to rub salt into the wounds of the Greeks' firm, we won the away leg 1–0. In so doing, Liverpool set themselves up for a mouth-watering European Cup final countdown with the Italiano Campionis of Juventus. The game was to be played in the lacy string undie capital of Europe, Brussels, in a rickety old Subbuteo stadium they called Heysel.

Now at the time the final was about to take place, a lot of

the original Annie Road End boys were locked up and doing sentences in the 'big houses' all over Europe. The fifteen, sixteen and seventeen-year-old beginners were now in their mid-twenties, European football veterans and head-workers supreme. When you start out on yer football travels having to work out how to get to Düsseldorf and back with a tenner, then certain techniques and improvisations are bound to become part of your make-up. Some of these young lads had seen at first hand that the grass really was greener, money-wise, once you left the confines of your Liverpool council home, and once those barriers to travel had eroded, then why not start hopping abroad to find a nice few quid? These were not lads who just got up one morning and said, 'I know, I think I'll go on the rob.' Or, 'Time to pick me wages up in Switzerland.' These were fellas who thought, *fuck this unemployment lark and having no dough*. Which in turn led to, *Vienna or Zurich looked nice with the Reds; I reckon a might find a few bob there*. A lot found good work and stayed. Going to see Liverpool in Europe, then not returning home, was a regular occurrence for young Scousers in the Eighties.

One thing led to another and before you could say 'take a Nelson on the tom shop' gangs of these early-doors lads were locked up and doing time in places like the sausage slammer in Frankfurt, the paella prison in Bilbao, the jewellery jug in Basle or the plain old nick in Dover. If the Dover port plod had wanted to teach a severe lesson to the scallies who gave them terminal grief, they should've chiselled a prison cave out of the huge white cliff that overhangs the harbour, put bars across the opening, then let the scallies watch as the boats pulled out every few hours; now that's real punishment. That was bound to take the wind out of their sails, and also stop them from thinking that duty free meant it was their duty to make everything on board free. Many of the young gangs who travelled to Brussels for the final against Juventus stopped off first, to visit imprisoned mates. With lads locked up in foreign tin cans all over Europe, some seriously strange routes were taken on the way to that final.

One of the strangest was undertaken by a young gang of Kirkdale kids who apparently hijacked a black Hackney cab and drove it to Berlin to see their close buddy, Tony Two-Ton, a good oul large but locked-up amigo. Two-Ton, it seemed, loved and lived on his chips, but they don't get served up in an East German slammer, so with three months of eating apples and the odd bratwurst sausage, Two-Ton had changed after four or five weeks into One-Ton, and as he neared the end of his gym-everyday sentence, he fully evolved into fourteen stone of pure Scouse muscle. The jail sentence had given him a goal, and even though he'd received a three-month term for trying to steal an East German travel agent's cash box that probably contained £1.50, he had few regrets. Any he did have vanished on a visit when one of his mates said that he hardly recognised him on initial contact, seeing as pre-slammer-days he'd been well on the way to becoming another Hattie Jacques. The mate added that he now looked a bit like Al Pacino in *Scarface*, and you've got to say that that is one hell of a transformation.

By the time the Gunters were ready to open the gates to release Kirkdale's answer to Al Pacino, he could have almost saved them the bother of looking for the keys by slipping through the bars himself. Time served, he returned to his ma and da's little house on the Mersey and a bouncing welcome home party that was in full swing. Women flocked up to him, and not around him anymore; he was the handsome star of the show. But not for long: six months later and dishy Al Pacino became Two-Ton Hattie Jacques once again. It was once those bastard chip shops turned their day-glo lights on just after last orders that he was well and truly fucked. You've heard of smackheads and cakeheads, well he was a chiphead, and it was only during his spell in rehab at an East German jail that he was able to keep off the spuds.

His three amigos, visit over, drove their black cab to Brussels, and on the morning of the final they stood about telling everyone the good news about Two-Ton and how he'd be a new man on the terraces next season. Brussels's main square, the Grand Place, was the setting for the pre-match sing-along and drinking shenanigans, and yet again the other team's supporters failed to impress. The bevvied-up Scouse army completely took over the centre of the Common Market capital, with the main square looking like another Liverpool trophy-homecoming outside St George's Hall on the banks of the Mersey. Thousands of scallies had already been enjoying a mini holiday in the Belgian coastal resort of Blankenberge, and for two or three days before the final the small seaside town resembled Southport on a sunny Bank Holiday back home, only with a lot more dodgy twenties in circulation. The bars along that shore got blitzed with one-legged money (count de feet); hopefully they passed it on to the French builders who were about to build a new pier. Everyone has their stories about Blankenberge before the Brussels final: bizzies with whips, post offices going west, bar owners pulling shotguns, but it's the morning of the game in the main square, and the place has just been turned into a massive Yates's Wine Lodge.

The hotels surrounding the Grand Place had flag after banner hanging from their ancient windows, and it goes down as the biggest drunken mob of lads I've ever seen assembled, before or after a football game, anywhere. The place was rocking, and every time a group of Juve supporters did show they were greeted by the sight of thousands of Scousers singing their European football ditties, followed by the usual cross-border banter, but no real malice was shown towards them. They were Eyeties, yes, but they were not Roma fans, fellas seemed to be saying, 'We'll take them as we find them, let bygones be bygones, forget last year.' With no real mobbed-up rivals on the scene, the drinking and partying continued in good mood.

> Every other Saturday is me half day off
> And off to the match I go
> I like to go walking down the Anfield Road.
> Me and me oul pal Joe
> We like to see the lasses with their red scarves on
> We like to hear the Kopites roar
> But I don't have to tell you that the best of all
> We love to see Liverpool score
> And when we won the European Cup in Rome
> Like we should've done years before . . .

CRASH! As everybody turned, a huge steel bench was sitting inside a jeweller's window, with the three or four scallies who had thrown it climbing right in behind. Within seconds, the Annie Road ants were swarming all over the shop, trying to retrieve their own little bit of golden toffee. It was gold fever again.

The legend of Brussels tells the story that the English had kidnapped the statue of Manneken Pis (the pissing boy) in 1745, in order to wind the Belgians up. He was their lucky mascot and was later returned. The cherubic permanent slasher was just around the corner taking his usual leak, while I was busy finding out that a part of the legend told of the time the little statue had pissed on the fuse of a lit bomb, placed with intent on the doorstep of the town hall, so saving the building from destruction. Well, the little fella was going to have to have some piss to drown out the gold fever at the foot of the same steps. From bubbling under, it had now erupted. The fuse had been lit with a park bench, and now up to sixty lads had thrown themselves into the tom shop window before all the hot potatoes were gone.

Pushing his way through, one lad threw a huge tri-colour Liver Bird flag over the glass and climbed inside. Everybody nearby could see his head above the main throng, as he was the only person facing the street. He looked like a market stallholder trying to sell his wares. This wasn't any old H. Samuels; the lads who settled down for a bevvy later on quickly learned that it was a very pricey establishment. Apparently, the lad in the window, ignoring the noisy alarm bell, had first filled his pockets, then lashed gold and diamond watches into the crowd, before clambering out and disappearing somewhere into the city centre. It was two or three minutes of pandemonium, and when it finally stopped, once the Brussels bizzies turned up, it was the cue for the singing and drinking to carry on. Far from being wary, the mob acted as though the police weren't even there. Another crash was heard, and a second jeweller's window was put in, with the same carry-on ensuing. Fifteen minutes later and the riot cops finally arrived in the square, only to see it utterly overrun with singing, dancing Scousers. Now not all of these fans were jewellery thieves, in fact the vast majority weren't, but as usual with this type of situation, everyone gets tarred with the same brush. Soon enough, the prodding with the riot sticks begins, innocent revellers start to feel the brunt, and indignation sweeps the square. As the riot plod got more and more heavy handed, little groups of lads came together on the perimeter, and once the bugle horn sounded, the riot plod felt the indignant force of the crowd and turned away to rapidly give it toes. They were not like riot cops in Britain, who are used to facing up to large, naughty football crowds. The closest the Belgians get are when students riot over the price of university croissants, or because the waffles are too hot to double up as cheap chessboards.

The Grand Place had now become a massive Liverpool shindig, and the fans started to party and jig as crate after crate of mainly Stella was carried from local supermarkets to the heart of the jamboree. Some of the revellers tried to bring the little pissing man to the party, but returned saying Belgian super-glue was the strongest in the world. Most of the boozers rapidly ran out of guzzle; they're never geared up for a true drinking session, are they? It was a lovely afternoon, and as I lounged back with a can in hand, I listened to the songs, the laughter, and the distant rumble of the Brussels city traffic. A song that could've been written all about that sunny European afternoon feeling was penned years later by Paul Weller. It was called 'Wildwood' and goes something like this:

> High tide, mid-afternoon,
> People fly by, in the traffic's boom,
> Knowing just where you're blowing,
> Getting to where you should be going.

Every time I hear that classic, it reminds me of the afternoons I spent in Europe waiting for the big 7.30 kick-off, the bit between two o'clock and the match, where the nerves and the tension build up. As that feeling swept over the Grand Place, thousands of Liverpool supporters left the riot cops behind and headed for the Brussels underground to catch the train to

Heysel. Here we go, Liverpool versus Juventus for the 1985 European Cup final; it sounded sweet to me baby.

On boarding the local train we came into contact with a few Italian fans and things were toddling along nicely, especially when we sang about Rome being shite and they all joined in as best they could. Liverpudlians wearing scarves were swapping them with the Juve fans and the banter and the songs were in full flow. Everyone aboard the train started to feel the rush of excitement as 'The Atomium' building came into view. Apart from a few vague notions, nobody knew what the building was for, what the design represented or what it was supposed to be based on. The large round steel balls reminded me of all the bootboys who had finally hung up their old army boots; they'd now given them over to the Common Market boys to have the toecap removed before being joined up with other rival toecaps to remind us that everybody could be at peace, unlike the violent bootboys of the past. The new European Union should be in the process of constructing their own similar building for their own meetings, only this structure should contain twenty different pairs of Adidas training-shoes, all stuck together in perfect hooligan harmony. Now that's an idea, a small building next to the new Wembley, to represent the Harmonious Hooligans of yesteryear, with loads of typical lying MPs all telling porkies about whose end they took. The lads that day were laughing when I explained why I called it the Bootboy Building; I suppose the new one could be called Scallywag Heights or for the Cockneys, No.1 Casual Court, with a special engraved earring as an ID card to get you through the door.

From the moment we left the train, I can honestly say that if the throng in the main square had been the biggest football mob I had seen gathered in a foreign town, then outside the ramshackle stadium was the biggest partying mob I have ever seen at a footy ground. Thousands of Redmen were drinking from wine and beer bottles as hundreds of little parties went on all around the stadium. It was a football version of Glastonbury; with Brussels in close proximity, every Redman and his Scouse dog had ventured across the Channel. And, as usual, the ticketless boys from the Bunkers' Elite were milling about looking for touts. The flashy Italian spivs didn't fail to disappoint.

The first tout approached and said in broken English, 'Liverpool yes, you all have tickets for the game, okay?'

'How much mate?'

A price was agreed before the touts, some with bodyguards, realised that this was not really a buying mob. One after another had their ticket stashes grappled from their greedy little hands. The flashy ones, with their crap Italian bodyguards, were ganged-up on and if they didn't hand over the desired booty immediately, they were beaten up. A lot of the spivs were Belgian-based, as the clueless teddy boys at UEFA had given the locals thousands of tickets for a final they had no right to be at, or to sell at. Once the remaining touts got wind of the marauding scallywag mob, they disappeared; I did not see or hear another spiv for the rest of the day.

Approaching the entrance to the stadium didn't give you the usual buzz of anticipation, as outside was scruffy and overgrown. From the moment I viewed the walls of the place up close, I knew that the stadium was an absolute shithole. It was crumbling, with huge weeds growing out of the waffle-strength walls. So those well-paid UEFA inspectors had given this place the green light, had they? I don't think so. Either the inspections had not taken place, the inspectors were all Mr Magoo's cousins, or they drew names from a hat, Brussels won, and they all thought, *well that's okay, it's the centre of the Common Market so it's bound to be a nice stadium that we won't have to check.* The one thing I do know is that the UEFA committee that allowed the final to be staged at this dump must have been the laziest bunch of overpaid amateurs to ever talk football.

It was only six o'clock and Scousers everywhere were walking in and out of the ground. It was the first European Cup Final in history where the ordinary supporters didn't need a ticket. I viewed ruptures in the wall big enough to climb through, but you didn't have to clamber through; next to these holes stood unmanned open turnstile gates with hundreds of unused tickets strewn on the floor inside the same openings. In fact, you didn't have to look for any turnstiles to get in, as the wall was a doddle to climb over anyway. I went in and out of the ground four times before I finally decided on a spec where me and my mates could happily view the game. If they'd filmed a Laurel and Hardy movie at Heysel and called it *Ollie and Stan and the Liverpool Fan*, the comic duo, performing with their usual brand of mayhem and teamed up with their new Scouse mate, Demolition Danny, could have levelled the place in an hour. People may think you shouldn't joke about such an occasion as this, but that's exactly what the place was, a fucking big joke. The Liverpool end was jam-packed but the daft authorities had decided to give an end section of Liverpool's part of the ground to the Belgian-based Italian/Juve community. The tickets had X, Y, Z, printed on them, with the Z felt-tipped out so the Italians could enter that section. It was all par for the course concerning UEFA's organisational skills. They'd had an age to print the tickets, and here we were at the felt-tip final. Great stuff.

I took my place for the game, sat high up on top of a wobbly back wall, above that dreaded Z section. From quite early on, the Italians, as some of them are prone to do, were spitting across the fence. The taunting that went on across the makeshift barrier was of the normal variety that you'd seen at hundreds of segregated ends – yeah, ends segregated with walls, fences and bizzies who don't run off when things get shady. As the spitting and taunting continued, some Liverpool fans started to rush at the chicken-wire fence that weakly separated them from the Italians. It's a different mentality with this spitting business, between say, a typical Southern European and a typical Northern European Scouser/ Englishman. Spitting, in our neck of the woods, meant outright war, and unless you were a yellow-bellied shitbag nobody accepted being spat at, especially full in the face across a flimsy fence.

Before long, large groups of young lads were gathering along the wire barrier and mounting charges to get at the Italians. I don't believe they intended to do more than chase off the spitting Juve fans, or get the police to take them to another part of the ground. Nobody was up for violence in a big way. It was the European Cup final and no supporter fancies getting collared and cuffed before that kind of game. In England, the police would have made a wide segregation space, with a heavy presence to keep the segregated divide at a comfortable width. Either that or they would march the much smaller group of supporters to a less volatile part of the ground, usually where their own fans stood or sat, and away from an unstable situation so any potential for trouble could be quickly defused. It's easy to say now, but I believe that Blackbeard and Flatnose, who used to police the Annie Road End, would have sorted the problem out in no time at all.

The Belgian police were absolutely useless; too young, too shaky, and too inexperienced. As the spitting and baiting continued, a few hundred lads eventually charged at the fence and the naive young cops legged it. As the Italians started to run away, with no real police presence between the two sets of supporters, an end section of wall collapsed. This fence-baiting had happened at hundreds of grounds before, but because of the state of the crumbling, shabby stadium, the end-section terrace wall immediately caved in and thirty-nine people lost their lives.

I sat at the top of that section and thought at the time that it was no big deal, just the usual taunting of rivals going on before me. I'd gotten used to it; I'd seen it 100 times before. I believed that the insults would soon die down once the match kicked off, or the Italians would eventually run away to the far end of the section, so the spitting and baiting would stop.

Now culpability is a big word, and in my own and most Liverpool supporters' view, the tragedy occurred for a number of reasons. The stadium was a decaying old slagheap, surrounded by walls you could climb over and through, with shale terraces that were breaking up under your feet. It was policed by untrained, inexperienced officers, usually referred to as novices. But the final and underlying cause stemmed from the fact that the game had been organised/disorganised by the inept, lazy, clueless UEFA officials, who deemed it okay to put two sets of passionate rival supporters just a frail fence apart.

Now if you want to blame the highly provoked Liverpool fans for charging at the fence, that's up to you, but it's like saying the following: if a large fight breaks out in a nightclub between two gangs – which would be a normal occurrence if someone spat in someone else's face – and one of the gangs ran away, starting a bit of a stampede towards the doors, and the walls or stairs collapsed because a few too many people were on them at one time, causing people to die, who would you blame? The person who spat in the first place? The gang who did the chasing? The gang who ran away? Or the stampeding people for trying to get away too quickly? It's none of them for me. I would say the blame lies squarely with the money-grabbing nightclub owner who may have not only skimped on the building and safety work but had also put on inadequate security before taking people's money to enter an unsafe environment. Skins and hoolies have been running at mobs and fences for years, but the dividing walls and boundaries never collapsed or crumbled underfoot, and police like Blackbeard and Flatnose didn't run away when things started to turn ugly, otherwise you would have had 1,000 Heysels.

As a footnote, I'd like to go on record as saying that no other mobs from England were involved, as some people tried to make out. It was really only Liverpool supporters on one side, with mainly Italians and a small number of Belgians on the other. Full stop.

The game eventually got under way, hours later, and was a farce. They gave Juventus a penalty for a tackle that was almost nearer to the halfway line than the penalty box. In the surreal, late-night circumstances the Italians won 1–0. It was without doubt the eeriest atmosphere ever at a football match. Nobody really knew throughout the game that fans had died. I was sitting with a grandstand view of the whole proceedings and I didn't know about the fatalities until later on, as only a few distorted rumours came filtering through during the game. The Belgian bizzies, finally getting their arses into gear, thought they could whip whoever they felt like on the way back to Ostende. You know what they say about the biggest cowards, always hurting the most ferociously. The yellow-bellied cops finally found the courage to whip the innocents, four or five hours too late. A lovely, but wild, daytime party had turned into a nightmare of a night. I didn't know it at the time, but it was the end of an era, a sort of closing curtain on the biggest European football party of all. Things would never be the same on the Continent again, but I suppose it was like the quiet Beatle had said, 'All good things must pass.'

God, how I miss those bouncing days in Europe.

PART FOUR

The Hangover

CHAPTER FOURTEEN

Double-Clicking

With Love Handles

WHEN YOU THINK that our lads were all forty-two games a season boys (plus a load of cup ties), then in the words of that piano-stomping music man Jerry Lee Lewis, that's a whole lot of bunking going on. After a number of years, some of the grounds finally started to wake up a little once the visit of Liverpool came around. One ground that woke up quite early to the sound of the bunking bells was Maine Road. Our little firm would usually venture over to where the home fans entered the ground, as in time it had become the easier jibbing option, seeing as they'd started to police the Liverpool end with greater numbers and a lot of those rugby-playing Manc plod had a big chip about Scousers.

We decided that the City parts of the ground were easier to jib, so around we went. Fast Eddie soon got caught double clicking, but got away. Next season, same fixture, this same head steward notices the same Scouse firm bunking in, and collars me. As soon as he ejects me from the stadium I promptly re-enter through another gate, but this guy sees me again as I'm lolling about eating one of those juicy Man City cow pies. Whenever that lady used to ring the bell at Man City I always thought she was telling all the home fans that the pies were ready. Anyway, the steward walks over on my blind side and goes, 'You never give up, you bloody Scousers, do you? I have to hold me hat off to yer for ingenuity, but tell me why you always bunk in here, why not in yer own end?'

'Cos our end's full of bizzies and youse don't expect us to jib in here, so that's why.'

'But how do you find a seat in the City part when it's all sold out?'

'We don't, we wait till it's near kick-off time and just wander onto the pitch and then jump into the Liverpool end.'

I knew he was quizzing me and gathering info, but I didn't care, I never did.

The head steward then surprised me, no shocked me, when he said, 'Listen lad, I'm not going to throw you out, 'cos you lot never give up. So listen, if you wait for kick-off time, I'll walk yer round. How's that?'

'Ah cheers, sounds alright to me mate.'

I bought him a cuppa and we chatted. He was an amiable fella, and reminded me of Reg Varney from *On The Buses* when he laughed, and believe you me, he laughed even more when I told him who I thought his twin was. The old Scouse-Manc banter was soon flowing freely and it seemed to me that he just wanted to leave the stewarding behind and have a good laugh with the boys. But back to work he went, and then for me, the reality of having no ticket kicked in. No sooner had he gone on his way than I walked into the front row of the main stand, hopped over the wall and out onto the pitch, then straight into the corner of the Liverpool end. I thought the steward was waiting for reinforcements, or else would have a change of heart and come bouncing back with the usual Officer Dibble in tow. It's just that we were always on our toes in the Bunkers'

Society, and we're talking about toes that seemed to have their own built-in steward radar.

The following season we were back at Man City. We parked up then headed straight around to the main car park. As we were weighing up which turnstile to double click, as in enter by pushing in behind somebody who has just produced a ticket, the same steward walked over. He came straight up to me and said, 'Not you lot again, you bloody Scousers never give up. Come on, I'm taking you all in.' Then he added directly to me, 'And where did you get to last year? I came back over but you'd disappeared.'

I'm thinking; *fuck me, what a memory*. 'I thought you'd be back with the bizzies mate, so I got off.'

'No, I always stick to my word me, mate, so if you're ready, come on, we're going in.'

We couldn't believe it. He took us right through the main away fans' gate, as other young lads we knew stared on while wondering, *what's with the freebie*? The guy was that true to his word that we went back every year until City got relegated. What a man. He was an old style Mancunian version of Reg Varney and he loved having a laugh just as much as we did. You don't get many like him knocking about, especially in this money-mad day and age, where pound signs and a Champions League placing are king and football trophies, glory and medals have all become secondary to the clubs' mega-rich owners and players. Joe Mac from the Kirkby Fusiliers had a small payday when he sneaked £400 in loose change from behind a turnstile gate. He couldn't move about too well with pockets full of silver, so he had to lighten his load by depositing £100-worth of coin into the Man City part of the ground. It wasn't simply for hoolie reasons, more for kecks-round-the-ankles reasons.

Me and my mate Frank from the Bunkers' Elite met a similar

guy at Maine Road a few years later. This fella couldn't get his head around the fact that we were sitting in the players' dug-out watching a TV series being filmed on the pitch. It had something to do with an actor playing a local football hero, and the same fella ended up in *EastEnders*. The actor was wearing a Man City top and had to run out to the crowd. As we were talking to him, just before he ran out from the dug-out, a steward approached and asked, 'What did we think we were up to?' Now this fella had been earwigging our conversation, so throwing a blag in his direction was a waste of time. We fronted him and told him straight: 'We jibbed in, we were having a laugh and that's all there is to it.' He laughed and was sound as a pound as he led us straight into the Platt Lane stand to join the rest of the Reds. Was it only Man City where all the stewards were custy? Or was it a coincidence? Coincidence of course, but don't give me any of that 'no wonder they were losing money' shit, as no five, ten, or fifty bunkers for that matter, ever bankrupted a football club. Bad directors, bad managers with bad buys and greedy, money-mad footballers do that job quite easily all by themselves.

* * *

The all-Merseyside FA Cup Final of 1986 was one of the more obvious examples of police reinforcements being drafted in at the Liverpool end of the ground. When we arrived at Wembley Stadium, we were a little dismayed to see so many police and stewards at the Liverpool end, which led to that famous scene of young kids risking their lives by swinging across to reach a friendly outstretched hand, before being pulled up to climb through a high open window. There was no animosity amongst the two sets of fans in those days, and in among our number were two ticketless Evertonians. They had automatically cottoned on to how under-policed their end of the ground was compared to ours, so that naturally became the entrance area of choice. By the way, BIG mistake by the London Dibble: Scousers are Scousers, and even though the red side of the city contained nearly all the top match grafters and the Bunkers' Elite, it wasn't as if their Evertonian mates were going to watch the Liverpudlians gain free entry to the Cup final while they stood around buying hot dogs all day on Wembley Way. But the fact remains that hundreds of Liverpool supporters bunked into the Everton end. Some of my old Road End mates got in with minutes to spare, when an unmanned turnstile gate was opened by a supporter and hundreds of fans got in free before the London Bill clicked what was happening. Other lads got in via a huge gate being used as a catering entrance at the Liverpool end of the ground. Most of these lads couldn't bear to spend the Cup final in the Blue part of the stadium, so they waited patiently at the van-sized entry point for an opening. Once the gate opened, the lads in waiting, numbering 100 or so, pushed past the stewards. As the first few through were chased, the rest walked quickly in behind. When this happened five or six might be caught, but the other 90 would be in. And with tickets always being so scarce, once you got into Wembley for an FA Cup final involving Liverpool, you felt like celebrating even before a ball had been kicked.

I entered the stadium for the 1986 FA Cup final in exactly the same way as I had for the 1978 European Cup final, by taking the tickets from a tout. This time I used the ticket myself and didn't sell to double click with a mate. This guy wasn't your typical tout, mind you, more like a Stateside spiv. I got to the top of Wembley Way and noticed a few people in suits milling about. Walking over for a closer inspection, I noticed from their accents that they were Yanks. One was holding tickets in his hand, so I ventured towards him and he started to look me up and down. I clocked the usual condescending glances that said, 'Who's this young rag-arse staring at, I'm with the suits, who's he with?' It was a look I'd grown used to and could tell a mile off, but it never failed to irritate. My brain went into overdrive. What were Yanks doing with tickets?

'Excuse me, are you selling any of those tickets?'

'Why yes, young fella, it looks like two of our guys are not going to make it.'

It used to drive me up the wall when this happened. Here I am at the top of Wembley Way, half an hour before the all-Merseyside FA Cup final, thousands of good supporters are about to be locked out, people like me da were stuck at home because they didn't have the slightest snifter of getting a ticket, and here's Robert de Niro sitting on two spares. I could feel my blood starting to boil, but the fella looked quite fit and agile; maybe he was a Marine or something? I was so amazed that I'd found two spare tickets that I realised I'd be quite happy to buy one, as I didn't fancy a wrestling match that could lead to me being nicked and missing the final. I asked him how much he wanted and was shocked when he quoted me five times the normal price.

'What! How much?'

He repeated the price and seemed unmoved by my tone. He added, 'This is a high profile game, I'm sure someone else would love to view the spectacle.'

Spectacle? Spectacle? What the fuck's this hot dog seller on about? My insides were going yankee-doodle fucking nuts. That was it; I swiftly decided that getting nicked was well worth the risk, but I didn't want to scare him away. So I said, 'Okay I'll take the two.'

He clocked me warily but still had the tickets in his hand, so to divert his attention away I said, 'Are these your friends? Do they have any . . .'

Snatch. We were off. As I'm running, I'm thinking, *fuck getting nicked and wrestling matches, go, go, goooo.*

I was running against the crowd marching up Wembley Way and with no clear pathway ahead I had to zig-zag to get through. I could hear a voice; fucksake, I could hear 1,000 voices. I must've been no more than a 100 yards away when I looked over my shoulder, and guess what? Nothing. Not a dicky bird was on my tail; great news. The Robert De Niro nugget hadn't bothered to run after me. Just to be sure I was in Freedom City, I walked back towards the stadium in the middle of the crowd. *GET PAID*, I was on one, glory hallelujah. No Catholic conscience came knocking with this one; he deserved it and I deserved these tickets. They were expensive stand seats and I'd have preferred terrace tickets, not just so I could lose myself in the crowd but because I wanted to be with the boys, the singers, the real supporters. I sold the odd one over to the first ticketless Red I knew, and believe me there were thousands to choose from. The lad still thanks me today when I see him; fucksake, it's more than fifteen years on. Fanatics or what? I entered the halfway line seating area and stood at the top of the exit stairs to keep an eye on the empty seat till ten past three. I could see the lad I knew sitting with an empty seat alongside, and with no suited-up Yanks in the vicinity I went down to join him. Lineker scored, but if he scores then Rush has to score two. We ended up scoring a third as the roof nearly came off. Once King Kenny had his hands on the trophy and I saw that familiar smile, it was the greatest feeling I've ever had at a football game. That night, did the dancing commence? Well did it? Ah well, let's just leave it there shall we; as they say, no need to rub it in and all that, the rest is history, fucking fantastic history.

In local football folklore, if that final went down as the game where you had to bunk in Everton's end, then the one in 1989 went down as the final where Reds and Blues alike literally hammered Wembley stadium with 'jarg' ten and twenty pound notes. The forged notes travelled down the tracks and motorways in their thousands before landing in the tills of 100 food, programme and scarf sellers. Some lads even ripped off their own Liverpool touts with jarg twenties, as the London touts, it seemed, had well given up the ghost on trying to make a fast buck at an all-Scouse final. Hundreds travelled to those two Wembley finals first class, as their new plastic friends paid for seats and hotel bills. Second class was always good enough for me, and I never needed one of those cards to get me to where I was going. Hundreds of Kop access cards were provided by a few light-fingered postmen, who I remember reading about later on when their little Visa venture ultimately caved in. It always does in the end.

Bunking into stadiums can become a fine art after you've spent a number of years gaining constant free entry to sporting events. Once you get caught a few times, you start to narrow it down to each individual stadium and its least guarded entrance points. Even the well-patrolled entrances can welcome you in if you're wearing the right clothes, carrying the right pass or speaking the right way. A lot of the old ways of jibbing in have become increasingly more difficult, with more seated venues, more cameras, more plod, and worst of all, the fact that the same Mr Plod will nick you if they suss that you're trying to get in for free.

* * *

Football fighting was almost solely the domain of bored working-class youths; lads with fuck-all else to do every Saturday except get down to the match to see if a different type kick-off developed other than the normal three o'clock one. Most of the victorious fighting stories are grossly exaggerated, because we were victorious away almost every second or third week for years, but I still struggle to recall all of those hidings and leggers we gave out, and only the biggest, wildest and craziest occasions still come through loud and clear. As I've said, a lot of tit-for-tat 'we legged you, nah, we legged you' books have been written on the subject, usually by Chelsea or West Ham. That's down to the fact that nearly all of the book publishers and main media are down in the capital; the two of them put together never had a mob worth mentioning at Anfield before Heysel '85, once the bizzies took over – get me? I always found places like Middlesbrough and Leeds far rougher than those two Cockney gaffs, but you don't see loads of books about those two northern nasties do you?

For me, being on the receiving end comes hurtling down the memory tubes like an unmanned runaway train, due to the fact that it happened so rarely. Maybe real fear stays with you longer. One case I have no problem recalling transpired at that friendly old place they call Millwall; you know, no-one likes them, they don't care. Millwall's firm are a bunch of fucking big scallies, no two ways about it, very similar to Liverpool in that on their day they can raise a mob of lads as big as anyone else in British football. Even more similar to Scousers is the fact that it depends on if they can be arsed to turn up on that given day.

A typical Stoke City nugget once said to me on holiday that I might be in for a bit of a shock if Stoke and Liverpool organised a fight somewhere midway between the two places on the M6, say Sandbach or Knutsford services.

So I said, 'That right mate? Shocked in what way?'

And he goes, 'Well, Stoke would have absolutely fucking hundreds there.'

'Well where's the shock in that?'

'Well how many Liverpool boys do you reckon might turn up?'

'Zilch mate, they couldn't be arsed getting out of bed, so you'd have the service station all to yourselves.'

I left his company quite quickly after that, as he had an empty, staring into space look etched on his gormless gob. What a fucking beaut.

What I'm getting at is that football is just another thing you might feel like doing on a Saturday for most of today's clued-up Liverpool boys. Most of the real Millwall boys are the same (though it must be easier to ignore their team). Whereas football was once lifeblood and meant everything to a young Liverpudlian, since Heysel and Hillsborough people view it differently. With silverware and travels galore etched in the memory, alongside sporting tragedy on a grand scale, they tend to see the bigger picture that most other supporters cannot. It's not the be-all and end-all it used to be. And with footballers and their agents taking the piss nowadays, a lot of the love for the game has been left behind on the old terraces. Now if the majority of Millwall's fans wanted to kick ten kinds of shite out of the opposing supporters every other Saturday when they were at home, then unless the police presence ran into many hundreds they could do exactly that. It's the same with Liverpool. But the vast majority of scallies just can't be arsed, especially with the heavy fines and jail sentences that now get dished out. But catch them on a bad day, or on a revenge mission, and you're in for as hard a time as you're ever likely to get. One day, a football team or its supporters are going to go a little too far at a Liverpool game and a naughty revenge mob will wreak havoc, mark my words. Although, after the things I've seen at football grounds, I sincerely hope it doesn't reach that stage, but I've got that gut feeling.

Come the 1988/89 season, the Millwall boys were about to sing their 'no one likes us' song in and around the First Division grounds up and down the country. Cascarino and Sheringham goals had seen to that, and I, like a whole load of wised-up Scousers, couldn't wait to drop in on the Den. Fuck the home game, it was New Cross Station and the other side of the Thames we wanted to visit. Then the FA Cup draw intervened, which meant we'd be going to Millwall a little earlier than the planned April league game. This was déjà vu. Ten years before, as the young Annie Roaders were planning to visit newly promoted Chelsea, the FA Cup draw had taken us to Stamford Bridge earlier than expected; now the same thing had happened for our visit to the Den. No sunny April game for us: first we had a January fourth-round cup tie in the afternoon darkness of mid-winter. Now those South London boys could plan a few surprises by jumping out from behind the Christmas trees they'd forgotten to take down; if they could fit one inside those tiny 500-grand houses. The moral is, never plan for a game long-term, it always takes the knock. Start taking a long cup run for granted and up pop Bristol City to beat you 2–0, away days over.

Every young man and boy who had ever played a part in the rise of the Scouse kingdom wanted to go to the fourth-round match, but as usual, small ground and whatnot, finding a ticket was like finding a young kid walking around Liverpool in an Everton kit. As usual, our firm wasn't thinking about the ticket situation, only the travel situation. In the end the coach was our chosen mode, due to the fact that the game was set for a Sunday kick-off, for TV reasons. It was the start of the fans getting used and abused big-time by TV scheduling, as anyone who has done serious mileage with the Redmen will tell you that trains on a Sunday from Liverpool to London are one big no-no.

Match arrives, bunk-ins occur, 4,000 boys could not be touched. It's not often that a mob that size contains nearly all boys, but believe me, this one did. Every young rogue who'd paddled in the Mersey was there; it was just one of those occasions when everybody was up for it. If the South of the River boys had attacked that day, they would have paid dearly. A little fella called Stanley Knife had climbed aboard the rag-arse special and Stanley was looking for action. In fact as Liverpool strolled home 2–0 the famous 'no one likes us' song got re-written, and seriously annoyed the Millwall boys:

> You are Millwall,
> You are gobshites,
> You are gobshites,
> From the Den.

The final whistle went and not a peep was heard, though I'm sure that the bizzies must have chased every one of those apprentice Charlie Richardsons home, as no one, especially South London's finest, likes having a few thousand Scousers piss-taking on their own doorstep. It was one of only a few times in almost thirty years of going away that a big mob contained nearly all up-for-it boys. It was in total contrast to the Tottenham quarter-final years before, but in all truth, police presence and crowd control had both gotten much greater since Heysel.

* * *

By the time the league game arrived in April, Liverpool Football Club were a few years into a six-year European ban, which truly wrecked my hoffman shenanigans. Now for the first time since I'd been hopping over the Channel, we were having to row in the same boat as everybody else: Spain for two weeks plus the odd international abroad. The Spain novelty had worn off by the age of twenty-one and, with all due respect, the internationals have always been shite. With the exception of those World Cup parties, you can shove the England games up your arse, sideways. Once everyone got in on the travelling abroad lark, then shooting across the Channel for an England game was not going to hold much joy for someone who was used to running wild and free. Being herded in and out of grounds, off boats and planes and around town centres by local riot plod was never my cup of tea. It was like having an army of tourist guides in tow, who would dig you in the ribs if you sang too loud.

Anyway, I'm back to Millwall for the league match, a slightly spooky midweek night-game (I always did like those games you were not supposed to go to). The half-time whistle went, and down at the tea-bar, I suppose to be expected, a few Millwall skins were jostling for position. Although it was in the open air and quite dark, I could see what was coming, so I backed away from the queuing crowd; *no sly digs, amigo, get right out in the open.* This one skin, with a bad set of Mick Jagger lips, wouldn't leave it alone, repeating over and over to anyone within earshot, 'Facking Scousers, all big-timers, just a bunch of big-timers.'

I'm thinking the mouthy cunt must be referring to the team's exploits, so as I weigh up the situation, one of them, who has obviously clocked me having a clock, steps up close and says, 'You one of the big-timers then?'

'What the fuck are you on about, gobshite?'

My aggressive response slows his motorboat lips down for a second, and a few of the 'box of toys' (boys) appear. Motormouth clocks this and instantly backs away to his corner. Looking over, I see him having a natter with a couple of his boys, so I tell the lads what's going on, and as the small Cockney firm starts to grow, we decide it's time to put them on the back foot. As we run at them, they back off in surprise, and I instinctively stick out a leg to trip up Lippy Lou, who awkwardly goes flying. A couple of lads are carrying Stanleys, and for a moment I fear the worst, but he quickly scrambles to his feet and makes haste. Wise-arse.

Five minutes into half-time and all's quiet on the Millwall front, but as I look out of the corner of my eye, the Mick Jagger lips are at it again, spouting ten to the dozen, 'Big-timers this, big-timers that, yap yap fucking yap.' I walk over and give him a serious dig – in truth it was blind-side – and he was done in. It was off again. We didn't realise just how many Millwall were mingling in at the tea-bar and instantly both sets of lads find their own group and number-up. Neither firm wants to back off, and for once it's a serious, proper fight. Punches and kicks are going in and a blade appears. The glint of the little yellow handle brings a few lads to their senses. As always, it's over in moments. The bizzies are here and the fighters move apart. This Cockney lad looks at the plod and goes, 'He kicked it off,' but the bizzie in question seems to know the gabber and tells him abruptly to 'shut the fuck up'. On moving away, Lippy Lou, sporting a bleeding lip but not badly hurt, tries to nudge me, so I butt him on the nose, not a good connection, only a nudge, but that's enough for Officer Dibble. I'm nicked.

The bizzies escorted me to this little interview room, took down some brief details, gave me a few warnings, then lashed me out of the ground. The copper's parting shot was street neat: 'Cheeky Northern cunt coming down here and throwing the head in, and don't try and get back in either or you'll be up to your neck in police boots.' The steward, ex-army-boxer type with a muzzy and a broken-nose, looked at me like he wouldn't mind going outside for a one-on-one. Little Barry McGuigan-faced fucker. Instead, he displayed his hostility by opening the gate before crashing it shut behind me.

I look back. It's not him I'm thinking about; the mouth and his crew are bang on my tail. *Surely they won't leave the match with the second-half about to begin?* I'd just decided to go round to Millwall's end, find a place to bunk in, then keep me gob shut till the final whistle, when the bastard steward, who obviously thought he was a bit of a South London gangster judging by the hardcase glares, waited for the bizzies to disappear before reopening the gate to let Lippy Lou and his boys onto the street. And here's me thinking the stewards are there for crowd safety. Ha.

Now this leaving at half-time lark is not something I'd consider unless the bizzies were seriously on me case or I was on an urgent mission. I suppose Fat Lips didn't like the fact that one of his gorgeous mud-guards was now split open. I always loved the footy and the laugh more than the fighting; for others though, it's the exact opposite. Steward McGuigan, who must have been matey with Lippy and his mob, not only opened the gate but also pointed me out in the dark, which automatically made me the fox and Lippy Lou and his hounds the hunters. No time for the Speedy Gonzales expressions – *I'm off, tatty bye.*

My arse cheeks moved up a gear as I eased into my Olympic

walking impression. No need to run full pelt yet, as a number of plod and a well-stacked meat wagon were close by in attendance. Some people would've instantly plopped and approached the van, but that was always a last resort for me (still going through that tough guy stage, you see). But I didn't have a clue where I was heading. All I could see were houses with a few kids playing footy outside, and the Cockneys on my tail were starting to do the Olympic walk. *Fuck it, Speedy Gonzales is back in town.* I'd clocked those Millwall lads up close and a few of them looked tastier than the mouthpiece, so if I got nabbed, rest assured I'd become their case-ball, and as anyone who's done a bit of decorating knows, a decent case-ball can easily be burst by a shiny new blade. It's the Russian Roulette of not knowing whether the hounds on your trail are carrying blades or not that always gets a half-wise footy lad's ringpiece twitching. Nobody wants to get their arse slashed down a South London jigger, and if you're a fighter who doesn't give in or lie down too easily, then a normal striping of the bum can become a whole lot worse. A Nicki Lauda facelift with a Chris Eubank nose and your Mars Barred up for life. It's the little worry in the back of your mind, that tonight you might be in for a bit more than the usual few slaps and kicks that your average hooligan crew dish out.

A speedy head count told me that eight to ten Cockneys had followed me straight out of the gate. I just hoped one of them wasn't the Rotherhithe Roadrunner, or an ex-South London marathon man who loved being a hooligan more than he ever loved being a half-arsed athlete. If any cross-country Cockneys were in among that crew, then the Scouse Speedy Gonzales was about to get mouse-trapped and twatted.

I could always sprint, so with a healthy lead I decided to slow down to ask a young-looking bizzie for directions.

'Hey mate, where's the nearest Tube to here?'

He can't understand me, as I'm panting for breath. He clocks me suspiciously.

'Fucksake copper, would I have stopped for directions if I was up to no good?'

He eventually speaks as I carry on by.

'Slow down mate, what did you say?'

'Arr, forget it.'

A final disdainful look from the YTS bizzie, and the distant but getting closer sound of the big-mouth crew, told me this thirteen-year-old in uniform was not about to come to my assistance, so off went the starting gun in my head again. *Bang! Tatty bye.*

While sprinting, I began to think about any bad cards I'd dealt out to rival supporters lately, and wondered if God was about to get me back. The oul Catholic Conscience Cup was back in town. A building that looked like a school or a library appeared, so I leapt the gates like a high jumper; funny the power you find when you think there's a danger of getting your arse ripped. I could hear voices getting nearer as I crouched behind a couple of huge steel bins, the type that dinner ladies and cooks throw slops into. There had been only two ways to run before I'd climbed the gates but now there was none. *Bad choice, bad climb, fucking bad move.*

The voices got louder. *There they are.* I could just make them out in the dark. The fact they had run this far told me just how much they wanted to use me as a mattress, yer know, bounce all over me till me springs came loose. *Maybe they might strip me and set my pubes on fire, like the Annie Road End Boys did to that Man U woolly on the train after the Maine Road semi-final. Those red pubes went up in an instant, a bit like that brush-like stuffing you used to pull out from holes in old bedding or settees on Bonfire Night. Lulu's pubes, we used to call it. But I hadn't lit the match, so come on Lord Above, give me a break . . . BASTARD, they're climbing over the railings.*

Lippy was making the biggest din, as usual, and it was just enough blabber to cover my noise as, foot on handle, I decided it was time to get in the bin. It pen-and-inks but I still slip inside. It's about a third full so I started to pull empty food boxes over my head. My brains working overtime as I think, *I'm sure I've seen this in a film.* I stop pushing down as the yakking has stopped. *Please don't let me be sussed.* I could feel the nervous laugh sitting in my throat; it always showed itself in these situations. The laugh knows how daft all of this is, but the brain's saying, 'Don't you fucking dare erupt.'

Then one of them speaks: 'He must have gone this way, there's nowhere else for the fucker to go.'

I still wasn't sussed – for the moment. I thought about springing out from my new London flat but I knew it would be a waste of time. In the two seconds it would take for them to realise I was not Top Cat, I'd be mashed. I could hear a ball being kicked about, and could visualise myself turning into that ball. They must have nabbed the kids' ball when they came running after me. It was one of my old tricks; I never could resist volleying a ball that passed by in the street, but then again I wouldn't have kept hold of it. The ball started hitting the bins, and out of the four why did it seem to hit mine the most? My arse went into double-twitch; it could only be a matter of seconds before I was sussed. My weird brain started to think of the Marx Brothers for some reason, the one where they're the stowaways on a ship, and the crew and passengers chase them into a large, dance-hall type room. The floor is highly polished and empty except for a few beer barrels in one corner. The Marx Brothers dive for cover under the barrels, and seconds later, as the crew and passengers enter the room, Groucho shouts out from underneath one of the barrels, 'Whatever you do boys, the Captain said don't look under the barrels.' So everybody in the chasing party has a quick look about, then they all leave the room.

Even in my position, inside this stinking bin, I still almost laughed out loud at the Groucho scene. Everyone reacts differently in a shady situation, and there I was thinking about something daft and just about ready to burst out laughing. Maybe I just didn't think they'd look in the bins.

Next thing, I could hear the young kids' voices, and they sounded tremendous to me.

'Give us the ball back, wanker.'

You tell him kid.

'Here, gimme the ball shithead, or you're dead.'

The crew of lads laughed at the youngsters' cockiness but otherwise ignored them.

'We'll have to go round the sides.'

'Check these bins.'

'Nah, he won't be in there.'

'Just fucking make sure.'

Finally someone looked right in my bin; I could feel and hear his feet clambering up the sides till his breath was inside the bin. No more jokes now. It was quite dark and there was still hope. *Don't move, don't move an inch, you never know, he might be climbing up to get a good view of the surroundings.* My last hope was that he was crap at hide-and-seek. Again I almost laughed. Weirdo.

'HERE'S THE CUNT, HE'S HERE, HE'S HERE.'

I knew I had to get out before they tipped the bin over. Amid the commotion I heard one of the kids say, 'Get the ball, quick, get the ball.'

Then it was a mixed-up chorus of the hoolie variety:

'Kill him.'

'Get him.'

'Fuck him.'

'Do the cunt.'

I stood on the edge of the bin but said nothing. Every time I tried to jump into a space, somebody cut me off. Two of them started to shake the bin and I had no choice but to jump. From the moment I hit the pavement, they steamed in from all sides. I could see Lippy Lou in front of me. Then I heard that chirpy Cockney kid's voice again, like the Artful Dodger in *Oliver*.

'It's the Old Bill, it's the facking Old Bill.'

The screech of brakes could be heard in the distance but these lads were seasoned hoolies and nothing was going to stop them from getting in a final few kicks. Kicked from behind, I hit the pavement and immediately curl up. *Cover yer noggin and protect yer eyes*. This is no daft Hollywood movie where the lone wolf hero suddenly becomes Bruce Lee King of the kung and kicks seven kinds of shite out of his eight attackers; nah, this is the bit where you just get done in.

Then one of the lads said, 'Here's the Bill, cam on, fack it.'

A few last wellies found their target but no steelies or blades, were used, thank fuck. The bizzies came over the gates, and as I peeped out from behind my arms I could see that the Millwall boys didn't look too concerned. The bizzies shouted something I couldn't make out, but just to show those London boys that I was okay I rose to my feet and tried to act nonchalant and unhurt, dusting myself down.

Lippy-Lou, the mouthpiece, looked back and said, 'We'll see you again Scouse.'

I went to laugh, until I felt the first golfball starting to grow on my forehead. I was too busy making sure everything was in working order to say anything back. The first bizzie approached.

'You alright mate?'

'Yeah I'm alright.'

The second bizzie said, 'You a Scouser then?'

'Yeah mate.'

'What you doing here then?'

'Getting used as a case-ball, what does it look like?'

'No, I mean how did you get down here?'

The sarcasm immediately takes over. 'Wakey, wakey, there's a football match going on just up the road, involving Scousers, yeah?'

'No need to get bloody stroppy. I meant what are you doing in these grounds?'

Meanwhile the Millwall skins slowly climbed the fence and walked off, shouting the odd obscenity.

'Lucky for you, you northern cunt.'

'Old Bill saves the day, eh Scouse?'

A third copper walked over. 'You been in trouble with the law before?'

Second copper goes, 'He's a Scouser, course he has.'

The smirks on their daft kippers told me it was time to go, but first, where was that Millwall firm? I turn to walk in the opposite direction to where they had gone, and on cue Officer Jim Davidson, the un-original second copper, goes, 'Where do you think you're going?'

'I'm going home, that's where.'

'Don't think so sunshine, you just wait here a minute.'

'I'm not waiting fucking nowhere.'

It's funny isn't it, when you reach that couldn't-give-a-fuck-anymore stage. A few lumps on your head, nothing serious, in fact it should have been a lot worse, spooky moment over, and now you haven't got a care in the world, and if Officer Davidson wants to be a smart-arse then you're going to be an even bigger smart-arse back.

'Watch your language and don't get stroppy with me,' said Davidson.

I was getting seriously pissed off. Here I was with a couple of golfballs growing on my head, the fellas who had done it had lazily walked off into the distance and it was me who was facing the questions.

'Look mate, it's obvious what's gone on. If you're gonna nick me, then nick me, cos I'm off.'

As I walked away, I overheard nice-guy first cop, who must have weighed up the situation properly, say, 'Let him go, it's the others we should be after.'

And bad-guy second cop, Jim Davidson, who won't leave it alone with the crap jokes, said, 'Nah, they've probably give him a kicking cos he was trying to screw the place.'

What an originally funny bizzie. I went to shout something smarter back but thought better of it. I could just imagine the prick at the annual coppers' Christmas do, telling those Scouse wheel-trim jokes, Scouser in a tie, Scouser in a mansion, etc. *Trust me to meet the Dickhead of Dock Green. That's it! That's what I'll shout. Nah, I'm off, I just can't be arsed being a smart-arse.*

I climbed over the railings and once I was off in the distance I started to laugh quietly to myself at my own jokes. If you'd have seen me, you'd have had me down as a Rampton escapee, but the inward laughing came to an abrupt halt when I thought, *get your head together, you're twenty-seven now, you're too old for all this. You'd be telling some away fan to fuck off home to the wife and kids if you knew he was the same age, you hypocrite.* The game was still in progress and I could see the glow of the floodlights, but I hailed the first cab on the road and told the driver in my best London accent, 'Good man, take me straight to Euston Square Tube station.'

My bubbly greeting told me the driver was one fat, miserable bastard who didn't have the energy to raise his jowls to form a smile. As I sat back in the seat, as far away from his deadpan gob as possible, my noggin went into overdrive. I started thinking, here's me with a head full of lumps, while miserable-tits up front contemplates suicide after listening to his Smiths albums all day. There and then and resume at I decided the old Euston tip-toes trick was looking good. I had to receive some kind of Cockney compensation for my ordeal. Sounds daft eh but it was my own Scouse logic at the time.

As the crabby cabbie sped through the South London streets before crossing the Thames, I shouted to him, 'Any score from the Millwall game?'

He answered in the flattest, dullest tone imaginable. 'Don't like football mate.'

'Forget it, it's alright.'

When we arrived we were facing west, ideal for the Euston tip-toes. Door open, round the back of the cab, Speedy Gonzales down North Gower Street. Next, it was right down Euston Street with its familiar spicy samosa smell, to the bottom, cross Melton Street and straight into Euston Gardens, where two Scotch paraffin lamps greeted me with toothless surprise as they held their own three thousandth Battle of Bannockburn party. Their scruffy, bearded, pleading faces let me know that I could join the shindig as long as I could spare the obligatory 10p. No problem, El Jocko.

The two old alkies were told to sit tight and I'd be back with the ale. I entered Euston, clocked the timetable and sure enough had forty minutes to kill. I went across to the other side of Euston Gardens and bought five tins of ordinary lager and five

tins of Special Brew, the liquid-toffee stuff that I knew the
alkies would love. Soon the party was in full-swing, as Paddy
and Coco (what a name for a Scottish tramp) regaled me with
their bad-luck life stories. I told them about my Millwall
shenanigans, which they surprisingly seemed to understand.
They offered me a swig from their own bottle but I declined,
especially when I saw that some of today's regurgitated food
was lodged around the lip.

As the ale took effect, I started to wonder about my close
escape and realised that there had to be more to life than
getting legged around a football ground in South London on a
Tuesday night. The melancholy feeling stayed with me for the
rest of the night, and even as I jumped the train home and
caught sight of some of the regular away boys, nothing could
lift me from the 'I'm getting to old for this shit' feeling. I
eventually made my way down to the front of the train to get
a bit of peace and shut-eye, which told me beyond doubt that
I must be getting old.

I arrived on our doorstep in the early hours of the morning;
my second taxi of the night had taken me through the deserted
streets of Liverpool to Walton, where my ma and da now lived.
My da had to get out of bed to open the door, as I had forgotten
my key, as usual. He looked me up and down as if to say, 'No key
again knobhead,' and chose this ungodly time and moment to
tell me, 'It's about time you had your own key to your own door,
don't you think?'

He's only right, you know.

* * *

After returning home from the shady Millwall game, my
thoughts about getting too old for all this shit lingered on until

the next morning. But they were soon forgotten by mid-afternoon when I thought about the build-up for the coming Saturday. It was the semi-final of the FA Cup, which usually meant that any foot-brawling took a back seat, as most lads on these occasions wanted to get behind their team to the full in the hope that they were cheering them on to a win at the last big game before the Wembley final. Little was I to know that this Sheffield semi-final was going to leave an indelible mark on me and thousands of others for life. If Heysel had brought our European party to a close, then Saturday's normally trouble-free, singalong semi was about to bring the curtain down on the whole shebang, a trophy-winning gala-party that lasted for nigh on fifteen years. It would also put a stop to a lot of the off-the-cuff scallywag capers we had been getting up to throughout every single one of those glorious, trophy-lined-seasons. Simply put, things were never going to be the same again.

Come the Saturday, I, like thousands of others, set off by car over the hills of the Peak District, via that well-trodden route, the scenic Snake Pass. Yet again, the FA (Fools Association) had shown their usual wisdom by allocating our opponents, Nottingham Forest – whose average home attendance was not far off half of ours – the massive Kop end of the ground (capacity 21,000). The police reckoned that with Liverpool being slightly to the north, their supporters would use the M62, then M1, to get to Hillsborough. They had failed to learn a simple lesson from a similar mistake made at a carbon copy of the semi-final fixture only a year ago.

Then, most Liverpool fans had driven over the panoramic Snake Pass that led you directly to the Kop end of the ground. So surely it would have made sense to give us that end? But a year on, Liverpool's supporters were once more given the much more compact Leppings Lane end of the stadium (capacity 10,000). When the tickets first went on sale, everyone round our neck of the woods was talking about how the Fools Association had unbelievably given us the smaller terracing again. As was customary with those office-bod controlling authorities, did they take into account ordinary people's concerns? Did they fuck. So off over the hills we go. Scenic route over, we join the Sheffield/Hillsborough traffic jam with the much smaller support of Nottingham Forest. Cars and coaches parked, they enter the massive Kop terrace, while we, the much larger travelling contingent, make our way around the ground to the smaller, paddock-like terrace. Sensible, eh?

Tickets had not been as hard to come by as usual, due to the game being a repeat fixture of the previous year's semi and also due to Forest struggling to sell their allocation. I was, and still am, a full-on terraces boy, who always loved to stand up at the game (lots of singing and shouting and no comfort for drifting off), but remembering how tightly packed the Leppings Lane terracing was and how much of a bad view it afforded you, had me paying for a seat five or six rows above that same claustrophobic end of the stadium. After a quick couple of pints, I didn't care, or should I say, I started to forget about the previous year's bad crush/bad view, and swapped my stand ticket for a terrace ticket. It was the FA Cup semi-final and I wanted to be with the main singers, in among the people, right there behind the goal.

Ten minutes later, with a couple of mates on my case and one lad in particular telling me that swapping my stand ticket was a big mistake – 'Remember last year, you couldn't see anything, and you know it's bound to be crushed again' – I eventually swapped back. Picturing myself with a bad view, packed in jam-tight, I relented. The guy I had originally agreed to swap with said, 'No problem mate,' and was unconcerned.

It was bedlam trying to enter the stadium. Both sides of Sheffield Wednesday's ground were hard to circumnavigate, so most people were trying to reach the Liverpool turnstiles 'down the hill' the same way. The previous year, the police had set up ticket checkpoints as you approached the stadium to ease and filter the crowds through, but this year, it was every man for himself as thousands struggled to reach the entrance gates. I eventually reached one of only a few operating turnstiles and had to use brute strength to struggle in. As kick-off approached, I looked down from my seat and was glad I had held on to my stand ticket, as everybody commented on how overcrowded the terracing below looked. Little did I know that the gladness I'd felt, a fleeting thought, would remain with me forever. I never knew that kid I'd almost swapped tickets with, and to this day I don't know what happened to him after we'd parted company.

As people were struggling onto the already over-crowded terrace, some never to return, down at the Nottingham Forest end there was plenty of space; in fact, it was almost exactly the same set-up as the semi-final the year before. The one huge difference was that the previous game had been supervised by Chief Superintendent Mole, an officer with renowned crowd control experience. As I've said, metal barriers and a police ticket-checkpoint had let the crowd filter through the year before. Not providing the same blockade control into the stadium this year meant somebody in authority had made that choice. IT WAS NOT AN ACCIDENT. This year though, the commander in charge was a rookie cop as far as football crowds were concerned.

The crush outside before the game became unbearable. I know, because I'd had to literally burrow my way to a turnstile gate, one among an insufficient number of entrance points available that day. The panicking police commander, newly promoted Chief Superintendent Dukinfield then gave the order to open the big gates. The man in authority had made that choice. IT WAS NOT AN ACCIDENT. Once that order was carried out and the heaving crowd moved through a short subway-type tunnel that led directly into the cage-like terrace pens Three and Four, ninety-six Liverpool supporters agonisingly penned-in behind the goal by huge steel fences were slowly crushed to death.

I looked on, helpless, while the police stood by. Some even had the temerity to push people back into the terrace pens as they struggled for life. As they worried about pitch invasions instead of trying to save lives, people were dying in front of their faces. IT WAS NOT AN ACCIDENT. Some of the officers on duty that day made that choice. Some people tried to escape the unfolding death trap by climbing over the high perimeter fences, but they were pushed back in. Minutes later, the first supporters to eventually fight their way out onto the pitch showed foresight and common sense by trying their best to pull those same fences down, so people had some sort of chance of survival. Yet again, they were stopped bluntly in their tracks by a police force not skilled, not trained and ill-equipped emotionally to deal with an unfolding tragedy of this magnitude. Once the steel fences could not be quickly torn down, the fans – mostly kids and young adults – had no chance.

It was later discovered that Sheffield Wednesday Football Club was negligent with its own stadium's safety procedures. The crush barriers in those dreaded pens were too weak, the capacity had been set twenty-two per cent higher than the pens could safely house and there was an inadequate amount of turnstiles for people to enter on the day. Were all of these safety issues also ACCIDENTS? Somebody must have thought so, because no prosecution of the club ever arose.

The cover-up and whitewash that followed was about as conniving, deceitful and low as any bunch of robbers' dogs could get. They tried to say the gate had been knocked down by Liverpool supporters, a MASSIVE lie, as Dukinfield – though only under pressure – eventually admitted. They tried to say the fans were drunk and lawless, in a headline story that was leaked to *The Sun* newspaper by a South Yorkshire police force ready to try anything to deflect the blame, another MASSIVE lie. They said the crucial videotape from just before three o'clock to just after three, showing the two corner sides of the Leppings Lane with SPACE and the two middle killing-pens vastly overcrowded, had mysteriously gone missing. I can bet it wouldn't have gone missing if an officer had been killed.

When Dunkinfield had given the order to open the gates, as he panicked about trying to ease the pressure outside, the supporters automatically walked straight through the tunnel that led directly into the two jam-packed middle pens. With that tunnel leading straight to the heart of the central part of the terracing, it was like walking into a deathtrap, a cage you couldn't get out of. You couldn't turn around, there was no going back, as the tunnel sloped down into the terraces. No police were on hand inside the gate and turnstiles to direct the in-coming supporters to the sides of the terraces where more space was readily available. Because people were not instructed about the already over-crowded middle pens (not even a simple announcement over the tannoy) or guided to the corners of the terracing, a now severely jammed crowd caused a weak crush barrier to collapse. The crush barrier couldn't take the crush. This resulted in people falling underfoot, many to never regain a footing. With Dukinfield's inexperience of crowd control, and the already poor state of certain safety features within and around the stadium, this was simply a tragedy waiting to happen. The fact that nobody has been brought to book or admitted full negligence is almost a tragedy in itself.

Families who had to go to Hillsborough to identify relatives later that day were unbelievably grilled about whether or not their loved ones had been drinking. The highly insensitive cover-up tactics had already started. All these shattered people wanted to do was to be left in peace to try to gather their thoughts. Can you imagine being asked questions about your son's behaviour, in a blaming tone, as he lay among the dead in the room adjacent, on the day he decided to innocently attend a football match involving his favourite team? The word insensitive sounds like an understatement to me. Subsequent public enquiries have seen police evidence doctored, lies admitted and Dukinfield retire on grounds of ill-health so he wouldn't have to answer accountability questions ever again. A 3.15pm cut-off point for evidence was also put in place, when it was later found that some people had died long after quarter past three. Let me make that clear. No evidence can be submitted to the court if it happened after 3.15pm that day. Yet surely, if some people had died long after that time, then the evidence of 'time, how and why' had to be listened to?

Somebody, later on in the evening after the tragedy had unfolded, entered the ground's security camera control office and removed evidence. Well, whoever you are, I hope you can look yourself in the eye when you remove that police helmet before washing your face at night. It all stinks. The pessimism I feel when writing, or even thinking about this, fills me with doubt and despondency about our so-called justice for all. So much so that I was all but ready to head a chapter like this:

HILLSBOROUGH: THE MASSIVE COVER-UP
End of chapter.

But I thought I had to speak up about something that is a part of every Liverpool supporter's make-up. I would like anyone who has ever been a true football fan to understand the basics of why some people are still fighting for justice fifteen years on. And if you are a football person like me, or just an interested human being with an inquisitive brain who would like to be a little more than just vague about the reasons why, then Phil Scraton's excellent book *Hillsborough the Truth* is all you need to read. Browse through to make sense of why justice to some people will always remain a myth.

For me, and most Liverpool people, it will always be the Great Cover-Up, so can you just imagine how people who lost loved ones feel, can you? I don't think I can; I can try but it hurts just trying, so imagine if it was real. For a brief moment, just try imagining how they feel about missing videotapes, hastily retired Chief Superintendents who tell huge fibs, more and more police lies to cover their own inadequacies, *The Sun* 'print anything that sells' newspaper, Sheffield Wednesday's failures, FA shortcomings, and lastly – and sadly – Liverpool FC for not wanting to have anything to do with the group of people who still fight for justice. Well, you know, they've got a business to run and all that.

Culpability, well, as I've said, that's a really big word. Negligence, well the authorities can't get their heads around that one either, or so they say. So tell me, if it was your child, brother, father, sister, loved one, with the reasons for their death being ignored, covered up and never admitted to, would you let it lie? Would you, your own flesh and blood?

Like most Liverpudlians, I knew a couple of the lads who

died at Hillsborough, but I wasn't close to them, you know, real close, so learning to forget comes easier for me. It took a long time for a lot of people to get over Hillsborough. A lot never did. I remember a kid from Norris Green who played amateur football with me called Dwayne Riley, an excellent footballer. The lad was racked with the horrors of Hillsborough and eventually took his own life. I was one of the lucky ones; I came away alive; and with my usual, but toned down, bounce-back-and-bite attitude, I was back on the terraces almost immediately. But thousands stopped going. I thought about packing it in but I was too far gone on Liverpool, it was in my blood. But if one of my family had died, then you can be certain things would've been different for me. Let's face it; my grief was nowhere near the same level. That may sound selfish or cold, but basically that's the bottom line.

Many of us try to suppress any thoughts of Hillsborough somewhere to the backs of our minds, except for the dreaded April 15, when it comes along too strong. You know what I mean, the 'I've got my own life to lead', selfish part of our minds. But for the grieving families, burying it away some place is not really an option, and will probably remain an impossibility, till one day somebody strong stands up to be counted by admitting negligence and to the fact that THEY who were running the SHOW, messed up large scale. Accident – ha, pull the other one.

CHAPTER FIFTEEN

From the Boys' Pen
to the Players' Plane

TRAGIC EVENTS WERE still fresh in the memory when we went on to win the FA Cup in that fateful year of 1989, beating Everton 3–2 in a final that would normally have sent me into ecstasy but felt hollow after what had just happened. Six days later, and with five minutes of the season to go, it looked like we were about to clinch the Double against Arsenal at Anfield, till Michael Thomas popped up to score with almost the last kick of the game. In reality, the end of the season couldn't come too soon. Throughout the summer, I remember distinctly feeling that my usual Saturday to Saturday existence was never going to be the same again.

All those years of partying at the football and stomping around acting cocky all over the place had come to a halt. The oul motto about enjoying it while it lasts had always held me in good stead, but now a new outlook was on the horizon. These were dark days for the people of Liverpool. Usually known for their humour and friendliness, it was a hard time to raise a smile. A new type of awareness could be seen around the city, and ordinary non-football people could see and feel things changing without even venturing to the games. When *The Sun* wrote those pathetic articles, condemning innocent people in the effort to sell more newspapers, it was a wake-up call for everyone, and the ordinary people of Liverpool rallied around their own magnificently. They organised whip-rounds, sponsored runs, in fact sponsored anythings as long as they raised money. I even remember Boris Becker presenting all of his winnings from a local tennis tournament towards the Hillsborough Disaster Fund, a fantastic gesture for which he will never be forgotten. Boris the Great, we salute you. One day I will meet that fella, thoroughly shake his hand and then challenge him to a game of football tennis, when Liverpool will once again triumph over Bayern Munich!

What had happened affected almost everybody, and for a lot of Liverpool families reared on football, it would take years, if ever, for the sunshine smiles to return and for the grey storm clouds to blow far beyond the Welsh hills. In the aftermath of Hillsborough, people like me were only too aware that some people had no new horizons to look forward to at all.

As I had done before, I bounced back to the match. It was in my blood. But for the following few years, a type of guilt would sometimes sweep over me if I laughed out loud at a Liverpool game. More than anything, I would visualise the heartbroken families whose children had not returned from a supposedly simple football match, and would wonder if they'd ever be able to smile and laugh at one of the games, the same way as me. The answer always came back as a big NO. It used to stop me in my tracks. Contemplation, eh.

Early in the new season it became apparent that there was a big change in most of the travelling lads. A lot of their normal away game aggression was absent and a lot of the other teams' supporters seemed to sense this, as a downbeat mood heralded in the early games. Whereas at one time the lads, including myself, wouldn't have thought twice about attacking an over-aggressive London, Manchester or Birmingham football fan, now, things were different. The tragedies at Heysel and Hillsborough had made Liverpool's supporters look at the bigger picture and see that football wasn't the only thing in life, and that fighting with other supporters seemed futile and a waste of time.

I would sometimes think of the title-winning Wolves game in 1976, when locked turnstile gates were opened up and huge holes were knocked in walls for thousands of Reds fans to gain entry, and then contemplate whether or not the only reason a tragedy hadn't occurred at that game was because the huge terracing at Molyneux could take the surge of in-coming people. Any adverse incident that day would undoubtedly have been our own fault. But Hillsborough in '89 was different. People had more money, they were not trying to knock gates and walls down, the terraces and entrance points were totally inadequate, and more importantly, Dukinfield had given the order to open the big gate that led to a caged-in pen. Enough said.

Around this time, acid house music and the so-called second Summer of Love were doing the rounds, and a lot of football lads who were attracted to the rave scene were turning their backs on their usual Saturday shenanigans. About time too, some would say. A lot of footy fans were dropping Ecstasy tablets on a Friday and Saturday night, so I suppose they were still 'loved-up' when they went to the match at the weekend, that's if they bothered to go at all. Being a bit of a chemical-free lad myself, that entire baggy clobber scene went right over my head. I don't think that bing-bong music had the same effect if you weren't into swallowing those disco biscuits. Quite a few of the original Annie Road End lads were wheeling and dealing in that world, and once they'd made their first chemical killing, some were acting as though the footy was below them by turning plazzy gangster overnight. Me, I just kept going; it was too large a part of the Red nugget that I was.

We were still banned from Europe, and Europe was always the icing on the cake for me. Most of the other real travelling lads felt the same. At times, I got fed up with going to places like Southampton on a Tuesday night, and often at the end of another forty-two or thirty-eight game season I thought about packing it in. But it was all just pre-season talk, and once we got back into Europa in 1992, it was like that crap group from Birmingham used to sing 'I was Hungry like the Wolf'. Come August, it was always 'Fuck the summer holidays! I'm turkeying for the ball to hit the net. Bring on the footy.'

King Kenny had won us the league again in 1990, but totally stressed-out, he spewed it in 1991. Graeme Souness and his still intact bushy muzzy took over and we won the Cup in '92, but he tried to change things too quickly, so he was shown his way to the main stand car park for the last time by our absolutely brewstered chairman, John Moores. Souey had signed some woeful players, and it was said that high on the new agenda for change was the players eating a lot more pasta. In fact they were eating so much Italian nosebag that the football they played was more akin to 'Pasta-parcel', as they quickly got rid when in possession. It was a no-confidence, shitbag thing to do, this getting rid of the ball, I mean look how much pasta the Italians eat and it never filled them with courage. It was no coincidence that he left not long after me and me oul mate Frank from the Bunkers' Elite had unfurled our 'Souness And Boersma Please Go Now' flag at Spurs away in December 1993. It was an act that no Liverpool supporter could be proud of, as we are without doubt the most lenient fans in football when it comes to getting on a manager's case, but once the 'Maggie Muzzy' gave those *Sun* interviews, a huge mistake in our book, there was no going back. I've got no regrets on that one. Like most professional football people, he thought of and loved the money more than he thought of and loved the fans. Quite normal in today's football climate by the way, but he'd overstepped my boundary line. I wish he'd stayed at Rangers, then at least I would only remember the fantastic footballer and captain he was.

A few months after he'd left, I walked into my local post office to send the *Pink Echo* to a mate in Australia, and who was standing two people away from me in the queue with a Giro in his hand – none other than Phil Boersma, Souness's long term sidekick. From one Kirkby fella to another, I was tempted to tell him about my flag and how it had helped put him on the dole, but the oul Catholic conscience kicked in, I felt a bit guilty, and the chance passed.

Too-nice Roy Evans then took over in 1994, and he was never going to be a 'big boss', not with footballers becoming pop stars and trying it on at being bigger than the club every week. The Me-Me-Me Brigade had arrived in town, Spice Boys to a man, and you had to be a bit of a cutthroat to manage these spoilt brats. The worst playing squad we'd had in donkey's years was also the biggest bunch of arseholes to ever walk through the doors of Melwood. Roy Evans always struck me as a really decent fella, but really decent fellas are always going to struggle to control white-suited Spice Boys. It got that bad that we nearly changed our name to Armani'd-up Beauts FC, and the training ground conversation went something like this.

Player: 'Want me to give a hundred per cent every Saturday?'
Too-nice Evo: 'Well, yeah.'
'See my agent. Want me to be on time for training?'

'Well, yeah.'

'Only after I've picked up my new Jag with my agent.'

Too-nice Evo: 'Razor, Babby, Stanley, Jamo, I want you to look real sharp today.'

'Well you'd better see our agents.'

Too-nice: 'But I only want you to try these Armani suits on.'

Players together: 'Oh, that's alright then.'

Too-nice Roy was never a cutthroat, and in the next five years we won fuck-all except the League Cup. In other words, truly fuck-all. We got knocked out of Europe early doors almost every year except for one. That was when we reached the semi-final of the Cup Winners Cup against Paris St Germain in 1997, where, along with the Strasbourg game a year later, I witnessed the shittiest performance ever put on by a Liverpool team in Europe. We were absolutely shizer and we knew it. In his heart of hearts, Roy probably did too. Outside the Parc Des Princes in Paris, it was going off all over the place. Fifteen or so years before, the only thing that had been going off were the Scouse turbo engines as they made off with a European Cup final ticket or two. As the PSG mob roamed the streets, breathing garlic on anyone who looked slightly Scouse, little Bucko, a well-known Bootle boy, got well and truly vultured by a mob of Paris skins and ended up in a French hospital for a day. For dinner, he was force fed shitty raw meat that probably came straight from a French poodle's arse, with frogs' legs and bacon and garlic-flavoured sausages for breakfast. He's never been the same since, and not because of the injuries inflicted by the black-flying-jacket crew; it was the poison Parisian tucker playing havoc on his Bootle belly. Maybe the hospital porter who served up le food had been up to the old toothbrush trick without washing his hands before wheeling out the nosebag.

Once they'd transferred him to a Scouse hozzy he was feeling a lot better after a few days of chips, Vimto and crusty cobs. The Liverpool away crew had feared for Bucko's health, but according to fellow red Danny Giles, Bucko was right as rain in Thailand pre-season 2003. From lying-down battered on the stinking streets of Paris to wearing a red thong on a beach in Thailand; now that's a true Scouse recovery if I've ever heard of one.

Similarly, the Italians didn't show any signs of being loved-up in 1992, when we played the sailors of Genoa on one of our first days back in Europe. Six-year ban complete, the attack by their Ultras came as a bit of a surprise, but it shouldn't have been. After quickly realising that peace on earth had not spread to big-booted Italy, a few tasty right-handers found their mark. Immediately following the unexpected altercation, our huge crew gathered and were up on their toes. A hundred or so dodged the police escort and chased the Eyeties clean out of sight – what's new? This made matters worse as police reinforcements turned up and we were baton beaten all the way to the gates of the stadium. Shit happens, but we hadn't expected this amount of shit.

Liverpool's reputation went before them and at every game in Europe that season we were herded and hounded by hundreds of police. At each match the bizzies had a bigger crew than the home support and unfriendly baton use became the norm. We had played Kuusysi Lahti of Finland, Auxerre of France and Swarovski Tyrol of Austria before we met Genoa, and on each occasion the police presence had been huge and overbearing. Why is it that European plod are so quick to baton-beat even the most-well-behaved of English club supporters, while English bizzies lay out the red carpet for visiting foreigners?

If anyone made a threatening move towards the Genoa skins, then it was truncheons away. It was getting so bad with Liverpool that it was likely to be truncheons away if you so much as whistled 'You'll Never Walk Alone' near the ground. Some things though remained the same; like in the third round in the city of Innsbruck when hundreds of scallies hadn't allowed for the cold alpine snap. It was one of the loveliest places we'd been, but the shops soon ran out of Berghaus coats when the Liverpool boys arrived. Most had travelled over in lightweight jackets and were not prepared for the snowy conditions. I think the ban had started to blot out parts of our early European education, but things like mountains and snow can soon massage your brain cells back to life. The Port Authorities at Dover also knew Liverpool had returned to Europe, when the boat went west once again on the way home from Genoa. The Pierhead pirates were back in town. Following the rough treatment we'd had in Italy, a number of lads were looking to do a bit of wrestling in the return leg at Anfield, but anybody who was looking for a revenge attack on the Genovese soon found that they first had to get through legions of Scouse bizzies, who would've had you lifted and nicked within minutes.

Euro cops are always heavy-handed and cause a lot of the foot-brawls themselves. One of the worst cases came when we played Olympiakos of Greece on our way to winning the UEFA Cup in 2000. The Greek cops were nut-jobs and were smacking kids with their sticks at every opportunity. At half-time they wouldn't let you use the toilets, and when people who were bursting complained, the kebab sticks instantly came out. After five or ten minutes of holding me plums while watching other desperate people sneaking a wee into a beer can, I decided enough was enough. On cue, me and this Peter Hanniford fella agreed it was time to wind up the Greeks by chanting for their hated local rivals.

'Panathaniakos, ch, ch, ch, ch, ch, Panathaniakos, ch, ch, ch, ch, ch.'

The dormant crowd began to rouse and rumble. So we repeated it: 'Panathaniakos, ch, ch . . .'

Nobody could hear the last part of the chant as hundreds of Olympiakos supporters had gone ape-shit. They set a Liverpool strip alight while thousands bounced up and down, before launching ape-like kamikaze attacks at the fence. The calm Athens night had been totally transformed. With the easiest ever wind-up complete, the cops steamed over to the fence to quell the disturbance and to hush me and Peter up, but as they did, 100 or so lads noticed the unguarded exit and shot to the bogs. I mean, come on, the things you have to do to have a burst in Greece.

After the Genoa game in 1992 we went on to win the FA Cup against Sunderland, and I'm sorry to say this, but it was shite. Either it still felt hollow or maybe we were spoilt. For me it was hollow. Winning the FA Cup for most supporters is only a dream; if that pile of shite manages to lift the famous old trophy just once, it usually goes down as their greatest football memory. But we were still living in the shadow of Hillsborough – and I'm not looking for excuses about how badly Liverpool performed in the Nineties here, because most teams would be more than happy with our Nineties record – but we were Liverpool, and the tragedy that had ended our fifteen-year party had left a black cloud over the club. That cloud took at least five years to blow over; for some it will always remain.

It was only by the middle of the decade that we showed signs of stepping out from under the clouds. Graeme Souness took over at a difficult time, that has to be said, but when we failed to qualify for Europe after his first full season in charge, the slippery slope to Doomsville beckoned, especially when he signed a number of players who were not up to scratch. Some of his signings, no matter how much pasta they ate, were never going to be able to play the 'Liverpool way'. Some Liverpool fans can be real touchy about giving players stick and think it's a cardinal sin to pillory anybody who has donned the famous red jersey. Seeing as that's the case, I'll do the sinning for them here. From Bristol and Bolton at home in the Cup, to sixth, sixth and eighth in the league, we were fucking garbage, and players who were signed on big contracts and weren't Liverpool class included: Neil 'arse like a taxi' Ruddock, Paul 'me legs are tied together' Stewart, David, 'fuck them crosses off' James, Julian, 'West Ham class' Dicks, Mark, 'Julie one-trick' Walters, Nicky 'sort your roots out' Tanner, 'Is he in the Van' Kozma, Torben 'nutty' Piechnik . . . I'm stopping here, it hurts too much.

When Too-nice Evo took over in February 1994, I thought, *oh well, things can't get any worse, at least he'll steady the ship*. I thought wrong. The good ship LFC was stuck in the Mersey and it looked like we could be changing our name again to Titanic FC, because as an anchor we'd signed Phil Babb. Now as far as playing football goes, he was definitely an anchor with a W. If anyone on the Liverpool payroll had checked out Babb over a number of weeks before giving their recommendation, they must've been Mr Magoo's Scouse cousin; either that or they were blagging Roy Evans that they'd been watching him, while all the time they'd been spending Kop cash in the lap-dancing gaffs of London and Coventry.

Another flop, the so-called hardcase, Julian Dicks, was sold after a year and soon took up professional golf. We always said he had a left-foot like a driver; yeah, a fucking fat lorry driver.

It was a good job really, because if he'd carried on I wouldn't have fancied making the flag that read 'DICKS OUT.'

* * *

With no Europe beckoning, no terrace battles of note to talk about and no big silver cups in May, my football adventures had ground to a halt. To get myself abroad, I did what the rest of the country's travelling football supporters had had to do for years: I went to the World Cup in America. That's how bad it had got. No wonder all those unsuccessful premier and lower division teams follow England; it's when your own team's crap, isn't it? That was why you'd see the likes of Stoke, Millwall and Birmingham flags all over the fences every time England played away. M1 and M6 boys, we used to call them. England had failed to qualify but I'd enjoyed myself at Italia 90 and I fancied seeing Disney on a dimsum breakfast, so I thought I'd give it a whirl.

Holland, Ireland and Mexico, along with the pot smokers of Morocco would all be playing games at the Orlando Citrus Bowl and I would be there with my red neck, red snooker ball nose and red Shankly t-shirt to watch the entertainment. The hotel accommodation had moved on a long way since my early jaunts into Europe and the football party held after each game at Orlando's Church Street Station beat Yates's Wine Lodge hands down. After the Ireland-Holland game, when the Irish goalie, Butterfingers Bonner dropped the ball, which led to defeat for the Irish, we bumped into Feed the World man himself, Sir Robert of the Geldof. An old autograph hunter, 'Frank of the Thousand Bunks', asked minty Bob if he was up for signing his 'Yanky proey', but Bob, who was buying a takeaway from the offy, refused, leaving Frank and myself with no other option than to call him a scruffy twat. I know that's a bit harsh but all that feeding of the 5,000 and he can't sign a piece of paper? Sir Robert wasn't easily riled, so the first jibe was followed up with, 'What, you can't even sign an autograph for a few lads, well I hope that was a bar of soap you've just bought, cos you look like you need a good scrub.' Sir Robert couldn't be arsed to offer an answer; he was used to rebuffing the hounds of the press, so we were an easy 'go away' for him to deal with.

Earlier that day, inside a roasting hot stadium, we'd bumped into Lou and his fucking fishcakes Macari, who had recently done well at Swindon. Lou, probably expecting the usual avalanche of football-related questions from a bunch of footy-mad Scousers, seemed quite surprised when I asked him if he'd opened a chippy in Swindon yet and if he thought the fish at the Old Trafford shop had nicer batter than TGI Fridays in the States; needless to say I was met with a blank stare as my chip shop enquiries went unanswered.

Game finished, off to Church Street Station we headed. The area around the stadium was rough to say the least; I wouldn't fancy taking a stroll around the Citrus Bowl on a normal day. With the Billy Bob Beggars out in force it looked high up on the shady scale to me. I asked a couple of Florida cops about the rowdy-looking down-and-outs and they said that, stadium apart, the whole area needed nuking; no sitting on the fence there then. I liked the way they didn't beat around the bush, but it made me think even the normal street cops were gung-ho.

With the games kicking off at midday and with it being so hot, people were suffering from dehydration and some even had sunstroke. The back of my neck felt like I'd been wearing a tightly knotted Liverpool scarf for two weeks; you don't think of putting suntan lotion on for a football match, do you? But help was at hand. Across the front of the approaching Church Street Station, the Americans had hoisted a huge banner which simply read 'Football Party'. And that's exactly what it was. As we walked through the gates, the festivities were in full swing. First boozer, thousands of Dutch and Irish drinking and singing in unison. This was good stuff, especially when one of the boys came back from Rosie O'Grady's bar with pitcher after pitcher of ale. Instead of pouring the ale into smaller glasses like everybody else, we decided to drink the ice-cold draught Bud straight from the large jugs, and after spending almost two hours in a hot, open-air sports stadium, it tasted like nectar. The 'Street of Boozers' was packed with football supporters from all over the world: Dutch, Mexicans, Brazilians, other small South American countries, Irish, the list was endless, and they gave a fantastic rendition of 'You'll Never Walk Alone' that nearly lifted the roof of the massive pub-cum-restaurant. I started the song when, after a few pitchers had found the spot, I took up the mike to get the crowd going. The Irish were good, but the Dutch were fantastic. I made a couple of mates that day and went on to enjoy some serious benders with those Dutch lads.

As the party spilled onto the street, the twenty-odd Scousers who had five or six Liverpool banners tied-up on the entrance gate got talking to Brendan Bateson of the Professional Footballers' Association, along with that lord of all suck-holes, the man whose tongue is always halfway up some footballer's brown rosette, Graham Taylor. After some idle chitchat about how we got there and our Liverpool flags, I asked Taylor to partake in a little game of keepy-uppy. I remembered him as a winger for Burberry City years before, when we'd beaten them 4–3 at Anfield, and told him he wasn't very good. After declining a few times, I kept ribbing him that I could have supplied better crosses for Bob Latchford and Bob Hatton than he ever could. I could see him wavering, so I said, 'You were one of those wingers who's never headed a ball in his life.'

'Right,' he replied, 'we'll see about that.'

Twenty Scousers quickly cordoned off a circle, surrounded by thousands of colourful football fans basking in the Florida sun, and up went the ball. I head it to Gordon and he heads it back. I head it back to Mr PFA and it bounces off the side of his head. So off we go again, by now a crowd has gathered to watch the two English jugglers but they must be thinking we're not very good as Mr PFA keeps messing it up. He was crap. In the end a Mexican substitute came into the circle and he was mustard. After he'd removed his sombrero, he performed like a seal. In fact he was so good that with the Budweiser now taking full effect, I decided to whack the ball up into the crowd as we reached twenty headers for the fourth time. The Mexican lad looked at me as if I was mad. I pointed at my noggin then the ale; it was a common language, this football-drinking thing, and he immediately knew the score. He passed me his sombrero, we shook hands and he disappeared into the crowd. Mr PFA gorra lorra lorra stick, but he took it all in good heart. He and Brendan Bateson both turned down a spliff offered to them by someone on the periphery of the crowd – there's always someone from the *News of the World* ready to stick their oar in.

The whole day was turning high profile on us when Liverpool's own Phil Thompson turned up. Thommo was sound and got the ale in for the lads. He enquired about my Bill Shankly t-shirt, which I offered to give him, but he refused, something about I was the right man for the shirt. I commented on his good tan, but wondered why his top lip was still white; he laughed out loud. Later on we met some of the Ireland players, who were brilliant to a man – even Dennis Irwin when H, a Liverpool lad in our company, asked him for his autograph. Irwin duly signed, only for H to turn round and say, 'What's this you've written here? I thought you were John Parrott.'

The only walking misery in the place was Mr Hardcase himself, Roy Keane, who nearly caused murder when he grabbed some young Scouse girl's backside and it almost went off between his entourage and the Scousers inside the boozer. Even a lot of the Irish fans inside the pub were saying he wasn't a happy drinker, and that he was the only Irish player on site who wasn't friendly towards the supporters. You could see he was a moody fucker when he was young; he's approaching mid-thirties now and still seems to be the same. It's called growing up, Roy lad, so stop thinking you're a hardcase among a load of poncey footballers, it's getting boring.

We had a great day and great World Cup. I hadn't met many Holland supporters before – in all my years of travelling I had never met anyone who could party like the Scousers and the Irish – but those Dutch took some beating. On one hungover day, the three cars we hired were driven for a beach day out to Sarasota, and the place was beautiful. After a game of beach-football, we hired jet-skis and raced them around the Mexican Gulf waters. As I clocked the Liverpool scallies zooming about in their cozzies, I'm thinking, *fuck me, this is a long way from Otterspool Prom*. Especially when a dolphin came right up to our jet-ski when we were half a mile out to sea. Myself and the Halewood lad I was sharing the jet-ski with stared in utter amazement. It stopped us dead in our tracks; I mean, you're looking at two lads who had only ever seen real animals in Chester Zoo, apart from the odd guard dog that is, as it tried to bite your arse as you climbed over the factory wall. We were so naïve about wildlife that we froze for a moment; we thought it was a shark! What a pair of Scouse nuggets. It remains a lovely memory and the lad who rode the jet-ski with me that day never returned; he jumped ship and has lived in Florida ever since. I returned home a few weeks later in rude health. All that sun, steak and salad had put me right in the mood for the new season. I still couldn't get enough of football, although the Reds, well, whisper it gently we were still shite.

To prove how poor the Reds had been performing, the funniest and best thing I did at Anfield all year had nothing to do with watching the football. It happened in the boring summer when I dived headlong over the building site walls of the knocked down Spion Kop. The dive reminded me of Franny Lee in his prime, when he'd legged Norman Hunter, and I bet oul Franny, the bogroll king, could tell you a few stories about the most famous terracing in the world. The mighty Spion Kop, the educator and the innovator to all good football fans, a place where thousands of Liverpudlians like me had served our apprenticeship, sung our hearts out and danced ourselves dizzy, as yet another League Championship was toasted.

One night in the summer, myself, Tony Mock and Stevie Spenner, three good Reds bevvied-up and up for a laugh, decided to climb into the ground and have a pretend football match inside. It was so quiet around The Shrine that every noise echoed. All we were lacking was an old burst ball, and the laughter boomed around the place when Tony said he regretted not keeping hold of the girl's head he'd copped off with last week. The barbed-wire fence and wall were an absolute bastard to climb but Tony Mock had been an England boxing international, so a swift few uppercuts up the arse of our jeans and me and Spenner were in. The aura and silence of the oul place stopped me in my tracks. At first, I tried to focus on the different parts of the ground, which was quite difficult under the light of a half-moon. I sat in the dugout where Shankly and Paisley had sat and thought back to the glory nights of Moenchengladbach and ten pence in the rain, St Etienne and Super-Sub, and a match like Auxerre, played three years before in front of a small, 23,000 crowd that had Anfield's foundations rocking, probably because the majority of the crowd were Scousers. Here it was, a pile of rubble flattened to the ground. The grass on the pitch was so deep that the three of us had a lie down. I went over to the Kemlyn Road and took a pretend corner, which Spenner gleefully headed home, before running to an ecstatic, imaginary Kop.

I thought about sleeping in the deep grass, but my soft mattress and Van the Man's *Moondance* album beckoned when the cocky watchman's light came on. I regret that I didn't have a good night's kip under the stars; it would have been nice to wake up at Anfield as the sun came up over The Shrine. So if anyone from the club is listening and the new stadium idea comes to fruition, how about a 'good night's kip on the Kop' amnesty, just for a couple of nights? Think what you want, before the old place goes, I definitely aim to take that dream snooze on the hallowed turf of Anfield. And while you're there Mr Chairman, any chance of a Scouse Kop at one end of the new ground, Liverpool people only? Go on Mooresy lad. Oh well, I suppose we'll all get blanked as usual. I've been back on a couple of drunken nights to take that kip, but me love handles lost a battle with the wall.

By the end of Evo's first full season in charge, we'd won the Mickey Mouse Cup against Bolton; this trophy changed its name to the FBC Cup in 2003, which stood for the Fucking Boss Cup because we beat Man United 2–0 (it reverted back to the Mickey Mouse Cup in 2004). Roy Evans did steady the ship in the end, and we pulled ourselves out of the mud by coming fourth, which meant we were back in Europe for the 1995/96 season. But like the lovechild of Woody Guthrie had said, 'The times they are a-changing' and the usual long and winding road was lashed right out the aeroplane window once the season got under way, as we drew Spartak Vladikavkaz and, without knowing where it was, we knew it was plane or bust. *Wahey! Jump aboard the older, and hopefully wiser, Rag-arse Express. We're off.*

The old way of travelling was over. Now that there was no more train and boat bunking, it no longer felt right; now it was all legit tickets for this, legit tickets for that, membership of travel clubs, club-affiliated tours – in other words, it was crap. A £300, two-day trip to Russia and what happened? Fuck all, except ale, ale, ale. This flying-in, flying-out took some getting used to, it was like going on a stag do, but at least we got through. Next up it was Brondby of Denmark and Liverpool took a huge firm over. No battles, loads more ale and a 0–0 draw. The only thing of note was when the captain of the plane threatened to turn back to Liverpool half an hour after taking off when, out of 250 passengers, about 100 were passing round baseball-bat-sized joints and the cabin crew were inadvertently getting stoned. Apparently those same stewards and stewardesses have been listening to Pink Floyd and old Genesis albums ever since. The Captain – probably half-wrecked – issued his threat and 100 joints were instantly stubbed out, to be saved up for Denmark. Me old mate Joey O reckoned the only time he thought turbulence was lovely was when he was stoned in a window seat, so maybe instead of puke-bags they'd be better off putting a small chunk of weed under each seat, either that, or hash cakes with your in-flight meal. While the biggest toker of them all, Bob Marley, was known for singing about 'Jamming', this was a case of jamming as many Scouse pot-smokers onto one plane as the travel arrangers deemed possible. Anyway, we got there, we got beat, we were out and we were still shite.

What made it worse was the fact that Not-A-Manc-In-Sight United were winning cups, and we'd laughed at them for twenty years. No wonder it's the biggest rivalry in England. One of the big differences between us was that when they would be doing well in competitions, you'd hear them constantly singing about Scousers whenever they had a European game on telly. Serious chip on the shoulder or what? When we ruled the roost, we didn't give two fucks for singing songs about them, not until we played them, that is. They are spookily not far behind our trophy haul these days: 4–2 in Euros and 18–15 in titles, so it's about time we got our arses into gear to see them off once and for all.

I had high hopes that we were finally getting our act together at the start of the 1996/97 season, after coming third in the league the year before. The season started at Middlesbrough, where the silver-haired pound-note collector Ravanelli scored a hat-trick against us as we drew 3–3. Even rough-arse Boro had gone all soft on us, with Cellnet this and McDonald's that; give me scary old Ayresome Park any day of the week. Once the Boro were watered down, it looked like the whole country had been diluted. No atmosphere, no boys and no big Boro boots, just loads of divvies in Ravanelli tops. If that's progress, give me a European trip to get me head together.

My new season really began at Mypa 47 of Finland for the first round of the European, Hoffmans on Aeroplanes Cup. The Finns were beaten both legs before we drew the Swiss mountaineers of Sion. We'd never heard of Sion but what a lovely place it turned out to be. It was like taking a break at an Alpine retreat, only with a footy match thrown in for an added bit of sparkle. Snow-capped mountains, friendly supporters in lumberjack boots and a nice mob of yodellers at the local boozer; this was great stuff. Sitting at the bar of the Ibis Hotel later that night, another well-travelled Red called Robbie Rogers remarked that although our team was not as good as it should be, the European away games didn't come much better than this. Well, I had to agree, but how was I to know that we were about to draw Brann Bergen of Norway, where we were given the red-carpet treatment from the moment the plane landed on the Vikings' runway? School kids were singing Liverpool songs in the centre of town, accompanied by a brass band, and as the young choir gave a sweet rendition of 'You'll Never Walk Alone', I turned to Bard, our local host and asked, 'What's all this about?'

To which he replied in the finest Scouse accent, 'Here, they love Liverpool and the Scousers.'

At last, somewhere where we were loved! Just kidding: Glasgow and Ireland have always made us welcome. Everywhere we went on that trip we were treated like visiting pop stars and we loved it. Speak to any well-travelled Red who ventured to the Bergen game and they will tell you this was one of our finest trips ever. They even laid on a nightclub in the city centre with subsidised ale. We had one of our finest bevvies of all time that night and by the end of the game I was thinking about emigrating and becoming a Scouse Viking for life. The place was so friendly that one lad in our company called Mark found he had a Norwegian Dale Winton on his tail, who wouldn't stop staring into Mark's twinkly eyes – till he booted him down the stairs. This Norwegian nonce, or 'Olaf Corkhill' as we called him, would not leave him alone. On the sly we think Mark was flattered and might have sloped off if we hadn't been about (just kidding), but it was just a small part of a lovely trip to a lovely place. Bergen, we salute you. But be warned, if we draw you again I'm bringing the kids and jumping ship, because we all loved that little place.

Bergen had given me that same old, sweet, European feeling: happy to be away, happy to be there, we were on the march. How wrong can you be? We played the Paris mob in the semis and we proved that we were still shizer. We were out. One minute I was in Bergen, lapping up the fresh air and feeling good, next minute, here's me conned into thinking we were getting back to our winning ways, but we weren't. We took a huge mob to Paris but the bastards drowned our noise by playing these loudspeakers at full-blast of their own fans' singing. That was a new one in my book. They only had this small singing mob but every time they chanted or sang the loudspeakers joined in and it came out like the Anfield Kop in 1965. English clubs take note, especially Newcastle, which used to be known for good atmosphere but today as soon as they go a goal down it's like being in Dracula's castle at one o'clock in the afternoon.

While I'm on the subject of noise, I recently returned from Ljubljana of Slovenia in the first round of the UEFA Cup, where their little band of supporters made a bit of noise only to be outshonc by Liverpool's legendary pyjama man, Stevie Martin from Huyton. This fella has been seen all over Europe for years in pyjamas and slippers, and at the game in question he first stripped bollocko, with just a red elephant's trunk on his nudger, stood on the high metal fence, then serenaded the riot cops for ten minutes. They couldn't work out what was going on. Now let's see the Hollywood version of Steve Martin do that for a laugh.

I'd seen Steve Martin the film star years before, after eating a nice breakfast in Harrods prior to a Liverpool–West Ham game. I sauntered over and asked him where John Candy was.

Was he lost on the Tube? And were the two of them still trying to get home for Thanksgiving? He looked at me as though I was Phil Mitchell in a pair of suzzies and a basque. With no jokes forthcoming from the man with supposedly two brains, I told him, 'I've seen you on that *Saturday Night Live* and you were coming up with all these off the cuff jokes and quips with ease, have yer got any jokes on board today Stevie?'

'No,' he replied, then added in his Yankee twang, 'Can I now get on with my shopping?'

'Well, no you can't.'

He gave me a strange look for the second time in a minute, this one being a little more serious.

'And why is that, may I enquire?'

'Cos, you big-headed ponce, here comes John Candy now,' and I pointed behind him. He looked puzzled as he scanned the shop floor. I was off, but not before I shouted back, 'One-nil, eh Stevie.'

Well, I'm thinking, *as I walked out of the shop, sorry for trying to have a laugh in his lordship's presence.* What is it with these phoney film stars anyway? Gimme the real Steve Martin any day of the week, at least the Pyjama Man wouldn't blank you. It was a real Dennis Pennis moment, long before the bespectacled Arsenal comedian made his name from sending up celebrities in a similar type of manner.

One of the first times I saw the Pyjama Man was outside Barcelona's Nou Camp, minus any footwear. He'd been jumped by jealous Spanish gypos who'd copped for his slippers and scarf; the cheeky cunts were only thirty years too late with the clobber-robbing. Didn't they realise that Arsenal and Chelsea are usually in Europe these days? If they'd set their sights on jumping a few Cockneys they might've copped for some tasty toilet seat earrings which were bound to look better hanging on a gypsy's ear than an oul tatty pair of slippers hanging on a caravan door. At least Stevie wasn't one of the Liverpool lads who mistakenly booked flights for Slovakia instead of Slovenia, which was only on the other side of Austria; otherwise we wouldn't have enjoyed his top-drawer entertainment at what was a boring game. The lads should have known better, but when you've travelled like the original Liverpool boys have travelled, it's sometimes easy to take routes for granted and get mixed up. Only recently I was talking to a lad at a pre-season tournament in Amsterdam and he was telling me about a cracking little boozer he'd found in Prague before the Slovan Liberec game. As he told me about the street, the boozer/restaurant next door and the friendly people, I had to interrupt him and tell him the place was really Sion in Switzerland from a couple of years before. We laughed out loud when he realised his mistake. With the amount of trains, boats and planes, plus countries, cities and stadiums we'd boarded and seen, it was easy to suffer with hazy brain syndrome now and again. God knows how some of those sports journalists keep abreast of where they've been.

The year after the French toothbrush tossers had knocked us out, we beat Celtic in the UEFA Cup first round before eventually going out to Strasbourg, who easily beat us 3–2 on aggregate, if you know what I mean. Me ma had always told me that 'after twenty-one it just flies by' and those shitty mid-Nineties seasons have already done just that. Whereas they got booted out of my brain with ease, something like Bruges '78 remains as clear and as sharp as a Stanley knife ripping through your undies. Big cups and great teams can sometimes do that to you.

The only reason I'm still clear about 1998/99 is because the lads finally ended up on the players' plane for the Slovakian

Kosice match, and we all went to Benidorm for the Valencia game. Only the players' plane was making the trip and it was expensive, but when the boys got itchy feet with those lambswool socks we were on our way the moment we started scratching. Gerry Blayney, one of the best Reds on the planet, was already a few drinks down the line and wanted to meet and greet the players but the stewards were having none of it. Gerry tells them, 'Have you ever felt the hairs on the back of your neck stand up?'

But the steward is not a football man, and doesn't get the gist of Gerry's convo. One of Gerry's buddies, Swanny, another Scouse Aborigine who'd been walking the planet for years in search of a Reds game, starts to encourage Gerry, who really doesn't need much encouragement. The man's house contains his own private shrine to Liverpool and Gerry was never shy in coming forward, but the first-class curtains have been drawn and the steward's having none of it. Is this what it had come to, footballers going all Mel Gibson, Bob Geldof and Stevie Martin on us?

When Bill Shankly started the Red revolution by taking Liverpool out of the old second division in 1962, he noticed how football daft the supporters were and how much of a part their fervour and passion had played in gaining promotion. It was a double act, a joint thing, in his words 'he was made for Liverpool and Liverpool was made for him'. Shanks always insisted all along that this was the people's club and there would never be any divide between players and Kopites. Clearly somebody had forgotten what the great man had said. Humbleness and togetherness were not flying to the cup-tie in Kosice. Shankly's slightly utopian dream of seeing the players and supporters marching together for the greater glory of Liverpool was not allowed to board the plane that day. Though we all have our own individual experiences to reminisce and talk about, in my mind, and I know I speak for a few other lads who went to Slovakia, despite the fact that it was 'just another one of those days' where the players seemed to drive off over the horizon in their 40-grand Jags, without giving a brief hello, the difference this time was that it seemed like it was for good. In my opinion, once you lose that common touch, that hands-on approach to ordinary people (who have relentlessly paid your wages and sung your name to the rafters), then that's the day you start to lose the plot.

Who were they to say that Gerry couldn't go through the curtain for a natter? Gerry had been there and back long before most of them were even born, and would still be there long after they had departed. As far as I was concerned, Gerry could go and sit upfront and play co-pilot if he wanted. He'd done his apprenticeship ten times over. That first-class curtain that separated supporters from club officials and players might as well have been the Berlin Wall in my book. I mean, if Nelson Mandela can take time out to speak with the supporters at a South African pre-season tour, I'm sure it shouldn't be too hard for a football club and its employees to do likewise.

Kosice were duly walloped both legs. Next up was Valencia, which meant that Benidorm was looking good for an Indian summer. I had seen hundreds of Scousers in the Costa del Blackpool before, but never with a footy mob in tow. It was funny entering holiday boozers and knowing almost everyone inside. That first night I sat on the balcony and watched a running battle between Liverpool's young urchin crew and the black-jumpered bouncers of Benidorm. Colonel Anthony was somewhere in the mix, as I could hear his voice all over the street. Though it was all across the local papers, it was no big battle, more of a seaside brawl than anything, and it eventually fizzled out. If a real Costa Del Rumpus had erupted, the lads from the balconies would've been down in a flash, but it was the papers exaggerating again. After a fine night on the tiles I nodded off to the distant sound of wailing police cars and drunken Liverpool songs. It was five in the morning, and I was rat-arsed. Through my Budweiser glasses, the Benidorm skyline might as well have been New York.

Boy did we celebrate when we went through on away goals after a 2–2 draw. That's how much our expectation levels had dropped; it was only an early round but we were dancing around like it was the final. This was fully brought home to the travelling supporters when we got knocked out by Celta Vigo of Spain in the next round. I'd never heard of Vigo, which was near the Portuguese border, but it was a nice place and we enjoyed a fine beverage on that trip. Vigo deserved to beat us, and should've scored more. From having seen Liverpool get truly beaten in serious competition once in about twenty years (5–1 by the Villa in December 1976), in the past three or four seasons I'd seen them get well beaten four or five times. It was hard to take. The bigger you are, the harder you fall.

In January that year we played the Septics in the FA Cup fourth round and were winning 1–0 till two late goals knocked us out. The reason I'm telling you this is because of the way the gorgeous Gary Neville celebrated the goals. He ran to the Liverpool end and was doing everything he could to start a riot. Hundreds of lads were trying to get over the fence as the Manc bizzies tried to defuse the situation, and Peter Schmeichel, realising this, sensibly pulled him away. Nothing was ever said about 'the players' representative' that day; I wonder if a Liverpool player had done the same thing, if the biased Manchester-based press would have kept the muzzle on and said nothing. The little shitbag tried to explain his celebrations by saying something about 'the rivalry involved' and his 'dislike for Scousers in general'. Realising that he had made himself Scouse enemy number one, he then came up with the whopper story that a load of Scousers had tried to tip his car over with him inside. This was the act of a complete coward, lying to deflect from what he had done on the pitch. Wasn't he supposed to be in a position of responsibility, setting an example to young kids and all that? If he'd have carried on like that outside the ground or on the terraces, he would have either been nicked or had his jaw broken in three places. It stank of one law for the pampered players and another for the man on the street. The truth is, nobody in Liverpool can find these fantastic car-lifters to give them their medals, so he deffo made that one up. If these untouchable footballers act the bollocks they should be brought to task, just like the rest of us. The player's representative nearly organised a strike before one game, in defence of Rio Ferdinand and all that palaver about a dope test. He was on the ball about the fact that the Peckham plonker shouldn't be penalised for not showing up for a dope test. Anyone who knew football knew Rio was a dope anyway, no test needed. As for strike – there's a few thousand Mickeys who'd like to teach him the meaning of the word strike.

One man who did get brought to task was the sheepshagger who was shouting the odds at us as we left the ground. It should be obvious from these pages that I'm not a person who loves going on about violence for self-gratification, but this beaut was asking for it. Once we were a few minutes away from the stadium we walked into a crew of Mancs, who could see we were in no mood to fuck about after a bad result. But seeing as the bizzies were everywhere and probably feeling it was his duty, this one nugget starts giving it the big one: 'Scouse cunts' this, 'Scouse cunts' the other and he won't shut up. Now there are a lot of bigmouths in a football crew, but why is there always one extra bigmouth who just can't shut up? As I got to my car parked at the back of that picture house in Salford Quays, I sat and watched the crowd disperse as we were gridlocked anyway. The crowd began to dwindle and I noticed the mouthpiece making his way over to the same car park we were in, before he darted into a nearby pub. I thought about sneaking inside to maybe cop for him. Moments later, he appeared twiddling a set of car keys and walked around to the back of the pictures. The lads knew what I was up to and told me to leave it, as there were cameras everywhere. Undeterred, I shot around the back and timed my run in so that he was just opening the car door as I lamped him. I hit him on the jaw so hard that I cracked a knuckle and probably his jaw in the process. The mouthy cunt went fast asleep and even though I was tempted to throw a few volleys to the head, I didn't. I take no great pride in telling you this, in fact I felt like a bit of a dickhead for letting a game of football and a half-arsed hooligan get to me that way, but as I've said, a result could sometimes do that to you. Usually I was well in control at the match, but the players' representative had more than put me in the mood with his antics on the pitch. The gob-organ was deffo a Man U hoolie and if he reads this he'll know it's him, tax disc out of date, red car, that's all I'm saying. Maybe he's finally learned to shut the fuck up, because if one thing is certain, one of his heroes, gorgeous Gary, still hasn't.

Too-nice Evo departed halfway through that year, to leave Gerard Houllier in sole charge. We ended the season by coming a miserable seventh. *Bastard, no Europe.* The Frenchman's first season in charge was a transitional one, as he tried to bring in new blood and sell some of the poorer players he had inherited. The best thing we did all year was sell David James. He was similar to the actor Wesley Snipes when he starred in *Blade*, because here was an Armani-clad black vampire who fancied himself as a stud, but was ultimately shit-scared of crosses. Here was an Armani-clad vampire who was truly scared of crosses. And Phil Babb, the worst player I have seen in a Liverpool kit. We'd been trying to get rid of him for a few years, and after several seasons of him picking up brewsters in the reserves, Houllier finally set him up with a nice little ice-cream stall outside Sporting Lisbon's stadium. The anchor with a W had finally gone. Centre-half, more like the centre of town, as you could drive a skip wagon through those legs.

The following year we were back in Europe, due to coming fourth in the league. It turned out to be the cup year of all cup years. I went to Bucharest, Prague, Athens, Rome, Porto, Barcelona and finally Cardiff twice and Dortmund to see Liverpool lift three big silver cups in one year. The places went like this: Bucharest – cheap and lovely; Prague – lovely and cheap; Athens – scruffy, smelly and bad bizzies wearing T.J.Hughes's wigs; Rome – still a shithole with a few old buildings to make it sound nice; Porto – the Bangladesh of Europe, say no more; Barcelona – another over-rated gaff, too spread out and that La Ramblas place was minty, even mintier after the Lacoste shop that got emptied by a mob of Scouse urchins; Cardiff – a tremendous city where the people were good to us, with a tremendous stadium, fuck Wembley, leave the cup with the Taffs. And finally on to Dortmund – a fine stadium that held about 45,000 Scousers among a 65,000 capacity crowd, so that place was always going to look good, rain or no rain.

Man of the year was the ageing Gary McAllister, who was used sparingly throughout the historic season to save his battered old legs. What a man; one day our manager maybe? It felt like we were back where we belonged, but some people are never happy, trying to say we were lucky and all that crap. Micky Owen's goals destroyed the old Arsenal FA Cup jinx and the celebrations after that second one went in past the pony-tailed ponce were as long and as hard as any I've seen.

At the League Cup final a large mob of Cardiff skins were walking around the city centre looking for any Birmingham skins, and whenever they bumped into any of the Liverpool boys they'd tell them so. Apparently the two clubs had a history of naughtiness; if so, it didn't spoil our two weekend benders, because I had a fine beverage at both finals. The UEFA Cup final in Dortmund was an all-day party and as we sat drinking at a bar in nearby Dusseldorf, nobody could believe it was our first European final for fifteen years. It felt like we had never been away, with all the old faces fifteen years down the line. The lounge we fell into inside the stadium at the end of the game was one of the finest I'd seen, and I've seen quite a few. By the time the Super Cup was lifted against Bayern Munich in Monaco and the Charity Shield against Man U in Cardiff, we were looking at five pieces of silverware. It was like the old taxi adage that you wait an age for one to come along, then suddenly there's five.

After such a fantastic start to the new millennium we were back in the European Cup, after finishing third in Gerard Houllier's second full season in charge. This new-look Champions Cup had way too many games; plus you could lose a couple of times and still win the cup. It also meant that fellas had to be choosy where they went, as by the time we'd reached the quarter-final against Bayer Leverkusen we had played fourteen games. The flying in, flying out method was all the rage, but is nowhere near as much fun as when you hit the road. We were only forty-five minutes from a Man U semi –

now that would have been good – but Leverkusen, who were a very good team at the time, knocked us out. I had spent most of the half-time interval singing, when I was convinced that we were through. The beauty of the game I suppose. My second surprise of the night turned up at Cologne Station, when a mob of 200 Cologne skins attacked the first Liverpool fans to arrive back there. It was totally unexpected, and innocent fans, being the first ones out of the door, were the first to meet the German golfballs head-on.

As we re-grouped, anyone who was a bit of a lad charged at the mob of Germans and they scattered. I was so up for it that I ran right through their mob. I caught this Turkish-looking hoolie who had been giving it the big one with a bottle in his hand outside the doors of the station, but as I gave him a few digs I realised that only three of us had kept on chasing them. The rest of the Liverpool supporters couldn't be arsed, and as soon as the Cologne fans ran, they simply left them to run. Suddenly, thirty or forty of them were directly behind me and two other Liverpool lads, with the rest of them scattered about roughly 100 yards up the street. The Turk/German starts screaming for help and without warning we found ourselves in no-man's land. The Cologne shitbags who had just run up the street without looking back realised what was going on, as the couple we had on the floor and the twenty or so behind us shouted them back. I knew this place, I'd been in no man's land before, but they were the years when Speedy Gonzales was still knocking about and I'd recently jibbed going to the gym. *Shit!*

While hitting the guy on the floor, I was already clocking which way to go. Looking beyond the twenty behind us, I became aware of just how far we had chased the German firm, as I couldn't see the station or the Liverpool supporters behind them. *Forward or back? Fuck it, sideways, ta-ra.* I shouted the other two as I felt the cobbles slipping under my feet: 'We're off, we're off, we're off in a motor car, sixty Germans after us and we don't know where we are. We turned around the corner . . .' The other two lads were laughing their heads off even with the German flying jacket crew right behind. The laughing stopped abruptly when a hammer sailed over our heads. We'd thought we were out of range, as the bottles they threw had smashed short of the target, but they obviously had the German national hammer thrower in that crew. We ran down a narrow street and I could tell it led somewhere. Any dead ends and it was three dead friends. As we ran full-pelt, I was thinking, *at least the oul legs have still got the speed when required*. After running for a few minutes we noticed this big mob up ahead. *Germans or Scouse?* Fantastic, it was the cavalry. They gave a brief chant and the flying jackets turned and fled.

The Liverpool crew charged past us, chasing the Germans. I instantly recognised most of the lads who were speeding past, but I kept my head down and kept on walking into the night. Quite a lot of the young lads who'd sped by had greeted me; they looked confused as I carried on walking against the flow. They knew me well and probably wondered where I was going and why I wasn't up for it, but the one thing they didn't know was that my brain was getting hammered with the same voice; it was my own and it kept repeating: *Who the fuck are you kidding? Get home to yer wife and kids, you dickhead, get home to yer wife and kids, you nugget*. I've never been a hypocrite. I knew it was over for me.

CHAPTER SIXTEEN

The Real King Billy

DURING THE 2001/2002 season I was boarding a plane home from Barcelona and a couple of kids bunked aboard for the ride back to pie and chips country. Before the plane took off, the crew knew something was amiss, so everybody was told they'd have to walk off the aircraft and onto the runway for a head count and baggage check. We were there for an absolute age as planes sailed into the evening sky all around us. After each passenger had identified their own bag, two or three were left standing on the runway. The cabin crew wouldn't go near the bags that were left over and, for whatever reason, nobody claimed ownership. The two or three hundred aboard the plane had gotten that fed-up waiting about that they toyed with the idea of sprinting across the runway en masse, as it was bound to be a right good laugh and the authorities would no doubt get their skates on, wanting to be rid of us off their own turf. We had already embarked and disembarked twice and as we weighed up doing a 'runway sprint', they finally boarded us and the plane took off. I don't know what happened to the extra bags, but what I do know is, the crew had sensed that people were getting fed up and something was about to kick off, so they decided, 'whatever extra was on-board' it was time to depart, NOW!

Sitting comfortably on the plane home, some younger lads

were reading those Cockney hoolie books, the 'we legged you' books. It was there and then that I decided a little bit of redress was needed, especially before some Welsh woollyback nugget came along to write all about the Liverpool Boys, or some Scouse lad that had been to West Ham twice and thought it had turned him into Know the Score Rory with his cock and bull story. I mean, you read some of these hoolie books, especially the 'cor blimey' London ones and you have to laugh. When their teams played at Anfield those match gangsters were as scarce around the ground as Liverpool–Man U tickets on the morning of the game. Soon as Officer Plodrington and his matchday marines turned up in force, after Heysel '85, they started getting braver and finally came out of the London smoke to venture past Watford Gap. Next thing is they're telling you they battered everyone. Truth is, the crews they brought before Heysel were almost non-existent, and considering the next ten years and the reputation they think they've got, well I've got to say more fish have been battered in our chippy on a quiet Monday night. It's like me oul mate Joey O says, 'I see the pearly kings of bullshit have got a new book out again.' It's like those Home Counties Chelsea hoolies acting the match gangsters at the England games. Most of *them* have been brought up in gangster-riddled outposts like 'orrible on top Oxford', 'rumpus and ruck riddled Reading', and even that place that remains top of the league for shitting yer kecks, the killer scallywag yard they call Tunbridge Wells. I mean, give us a break. Now they've gone on to sell their team to a Russian in the hope of hope and glory. I wonder how that feels? Not very English, I would imagine.

Well, me and me brethren had a different upbringing than the majority of those plastic match gangsters. We got hooked on the football full-time, and not for just something to do, when we first saw and heard King Billy Shankly.

I got hooked on the football when I saw and heard Bill Shankly, backed up by a singing, swaying Kop. For us, politics, life and football were all intertwined, like a sole existence, not just certain hats you wore at the weekend. When I look at who the characters are in football today, I'm struggling. It's all so serious, on and off the terraces, with TV cameras watching the mega-rich players' every move and stadium cameras focused on making sure the fans don't move. It'll be like Communist China soon: clap politely, but you'd better sit still if you don't want a ban. A lot of the seriousness is due to faceless money-men (agents and overpaid executives) and players bleeding the game dry; it's become a moneyman's game, with contracts and cash being far more important than medals and cups. And the rule makers have started down the non-contact route, and football with no contact is like sex with no contact – you might be up for a dabble, but it's a lot less pleasing. If a player gets slightly aggressive in his tackling or passionate about the shirt he's wearing, he's instantly penalised. So nearly every time you see a good hard tackle, or a player hunt down the ball with effort, causing you to roar him on, the woeful referees blow the whistle and the whole thing dies a death. It's passionless. Whereas a game would ebb and flow, continual petty stoppages are like putting a spanner in your Raleigh Chopper chain; it cracks me up. The politically correct brigade have also found their way through the turnstiles and have been hitting everyone over the head with that big fat Liberal lollypop for years now. Things like kicking the ball out every time some one goes down with a broken toenail, fuck all that, we want you to play on; only stop if it's deadly serious, like his head has been chopped off.

Don't sing this, don't sing that, sit down, don't stand up, don't 'fucking' swear, don't be aggressive, there are women and children here, don't raise your banner too high we can't see, and don't let it hang over the Kellogg's Fucking Cornflakes advert while you're there. It's watered down football being played in front of a watered down crowd. But if you're well wedged-up and enjoy a nice, sterile, non-existent atmosphere, and it doesn't bother you if you're sitting next to some Mars Bar in a jester's hat who's busy telling mummy to have his tea ready on his top of the range mobile, then you've found your ideal place to watch the match.

I recently went to watch my first Sunday League game in years, thinking it might be different. It was: I got covered in mud and all the players looked like Johnny Vegas. I got hooked on a much tougher, noisier and rowdier game, with bouncing, singing mobs and players who were more accessible and down to earth. But with football stars today becoming more and more aloof, as the 'do not disturb' signs go up on their new security gates, it's getting harder to feel or build an affinity. And with those same players buying Buckingham Palace-style mansions, times two (they have to have one abroad as well), with five Mercedes Jeeps parked on the football pitch they call a paved driveway, while Mary-Ellen indoors is hanging up her diamond-encrusted Prada knickers for the neighbours to try to rob, it's all gone arse over tit. The way it's going we'll end up with £500,000-a-week players with mansions on the moon, who only 'beam down, Scotty' at the weekend to put in an appearance, soon to be followed by a load of books telling you how Chelsea took Jupiter's end. Either that or it will self-destruct. Ah well, what can you do? For a little bit of sanity for the over-thirties, let me tell you a little story about how I 'disturbed' the Liverpool manager one day, but it wasn't at all like today's script, nah, no getting blanked for me boys, let me give you the S.P. on a different kind of football man.

Me and my brother, when we were nine and ten, jumped off the bus outside Anfield late one night. It was winter, freezing cold and dark. As we entered the Liverpool FC car park there was no-one about and under that massive Kop roof it all looked a bit spooky. We went over by the players' entrance and stared through the large window, steam rising from our mouths. As we whispered quietly, the window misted over. Suddenly a door opened and the noise was magnified tenfold in the crisp stillness of the night. We jumped behind a wall but the person who opened the door had seen us. I could see two fellas coming out.

'Quick, get in here and hide.'

It was no use, we knew they'd seen us. As we walked out, a Scottish voice said, 'Hey, what are you doing there?'

It was Shankly and following close behind was Ian St John. I'd know those two faces a mile off.

'Shanks, we've come to see you.'

'And where have you come from son?'

'From Kirkby. On the bus.'

'Does your dad know you're here?'

'Err no, we never told him.'

St John spoke up, 'It's a bit late to be down here isn't it boys?'

'Yes Saint, er Ian, er, Mister John.'

'Take it easy boys, you're not in any trouble.'

And Shankly goes, 'I think you boys better be getting on that bus back home, what d'ya say?'

'Yes Bill, er Shanks . . . er yes, Mister Shankly.'

They both signed their autographs and were giggling away

about something. Meanwhile, I was staring at Shankly like he was God. Then he spoke again.

'Come on, you boys get back down the Valley for the bus to Kirkby.'

The two of them walked us to the jigger by the Albert pub, and for a moment we hesitated as they walked away. We wanted to go back, but Shankly saw this and said, 'Now get home, your mother and father will be worried.'

I'm thinking, *you're not kidding, me da would have a fit if he knew we were here.*

'Okay Shanks, er Mister Shankly.'

And we were off. We sped all the way down the hill to the bus stop without speaking; it was the budding Speedy Gonzales showing some early potential in the sprinting stakes. From the moment we stopped, we acted like we'd just met Jesus himself: all nervy and jangly and floating on air. In fact, it wasn't like he was the son of God; for us at the time, he was the one true God, one who we'd seen and touched.

The next time I spoke to Shankly was in the Kop five years later, five years that went in a blink. We were playing Coventry at home and he had recently retired and decided he would like to stand with the singing supporters on the Kop. He was wearing a light cotton mac and I was on the barrier directly behind him. Nobody would touch him, and as the Kop swayed back and forth, they made a small circle around the man, even though he complained and said they didn't have to. The Kop understood his gesture, as they sang constantly throughout the game, to the tune of 'On Ilkley Moor':

> You'll always be our king
> You'll always be our king
> You'll always be our king.

He later said, 'I got my red and white scarf from a boy on the Kop and brought it home. I am a citizen of Liverpool and I wanted to go there and see the fans who have done so much for me. The handshakes are real, they aren't false. It was an enjoyable experience and not as tiring as you might think.'

Earlier in the Sixties, the man had walked down the pitch and climbed into the Kop during a game. He asked the surrounding Kopites about tactics, team selection and who we might buy. He was getting a feel for the place and wanted to see where the people were coming from. Where do you see fellas like that today? Nowhere. This lot are all too busy living in big, glass mansions that'll one day crack. A lot of stuff about the great Bill Shankly often gets romanticised, as it does with other people of legend. At times, it can be a Liverpool trait, but there's no harm in that. We didn't care. We loved him, full stop and always will.

A few years after Shanks had stood on the Kop, I was in Glasgow to watch Liverpool play Celtic for Danny McGrain's testimonial. Before the game we ventured over to Ibrox Park, so we could say we had seen both grounds. A little gang of us walked straight into the trophy room and were wandering around inside the office part of the stadium when we bumped into the Rangers player Derek Johnston, who asked us what did we think we were doing. He ushered us out before showing us around the pitch and the terraces. He seemed like a decent fella. As we ran onto the pitch he told us we'd better get off, as the pitch was sacred. He then led us to a small supporters' shop, where we binned as many scarves hats and badges as we could once his back was turned. This was all good stuff for a bunch of young, football-loving rag-arses. His parting shot as we left the stadium confused us a little, as we were only going to a testimonial.

'Cheers Derek mate, thanks for that.'

'Nae problem boys. Oh and by the way. I hope you hammer those Fenian bastards tonight.'

Half the lads didn't have a clue what he was on about, while the other half looked at him in mild amusement, till one of the lads shouted, 'Shut up, you King Billy bastard.'

And he smiled the smile of recognition. All that stuff sailed right over my head at the time. Most of us were young Catholics of Irish/Liverpool descent, but we weren't into all that shit. I suppose things would've been different had we been born in Northern Ireland. Mind you, some of the lads were of Protestant, English descent, so we wouldn't have even been together if that had been the case. Bollocks to all that. Togetherness is what it's all about; fuck all that divide-and-conquer Tory shit. It was a strange thing to shout to a bunch of young Scousers and I'll always remember what he said. The testimonial at Parkhead that evening was a Glasgow education in itself, when a number of Celtic fans grabbed me bunking in to the side of the ground they called The Jungle (Celtic's home end), and were telling me to pay in properly and give my money to Danny's fund, then laughing when I replied, 'What fucking money?' And me asking the same crowd 'What the fuck are macaroons?' as some guy constantly walked past trying to sell these small Scottish toffee bars.

From then on, I'm all over the place. I'm chasing Mancs outside the huge Tivoli Fair, pre-season in Copenhagen, Denmark, late Seventies; now that was a decent battle, as they tasted the dust from a Danish building site. I'm singing 'You'll Never Walk Alone' to interrupt the National Anthem before cup final after cup final; it was never happening, that 'God Save The Queen' song, for the Liverpool fans. Then I'm bang out of order as me and me mates batter these Forest fans because we thought they were all 'scabs', with the lads in question repeating that they didn't know what the fuck we were on about (or so they said). It's European Cup finals in London, Paris, Roma, Brussels and Dortmund, semi-finals and pre-seasons from pillar to post, forty-two-game seasons year-in, year-out, fighting with men, boys and even a woman once who attacked me in Chelsea's Main Stand. I couldn't hit her back but I gave her a right mouthful (remember love, I said you only hit me because you fancied me and you went nuts?). Then we've got Jegsy Dodd, the local man of rhyme, telling me to pull down the window shutter, seeing as we're reaching the dodgy part of the line at Man U, and just as he tells me, a brick comes through the window and hits him square in the mush. I'm viewing a wedding near the Hawthorns as it gets totally ruined because West Brom and Liverpool fans have laid siege with a massive rock fight while the congregation has to hit the deck. Leaving Highbury by Tube and hearing that a number of police horses had been slashed outside Arsenal's ground; now that was weird. Standing outside Upton Park in 1978, as West Ham get relegated after we beat them 2–0, and their fans go Landon loopy. Guinness, the only black lad I've ever seen in Liverpool with red hair, trying to walk back to the station with me from Middlesbrough's Ayresome Park in 1979 after we'd missed the main mob, and I'm thinking, *fuck that Guinness lad, if you stand out in Liverpool, imagine what you look like here.* Sometimes that kid was called Jaffa or Cigar. Then there was the Jocky Wilson testimonial game (kidding) as it rained darts in Manchester City's Kippax; I'm saying, 'Don't throw them, they're only going to come right back,' and they did. Man U getting battered all over the place at Goodison; as if they didn't hate us enough before that 1985 semi. Lads like Sully and Hally, two Alan Whicker-type Reds, coming back from

Galatasaray dressed to the nines in jarg clobber; Liverpool's hairdressing mob, the feather-cut burners, giving out flame-coloured highlights to any Chris Waddle lookalikes; getting back into Europe in 1992 after the ban and the boat going west after the Genoa game; asking Joe Royle at an Oldham game if he'd ever thought of wearing a Ford Escort wheel-trim for a hat, after taking into account the size of his big, fat head, and wondering if Joe still wanted to do that Tommy Cooper impression at the Chrimbo do, as I was still keeping hold of a big oil drum he could use as a fez. Burt Lancaster, the famous actor, telling us to get to fuck in Harrods when we asked him if he'd enjoyed swinging on a trapeze with Tony Curtis. Turning up at a Newcastle boozer where we'd enjoyed a drink for the past few years before the game, only for a bouncer with a sovereign ring on every finger to tell us it had recently become a gay boozer, and me replying, 'Fucksake, I didn't think there were any gay Geordies.' Swiss and German bar tabs throughout the Seventies and the Eighties that let you drink all night for free, providing you could still run at the end. A Man City fan getting the arm ripped off his new sheepskin at a service station, when we tried to turn it into an *Emmerdale Farm* body-warmer as he almost burst into tears. The 'Frank Bruno – You Tory Prick' banner causing uproar in Rome. Emptying the fridges inside a couple of those corporate boxes at the Villa, then watching the Liverpool crew devour the food. A top 'tom pepper' claiming he got followed into Zurich Airport by 'snides' because he was carrying stolen jewellery; apparently they followed him right onto the plane, so he threw the evidence out the window after it took off (he was serious). Twenty Liverpool fans in new Berghaus coats at freezing-cold Innsbruck, standing together inside the ground looking like a page from the catalogue. I could go on and on and on.

Jumping into the mid-Nineties and I'm in the lounge at Anfield enjoying a bevvy, when up pops Robbie Williams,

'What's a Manc from Take That doing at a Liverpool game?' I ask.

And famous balls goes, 'I'm no Manc mate, I'm Port Vale me. I fucking hate Mancs.'

So I go, 'I'll bet you wouldn't say that if your pop star mates were standing here.'

'Oh yes I would mate, Port Vale, me pal.'

After talking to him for ten minutes, he seemed alright. So much so that me and me oul mate Frank were thinking about going out on the ale in Liverpool with him, which he said would be a pleasure. We thought about it, he seemed genuine enough, but then we had to decline and make a joke out of it – his drinking buddy had walked in and it was Phil Babb. Now I'm not going to give Babb any more stick about his playing credentials than I already have, and for all I know he might be a nice fella and all that, but the football always came first for me, and I didn't want to act like some back-slapping hanger-on so I would have ended up telling him that he was shit, end of. And that's no way to enjoy an evening's bevvy.

It showed me how much football was changing, and changing fast. I'd bunked into the lounge one week, and after a few weeks of doing the same thing the steward on the door had started to give me a wink on the way in. He thought I was a regular, a face, a somebody who he was happy to wink to. I'd only started entering what we termed the back-slappers' bar in the first place because it was easy to get served in, as the two stands at Liverpool are nigh-on impossible at half-time and the local boozers are the same at full-time. You'd see all the freebies, the hangers-on and the phoney Liverpool supporters giving it the big one. Acting the fan, me mate used to call it.

I began to realise that some old heroes of mine, people like Kevin Keegan, were just money-hungry mercenaries, professional pound-note men who only loved the club that provided the next pay cheque. He'd said, 'I love Liverpool,' then, 'I love Southampton,' next it was, 'I love Newcastle more than anyone, me,' and at the time of writing, he loves Man City. I mean, make yer mind up. People like me love one club, and when the little Yorkshire nugget started pandering to the Manchester press by joking that he risked getting his wheel trims stolen when he went to Robbie Fowler's house to get him to sign for City, we all instantly knew that the little phoney was money mad. It wasn't the daft, boring, Jim Davidson joke we were bothered about; nah, those robbing jokes are just that — they're a joke. It was the way he was trying to say to the Manchester City fans and the press, 'Look, I'm one of you, I'm giving the Scousers stick, can you hear me?' Crying Kevin Keegan eh — just another blowse with more money than sense, and to think when I was a kid I used to love him. You have to laugh though; the people who he joked might steal his wheels were only the ones who put him on the map in the first place. Short memories, these pound-note men. He'd still be selling socks and undies in Doncaster market if it wasn't for Shankly and the people of Liverpool. Mind you, money-hungry Yorkshire pudding that he is, he'd end up owning the whole fucking market, so he'd still be loaded anyway.

Oh well, another nail in the coffin for the oul football fanatic in me. But for all my cynicism I'm never gonna let a Doncaster perm and a load of poncey pop stars stop me from going the match, oh no. I've been bevvying all over Europe for too long, it's in me blood. If there's a ban in the air, bring it on, but for now I'm off to Bucharest for Bonfire Night, cheap Rumanian rockets, boxes-full for two bob I believe, supposed to be the very best for lighting up the sky. I wonder if I'll find some Catherine Wheels. Oops, I've just remembered they're the German brasses shoes we ran off with down the Reeperbahn. A least I might find some Roman candles. At least I'll be able to find some bangers? Aagh, I'm getting totally confused here, they're all parked outside Old Trafford. I know, keep it simple with rip-raps? Oh forget the fucking fireworks, whatever they've got, I might bring some home for next year when we win the League (in me dreams). Where's me pazzy? Beam me up Scotty.

P.S. Whisper it gently, I've just heard West Ham have legged half of Saturn, watch out for the book next year.

CHAPTER SEVENTEEN

The Final of all Finals

TREKKING ACROSS THE rocky, goat-infested hills of outer Istanbul, the Ataturk Stadium loomed surreally in the distance. I'd dreamed of us winning the league, but this dream was streets ahead – Istanbul streets ahead. This was the mythical gateway between Asia and Europe, where two cultures collided, and if the truth be known, quick right turn into Syria and Lebanon, then Israel, and you were in Northern Africa. Here was the melting pot on the Bosporus, the ancient home of the Empire of Constantinople and the Ottaman Turks, and guess what cultural identity the locals were viewing all this week? Yeah, 'Them Scousers Again,' as one huge red and white banner proclaimed.

They were here in their legions to help create and hopefully witness a new slice of their beloved clubs oh-so-glorious football history. Twenty years on since Liverpool's last final, this was the European Cup for keeps! Hundreds of yellow taxis and green buses were transporting the Red army from the ancient city centre, with its Golden Palaces banking the Bosporus River, its beautiful Blue Mosque and its Grand Bazaar (selling everything from Viagra to Malcolm Glazer masks), upward and outward to the barren wilderness of outer Istanbul. The pilgrimage was being clapped and cheered by thousands of Turks every inch of the way. It was as though the people from the city by the

Mersey were some kind of football royalty. Children in school uniforms were jubilant as Liverpudlians threw them hats and scarves and other small trinkets. Their brown skin framed and magnified their brilliant white smiles. They were the happiest street lights I'd ever seen. I will never forget the joy etched in those schoolkids' faces.

Meantime, our little firm had jumped bus and like thousands of others on that long and winding road, we were now 'bus surfing' our way to the Ataturk in the sky. As the early evening breeze lifted dust with each step, it looked like the futuristic stadium was floating among the haze on some far-off distant horizon. The different streams of fans eventually ran out into one huge red reservoir down in the valley. The reservoir was swarming with red ants and swaying from side to side. Their party rumble beckoned us as it echoed up into the rubble-strewn hills. Bit of a walk, jump bus; another short walk, jump bus. Along the trail, the greetings and spontaneous hugs from people you knew back home were heartfelt and for real. This felt like our road to Damascus, a Scouse Biblical epic, our Five Star holy grail, and yeah, ticketless, as usual, nobody was gonna stop me and my brethren from witnessing those red jerseys lift that Big-Eared Fucker for keeps.

Gilly, Jegsy, Riley, Sante, Whacker Carney from the HJC, Sully and Hally, some of the Kirkby Fusiliers, a few of the Huyton Baddies, Murphy and Gilesy from across the Mersey, Macca, Garner and Davie Bunnymen from the Halewood Chains crew, they were all here for one thing: to see the big one get lifted before being gift-wrapped and taken home for good to the Shrine on the banks of the Mersey. Seeing all these oul' faces – some with bin-lids in tow – alongside the new gave me the feeling it had all come full circle, like a slice of football destiny was taking place. Lads, normally nattily dressed, were noticeably badged- and scarfed-up for proceedings. Should think so!

The stadiums two GTi spoiler roofs drew near. First tout shows face. It's the face of . . . no, wait. No lookalike there, just a scrunched-up face of Special Fried Rice with a Polo-sized hole for a mouth, and it's shouting, 'Anyone looking for tickets?'

I am, so I go, 'Yeah, over here mate. Where are they for?'

'Upper tier, most expensive seats.'

'How much are you looking for?'

'A little extra.'

'What's a little extra, squire?'

Before he could answer, I noticed his accent was coming back all Southern Fried England to match his Special Fried Rice kipper. I didn't get to hear how much bump-up he was looking for, as Waller, a mad Red of a mate, jogs in with,

'Let's have a look what section they're in.'

Making his first mistake, the Fried Rice tout half hands them over, while keeping a slight finger-pinch on the ticket corners.

Waller goes, 'Don't worry mate, we're not gonna snatch them. I just want to see if it's anywhere near me mates.'

The fella, loosening up, loosened his grip.

Waller says, 'Alright mate, now start walking that way.'

The fella eyed him up and down, confused, before glancing round at the red hordes on the rocky road to Damascus. As the penny dropped, his own reality game show kicked in. Realising he was in a total no-gain show, with not a Turkish truncheon in sight, the tout changed tack – fast.

'Okay, just give us face value. It's in Euros on the front.'

Waller scanned the ticket, then repeated his directions, 'Alright mate, now start walking that way – right now!'

This time the threatening overtones went up a notch. Special

Fried Rice looked around for moral support, but he might as well have been looking for a copy of the *Sun* newspaper among the Reds supporters. Sky and its Big Brother cameras moved in towards the commotion, only to be locked out by a blank red wall. Fried Rice turned on his wheels. Waller had his tickets. Fair game if you ask me. But doesn't that Big Brother with his big fuck-off lenses get everywhere! I'd done the same de-briefing to a similar lard fringe at the '78 final in London, in Trafalgar Square, before the game. Cameras aside, this was feeling more full-circle by the minute.

Whoa! There's more. A French TV crew nudged their way in to ask our opinions on the outcome of the game. A drunken song and dance man, dressed-up like the Pope, pushed in to answer the boys from channel Ooh La La. On cue, we happily merged into the marching hordes before Mr Tout had the chance to return with a few Turkish truncheons in tow.

Ticket-wise, we were all sorted. I sat down to witness the scene. *'Stadium to the right of me, hills full of Reds to the left, here I am, stuck in the middle with you.'* The old Steelers Wheel song rattled round my brain for some reason. A huge stage had been temporarily built next to the ground to showcase some new Liverpool bands before the Big One started. It was being rocked by thousands of singing, dancing fans, with a compere pleading for people to leave the stage, as it was about to collapse. This only made them dance some more and it started to bounce as Johnny Cash's 'Ring of Fire' hit the early evening air for the umpteenth time.

The stage and its scaffold had been decorated by the supporters with hundreds of different Liverpool flags. 'We all dream of a team of Carraghers,' said one. 'Pete Price is a cunt,' leathering a local radio DJ, read another; while one of the funniest for me said, 'Boris Johnson, Gorgeous, Blonde and a public school wank veteran.' Young kids, wearing their young Scouse uniforms (Lacoste trackies), were throwing stones at the moving goat targets as droves of red ants came over the Turkish hills. The pilgrimage was one of the greatest sights I'd witnessed in thirty-odd years of footy. I sat mesmerized – as I often was by our supporters. Sometimes I loved them more than the team. It was then that I wondered how we'd gotten to this mystical place . . .

The group stages had been like the league: all stop-start, stop-start. Grazer AK: win away, lose at home. Monaco: win then lose. Olympiakos: lose then win. We ended up having to score three goals in the second half against Olympiakos to get through to the knockout stages, the REAL part of the European Cup. Once Stevie Gerrard had banged in another screamer against the Greeks, with only minutes to go, the crowd sang their hymns of praise knowing we were through. But, at that joyful moment, you never once envisaged ending up in 'The Bul' for the final. Not me, anyway, or the lads who booked end-of-season May family holidays thinking, *this team are going nowhere in Europe*.

From Olympiakos onwards, each game of the knockout stages was treated like a final itself. Bayer Leverkusen, who were funded by pharmaceutical supplies, were first up. Revenge was badly needed after Ballack and Co. had drowned our dreams of lifting the biggest trophy in world club football in an ocean of Night Nurse just three years earlier. We were soon 'Rocking all over the World' when we hammered the German headache tablets 6–2 on aggregate. Bayer was always a good place to visit, although you needed a knob-Aspirin when you eventually found the ground, seeing as it was such a ballache to find. Once you were there, Leverkusen's fans, though wearing those daft, brightly-coloured, German weightlifter kecks and small in number, were vociferous and definitely of the warm, welcoming variety. I tip my jester's hat to them.

Though the red Rafalution was gathering pace, we were still looking a long way off Istanbul, especially when we drew the vengeful, zebra-topped Juventus in the shit-hot quarter-final. It was the first time the clubs had met – almost twenty years to the day – since the Heysel tragedy. Half the journalists on earth were trying to contact me because of my years in Europe and this book, I suppose, asking whether a battle was on the cards and all about that fateful night in '85. I got bored talking about 'the past'; I wanted to talk about 'the today'. These were the raucous type games that got me hooked in the first place. It was making the sporting headlines for all the wrong reasons. Excuse the crap pun, but 'Turin trouble' if you're a footy lad and you're not buzzing for these ones.

Big noises were being made about revenge and what was going to happen to you if you risked travelling to Northern Italy, especially without a piece of paper (ticket). Well, I'd heard that one before! So, when you're told not to go, and threats from Match Gangsters don't have you quivering in your Adidas, then that's when you want to go even more, isn't it? Always was for me anyway. It was funny to hear the same oul' shitbags, the football worriers, preaching to young lads about how iffy it would be and how they certainly wouldn't be going. Worriers apart, those battles, like where Man U got jumped on Scotland Road in the 2005 FA Cup quarter-final, are few and far between these days. It tends to be all Prada bags at ten paces, with hundreds of bizzies and cameras looking on. If you got nabbed, you could be looking at more jug than the Great Train Robbers got. And when you think about the football worriers and seventeen-year-old kids fighting with Jerry on the beaches in Dunkirk, it's quite laughable really.

In the first leg at Anfield, an olive branch of friendship was offered by some, only to be treated as though it had been dipped in dogshit by Juve's hardcore Ultras. The Kop belted out a mighty rendition of 'You'll Never Walk Alone' before creating a giant mosaic that read, 'Amicizia' (Friendship). It was greeted with a back-turned, one-fingered salute from the lard-fringed, sunglasses-wearers in the Anfield Road end. I wasn't surprised by their reaction. Myself, I wasn't up for that hand of friendship malarkey, it was always going to be thrown back in your face anyway. Strange thing is, the people most affected by the disaster, those who lost loved ones, had proved to be the most forgiving of all, mainly because they've seen the bigger picture an' all that, and I mean, most of these one-fingered salute beauts weren't even about in '85. Ultras, ha ha ha! Hundreds upon thousands of soft-arse-fans-abroad hiding behind that logo isn't there. Those back turners seemed more like the John Travolta, Ultra fishcake firm if you ask me, and were probably still swimming around in their da's ball sacks in '85, telling the other hoolie sperm they better watch out or they'd be swimming with the fishes.

The naïve and plainly out of touch *Liverpool Echo* had a front page headline proclaiming 'a big apology' from 'everyone within the city'. It enraged people like myself who thought that some half-arsed, university educated journalist, who wasn't even at the game, had the temerity to think he and his Tory rag could take it on themselves to apologize for all the supporters and the city of Liverpool in general. It was a tasteless, worthless, empty gesture, aimed at headline-grabbing only, and I, along with others, sent words in stating this, but, as usual, they blanked the opinions of the ones who knew the truth and were there. Academic, no-all, no-nothings! What can you do? They basically monopolize the whole city, that newspaper.

The crowd and team were as one that night and Juventus were blown away in the first half, which ended with Liverpool two up. A mistake by our young goalie, Scott Carson (who looks a good 'un to me) gave Juve a second-half goal to leave the tie hanging in the balance for the return leg at the Stade Del Alpe. I believe some of the Ultra fishcakes got cocky and started to look for trouble in Stanley Park after the game, only to end up legging it to their buses when a large Urchin firm showed face.

* * *

Threats by those same Ultras were levelled at travelling Liverpool fans, through internet sites and through messages sent to various media. The thing about large-scale 'football threats' is that they usually narrow an away support down to its more hardcore brethren. Looking about John Lennon Airport on the morning of the return leg, a high percentage of the travellers seemed to be young, gifted and clobbered-up in black. The first and last descriptions take care of themselves, but when I say gifted I mean in the witty statement department, as I heard one young lad saying openly, 'Its like when they tell you not to go, you know, that's when you've gorra go.' Adding, 'Like when a bird says she won't let you near trap two, so you know that's where you're dabbling.' The Cockiness of youth, eh!

On the plane to Trap Two, a young lad came over to me and showed me another one of those Cockney sponsored hoolie books (some things never change) where some Manc hotdog seller was having a pop at me for not being 'well known' – which I take as an absolute compliment by the way – and that he knew some of the top Liverpool boys and they'd never heard of me. Being a footy gypo of some mileage, I gathered they must be the Liverpool boys from Salford then. This Homer Simpson went on to say that in the '70s and '80s Not-A-Manc-In-Sight United were the kings of Europe and he was the king of the jibbers, ha ha, ha! More like the king of the fucking fibbers. While Liverpool won four European and two UEFA Cups, and they won nothing, they were still the kings of Europe according them. Don't they realise that kids are all computered-up these days and can easily see through the hooligan bullshit with the power of the microchip? He was going on about Man City being jealous and bitter, but his generation of Milltown Cranks was always jealous and bitter about Liverpool, due to us bouncing all over Europe and normally being a good two years ahead of them in all things wise. This was the beaut who barricaded himself in on the train when the Scousers turned up and who must've been getting home leave every weekend to watch the Red Devils, as he started bragging about how much jug he'd done.

I told the lad, who was eighteen, that this type of 'shit-chattin' and jealous football fabrication was the main reason I wrote this book. As a footnote, David Cooke and Paddy Barret, two mates who were on the train in Portugal for Euro 2004, bumped into this fella and he apparently said this book was a good read. Confusing or confused? Who cares?

Landing in Turin, the Quick to the Sticks (Italian bizzies) were numbered-up and ready to rock 'n' roll, but the people on the incoming planes were mostly experienced football gypsies like myself and knew that the caribineri were one of the most heavy-handed forces in Europe. So, leaving the plane, then the airport, people were under starters. Almost as many reporters and newspapermen were hovering outside the police cordon, just aching for a kick-off. Unlike England's

No Surrender Boys, who normally act up and reach for the plastic chairs on cue, everyone stayed calm and lip-sealed. Surprisingly, even the Quick to the Sticks seemed to be laid back and let a couple of young lads re-board the coaches outside the airport after the sniffer dogs had found their day's pot provisions.

On the way to our midday destination, Mussolini's castle for a nosebag, passing cars and vans were giving us the cut-throat gestures, which made everyone laugh, especially when a wrinkly oul' Italian biddy started giving it the bifters. It still let you know how the locals felt though. I love it when a game has an edge like this and I knew the 4–500 aboard the buses felt the same. It's the Rangers–Celtic thing, where you know sectarianism is idiotically wrong, but it's all a main part of what makes that game such a raucous occasion. Once we reached the castle, each coach was seated in turn. The manager, Danny De Vito in stack-heels and a waistcoat, informed us from a microphone that 'dinner will be served.' Well, the macaroni cheese served up was elephant sponk, the wine poured was cat piss and the bread sticks chomped on were like robbers' coshes, while all the time the massive eating hall was full of some of Liverpool's maddest lads just dreaming about the chippy. Basically, Peroni ale is what we needed. We were told that no more alcohol would be available once we'd drunk our allotted two cans and a bottle of wine each. See, organised trip with no other option and that's how they treat you. Bollocks to that! A scout was sent to a hole in the castle wall to meet a wise-arse villager from the offy. Soon hundreds of Euros were being turned into crates of Italian sherbet. But warm ale – nah! Some lads enjoyed the cat-piss-vino more than others; like Sante, who readily smoked a fat breadstick joint – on fire at one end – when it was offered to him by Joey O'D. Only when everybody burst out laughing did he realize he was Bob Marley on breadsticks.

Two slow-supping, sunbathing hours later and we were back on the buses towards the stadium. One lad took the microphone and sung a lovely version of 'Redemption Songs'. The cut-throat gestures were back and coming from every Fiat displaying a black and white barcode. All the lads wanted to get off and walk to the ground . . . with this mob you'd walk through any town anywhere in the world. The Quick to the Sticks were having none of it and hurried hundreds back aboard the coaches after motorway traffic got an eyeful of 400 unzipped Scousers having a lag. Boy, were we in the mood for this one! Reaching the stadium was like entering the battle zone, as helicopters twirled noisily in the early evening sky. Riot cops had apparently been battling with the Ultra John Travoltas all day and those same gun-carrying Darth Vaders were now trying to hustle us through the turnies as some straggling Juve skins got legged.

One young lad piped up, 'Imagine the full-on battle we could have if the bizzies disappeared.' It's not hard to imagine. Entering the Stade Del Alpi we were greeted with a torrent of whistles, catcalls and firecrackers, while a new mob of Ultras, the Ultra Stadium Destroyers, ripped out seats to use as Frisbees. This was all good stuff – bit more rowdy like the oul' stadiums. There were three levels you could stand in the Curva Nord; I chose the middle tier for atmosphere and view, and seeing as you had to have one eye on the ball and one trained Dalek eye on the flying coins, seats and fireworks in the neck-stretching bottom tier. Anyway, I never did fancy a bottle of olive oil (Italian piss) as a quick fringe conditioner. The top view gave you Diddyman binocular footy and got christened Glastonbury because it's where the LFC pot smokers decided to camp out.

A female announcer brought a loud collective laugh from the whole Liverpool mob when she stated, 'Anyone throwing missiles could face up to six months in prison.' At least two chokeys full of lags ignored the plea and continued to lob everything at us. The Quick to the Sticks remained motionless. It's as though one 'throw what the fuck you like' law for Italy and one 'fart too loud in the ground and it's a three-year ban' law for the UK was in place. Some Liverpool fans who'd had enough started to lash stuff back. I cottoned on that the last time a police force remained as apathetic as this, at this fixture, a serious tragedy unfolded. For a short while it was looking like a major kick-off was about to progress, as both sets of fans charged at the fence. This time, though, the barricades were not made of imported Belgium chicken wire. When the caribineri finally regained order (only when Liverpool started to kick off, not before), the inflammatory Hillsborough flags came out like clockwork, along with some 'Fuck the Queen' and 'Ugly Camilla' ones, which were funny but also meant to wind us up. As if – dickheads.

The team in red played keep-ball to the end and we roared them home. Red tackles were cheered like goals and 3,000 loons were disco dancing to 'Ring of Fire'. The final whistle was greeted like a last-minute derby winner, as strangers hugged, danced and cavorted. Fucksake, you could tell this red choo-choo was gathering steam when even the iPod wearing pot smokers in the top tier started to wake up and sing. Hundreds of caribineri managed to maintain an unstable peace and the last chance for a battle of Turin failed to materialize. We were definitely on the march under this Rafa fella, and arriving at JLA in the early hours of the morning, nobody showed signs of weariness as we bounced out of the airport and home to our flocks.

All I can say about Chelsea in the semi was that there was only going to be one winner. The 'imagine ifs' and the 'imagine thats' were doing the rounds in Liverpool once more. People were being tempted to dream again, and once you fan the dream embers of success-starved Liverpool supporters, fact is, they normally get fed, then turn into a blaze. On the other side of the Kop roof, the Chelsea support these days is full of glory-hunting, pop star wannabes, and listening to their silence throughout two European Cup semi-finals and an earlier season Coca Cola Cup final, tells me which supporters were brought up on football for breakfast, dinner and tea. To see the changing face of corporate footy, look no further than Stamford Fridge: the cold, passionless graveyard of today's footy-yuppies. In the first leg they should have given the Scousers more tickets, just to teach the Fridge how to defrost and sing. A hundred thousand turned out to see them tour the Championship trophy for the first time in fifty years, whereas almost 750,000 lined the streets of Liverpool to get a glimpse of Big Ears – need I say more.

For a bit of first-leg nostalgia, the lads met at Trafalgar Square, where an outdoor party began as bottles of red dye were dropped into the fountains. The London Plod soon called a halt, yer know, seeing as the tourists were enjoying the spectacle and taking too many photos. Meantime, a banner that read 'London Stinks of Cat's Piss' seemed to 'Kill the Bill' and their ability to get into the swing of things. The tourists moved on to find more attractions while the Reds supporters moved on to find boozers. The game was as drab as the home support, as 3000 bottom-tier Liverpudlians sang their hearts out and dreamt some more.

The return game was edge-of-your-seat, arse-twitching time, as you could almost smell the kebabs. Anyone who witnessed the second-leg would struggle to describe the passion in and around Anfield that night. The cobbled roads were like a riotous street carnival, while the ground itself felt electrified, like it was ready blow at the seams. Tickets, as usual, were as scarce as big silver trophies at Goodison and fellas with no tattoos in Newcastle, and eBay and internet touts were charging up to a grand. Be nice if it was easier to meet and de-brief a few of those internet spivs. The street carnival led straight to the gates of The Shrine. Once you were in and you glimpsed the pitch, a typhoon of noise twatted you square in the chest. Forty-odd thousand fantasists were under starters!

Once the ref blew his whistle to continue the fantasy, the Kop and all its dreamers vacuum-sucked Luis Garcia's shot over the line (by the way, I was on the edge of the six-yard box and it was well in, end of) then blew noise out like you've never heard in your life. They were still blowing it out with minutes to go, when they blew Gudjohnsen's shot off the line and the Chelsea fans clean out of the stadium. We were so up for the cup that incredible night that an army of *Big Issue* sellers would have struggled to stop our unyielding march. By the way, I'm glad the Chelsea Roubles couldn't afford that crowd of vagabond street traders for a defence, as they were about the only people on earth who had a chance of stopping us. Mind you, how do you stop a spiritual journey to destiny?

We were there! Or should I say here, on this Bulgarian beach where I'm finishing what I started to tell you prior to kick-off. I was going to finish the day after the final but I've been on a four-day bender with roughly three hours kip a night to get me by. A full four days after probably the greatest final ever and I'm still buzzing off me cake like a demon speed freak! And for some reason, I keep getting in at five o'clock in the morning. The day and night of the 25th of the fifth, 2005, will live with me and the 45,000 other Liverpudlians who were there, forever. It's getting scary how many times that number five has showed face. Five people in our party, five stars on the Central Bar sign where we end up partying every night, fifth win, fiftieth final, going down to five pens and somebody has just told me it was the fifth time Milan had worn the white.

Requiring a dip in the Black Sea, we'd hastily booked a week in the Sunny Beach resort of Bulgaria, as people booked flights via all corners of Europe from the UK. Istanbul flights were gone in days, so the new route and travel agent enquiry was, 'Via anywhere please!' The Bulgarian coastline, and Sunny Beach in particular, had become Southport with sunshine, accompanied by food, clobber and wallop that was, in the words of that wrinkly antiques fella with the orange face, 'Cheap as chips!' Things are happy-hazy at the moment as though it was all a dream. Funny how footy can lift people that way, yer know, give them that all over buzz like a kid whose tableted off his tits. I suppose you'd had to have had football as an on-going lifetime agenda to know where I'm coming from.

Anyway, for all those football loons who've never had and probably never will have the pleasure of the Big One, here's a quick shufti of how a European Cup Final trip goes. And let me tell you that what has taken place in the last few days feels like another lifetime since my first skedaddles abroad. No more season after season of bunking the rattler and the boat with no passport or dough, having Jaffa Cake crumbs only in the lining of me pockets, with 'No sleep till Brooklyn' on flea-ridden mattresses, where minus-two-star Hotel Shithole always had to have an easy sash window to climb out of. For a lad whose body could bend its way past any hotel receptionist when Liverpool were in town, or swerve its way into any football stadium on earth, this all used to be the lay of the land. Not now. Now it's all few quid in yer bin, step aboard nice flights, drink loads of ale then dive into yer king-size springy flock. Oh yeah, Hotel Shithole has to be at least a three-star, with a name like De Palace Royale El Brewsters, before you'll rest your tatty barnet inside. Not that I'm arsed about the upgrades myself, but everyone else seems to be. It's what you're used to I suppose, and seeing as I've kipped in streets and car park lifts . . .

One thing that seems to be permanently set in stone is the ticketless situation, because I'm not joining some daft, club- or government-sponsored travel organization. Nah, leave the football to the club and the travelling to the football gypsies. Anyway…

Arriving here, at our all-inclusive five-star hotel (that number again), on the Monday before the final, we ordered a pint or three before downing bags in rooms on the fifth floor – serious. Tuesday night we met Jimmy Hollywell, John Davies and Phil McGreal, who had sorted a charra for us to get to The Bul. It was leaving at 4.30am, so a half-arsed curfew was put in place in the hope of getting some much needed shut-eye. We eventually got in at two bells. Falling onto the charra, other crews of lads were picked up at different points around Sunny Beach, before we headed off to the hills of the Bulgarian/Turkish border. Wise travellers had brought their pillows from the hotel rooms for the tarmac-less, dirt road tour.

We reached the border at half seven. It felt like we'd been stuck on the Big Dipper in the misty morning mountains of Outer Mongolia – that's what my arse felt and the place looked like. As we stopped at the Bulgarian side, most lads swerved the holes-in-floor toilets and used the mountain fields instead. I thought I was being wise by sneaking into the ladies' bogs, as a few Liverpool girls laughed at my cheek. But it smelled like Bernard Manning's Y-fronts, and was even mintier than the men's. The woman collecting coins outside the holes in the floor had a better beard than Georgie Best and got blanked every time she put her mitts out. Soon a huge traffic jam of commissioned Liverpool taxis, vans, hired cars and coaches were stood still, weaving a path way up through the misty mountains. Flags were being waved out of windows, songs were being sung, while others were having yodelling contests. It deffo rated as one of the weirdest scenarios I've seen at the footy.

Once we reached the Turkish customs, some two hours later, the putrid holes in the floor had been nicknamed the Devil's Doorways and the new bearded lady on the Turkish side couldn't understand why she was getting blanked, as everyone started pissing into the trees. The Turkish bizzies created a total gridlock by trying to extract whatever coinage they could from every supporter. They wanted £10 from everyone stood in a line where you had to show tickets and passports. People were telling them to fuck off, but in the end, with a European Cup Final to go to, everyone paid up. A Turkish interpreter tried to make out it was a hooligan checkpoint – an' I know, yeah! Half the people never had match tickets, but a photocopy was adequate proof. Hundreds were soon queuing at the one photocopying machine to sort copies for their mates, as a large pass-the-ticket-back operation got under way.

I went for a piss against some brand new Mitsubishi jeeps, which I presumed were imports, seeing as they were covered in cellophane. Suddenly, what looked like seven or eight Taliban were staring out at me while I tried to spray LFC on the side doors. Wiping the misted windows, I double-clocked the Taliban adults and swore I could see Taliban tots hiding underneath their ma's and da's beards. It was getting weirder by the minutes. I'd heard all about the Third World, but I didn't know it was in Europe.

Although hundreds were starving, nobody would eat the Alsatian sarnies or jarg Twix's on offer. Some young fella who'd driven his car over was almost in tears, because they told him he was not getting through. Another lad was having a serious snarl with the photocopier owner (Tattoo off Fantasy Island) because he'd given him no change from about fifty quid. It was deffo turning League of Gentlemen. Just as some people were contemplating a runner across the hills, for the fun of it, the penny-pinching, muzzied-up arse-bandits finally let us go.

The rocky road to Damascus continued for five more hours, with two more stops at Devil's Doorways, where Cocker Spaniel sarnies and jarg Fanta were on offer. Magnum ice creams were all we could find, so I had a three course Magnum dinner, but ended up lashing the third one at a three-legged Cocker Spaniel who was tied up in the corner of the Devil's Doorway. It had definitely had its other leg ripped off for the service station sarnies. This Turky lurky place, so far, was looking like one rough gaff! I liked it though, it was different.

We finally hit the motorway and arrived in Istanbul at around two o'clock. Alex, who was seven, asked me about the all the missile rockets that were pointing to the heavens on the city skyline. He was told they were Taliban rockets ready to be fired at anyone in the world who kicked off on the Muslims. He looked worried, so he was truthfully told they were the pointed towers of mosques. As we passed yet another sky rocket, the Ataturk Olympic Stadium came into view. We were so joyous at finally viewing the Promised Land that we impatiently jumped coach, not knowing we were still five or six miles from Taksim Square in the city centre (the meeting place for the Big Red Party). It was early enough, seeing as the game didn't kick-off till quarter to ten local time. Yellow taxis were everywhere and from the moment we jumped ours, we were in the Turkish Wacky Races. No lanes, pure 70mph, fairground bumping cars, with loads of taped-up wing mirrors. Our driver, who looked like a smackhead from Blackburn (half woollyback, half Pakistani and half asleep), was nuts, and so were the other drivers.

Reaching Taksim Square was a vehicle maze, with crawling traffic being needle-threaded by banana coloured taxis that were slip-sliding all over the show. But once the red legions and their banners led us directly to the gathering, we bid our farewells to mad-arse Tony Blackburn. A fella who looked like Super Mario instantly popped out of the maze of streets and tried to sell us match colours, but he looked confused when we asked him did he have any bushy, stick-on muzzies like his own. Finding our way through the maze, we hit the Square. Or should I say the Square hit us. It was absolutely rocking! The streets and buildings were dripping with red as song after song bounced of walls and down side streets. We dipped into one of those side streets, into a bar called the North Shield. It felt like we'd stepped into an oxygen artery, while the main streets were blocked veins and needed a bypass. The Big Red Party was in full swing and after 100 Scouse hugs and 1,000 'how are yers', I looked around and breathed it all in. It was that Paul Weller 'Wildwood' moment: 'High tide, mid-afternoon. People fly by, in the traffic's boom. Knowing just where you're blowing. Getting to where you should be going.' The gorgeous sunshine, the afternoon reverie and the tickle of the butterflies in me Levis that only a game of this magnitude bring to your being, was washing all over me. For a passing moment I drifted back to sitting astride a couch in a Parisian boulevard with a street full of hotel furniture before me, Rome and the frontline Lazio scallies, beating Jean-Claude in the 400m around Trafalgar Square in '78, the clattering of tom shops and the party at Grand Platz Square in Brussels, Munich and the caterpillars cufflinks, Vienna and the Snowbound Skinheads, it was endless. It was time to breathe in Istanbul, 2005...

Jumping on the buses back to the Ataturk, I joined in with the people singing and banging on the roof, and as our green bus was swallowed up by the vehicle maze to take part in the Wacky Races once again, I silently thanked the lord I was born a Red!

* * *

About that game, well, what can you say? Here was a piece of pure theatre about a dream of destiny come true. The miracle of Istanbul re-wrote football history, stating that no cause need ever be lost. You can already hear it around the ale-gut-packed Sunday League fields of Britain: 'Come on, we're only three down, let's do a Liverpool.' Can words do justice to such an occasion? I think not. But this is a book about Liverpool supporters, so I'll try and keep it brief. We were being turned over by a fantastic team, 3–0 at half-time. Personally, I never had a notion about 3–1 or 3–2, never mind 3–3. I just wanted a goal to go home with and to give us some pride to take back to Liverpool. I already thought we'd done brilliantly to get this far. I mean, nobody thought we'd score three in the second half against Olympiakos, or have an earthly against Juve or Chelsea, but once you're three down at half-time against maybe the meanest defence in the world, what can you do?

Thing is, it seemed a shame that the dream for the religious fanatics (Liverpudlianism) who populated three-quarters of the stadium had to end in such an abrupt manner. The smacked arse we got in the first-half didn't surprise me, nothing much does these days, but the uppercuts in the second that we marmalized Milan with? Those blows emanated from a supreme will to win on the field, from the likes of Gerrard and Carragher, and from a ferociously loyal backing, who refused to give up on there team, off it. To those supporters who sang 'You'll Never Walk Alone' so sweetly at half-time, I can honestly hold my hands up and say I was stretching me legs in the bogs, not the Devil's Doorways mind you, the proper modern bogs, and when I heard that football anthem that has no equal in the world, being sung in line with a heavenly choir, I wanted to climb the GTi spoiler roof and bail out of the stadium.

I'd spent the first half in the bottom tier, standing next to Corky from Huyton, a boss Red I'd seen 100 times over the years. Our crew was in the top tier. So thinking, *bottom tier's a jinx,* like you do, and so as not to lose anybody, I joined the lads in the clouds for the second half. When those uppercuts went in – Gerrard, Bang! Smicer, Bang! Alonso, Bang! – and the somersaults started and bruises and cuts were attained without the feeling of pain, an electrical current of intense emotional fervour bathed 45,000 Liverpudlians, to send them into raptures you'd be lucky to ever see again. Win, lose or draw, after 3–0 down, who cared? But once those pens kicked off, that intense euphoric feeling kicked in for the second time. I was on such an emotional high up in those Turkish clouds, that only a few days after the game I'm struggling to remember anything clearly. I remember young Scouse kids, heads in their hands like Katie my niece, or weeping tears of sadness like Alex at half-time, miraculously turning into heads aloft and tears of joy the moment Jerzy palmed away Shevchenko's pen. Grown men were hugging, dancing and weeping, all at the same time. I'd never seen an outpouring of unadulterated euphoric joy on this scale before. People were totally letting go in wild abandonment. Now that was a sight to behold, and the tear-fest, that was a definite first on me!

There you go, maybe I can be surprised. See, once Murdoch came along and the game was engulfed by silly money and players who didn't seem to give a shit, then along came the corporate whores and their oh-so-correct new crowd rules: don't swear, don't let your flags hang over our adverts, don't do this, don't do that, I'm thinking, *yeah, the footy, it's well and truly fucked up the hoop* – and to a certain extent it still is. Then along comes a weird, inexplicable night like Istanbul, with soldier Carragher leaping into the crowd to interrupt your cynical view, and it gets you re-thinking things over in your battered barnet. So what I'm saying is, yeah, season tickets, travel clubs and wearing a blazer or a badge the club or government tell you to, I'm swerving those things forever; but European nights, in mystical settings, where crazy things happen and dreams can come true . . . well, I'm already there, it's become part and parcel of my being. Trips to Europe, eh, and places where a lad can still roam like a real football gypsy. That's the gaff for me.

To all those young lads, and players, who'd probably gotten fed-up listening to all us arl-arses going on about those magical nights in Europe, well I seen the tears in your eyes and the joy on your faces. We told you it was a bit special, didn't we? If not being part of the Right Blazers Association is going to make it more difficult for me to roam in the future, then so be it, but I'll tell you this, I was having a lovely dream the other day and the Rafa fella was talking to me about the magic that crackled on a hazy May night in Istanbul and how victory was wrought by a team with a band of supporters who really made a difference. He added that there were a lot more ancient cities worth a visit with the Boys in Red. Then sadly, I woke up. I checked the papers again to see if we'd won the Big Eared Fucker. We had! Funny life, isn't it, yer know, it taking a wise-arse fella from Spain to make you believe in your dreams. And to think that they say a lot of Scousers are romantic dreamers, well personally, I'd rather stay up in the Turkish clouds than go to shitty Millwall on a rainy Tuesday night. European Champions, eh! My team, my city, my Liverpool . . . I'm tingling, who'd have believed it? Me from now on.

I'm off to spend the last of me Bulgarian Levs. Catch yer later!

PPS . . . I wonder if all those chipped-up match gangsters will put this in their brand new soccer story books, yer know, seeing as they always seem to have a 'made-up' chapter about us Mickeys. It's great life, innit . . .